The Hermetic Brotherhood of Luxor

THE HERMETIC BROTHERHOOD OF LUXOR

**Initiatic and Historical Documents
of an Order of Practical Occultism**

Joscelyn Godwin, Christian Chanel, John P. Deveney

SAMUEL WEISER, INC.

York Beach, Maine

First published in 1995 by
Samuel Weiser, Inc.
Box 612
York Beach, Maine 03910-0612

Library of Congress Cataloging-in-Publication Data
The Hermetic Brotherhood of Luxor : initiatic and historical docu-
    ments of an order of practical occultism / edited by Joscelyn
    Godwin, Christian Chanel, John Patrick Deveney.
        p.   cm.
    Includes bibliographical references and index.
    1. Hermetic Brotherhood of Luxor--History--Sources.
2. Hermetic Brotherhood of Luxor--History.   3. Occultism--
History--19th century.
I. Godwin, Joscelyn. II. Chanel, Christian.
III. Deveney, John Patrick.
BF1429.H47   1995
135'.4--dc20   95-15313
                                                                CIP

ISBN 0-87728-825-9 (Hardcover edition)
ISBN 0-87728-838-0 (Paper edition)
EB

Typeset in 11 point Palatino

Printed in the United States of America

The paper used in this publication meets the minimum requirements of the American National Standard for Permanence of Paper
for Printed Library Materials Z39.48-1984.

TABLE OF CONTENTS

PART 1. AN ORDER OF PRACTICAL OCCULTISM

PART 2. THE SECRET MANUSCRIPTS

PART 3. THE HISTORY OF THE H. B. OF L. IN DOCUMENTS

ILLUSTRATIONS

PREFACE

The Hermetic Brotherhood of Luxor was an order of practical occultism, active in the last decades of the 19th century. It taught its members how to lead a way of life most favorable to spiritual development, and gave them detailed instructions in how to cultivate occult powers by working on their own. It differed from contemporary movements such as the Theosophical Society (founded 1875), whose teachings (at least after its earliest phase) were philosophical rather than practical, and the Hermetic Order of the Golden Dawn (founded 1888), whose activities were social and ceremonial.

The "H. B. of L." (as it was always known) succeeded in enrolling a surprising number of influential people, who carried forward its training and its doctrines into many other esoteric movements of the 20th century. Its private and individual nature, and the mystery that still partially surrounds its Grand Master Max Theon, are among the reasons why it has remained so obscure. Writers on the history of the Theosophical movement dismiss the H. B. of L.; Golden Dawn scholars ignore it. Most of the information available up to now comes from inadequate or untrustworthy sources.

We hope to have remedied the situation with this dossier, which has been compiled from a scholarly point of view and in the interests of intellectual history. Part 1 gives an account of the H. B. of L., its principal characters, its relationship to other groups, and its doctrines. Part 2 presents (where available) the original English texts of the manuscript instructions that were circulated to the membership. Part 3 is a historical dossier, comprising some fifty items that illustrate the changing fortunes of the Brotherhood, its internal affairs, and especially its conflict with the Theosophical Society. With this material now made available, the importance of the H. B. of L. will no longer be in question, and future studies of it can be conducted on a firm documentary basis.

Our work is the result of cooperation across the boundaries of language, nationality, and the professions. Mr. Chanel is the author of a doctoral dissertation, "De la 'Fraternité Hermétique de Louxor' au 'Mouvement Cosmique': l'Oeuvre de Max Théon (contribution à l'étude des courants ésotériques en Europe à la fin du XIXème siècle et au début du XXème siècle)," accepted by the Ecole Pratique des Hautes Etudes, Sciences Religieuses (Sorbonne), in 1994. Graduated from the Ecole Nationale d'Administration, he is a Judge in the Administrative Appeals Court of Lyon, France. Mr. Deveney did graduate studies at the University of Chicago under Mircea Eliade before entering the profession of law. Formerly Assistant United States Attorney in New Orleans, he is now in private law practice in New York City. Mr. Godwin was born in England, came to the United States in 1966, and is Professor of Music at Colgate University, New York State. He has published widely on music and the Western esoteric traditions.

A Note on Sources

Public discussion of the H. B. of L. began with two early books by René Guénon that have never been translated into English. References to it are to be found in his books on Theosophy (Guénon 1982, 14, 23-26, 31, 36, 95, 99, 118, 120, 138, 207, 299-300, 319) and on spiritualism (Guénon 1952, 20-21, 233). Guénon hints in these books about what the H. B. of L. was and who belonged to it, probably basing his statements on the very documents that are now in the Bibliothèque Municipale de Lyon (see Introduction to Part 2), as well as on what he learned from Barlet, Narad Mani's article, and C. G. Harrison's *The Transcendental Universe* [see B.9.c,e]. Even given these sources, it is impossible to see how he came by some of his conclusions—and confusions. Guénon's account of the H. B. of L. has been treated as canonical by most French writers on the subject.

The second source of information is in the works of R. Swinburne Clymer, founder of the Rosicrucian Fraternity based in Quakertown, Pennsylvania. Clymer had access to documents of the H. B. of L. and to information from ex-members of that and of Randolph's group. But his object in writing about the Order and its leaders in his three-volume survey of esoteric movements (see Clymer 1947, II, 80-82, 215-232), was not to serve the needs of scholars, but to support his own claim to be the chief holder of the Rosicrucian lineage. For Clymer, the H. B. of L., and the H. B. of A. L. and E., to which he belonged, were merely "exoteric" doors to the esoteric truths taught in his Rosicrucian groups.

A primary source has appeared recently in French (H. B. of L. 1988). Edited anonymously, this is an edition of the H. B. of L.'s manuscripts as circulated in French during the 1880s and 1890s. It has an anonymous Introduction based uncritically on Guénon's statements and containing other errors. Mr. Chanel's review of this publication (Chanel 1989) shows that the manuscripts were obtained from Paschal Thémanlys and members of the Movement Cosmique and completed by those in the Lyon collection—without any acknowledgment. Dr. Massimo Introvigne has called our attention to another anonymous edition of the H. B. of L. manuscripts in the Lyon collection: *I manoscritti della Hermetic Brotherhood of Luxor: scopi e pratiche* (Milano: Agape, n.d.). Another translation, with minor variants, from the Lyon manuscript is Peter Davidson, *Gli Specchi Magici. Leggi e technica operativa* (Genova: Phoenix, n.d.).

ACKNOWLEDGMENTS

The three editors would like to thank the following individuals and institutions for their assistance, while assuming responsibility for any errors in this work:

Mr. Christopher Bamford (The Lindisfarne Press);
Mr. David Blackley Board (The Smithsonian Institution);
M. Jean-Pierre Brach (Ecole Pratique des Hautes Etudes);
Bishop T Allen Greenfield, D.D. (Atlanta);
Mr. John Hamill (Grand Lodge Library, London);
Mr. Glen Houghton, of Samuel Weiser (Antiquarian), Inc.;
Mr. Paul Johnson (South Boston Public Library);
M. Jean-Pierre Laurant (Ecole Pratique des Hautes Etudes);
The late Mme. Jackie Séménoff, for permitting Mr. Chanel to consult the archives of Max Théon;
M. Pascal Thémanlys (Jerusalem);
M. Laszlo Toth (Paris);
Colgate University Research Council, for a grant enabling Mr. Godwin to study the H. B. of L. documents in Lyon;
Bibliothèque Municipale de Lyon;
Grand Lodge Library, Freemasons' Hall, London;
The Houghton Library, Harvard University;
The Theosophical Society, Adyar, Madras.

PART I

AN ORDER OF PRACTICAL OCCULTISM

1. First Public Appearance of the H. B. of L.

The H.B. of L. first came to notice in the latter part of 1884, when a discreet advertisement appeared in an English edition of *The Divine Pymander of Hermes Mercurius Trismegistus*. It invited aspirants to contact a mysterious personage called Theosi or Theon, in the care of the publisher or an American agent [see items A.1.a and B.3.b in this dossier]. The curious would-be occultist would then receive a letter from an individual acting on the "Grand Master's" behalf, asking for a photograph and a natal horoscope, so that it might be seen whether he or she was suited for occultism. Failing that, the aspirant was to send the necessary information for drawing up a horoscope, together with a small fee for the service [see B.7.a,c]. No list of members survives, but we know that some applicants were rejected,[1] which lends at least an appearance of good faith to an organization that was frequently dismissed by its enemies as a money-making fraud. While most European members were men, women predominated in America.

Those who were accepted as neophytes received in due course their initiatic materials: pledges, questionnaires, and the revelation of the H. B. of L.'s true name and degrees. The name was given on a slip of paper that was to be burned after reading. After a delay sometimes amounting to years, the rituals for self-initiation were disclosed [A.1.e].

Having established contact with a named representative of the Brotherhood, the neophyte would enter into regular correspondence with his or her mentor, who in turn would dispense a series of manuscripts setting forth the doctrines and occult practices of the Order. The basic manuscripts were already circulating by late 1884. Over the years they were supplemented by additional ones. All were designed to prepare the neophytes for their eventual initiations and to aid them in progressing through the degrees and grades of the Brotherhood—degrees and grades

---

[1] One of these was the publisher R. A. Campbell [see B.3.b]. Others were T. H. Pattison, later a member of the Golden Dawn (letter from W. A. Ayton to an unnamed American neophyte, 2 July 1885), and Elliott Coues (letters from S. H. Randall to an unnamed American neophyte, 14 and 21 October 1885). Unless otherwise noted, all letters cited are in private collections.

which were seen as paralleling the possibilities of the human state [see Section 11, below]. These manuscript teachings were given under a pledge of secrecy which was almost universally preserved inviolate. It is thus only by great good fortune that an almost complete set of them survives.

In many cases, the mentor would be someone already known to the neophyte, and their relationship would be friendly and often face-to-face. Such was the situation in England, where the H. B. of L.'s agent was the Rev. William Alexander Ayton, a man of wide acquaintance in the worlds of occultism and "fringe" Masonry, and in France, where the agent was the similarly well-connected Albert Faucheux (known as "F.-Ch.Barlet"). Both these men encouraged their confreres to join the new Brotherhood, and explained its workings in easy and informal terms [B.7.d]. When they could not answer their neophytes' questions, someone higher up in the Brotherhood might respond personally [see B.7.e].

The world of the occultists was a small one, and a single person might well belong to several different societies and have a passing acquaintance with most of their members. Word of the H. B. of L. would have got around quickly in these circles. But the object of the H. B. of L. was not to become yet another clique in London or Paris. It was to teach practical occultism to individuals, and this was why it appealed not only to lonely aspirants living far from the metropolis, but also to people who were already in the occult network. The fact that its practical occultism might involve not only the development of clairvoyance through using the "magic mirror," but also sex and drugs, explains why it was veiled in secrecy, and why, when this veil was penetrated, it aroused strong emotions.

There is no mystery about the people behind this effort of the period 1884-1886. Until mid-1886, the "Provincial Grand Master for the North" was Peter Davidson,[2] based in Banchory, Kincardineshire, Scotland. The "Provincial Grand Master for the South" was the aforementioned Ayton, who was Vicar of

---

[2] On Peter Davidson, see Section 6, below. He is not to be confused with Thomas Davidson (1840-1907), the Utopian and Platonist who was active in both America and England during the 1880s, on whom see Webb, 228-229.

Chacombe, near Banbury, Oxfordshire. Thereafter Davidson became "President of the Eastern Section," and moved to Loudsville, White County, Georgia, U.S.A. The Secretary of the Order was another Scotsman, Thomas Henry Burgoyne, who likewise moved to the U.S.A. in 1886.

During 1885-1886, Davidson and Burgoyne produced *The Occult Magazine,* a monthly journal in which the H. B. of L. addressed a wider public. They wrote many of its articles under pseudonyms, but in correspondence with neophytes and initiates they used their own names. In short, we know how the H. B. of L. operated from the time it announced its existence. But in the background, and apparently superior to Davidson and Burgoyne, there was the "Grand Master of the Exterior Circle," known as "M. Theon."[3] And there were many reminders that the Brotherhood had not arisen overnight.

---

[3] Theon is always identified thus in English-language sources, without the name Max and without the accent present in French sources, where he is "Théon."

2. THE QUESTION OF ORIGINS

The H.B. of L. told its neophytes that they were joining the Exterior Circle of a very ancient initiatic order, which had existed since before the time of Hermes Trismegistus (given as circa 600 BCE). What distinguished it from other historical orders, such as the Rosicrucians, was that it had always stood outside any religious affiliation [A.1.c]. As such, its nearest relative in the West was Freemasonry. But whatever Freemasonry might once have been, by the later nineteenth century it was certainly not a source for occult teachings.

The H. B. of L.'s history as written by its leaders was naturally an exercise in myth-making, and as such is no better or worse than the foundation legends of Freemasonry itself (Solomon's Temple, the murder of Hiram Abif, etc). The very dating of the Order's supposed foundation—4,320 years before 1881—is symbolic, the first figure belonging to one system of cosmic cycles [explained in A.2.b], and the second to another, interlocking system [A.2.c,d]. This auto-mythology served to place the H.B. of L. in its appropriate historical current, and also to show which currents it did not want to be identified with.

The question of the H. B. of L.'s foundation date is nonetheless an important one, for reasons arising out of its rivalry with the Theosophical Society. H. P. Blavatsky and Colonel Olcott, who founded the Theosophical Society in New York in 1875, were Buddhists who acknowledged the guidance of certain Mahatmas or adepts in Tibet. From their point of view, the H. B. of L., which they first heard of in 1885, was a sinister order of low-grade occultism, newly invented as a mockery of the "real" Brotherhood of Luxor which had inspired their own society ten years earlier [B.1.a-c].

While freely acknowledging the existence of adepts in the East, the H. B. of L. stressed that it was a Western order, owing nothing to the "Esoteric Buddhism" of the Theosophists. From the H. B. of L.'s point of view, it was older than the Theosophical Society—not so much by virtue of an antiquity that was clearly mythological, but simply because it claimed to have begun this phase of its work in 1870 [A.1.c]. In this view the "Brotherhood of

Luxor" that brooded over the early Theosophical Society had been the work of the same person or persons.

Whether there was in fact any connection between the two brotherhoods is one of the unsolved questions of esoteric history. Its solution probably lies in an investigation of the state of Western spiritualism in the decades prior to 1875, which we will discuss in Section 13.

What is certain is that once its public work began in 1884, the H. B. of L. developed with almost incredible speed into a powerful rival of the Theosophical Society. A majority of the American Board of Control of the latter had joined the H. B. of L. by 1886: they included Mrs. Josephine Cables, Elliott B. Page, Thomas Moore Johnson, Dr. Jirah Dewey Buck, and William B. Shelley. The future leader of the Society in America, William Q. Judge, either refused to join, as he maintained, or else was rejected, as the H. B. of L. claimed [see B.5.b]. Less information is available about the British Theosophists, but even Countess Wachtmeister, the faithful companion of Blavatsky's last years, approached Ayton about joining.[4] Even more than the rival order of the Golden Dawn, it was this mass movement of Theosophists to the H. B. of L. that forced Blavatsky, against Olcott's will, into founding an "Eastern or Esoteric School" within the Theosophical Society in 1888 as a school of practical occultism under her control—though her notion of "practical occultism," as her students soon found out, was far more cerebral than that of the H. B. of L.

This enrollment of so many important Theosophists could not have been achieved without some prior groundwork. Davidson was a member of the Theosophical Society, and was making his own reputation as an occult writer by the end of the 1870s. But before we describe his life and work, we must establish the role of the *éminence grise* behind the whole affair, whom *The Occult Magazine* called the "exalted adept, M. Theon."

---

[4] Ayton to unnamed American neophyte, 28 September 1885, mentions Page and Wachtmeister. Shelley's pledge is dated 8 June 1885. The Judge question is in S. H. Randall to unnamed American neophyte, 6 July 1885.

3. IDENTITY OF MAX THEON

Better known through his later work, Max Theon is an enigmatic character. The rare surviving photographs of him seem to depict an initiate, while his life and actions seem less akin to those of modern mages than to Nietzsche's Zarathustra. Since the second phase of his initiatic work (the "Mouvement Cosmique," which published his ideas under the name of "Philosophie Cosmique," through the journal *Revue Cosmique* and works such as *La Tradition Cosmique*) was mainly directed under the pseudonym of Aia Aziz, the link with the H. B. of L. has been largely ignored. This is true even in France, where the movement was launched in the first years of our century, and where it has had a powerful, if subliminal influence. The Mouvement Cosmique, although public in character and more theoretical than practical in appearance, was conceived by Theon and his wife as the continuation of the H. B. of L. What we know of Max Theon's biography comes mainly from there, in particular from his successor in the movement L. M. Thémanlys, and from the latter's son Pascal Thémanlys [B.2.c].

Despite their information, Theon's identity remains as unclear today as it was to his contemporaries. In 1907, a French journalist believed that he was right in saying that Theon was Jewish, and originally from the Levant.[5] Mirra Alfassa, whom Theon trained in practical occultism at Tlemcen, Algeria, during 1906 and 1907, and whose knowledge thus gained was so important to Sri Aurobindo and the Pondicherry Ashram, recalled that he had never told her his age, his place of birth, or who he really was. She thought him to be a Polish or Russian Jew.[6] When Theon was married in London in 1885, he was obliged to fill out the marriage certificate [B.2.a] with his father's and his own name, and his age. These confirm the Polish Jewish identity, yet his age, given as 30, contradicts all of the three dates of birth that are recorded elsewhere: 17 November 1848, on his death certificate;[7] 5 August

---

[5] Brieu, 139.

[6] Alfassa, I, 228.

[7] Undated letter to Mr. Chanel from the daughter of M. Benharoche-Baralia, confirmed by information received from Pascal Thémanlys.

1847 on the Algerian Census of 1911;[8] 1 June 1850, according to an Algerian rabbi.[9] The local paper in Algeria gave his age at death as 76, in March 1927, which agrees only with the last date.[10]

Even Theon's original name is uncertain, for the "Louis Maximillian Bimstein" of his marriage certificate is only one of several versions that are met with, depending on whether the names are transcribed into English, French, or Hebrew. The surname also appears as Binstein and Beinstein, though Bimstein (meaning "pumice-stone") seems the most likely.[11] One concludes that Theon must have spent much of his existence under false names or false identity papers, and that he did not hesitate to give wrong information to the authorities. The errors on his marriage certificate, especially concerning the date of birth, suggest that he might have been compelled to assume a false proof of identity. East European Jews often had to do this in order to escape the Tsarist or Austrian repression.[12]

Various remarks attributed to Mirra Alfassa by her biographers connect Theon with Madame Blavatsky's first attempt at public work: the "Société spirite" she started in Cairo in 1871. But they are too insubstantiated and contradictory to allow us to accept them.[13] While it is not impossible that Theon was in Egypt in 1871-72, and there met Blavatsky and her former teacher, the Coptic magician Paulos Metamon (sometimes rumored to be Theon's father!—see B.9.e), it seems unlikely, especially if he was in Paris in 1870, and in England by 1873.[14]

---

[8] Nahar, III, 51. This book contains information on Theon sometimes derived from Mr. Chanel's researches, but mixed with Nahar's own errors. As regards this birthdate, the fact that Theon filled out the census with his pseudonym, "Max Théon," does not reinforce the credibility of the other information he gave there.

[9] Letter from Pascal Thémanlys to Mr. Chanel, 5 December 1989, where the information is credited to an Algerian rabbi named Morali.

[10] "Etat civil de Tlemcen du 27 février au 5 mars 1927," in Le Petit Tlemcénien, 45th yr., 10 March 1927, 2.

[11] Undated letter from the daughter of M.Benharoche-Baralia to Mr. Chanel. M. Benharoche-Baralia was in Algeria around 1935.

[12] Mirra Alfassa notes that "he was of Jewish origin, and had had to flee his country on that account." Alfassa, II, 74.

[13] They consist of remarks made in conversation by "The Mother" concerning events of fifty years before. See Satprem I, 180-181, repeated in Nahar II, 48, 51.

[14] Paris 1870: Thémanlys informed Mr. Chanel, on the basis of notes taken by Madame Perrault-Duban, who had been to Tlemcen. Thémanlys' surmise that Theon was in England in 1873 is based on the "Origin and Object" [A.1.c].

Max Theon. (Reproduced by permission from *H. B. of L. Textes et documents secrets*, Milan: Archè, 1988.)

4. THEON'S EARLY ACTIVITIES

When Theon writes that he was initiated at eighteen, Pascal Thé-manlys regards this as an indication that Theon's initiation took place in Hassidic circles before he left Poland. In any case, he soon broke off relations with his initiators. This is a common pattern among occultists who engage in public work, serving on the one hand to ensure their own independence, and on the other to avoid compromising their initiators, who always remain unidentifiable. In a description of initiation from the *Revue Cosmique*, that is attributable to the Theons; we read the following description of initiation:

> This exiting of the initiates by ten stages was an invariable rule in the Sacred Hierarchy, because it was from among them that the invisible Archpriest and psychic King was chosen, or at least a deputy who could fill the office until the Elected One was found. And from time to time, among these invisible Archpriests and psychic Kings, the Keves was chosen who, in union with the Divine Holocaust, would offer himself in hierarchical order for the restitution of the emotional, spiritual, intellectual, and vital energies of the Initiates. That is why it had been judged illegitimate for any man to devote himself to such a high function among the initiates without having first returned to live again in the world, for fear that he might be influenced, even unconsciously, by those who had taught and evolved him.
>
> The new initiates would therefore leave as poor men, taking with them nothing but provisions for the journey and a change of clothes. They went to the place where they intended to reside, greeting no one and speaking with no one on the way. Their first dwelling was usually in a large city, where they lived in poverty, selling some trivial merchandise so that no one would question how they earned their daily bread. However, there was always an envoy of the Sacred Hierarchy living in the same city, to look after their wants in case of need. Those who had sent them there from so far away

were well aware that worrying about food, clothing, and lodging is incompatible with psychic development.[15]

The end of this passage, with its Rosicrucian connotations, is curiously evocative of Blavatsky's situation in July 1873, when, as Henry Olcott recalled, "she told me she had taken lodgings in one of the poorest quarters in New York—Madison Street—and supported herself by making cravats or artificial flowers—I forget which now—for a kind-hearted Hebrew shopkeeper."[16]

In addition to Hassidic Kabbalism, Theon must at some point have gained access to Indian (or Tibetan-Indian) teachings, for the Philosophie Cosmique, some of whose texts clearly refer to ancient Indian thought, is, among other things, a synthesis of the two esoteric streams. Mirra Alfassa said that he had been in India, and had a thorough knowledge of Sanskrit and the *Rig-Veda*.[17] He also had inside knowledge of Western spiritualist circles. But this probably counted for less than his own investigations of magnetism, or so one assumes from the novel *Ben Malek*, discovered among the archives from Tlemcen. A passage in this book shows how he lost no time in setting his spiritual sights, so as to be able to influence occultist circles without being influenced by them:

I have the power of magnetizing, or rather "pathetizing," as we call it. I will search for sensitives and test my power. Evolution through contemplation, which can induce a profounder state of sleep, is not allowed to one who is alone and unprotected. It would interest me very much to frequent the Western occultists and to learn from them." Henri Delisle smiled: "You may well frequent them, for they have a passion for anything oriental! As for learning from them, that's another matter.

---

[15] "La quatrième évocation," 230-231. Virtually all the articles in the *Revue Cosmique*, which appeared monthly from 1901 to 1908, were anonymous. They were essentially the work of Madame Theon in collaboration with her husband.

[16] *ODL*, I, 20.

[17] *Agenda de Mère*, I, 228.

They are bogged down in the swamp of mysticism. Even the best have no master who can show them the path of knowledge..."[18]

Theon succeeded in maintaining a personal obscurity verging on invisibility. However, we do have an idea of how he lived in London during the 1880s from a classified advertisement for a psychic healer in the spiritualist magazine, *The Medium and Daybreak* [B.2.b]. We know that they were the same person, for the healer's address in St. John's Wood is the same as appears on Theon's marriage certificate [B.2.a]. "Theosi" may have been the first version of the pseudonym he adopted for this stage of his work, and the change to the Greek "Theon" the result of his wife's enthusiasm for ancient Greece.

In the later phases of his work, Theon kept close control of his public image, breaking cover only on a few deliberate occasions. In autumn of 1899, when he had begun to publish articles in the *Journal du Magnétisme et de la Psychologie*, he felt obliged to denounce the dangers of spiritualism in the face of the overwhelming influence of Kardecist "Spirites" on the coming Congrès Spirite et Spiritualiste International in Paris (1900). The Spirites reacted virulently to his statement that their practices put unprotected mediums in contact with diabolic forces eager to possess humanity, leading Theon to lift the veil slightly on his former practices by describing himself thus: "As a person who for most of his life has consecrated his being and all his energies to the study of pathotism, and who for twenty years has practiced the modest science thus acquired, I can speak on all these questions practically, sincerely, and conscientiously."[19]

By the word *pathotisme*,[20] which he said had denoted magnetism in antiquity, Theon meant the natural force subjected to the cosmic law of duality, or as he put it, "the infusion of the active psychic being into the passive psychic being, and the consequent development of the passive sensitive to the highest per-

---

[18] *Ben Malek*, unpublished manuscript, 13.

[19] Theon 1899, 62.

[20] Theon also uses the terms *pathétisme* and *force pathétique*, meaning love as the most powerful force in the cosmos.

fection of which she is capable in every state of her being."[21] This is a technique of meditation involving an active and a passive being, whose most desirable form involves a man and a woman.[22]

Theon's practice fits within a tradition of spiritual research conducted by a man controlling a psychically gifted woman. In the West, it is at least as old as the Delphic Oracle, in which the ecstatic speech of the "Pythoness" or priestess was interpreted by the priests. Theon believed that by this collaborative method, spiritual vision could be subjected to intellectual and critical control, as was not possible when scribe and seer were one and the same person. Theon's method consisted in protecting his wife (or a "sensitive") during her passage through progressively more subtle bodies, and in guiding her, for example by indicating or confirming what state and degree of subtle matter she was in. During the process of exteriorization, Madame Theon managed to speak faintly but audibly, and to converse with her husband. (To judge from various passages in her *Agenda*, Mirra Alfassa also experimented with this.) The Theons used the information thus obtained to write the texts of the Philosophie Cosmique, totalling more than 10,000 pages of partly unpublished material.

Among parallel examples of a man obtaining esoteric knowledge through his wife's mediumship, we might mention the collaboration of Laurence and Mary Oliphant, who produced a mystical treatise called the *Sympneumata* in 1882-1883; that of S. L. McGregor Mathers and his wife Moina Bergson, which gave birth in 1891-1892 to the rituals of the Golden Dawn; and, at a somewhat later period, *A Vision* by William Butler Yeats and his wife Georgie.

The Theons later emphasized how important it was for the "sensitive" operating in the invisible world to benefit from the best possible conditions for the unfolding of her powers:

Trance is the supreme development of passivity, a development whose nature and goal are lost in the

---

[21] Théon 1899, 62.
[22] Thémanlys, 19.

night of prehistoric times. A trained sensitive, intellectual and refined (for one must remember that there is a psychic royalty and a nobility, just as there are a royalty and nobility of talent, of birth, and of wealth) can be compared to a priceless instrument, finely tuned, of such delicacy that its harmony may be destroyed if it is roughly touched. Such a person is the most precious of beings, for if she is entrusted to a person who by his nature and his own knowledge can develop her, he may through her agency arrive at communication with the highest intelligences, acquire the secrets of life and death, read in the cosmic book of the universe whose pages are open, and dominate the forces of nature, not to mention many other things not yet touched upon.[23]

Theon explains that as a function of this psychic rank, sensitives can awaken in states and stages that correspond to those of their own being and which are recognizable through their unvarying colors, which allows the magnetizer or *pathétiseur* to find his bearings in the invisible cosmography and to guide them with ease.[24] However, these states and the degrees they imply cannot be attained without passing them in order and by following a special process, even if the sensitive is not necessarily conscious of the stages traversed.

Theon's originality consisted not so much in having described in fairly concrete and accessible fashion the hierarchy and characteristics of these states and degrees, as in having drawn attention to the importance and dangers of the "Nervous State" (*Etat nerveux*). With great precision, he describes this as being a region largely occupied by the *Hostile* (equivalent to Satan), and hence as an abyss that has to be passed over before the higher regions of the soul and spirit can be reached. Just beyond the Nervous State is the region of the souls' repose, where they rest two by two, sleeping under the protection of guardians, and

---

[23] Théon, 1899, 61-62.
[24] Max Théon, "Le magnétisme et le psychisme," in *Journal du Magnétisme et de la Psychologie*, 27/4 (20 February 1899), 82-83.

from which they sometimes come down, traversing the Nervous State, to incarnate or reincarnate together on Earth.

In the Philosophie Cosmique, Theon explains that just as the "nervous degree" (so called because it corresponds to the nervous system; later Sri Aurobindo and "The Mother" call it "the Vital") is the most fragile part of man and the most liable to unbalance, yet is the obligatory link between the tangible body and the realms of soul and spirit, so those higher regions are linked by this abyss to the dense material world. Thomas Burgoyne (see below) seems to have been well aware of the difficulty of attaining the higher states, for he denounces the "esoteric Buddhists" (meaning the Theosophists) for knowing nothing about these regions, being unable to go beyond the astral zones.[25]

---

[25] *LOE*, I, 48. The astral zones of occultist theory are very close to what the Philosophie Cosmique understands as the nervous state.

5. THEON AND THE H. B. OF L.

Theon's title of "Grand Master of the Exterior Circle" of the Order implies the existence of an Interior Circle. In the published texts of the Philosophie Cosmique, Theon and his wife use the terms *cercle extérieur* and *cercle intérieur* in such a way as to avoid creating any mystery about the latter. The *cercle intérieur* seems to mean simply the few people directing the society, while the *cercle extérieur* comprises the members who look after diffusing its ideas in public.[26] This was not quite the case in the H. B. of L. as it developed. Here the Interior Circle was not supposed to be on the physical plane alone, but to consist of adepts on both sides of the grave,[27] and was to be contacted through the occult power of clairvoyance, especially with the use of the crystal or mirror, which the H. B. of L.'s instructions were designed to develop.

As an adept himself, Theon was presumably able to put others in touch with this Interior Circle. His primary contribution to the Order was the initial training of Burgoyne and Davidson, or even of Burgoyne alone. In this view, Theon was the initiator of the H.B. of L. in the true sense. Once he had given it the link with the partially-discarnate Interior Circle, his outward task was done, though as a member of the latter he remained as a potential helper.

It was always Theon's policy to allow his pupils and associates a broad freedom of action. Davidson and Burgoyne were free both in the practical organization of the Exterior Circle and in the choice of doctrinal articles for the Brotherhood's magazine. They, too, may have made a deliberate break with their initiator. To judge by remarks in Theon's letter of 1915 [B.2.c], this may have occurred even before the formation of the H. B. of L. as a public organization in 1884. The covering letter of Theon to Thémanlys that accompanied the bilingual version of "Origin

---

[26] On the *cercle extérieur*, see *Revue Cosmique*, III/10, 584. On the *cercle intérieur*, see ibid., 633 (in relation with esoteric science); III/2, 94 (interior circle of the sacred Hierarchy); VII/9, 556 (interior circle of a society). Sometimes the use of the expression *cercle intérieur* refers to the innermost circles of ceremonial magic, i.e., the circle of four, which may perhaps refer also to the four persons who are depositories of the Tradition on earth: see *La Tradition Cosmique*, II, 328.

[27] See *LOE*, I, 149, and Section 8, below.

and Object of the H. B. of L." seems to cast him in the role first of neophyte (in 1873), then of adept and Grand Master of the Exterior Circle.

Theon does not seem to have been interested in making his own philosophical ideas available to the Order. No manuscript teaching and no article in the *Occult Magazine* bears his name. The one piece in the *Occult Magazine* devoted specifically to Kabbalah—a subject of which he was hardly ignorant—is merely a digest based on Ginsburg's book.[28] In the early numbers of the magazine, subscribers were invited for a series of cheap editions of Hermetic works with "explanatory notes by the eminent Occultist, M. Theon" [B.3.e], but these never appeared.[29] The only articles that bear the definite stamp of his influence are two short essays on mediumship, called "Flashes of Light" and signed by "Eos,"[30] which sketch some of the ideas that would recur in the Philosophie Cosmique. Parts of them would be reproduced word for word in Burgoyne's *The Light of Egypt* (see Section 8).

Unlike so many self-proclaimed adepts and cult-leaders, Theon evidently had no personal need for the H. B. of L. He gave initiation to whomever he chose without having to go through an Order with a system of degrees (as one can see in the case of Mirra Alfassa), and had plenty of his own knowledge to draw on without needing to borrow from Randolph or anyone else. His later conduct with the Mouvement Cosmique showed that he could well protect himself from inquisitive and annoying persons without needing the cover of a secret society.

Given all this, we can best understand Theon's role in the Order with the help of the Sufi concept of the spiritual master as *Qutb*, the term for the unmoving Pole around which, and by virtue of whose presence, everything turns. When a person func-

---

[28] J. W. F., "The Kabala," in *Occult Magazine* II/15 (April 1886), 25-26; II/16 (May 1886), 33-34. The author is probably Burgoyne.

[29] In *La Tradition Cosmique* III (1906), there is an appendix explaining certain terms that had been announced in *La Revue Cosmique* as written by Théon. The use of this name is exceptionally rare in the "cosmic" period.

[30] *The Occult Magazine* I/5 (June 1885), 37-38, and I/6 (July 1885), 45-46. Eos is Greek for "dawn." These two articles were also published in French: see *Le Magicien* (Lyon) IV/70 (10 May 1886), 541-545.

tions as *Qutb*, his spiritual influence suffices to inspire and sustain the aspirations and actions of others, without his having to become involved in their affairs—or their errors. One finds in the Philosophie Cosmique the idea that a sage can act psychically, especially during his regular periods of meditation, both for the good of the world and for the specific aid of those close to his own work. The same idea, and its practice, would recur with Sri Aurobindo.

Mirra Alfassa, who was not one to scatter praise indiscriminately, describes Theon as a man of enormous occult power, knowledge, and perception. He first told her, she says, of the God within and taught her how to open herself to that God. He taught her dream consciousness and explained to her the power of performing a variety of phenomena, such as quelling serpents, calming the stormy sea, and diverting lightning bolts. Most importantly for our present purposes, he taught her practically how to "exteriorize" herself and leave her body to explore successively the "vital," "mental," and other progressively subtler states of being or consciousness in the search for knowledge and power, and to relate her experiences to others while in trance.[31]

Mirra Alfassa is even more lavish in her praise of Madame Theon, formerly Mary Christine Woodroffe Ware. Mirra attests to Madame Theon's possession of extraordinary gifts for producing phenomena, greater than Theon's own. This is corroborated by Pascal Thémanlys' parents. We do not know when the Theons met, but it may have been in London the year before their marriage in Westminster on 21 March 1885 [B.2.a]. Curiously enough, this meeting seems to have occurred simultaneously with the first public manifestation of the H. B. of L. in autumn, 1884. Mary Ware, under the pseudonym of "Una" (taken from Spenser's *Fairie Queene*), had founded in July 1884 the "Universal Philosophical Society," in which she gave lectures that are reported in the spiritualist journal *The Medium and Daybreak*, and

---

[31] Nahar, 203-204. For further excerpts from the talks of The Mother on Theon and his powers, see chapter 5 of *Glimpses of the Mother's Life*, compiled by Nilima Das (Pondicherry, 1978).

published brochures.[32] The very name of this society, and many of its ideas, anticipate the future Philosophie Cosmique, and confirm that Una was indeed Mary Ware and the future Madame Theon.

The psychic cooperation of the Theons, furthered by their settling in Algeria in 1888, led to the elaboration of this initiatic philosophy, which was not completed until the beginning of the twentieth century. Once their collaboration had begun, the Theons had the choice of either putting their energies into the H. B of L., or of working on the development of their own ideas; in either case, they wanted their anonymity protected. In view of the ongoing success of Una's lecturing, at least until she bade farewell to *The Medium and Daybreak* in January 1885, Max Theon may have not wanted the H. B. of L.'s activity to interfere with hers. Consequently, during the heyday of the H. B. of L. in the mid-1880s, Theon had little or no part in the day-to-day running of the Order. Even the Provincial Grand Master Ayton could find out nothing about him, and, after his disillusion, came to believe that Theon was the alter ego of an Indian adventurer, Hurrychund Chintamon [B.6.k]—an opinion later adopted by Pierre Duvar [B.7.h], A. E. Waite [B.9.d], René Guénon [B.9.e] and others. Davidson himself had to reassure the American neophytes that Theon was real and that he had actually met him.[33] If the "confessions" of Burgoyne and Davidson to Gorham Blake in the summer of 1886 [B.6.k] are true, Theon had disappeared after training Burgoyne who had up to then been visiting him every day.

The Theons, then, left England for France in March 1886. We know of this from the diary (in a private collection) of Augusta Rolfe, a young Englishwoman who accompanied them as Theons's secretary. She wrote on 23 July 1885: "I am allowed a year's trial under Theon." In fact, she stayed with them for the rest of their lives, nearly until Max Theon's death in 1927.

---

[32] Mr. Chanel's thesis gives further details on this society and its publications.

[33] Peter Davidson to an unnamed American neophyte, 7 August 1885.

From this point onwards, Davidson and Burgoyne answered correspondence in the Grand Master's name, perhaps in the same spirit that allowed H. P. Blavatsky, at around the same time, to write letters in the names of her masters. The parallel is more than a casual one. During these same 1880s the most famous of the Theosophical Mahatmas, Koot Hoomi and Morya, made it plain that the Theosophical movement was Blavatsky's responsibility alone, and that, while willing to help, they were not going to put in a personal appearance, much less clear up any mess she might make of it. And at the moment of crisis, in 1886, they vanished.

6. PETER DAVIDSON IN SCOTLAND

Peter Davidson (1837-1915),[34] was a violin-maker who lived in Forres, near Findhorn, Scotland. Believers in the *genius loci* will appreciate the fact that he came from an area that would later become famous in the lore of the "New Age." Later he lived in Banchory, southwest of Aberdeen. Local tradition in Loudsville had it that Davidson set out to become a priest, but lost his vocation when he met a woman on the train to Rome.[35]

The fruit of Davidson's original trade was a historical and technical introduction to the instrument, *The Violin* (Davidson 1871), a manual that served its purpose so well that it went into five editions. The book does little to dispel the obscurity shrouding Davidson's early life, but it suggests a possible date for his abortive journey to Rome, for he mentions having seen a certain violin in Paris in 1859.[36] The only other information we have at present is that he married Christina Ross in 1866.[37]

For all his Highland isolation, Davidson was in touch with people in the thick of the London occultist scene: members of the Societas Rosicruciana in Anglia, of "fringe" masonic groups, experimenters with magic mirrors, etc. A friendly letter written to Davidson in 1884 by Hargrave Jennings (author of *The Rosicrucians, Phallicism,* etc.) says: "I have known you, now, for a good many years..."[38]

Long before the formal appearance of the H. B. of L. in 1884, Davidson was already hinting at his initiation into an unnamed occult order, and at his visitation by angelic beings. In an exchange of letters with Captain F. G. Irwin (a leading "fringe" mason and occultist) in November 1877, he gives a series of fascinating glimpses of his early life: "I have been a student of occultism for several years now. Spiritualism gave me an extra stimulus. I became an initiate and go on advancing as time allows

---

[34] Dates on Davidson's gravestone, Cleveland, Georgia, photographed by Dr. Greenfield. The Library of Congress Catalogue gives the dates as 1842-1916.

[35] Information given to Mr. Deveney in Loudsville.

[36] Information given in *The Violin*, third ed. (London: Pitman, 1881), 90.

[37] Facsimile of certificate provided by Dr. Greenfield.

[38] Letter from Jennings to Davidson, 11 January 1884. Copy provided by Dr. Greenfield.

me for I have a business here [...]" He hints rather mysteriously that he was no Rosicrucian *in the modern acceptation of the term,* and boasts that he had:

> had the visits of bright angelic beings, shining in their radiance and glory of the Astral Light—coming to me, my wife and children within our room, and be it remembered, not by *physical Mediumship, cabinets* or any appliances or aids used and in the manner Mediums generally adopt [...]
>
> I need scarcely tell you it is *White Magic* I have studied as I have the utmost repugnance to the communication with the Elementaries etc. by Invocations, Circles, etc. such as described in the works of Agrippa, Barrett, Peter de Albano [sic], etc., etc.[...][39]
>
> With reference to my pursuits you must understand *any one* sees the spirits in my room, but of course I never have allowed any one in this outlandish place to know except my wife and children, who have often, often seen them. No physical Mediumship, cabinets, veiled corners or such like Mediumistic trumpery [...] These things are only a preliminary however upon the [spirits'?] part as better and higher stages are fast in progress which I hope to be able to report to you soon.[40]

In Davidson's history of the H. B. of L. [A.1.c], the first mover is an oriental adept, who was in England in 1873 and in Tibet by 1887. Davidson's own initiation came, he suggests, directly from the same oriental adept, for he told Ayton in 1887 that "he had met with an Oriental Adept or some such person who had appeared to him in the Astral form &c., and that he was about to

---

[39] See B.7.a for a letter in which Davidson is offering a copy of Barrett's *Magus* for sale. This book included the treatises on magic of Agrippa and Peter de Abano.

[40] Mr. David Blackley Board, following the indications of the late Ellic Howe, located these fascinating letters in the Irwin papers at Grand Lodge Library, London, and made this first attempt at deciphering Davidson's handwriting. Davidson also mentions Ayton in the letters, but appears not yet to have met him.

revive or add to an Ancient Order [...]" Davidson added that the adept was then (that is, in 1887) in Tibet.[41] In Davidson's mind, this "astral" contact gave him an effective initiation into the mysteries of the H. B. of L. It also accounts for his attitude to the Theosophical Society. His original idea seems to have been that the H. B. of L. (in its Interior Circle, of course) was responsible for the setting up of Blavatsky and Olcott's Society. Later the Theosophists fell away, coming under the control of beings who were either lesser adepts of the same fraternity, or what he unfairly calls Buddhist fanatics (see Sections 12 and 13, below).

By the time Davidson was writing to Irwin, he was familiar with the current explanations of such experiences by the "higher spiritualism," and was trying to reconcile them with Christianity—as he would do all his life—in an essay on "Astrology and Scripture."[42] His view was that "the best and most reliable digests of Cabalistic wisdom are to be found in the songs of Orpheus, the philosophy of Plato, the doctrines of Pythagoras, Apollonius of Tyana, and the modern mystics Van Helmont and Behmen." In other words, he was reading not the Hebrew Kabbalah but the translations of the Platonic tradition by Thomas Taylor, and had encountered the venerable English tradition of spiritual alchemy, largely based on the writings of J. B. and F. M. van Helmont and of Jacob Boehme.[43]

For all his poverty and family responsibilities (he told Irwin in 1877 that he worked in a distillery[44]), Davidson was able in 1878 to publish The Philosophy of Man, which showed his interest in alternative medicine, advertised his membership in numerous European and Asian secret societies, and seemed to be inviting fellow occultists to contact him. By April 1880 he had also discovered the early writings of the Theosophists, and joined their

---

[41] Ayton to an unnamed former neophyte, 30 March 1887 (private collection). In "The Hidden Hand" (Godwin 1990-91), Mr. Godwin drew conclusions about the identities of the "adept" and the "neophyte" based on the faulty French translation of "Origin and Object of the H. B. of L." Since then, thanks to Pascal Thémanlys, the English original (presumed lost) has become available to us [A.1.c], and with it a definitive statement of who was who.

[42] Printed letter by Davidson, Forres, 17 July 1877; copy provided by Dr. Greenfield.

[43] On this tradition, see Godwin 1994, 227-246.

[44] Davidson to Irwin, 10 November 1877.

Society.[45] In the following year, he enlarged the third edition of *The Violin* by adding to it a bewildering quantity of occult and spiritualistic material. However irrelevant this was to the theme of the book, it served to attract attention to him as an authority on these matters as well.

We do not know how or when Davidson met Theon and Burgoyne, and embarked on the adventure of the H. B. of L. Burgoyne was seeking instruction from occultists by 1881 (see below), and Davidson may have been one of them. The next stage of Davidson's program of exteriorization was the appearance of a magazine. After a few failed attempts in the latter part of 1884 [B.3.a, c, f], *The Occult Magazine* began in February 1885 to appear as a monthly, with the help of the Glasgow publisher Hay Nisbet.

---

[45] For the acknowledgement of Davidson's subscription or contribution, see *The Theosophist*, April 1880, 192.

7. PETER DAVIDSON IN AMERICA

No sooner was *The Occult Magazine* up and running than Davidson became taken with the idea of emigrating to America and
starting a utopian colony there, perhaps lured by the success of
Thomas Lake Harris's establishment in Santa Rosa. Max Theon
was said to have had an interest in such things [B.4.a], and may
have approved the project. For a short time it seemed as if it
might become a serious financial venture, with an issue of shares
[see B.4.a, c]. But it did not enjoy the success of that other step-
child of Theon's, Auroville (founded by Mirra Alfassa in 1968 to
crown the success of the Pondicherry Ashram). The H. B. of L.
attracted neither investors nor fellow-settlers, and the projected
"colony" became merely the Davidson family homestead in
Loudsville, Georgia.

According to the White County Board of Commissioners:

> The Dr. Peter Davidson Family came to Loudsville,
> White County, Georgia from Edinburgh, Scotland in
> 1889 [sic]. Dr. Davidson was married to Christina Ross.
> They had five children: Peter Jr., John, Alex, Jim and
> Tina. All the children came to America with their par-
> ents except Jim, who remained as a private guard to the
> Queen. Christina Ross Davidson died several years
> after the family came to White County and Dr. David-
> son married Jessie Mantoch from Scotland.[46]

Soon after emigrating in the spring of 1886, Davidson and Burgoyne went their separate ways. Davidson kept the H. B. of L.
going in France and a large part of the U.S. from Loudsville.
Much of the enrollment and correspondence was delegated to
the national presidents [see B.7.c, d], but the fees came to Davidson. His correspondence with French members shows the difficulties of getting these small amounts transferred from France to
his local post office.[47] These, together with the sale of books,

---

[46] Letter to Dr. Greenfield, 12 February 1992.
[47] See letters of 23 November 1888 and 10 January 1889 from Barlet to Arnould (Fonds
Papus).

crystals, and magic mirrors [B.7.a], probably gave the Davidson family just enough to live on until they became established in the area [B.4.f]. By 1895 Davidson could call himself:

Author of "The Caledonian Collection of Music," "The Philosophy of Man," "Masonic Mysteries Unveiled," "The Book of Light and Life," "The Mistletoe," "Mountain Musings," etc. Editor of "The Morning Star." "Member of the American Society for the Prevention of Cruelty to Animals," Hon. Member of the Poona "Gayan Samaj," Hon. Member "Bengal Academy of Music," etc., Hon and Cor. Member "Groupe Indep. d'Etudes Esotériques," Member "Frater de l'Etoile," "S∴I∴" etc.[48]

By explaining some of these titles and abbreviations, we can give a fair idea of Davidson's activities. *The Morning Star*, published monthly from 1892 to 1910, began in the style of *The Occult Magazine*, with translations from Hermetic works, spiritualist teachings, and answers to correspondents who wrote from all over the English-speaking world. *Mountain Musings* was the more exoteric part of Davidson's enterprise, being aimed at the local readership and couched in the Christian terms familiar to them.

The H. B. of L. was far from being Davidson's only activity, but his links were now more with France than with Britain, where the Burgoyne scandal (see Section 8, on page 33) and its exploitation by the Theosophists had ruined his reputation and that of the H. B. of L. Most of Davidson's dignities mentioned in the above list are French. The "Groupe Indépendant d'Etudes Esotériques" was a creation of Papus, who had entered the French occult scene like a meteor in 1887, charmed Barlet, and taken over every group in sight.[49] It was a catch-all group which served as a recruiting-ground for the H. B. of L. The abbreviation "S∴I∴" stands for "*Supérieur Inconnu*," or "Unknown Superior," the title used by members of Papus' Martinist Order. This order

---

[48] Title-page of Davidson, *Vital Christianity* (*Mountain Musings*, no.III), Loudsville: Davidson/Glasgow: Bernard Goodwin, 1895.

[49] See Godwin 1989, 23-27.

presented itself as the continuation of the 18th-century illuminist tradition founded by Martinez de Pasqually and Louis-Claude de Saint-Martin. *The Morning Star* served for a time as their official organ in America, and carried translations of articles on Martinism and Freemasonry. The "Fraternité de l'Etoile" was founded in 1889 by René Caillié (1831-1896) and Albert Jounet (1863-1923), two Christian esotericists, to counter the "atheistic neo-Buddhism" of the Theosophical Society.[50] Caillié was a member of the H. B. of L.[51]

Davidson was embroiled in the mid-1890s with a difficult character called Edouard Blitz. This apostle of Martinism to America did his best to discredit Davidson in the eyes of Papus and the French occultists by telling them that the H. B. of L. was not flourishing in the New World, and that Davidson's isolation made him incapable of helping the Martinist cause. Although Davidson had born the title of *Supérieur Inconnu* at least since 1892,[52] Blitz wrote to Papus in 1895 that Davidson was still hesitating to join the order because he was not a Freemason.[53] One could be a Martinist without being a Mason (Papus himself was a case in point, though Blitz may not have known it). But this raises the question of whether Davidson himself was ever initiated into Freemasonry. Dr. Greenfield's Loudsville informants say that he was; Mr. Board's state quite adamantly that he was not. And there we must leave it.

Most of our knowledge of Davidson's life in Loudsville comes from the conversations that Mr. Deveney and Dr. Greenfield have had with local people there, including Davidson's descendants.[54] The locals knew Davidson mainly as a practitioner of "alternative medicine," having a deep knowledge of herbs,

---

[50] See Godwin 1989, 20.

[51] Unpublished notes by another French H. B. of L. member, Louis Le Leu, transcribed by L. M. Thémanlys [B.2.c]; copy provided by Mr. Chanel. We have not included a translation of these notes, partly because of their fragmentary form, and partly because they are largely a summary of Guénon's articles [B.9.c, e]. Caillié was the son of the famous explorer René Caillié.

[52] See title page of Davidson 1892.

[53] Letters from Edouard Blitz to Papus, 8 March 1895, 14 September 1895, in Bibliothèque Municipale de Lyon, Fonds Papus, Ms. 5489.

[54] Beside personal communication, we also draw on Greenfield 1992.

drugs, and poisons (as demonstrated in his book *The Philosophy of Man*, and to a lesser extent in *The Mistletoe and Its Philosophy*). Among the surviving documents is a homeopathic Pharmacopeia, with notes on case results. Relatives also recalled Davidson as sending ginseng hunters into the woods, and distributing an "elixir of life." Loudsville lore records that the ex-distiller made the best moonshine around.

Davidson's activity as a healer caused him the one embarrassment of his American period, for it aroused the ire of the local medical establishment, such as it was in North Georgia at the time. He was arrested for practicing medicine without a license, but was acquitted and suffered no further annoyance.

The Davidson family attained local respectability by way of the small-town newspaper of nearby Cleveland, called *The Courier*. The paper was edited from 1897 onwards by Davidson's son Alex, who also became the local postmaster. Its printing press served for *The Morning Star* and Davidson's other publications. Later the editorship passed to Alex's son James P. Davidson, then to James' son Richard Davidson, remaining in the family until recent years.

During the last decade of the century, Peter Davidson's inclination was toward an esoteric Christianity with a strongly apocalyptic flavor, using "Christ" as a generic term more or less equivalent to "Mahatma." The teachings of the H. B. of L. concerning historical and cosmic cycles [A.2.b-d] had already contained the idea of a New Age having begun in 1881. Now, in 1897, Davidson wrote in his magazine of how the invisible Soul World was approaching the mundane plane, furthered by the work of the Martinists and Rosicrucians, and that the "Coming Kingdom" could not be far off.[55] His later work concentrated on two other themes: a mysterious alchemical transmutation of the human body into something more "immortal," and the "Sleep of Siloam" or mystic trance as a transformative experience,[56] on which see Section 15, below.

---

[55] "The Coming Kingdom," in *The Morning Star* VI/4 (1897), 61-63.

[56] See the documents collected by Dr. Greenfield in *Lashtal* V/1 (1993), unpaginated.

As one might expect, Davidson accumulated a rich occult library. His grandchildren remembered him going to it daily "to meditate or something." A few years after Davidson's death his family had a huge bonfire of his papers in the yard, but among the relics that survived were some stereoscopic pictures of Algiers or Tunis. We can associate these with the fact that after the turn of the century, Davidson and Max Theon resumed relations.

By the late 1890s the revelation to the Theons of the Cosmic Tradition was nearing completion.[57] Theon's first attempt to publish this work had been in 1899, with his articles in the *Journal du Magnétisme et de la Psychologie*, but, as we have seen, this came to grief because of the offence taken by the spiritualists. The next attempt was more successful. F.-Ch. Barlet, who was the H. B. of L.'s representative for France, launched the *Revue Cosmique* in January 1901. He was helped by Pierre Deullin, who was a Martinist and soon became (31 May 1909) the brother-in-law of Papus. Barlet and Deullin had both visited the Theons in Algeria in 1900 (and Barlet again in 1901). As well as being the journal's first editor, Barlet helped with the publication of the first and second volumes of *La Tradition Cosmique* (1903, 1904), which tell in allegorical form of cosmic evolution in "the seventh epoch of the classification of matter."[58] He resigned the editorship in the autumn of 1902. From 1904, the official editor was Max Theon, under the pseudonym of "Aia Aziz."

Davidson's connections in France naturally made him aware of the Mouvement Cosmique, and from 1905 onward he offered his *Morning Star* as the vehicle for it in the English-speaking world.[59] *La Revue Cosmique* returned the compliment by publishing a long and appreciative review of Davidson's *Le gui et sa*

---

[57] A simplified version was given in 1899, but differs noticeably from the work published in late 1902 or early 1903.

[58] The catalogue of the Bibliothèque Nationale wrongly lists Barlet as the author of this work.

[59] See "The Cosmic Philosophy: its Aims and Objects," in *The Morning Star* XIII/10 (February 1905), 199ff. We retain the French term, Philosophie Cosmique, to avoid confusion with other uses of the expression.

philosophie,[60] and by announcing that it had no connection with any other magazine "except the section of the Morning Star published in the United States by Peter Davidson."[61] Just as Davidson had accepted the authority of Theon in the 1880s, now he found in the Mouvement Cosmique the best exposition of the mysteries that had occupied him throughout his life: those of birth, death, rebirth, and the Fall and Regeneration of Man. *The Morning Star* and some books translated and edited by Davidson (such as *The Chaldean*, 1911) remain the sole source of these teachings in the English language.[62]

---

[60] This was the French translation of Davidson 1892. The review is in *La Revue Cosmique* IV/4 (April 1905), 247-254. However, in a review by ETLEC ("Bibliographie," in *Le Voile d'Isis*, 25 June 1896, 3-4) it is stated that part of Davidson's work is copied from various works known to occultists, and taken word for word from *Nouvelles éthymologies médicales tirées du gaulois* by Lenglet-Mortier and Diogène Vandamme. Stanislas de Guaita recalled humorously that certain passages in his own works had been copied by Davidson.

[61] *Revue Cosmique* IV/10 (October 1905), 637.

[62] Mr. Paul Johnson has kindly brought to our attention a summary of the Philosophie Cosmique based on Mirra Alfassa's writings and discourses: Levin 1988. In recent years, Argaman (Jerusalem) has published some texts of Theon in English.

8. THOMAS H. BURGOYNE

Unlike the case of Peter Davidson, there are no descendants or local historians anxious to bear witness to the virtues and achievements of Thomas Henry Dalton (1855?-1895?[63]), better known as T. H. Burgoyne, whose misdemeanors are amply chronicled in the Theosophical literature [B.6]. The "Church of Light," a still active Californian group which descended from Burgoyne's teachings, disposes of his life up to 1886 as follows:

> T. H. Burgoyne was the son of a physician in Scotland. He roamed the moors during his boyhood and became conversant with the birds and flowers. He was an amateur naturalist. He also was a natural seer. Through his seership he contacted The Brotherhood of Light on the inner plane, and later contacted M. Theon in person. Still later he came to America, where he taught and wrote on occult subjects.[64]

While this romanticized view cannot entirely be trusted, there is no doubt that Burgoyne was a medium and that he was developed as such by Max Theon. Burgoyne told Gorham Blake that he "visited [Theon's] house as a student every day for a long time" [B.6.k], and gave this clue to their relationship in *The Light of Egypt*:

> ...those who are psychic, may not know WHEN the birth of an event will occur, but they Feel that it will, hence prophecy.
> The primal foundation of all thought is right here, for instance, M. Theon may wish a certain result; if I am receptive, the idea may become incarnated in me, and under an extra spiritual stimulus it may grow and mature and become a material fact.[65]

---

[63] Date of birth deduced from prison records; death record searched for, without success, by Mr. Deveney.

[64] "The Founders of the Church of Light," [1].

[65] *LOE*, I, 189.

Very Truly
T. H. Burgoyne.

Burgoyne was making enquiries in occult circles by 1881, when he wrote to Ayton asking to visit him for a discussion of occultism. The clergyman was shocked when he met this "Dalton," who (Ayton says) boasted of doing Black Magic [B.6.f], and forthwith sent him packing [B.6.k]. Later Ayton would be appalled to learn that it was this same young man with whom, as "Burgoyne," he had been corresponding on H. B. of L. business. Having decided that the mysterious Grand Master "Theon" was really Hurrychund Chintamon, Ayton deduced that the young Scotsman must have learned his black magic from this Indian adventurer.

Hurrychund Chintamon had played an important part in the early Theosophical Society and in the move of Blavatsky and Olcott from New York to India. He had been their chief Indian correspondent during 1877-1878, when he was President of the Bombay Arya Samaj (a Vedic revival movement with which the early Theosophical Society was allied). After Blavatsky and Olcott arrived in Bombay in 1879 and met Chintamon in person, they discovered that he was a scoundrel and an embezzler, and expelled him from the Society. Chintamon came to England in 1879 or 1880, and stayed until 1883, when he returned to make further trouble for the Theosophists in India. Perhaps the fact that Chintamon was in England when Burgoyne first met Theon led some to conclude that they were the same person.[66] But this cannot be the whole story. Ayton claimed very clearly and repeatedly that he had proof of Burgoyne's being in company with Chintamon. In a letter in the private collection, Ayton writes:

> I have since discovered that Hurrychund Chintaman the notorious Black Magician was in company with Dalton at Bradford. By means of a Photograph I have traced him to Glasgow & even to Banchory, under the alias of Darushah Chichgur. Friends in London saw him there just before his return to India. This time coincides with that when I noticed a great change in the

---

[66] See Ransom, 115-116, 120-121, 175.

management. Chintaman had supplied the Oriental knowledge as he was a Sanskrit scholar & knew much. Theon was Chintaman! Friends have lately seen him in India where he is still at his tricks.

Before her disillusion with Chintamon, Blavatsky had touted him to the London Theosophists as a "great adept." After the break that followed on her meeting with him in person, Chintamon allied himself to the rising Western opposition to esoteric Buddhism exemplified by Stainton Moses, C. C. Massey, William Oxley, Emma Hardinge Britten, Thomas Lake Harris, and others. From this formidable group, Burgoyne first contracted the hostility towards Blavatsky's enterprise that would mark all his writings.

Chintamon also appears in connection with "H. B. Corinni," the otherwise unidentifiable (and variously spelled) "Private Secretary" of Theon, who was thought by the police to be just another of Burgoyne's aliases. Ayton, however, believed Corinni to be Chintamon's son, who he said offered Blavatsky's old letters for sale to the President of the London Branch of the Theosophical Society, Charles Carleton Massey.[67] The flaw in Ayton's thesis is of course the existence of a real and independent Max Theon, of whom we, unlike Ayton, have documentary evidence. Nonetheless, after more than a hundred years, the whole tangle of misidentifications involving Chintamon, "Christamon," and "Metamon" [see B.9.c-e] with the Order cannot be entirely resolved.

By October 1882, Burgoyne was in Leeds, working in the menial trade of a grocer.[68] Here he tried to bring off an advertising fraud [B.6.d] so timid as to cast serious doubt on his abilities as a black magician! As a consequence, he spent the first seven months of 1883 in jail. He had probably met Theon before his incarceration, and, as we have seen, worked for a time in daily sessions as Theon's medium. On his release he struck up or

---

[67] Ayton to unnamed American neophyte, 11 June 1886, based on what he had been told by Massey.

[68] This is the trade ascribed to him in the court records. The records of the Leeds Constabulary call him "medium and astrologer."

resumed relations with Peter Davidson, and became the Private Secretary to the Council of the H. B. of L. when it went public the following year.

Burgoyne contributed many letters and articles to *The Occult Magazine*, usually writing under the pseudonym "Zanoni." He also contributed to Thomas Johnson's *Platonist* [see B.7.c], showing considerably more literacy than in the letter that so amused the Theosophists [B.7.b]. But he never claimed to be an original writer. In the introduction to the "Mysteries of Eros" [A.3.b] he states his role as that of amanuensis and compiler. The former term reveals what the H. B. of L. regarded as the true source of its teachings—the initiates of the Interior Circle of the Order. The goal of the magical practice taught by the H. B. of L. was the development of the potentialities of the individual so that he or she could communicate directly with the Interior Circle and with the other entities, disembodied and never embodied, that the H. B. of L. believed to populate the universes. If Gorham Blake is to be credited [B.6.k], Davidson and Burgoyne "confessed" to him that Burgoyne was an "inspirational medium" and that the teachings of the Order came through his mediumship. Stripped of the bias inherent in the terms "medium," and "confess," there is no reason to doubt the statement of Burgoyne's role. In the Order's own terminology, however, his connection with the spiritual hierarchies of the universe was through "Blending"—the taking over of the *conscious* subject's mind by the Initiates of the Interior Circle and the Potencies, Powers, and Intelligences of the celestial hierarchies—and through the "Sacred Sleep of Sialam" (see Section 15, below).

Shortly after arriving in Georgia, for all the Theosophists' efforts to intercept him [B.6.l], Burgoyne parted with Davidson. From then on, the two communicated mainly through their mutual disciples, squabbling over fees for reading the neophytes' horoscopes and over Burgoyne's distribution of the Order's manuscripts, with each man essentially running a separate organization. This split may be reflected in the French version of "Laws of Magic Mirrors" [A.3.a], which was prepared in 1888 and which bears the reference "Peter Davidson, Provincial Grand Master of the Eastern Section."

Burgoyne made his way from Georgia first to Kansas, then to Denver, and finally to Monterey, California, staying with

H. B. of L. members as he went.[69] According to the Church of Light, Burgoyne now met Norman Astley, a professional surveyor and retired Captain in the British Army. After 1887 Astley and a small group of students engaged Burgoyne to write the basic H. B. of L. teachings as a series of lessons, giving him hospitality and a small stipend. Astley is actually said to have visited England to meet Theon—something which is hardly credible in the light of what is known of Theon's methods.[70] We do know, however, that Burgoyne advertised widely and took subscriptions for the lessons, and that they were published in book form in 1889 as *The Light of Egypt; or The Science of the Soul and the Stars*, attributed to Burgoyne's H. B. of L. sobriquet "Zanoni."

With *The Light of Egypt*, the secrecy of the H. B. of L.'s documents was largely broken, and they were revealed—to those who could tell—to be fairly unoriginal compilations from earlier occultists, presented with a strongly anti-Theosophical tone. Only the practical teachings were omitted. The book was translated into French by René Philipon, a friend of René Guénon's, and into Russian and Spanish, and a paraphrase of it was published in German.[71] We present [B.8] the most important reactions to this work, which has been reprinted frequently up to the present day.

Burgoyne's last years were spent in unwonted comfort if, as the Church of Light says, Dr. Henry and Belle M. Wagner—who had been members of the H. B. of L. since 1885—gave $100,000 to found an organization for the propagation of the *Light of Egypt*

---

[69] Itinerary based où letters from Burgoyne as he progressed West.

[70] "The Founders of the Church of Light," [2].

[71] *La lumière d'Egypte où la science des Astres et de l'âme en deux parties* (Paris: Chamuel, 1895); Philipon's identity as the anonymous translator confirmed in *Stanislas de Guaita*, 16. Philipon also translated Burgoyne's *Celestial Dynamics* as *La Dynamique Céleste, Cours de Métaphysique astrale* (Paris: Chacornac, 1899, reprinted Genoa: Phoenix, 1982). There is an anonymous French translation of *The Light of Egypt* in Lyon, Fonds Papus 5.491.-II (27). Spanish translation: *La luz de Egipto o la ciencia de la alma y las estrellas* (Buenos Aires: Editorial Kier, S. A., 1978). Russian translation by the astrologer V. N. Zapriagaev: *Svet Egipta, ili nauka o zvezdakh i dushe* (Viaz'ma, 1906; 2nd ed. 1910); see Maria Carlson, *"No Religion Higher than Truth." A History of the Theosophical Movement in Russia, 1875-1922* (Princeton: Princeton University Press, 1993), 211, n.12. German paraphrase by "Raphael" (Paul Köthner): *Hermetische Lehrbriefe über Sternenweistum und Alchemie* (Leipzig: Theosophisches Verlagshaus, 1908, 1924).

teachings. Out of this grew the Astro-Philosophical Publishing Company of Denver, and the Church of Light itself, reformed in 1932 by Elbert Benjamine (= C. C. Zain, 1882-1951).[72] Beside Burgoyne's other books *The Language of the Stars* and *Celestial Dynamics*, the new company issued in 1900 a second volume of *The Light of Egypt*. This differs markedly from the first volume, for it is ascribed to Burgoyne's spirit, speaking through a medium who was his "spiritual successor," Mrs. Wagner. As the spirit said, with characteristically poor grammar: "Dictated by the author from the subjective plane of life (to which he ascended several years ago) through the law of mental transfer, well known to all Occultists, he is enabled again to speak with those who are still upon the objective plane of life."[73]

Max Theon wrote to the Wagners in 1909 (the year after his wife's death), telling them to close their branch of the H. B. of L.[74] By that time, the Order had virtually ceased to exist as such, while the Wagners continued on their own, channeling doctrinal and fictional works. Their son Henry O. Wagner told Mr. Deveney that he, in turn, received books from his parents by the "blending" process, to be described below. In 1963 he issued an enlarged edition of *The Light of Egypt*, which included several further items from his parents' records. Some of these are known to have circulated separately to neophytes during the heyday of the H. B. of L. (see Section 10, below), while others were circulated by Burgoyne individually on a subscription basis to his own private students (all of whom were in theory members of the H. B. of L.) from 1887 until his death. These include a large body of astrological materials and also treatises on "Penetralia," "Soul Knowledge (Atma Bodha)" and other topics. They are perfectly consistent with the H. B. of L. teachings, but appear to have been Burgoyne's individual production, done after his separation from Peter Davidson, and they are not reproduced here.[75]

---

[72] "The Church of Light."

[73] *LOE*, II, xi.

[74] Information given to Mr. Deveney by Henry O. Wagner.

[75] As a companion to the printed version of the "Mysteries of Eros" circulated by Dr. Henry Wagner to the Denver group of the H. B. of L., a silk-bound pamphlet was issued containing "La Clef Hermétique," "La Clef," "Naronia," "Soul Knowledge," and "Penetralia," all of which are found in the augmented *LOE*.

9. PASCHAL BEVERLY RANDOLPH

We have now surveyed the H. B. of L.'s origins as a semi-secret order for teaching practical occultism, and described the roles of Theon, Davidson, and Burgoyne. For all the vaunted participation of celestial hierarchies, the more immediate source of almost all the Order's teachings is more plebeian, and demonstrates the truth of Burgoyne's claim to be merely a compiler. René Guénon suggested that one should look for the antecedents of the H. B. of L. in a "Brotherhood of Eulis," which he rightly says was founded about 1870 by Paschal Beverly Randolph.[76] Even a glance at the practical instruction embodied in the "Laws of Magic Mirrors" and "Mysteries of Eros" reveals the enormous extent to which the Order mined the works of this unique and underrated character.[77]

Randolph (1825-1875) was an African American man who had a reputation by the early 1850s as a typical "trance speaker" who would act as the unconscious medium for various reform-minded "spirits." This began to change in 1855 when he traveled to Europe and mixed in the Mesmerist circles in France around Baron Jules Du Potet de Sennevoy and Louis Alphonse Cahagnet. Unlike most American spiritualists, the French Mesmerists were well versed in the Western magical and occult traditions. Also, and most especially, they used in their spirit evocations magic mirrors or crystals, and drugs, especially hashish. All this was a revelation to Randolph.

In 1857, and again in 1861, Randolph was in Europe visiting the same circles, but also venturing to the Near East (Egypt, Palestine, and Turkey as far as the borders of Persia), where he came to know a different sort of magic among the wandering dervishes and "fakirs" whom he met on his travels. Returning to America after his first trip to the East, he publicly denounced spiritualism, and especially the role he had hitherto accepted: that of a passive and unconscious medium for the "spirits." In its place he now taught a complete system of practice and theory, of which these are the main points: A) Myriads of divine "monads"

---

[76] Guénon 1982, 313; Guénon 1952, 21.

[77] This section is condensed from Mr. Deveney's forthcoming study of P. B. Randolph.

are continuously being spun out from the vortex of the Divine Central Sun. The goal of every human monad is to become first individuated, then a divine individual, and then to progress perpetually as a god through infinite universes. The inhabitants of these universes are not limited (as the spiritualists thought) to the "spirits" of the human dead, but include vast hierarchies of "elementals" and of the progressed dead and of the never embodied, with all of whom men on earth can be taught to communicate. B) There is no reincarnation in the sense of rebirth on this earth, with the exception of abortions, mental defectives, and those who die before the "soul" really comes into being. C) The goal of divinization can be attained by many people here and now, through clairvoyance achieved by means of the magic mirror, drugs, and sexual magic.

Whatever René Guénon may have urged to the contrary, both Randolph and the H. B. of L. were firm believers in communication with the dead. But Modern Spiritualism, in Randolph's mature view, was up a blind alley in trying indiscriminately to contact what it took to be the spirits of the dead, and in encouraging passive and unconscious mediumship. What should be contacted was adepts and beings in the celestial hierarchies, and what should be cultivated was conscious clairvoyance and the will.

Originally Randolph characterized his teachings as "Rosicrucian," though by that he did not mean exclusively the Rosicrucians known to history. These were merely a small part of the real Order, which Randolph called by various Oriental names ("Gate of Light," etc.). This extended on both sides of the grave, among men and among the earthly and celestial hierarchies, and contact with it was on the clairvoyant level. Randolph spoke variously of his contact with Ramus/Thothmor, a dead Egyptian pharaoh, and with Pul ali Beg, a Persian who, it seemed, was still alive. The earthly extensions of the Order were in the Near East, though there appears to have been a center in Paris.

Randolph places great emphasis, both personally and as an occultist, on a state he calls variously "Blending" or "Atrilism"— a state in which a person, while still conscious, is totally taken over by another being, human or never human, and indoctrinated or used for some purpose. This was the very essence of the

Paschal Beverly Randolph

H. B. of L. A parallel process is to be seen in the relationship of Blavatsky with the "Brothers" who wrote much of *Isis Unveiled* through her: Colonel Olcott remarked on how she would sometimes assume, while writing, an entirely different and masculine personality, which did not seem even to recognize him.[78] Another case relevant to our topic is that of Emma Hardinge Britten (see Section 13, below), who from 1857 onward found that she could lecture in full consciousness on virtually any subject without any preparation, thanks to an apparently omniscient force that used her voice.[79]

The Philosophie Cosmique explains that entities not living on earth can materialize in the aura of certain persons, through "reciprocal affinity." Randolph himself had been aware of the dangers of "Blending," and Theon's warnings were even stronger. He called it "confusion of being" and identified it as one of the most dangerous sources of unbalance, especially when it concerned non-human entities. He denounced it vigorously as one of the dangers of spiritualism. On the contrary, Theon says, the magnetizer should respect the medium as he would a rare Stradivarius violin, and leave her in full liberty, since it is the medium's own sincerity that enables her to reflect the higher worlds. For this, it is essential for her to be free from any imposition by another. The role of the "pathetizer" in Theon's method is simply to protect and guide the medium, and to obtain knowledge for the good of humanity.

From his earliest days, Randolph was fascinated with sex, both personally and as a physician. He claimed to have found in the Near East the true secret of sex, and began in the early 1870s to distribute a series of manuscript teachings on his sexual magic. The organization which he formed for this purpose was the "Brotherhood of Eulis," mentioned by Guénon as the place to look for the origins or antecedents of the H. B. of L.

After Randolph's death, his wife, Kate Corson Randolph, and followers continued his work. In the early 1880s the Bath bookseller Robert H. Fryar was the agent in Britain for the sale of

---

[78] *ODL*, I, 236-254.
[79] See Britten, 50-51.

his manuscript teachings, of which the most important was the "Mysteries of Eulis." When Fryar had first come into contact with Randolph is unknown, but the relationship probably dates back to Randolph's friendship in the early 1860s with the circle of "Christian" spiritualists around the *London Spiritual Magazine*. Hargrave Jennings, never good at chronology, wrote to Fryar in 1887: "I first knew Randolph the American thirty-five years ago..." Fryar's edition of *The Divine Pymander* (with Jennings' Preface), in which the H. B. of L. first announced itself, was the first edition of the *Corpus Hermeticum* to appear since Randolph's own edition of 1871, and typographically almost identical with it.[80] We conclude that the H. B. of L. started to function within a small Randolphian coterie already existing in England, of which Fryar was the center.

Nowhere in the surviving H. B. of L. material is the exact relationship between the Order and Randolph, or between Randolph and Theon, spelled out. That Randolph was called "half-initiated" implies a real connection somewhere with the H. B. of L.'s putative antecedents or siblings, as does the Order's wholesale appropriation of his practical magic, but the exact connection is never made explicit. Perhaps Guénon's theory that the antecedents of the H. B. of L. were to be sought in Randolph's Brotherhood of Eulis [B.9.e], with its supposed Near Eastern source in the Isma'ili Nusairi, is an echo of the Order's own attempt to explain the relationship. What is demonstrably certain, however, is that the entirety of the H. B. of L. manuscript material, with the exception of the purely doctrinal works, "The Key," "The Hermetic Key," and "Symbolical Notes," is essentially derived from Randolph. The indebtedness, moreover, is greater than is apparent from the texts as published here. In the early days of the Order, manuscript copies of the "Mysteries of Eulis" were circulated to the neophytes as such, and the First Grade of the Order was known as the "Grade of Eulis." But the H. B. of L., though it valued very highly certain parts of Ran-

---

[80] Both editions of *The Divine Pymander* have been reprinted in facsimile: Randolph's (in the reissue of 1889) by Health Research, Mokelumne Hill, Ca., 1972; Fryar's by Wizard's Bookshelf, Minneapolis, 1973. The H. B. of L.'s advertisement [B.3.b] has been eliminated from the latter.

dolph's teachings, did not so admire the teacher. By his own account, Randolph was an extremely unhappy man, frequently out of control and sometimes on the brink of insanity; he died by his own hand. The H. B. of L. cautioned its neophytes that he was only "half-initiated" and that he had fallen into black magic. Gradually "Eulis," with its strong echoes of Randolph, gave way to "Eros" or "Erosa," as the Order distanced itself from Randolph while continuing to use his work. This, rather than simple plagiarism, accounts for the suppression of his name in the documents adapted from his writings.

Randolph's distinction lies primarily in his practical instructions on personal development: mirror practice, drugs, and sexual magic. His methods, learned (as he variously claimed) in the Near East or from personages of the celestial hierarchies, or made up from his own creativity, provided the essential element missing from the occultist *koiné* of the period: the practical key to an experiential realization by the individual neophyte of the mysteries expounded endlessly in the wordy occult compilations and theories of the age. With the exception of the French and English Mesmerists and the related mirror-magicians of the mid-century—whose practical experiences were in any case secondhand at best, mediated through the visions and reports of the medium or seer—Randolph provided practical instruction for a person seeking to realize directly the truths of occultism. His works outlined a variety of means of achieving personal experience: mirror magic to develop clairvoyance in the individual using the mirror; the three principles of practical magic (Volantia, Decretism, and Posism); sexual magic; "Blending" as the means of communication with the celestial hierarchies; the Sleep of Sialam, and the use of mind-altering drugs.

These practical means were taken over wholesale by the H. B. of L., and it is these that constituted its attraction for the occultists of the time—especially for Theosophists "who may have been disappointed in their expectations of Sublime Wisdom being freely dispensed by Hindoo Mahatmas."

10. THE SECRET DOCUMENTS

While individual teaching manuscripts bear the name or initials of Peter Davidson, the Provincial Grand Master of the North of the H. B. of L., or of T. H. Burgoyne, the Secretary, it is clear that these works were largely common efforts, produced or edited by both of them. Their individual hands and roles, however, are discernible in different works. "Symbolical Notes to the First Degree" [A.2.a], which is an exposition of the theory of the role of sex in the soul's descent into matter and reascent to the heavenly spheres, clearly shows the hand of Davidson in its rehashing of the ideas of Hargrave Jennings, Emma Hardinge Britten, and H.P.Blavatsky. The same is true of the material from Agrippa and from Barrett's *Magus* that has been added to Randolph's mirror instructions in "Laws of Magic Mirrors" [A.3.a]. Davidson had all of the obscure learning so dear to the hearts of most 19th-century occultists. Burgoyne, on the other hand, was no scholar, and the compilations mixed with polemic embodied in the "Hermetic Key," "The Key," "Naronia," and "Reincarnation" undoubtedly bear his stamp.[81]

The part of the H. B. of L. corpus that Davidson and Burgoyne chose as accompaniment to the Randolph materials is surprisingly nondescript, being variations on the prevailing occult themes of the day, largely theoretical or antiquarian, lacking both the practical purpose and the personal conviction and experiential basis of Randolph's work. These "original" items, again excepting the purely doctrinal expositions such as "The Key," consist primarily in the addition of the elements of traditional Western ceremonial magic (paraphrased mainly from Barrett, the *Comte de Gabalis*, and Agrippa) and the traditional correspondences of colors, metals, astrological times, etc., appropriate to various ritual acts or explanatory of various cosmological theories. Examples of this class of material are the rituals for initiation into the Order and the theoretical additions to "Laws of Magic Mirrors" [A.1.e,f; A.3.a]. The eternal refuge of the non-visionary who suspects the existence of mystery and desires to participate

---

[81] Even though Burgoyne himself attributed the "Hermetic Key" to H. B. Corinni, Max Theon's Private Secretary. See A.2.b.

in it is bookish elaboration, dogmatism, and the working out of the permutations of a theme. The additions to Randolph's work made by the H. B. of L., especially those by Davidson, largely reflect such elaboration. The tendency to romantic detail is obvious, for example, in the insistence in the H. B. of L. additions to "Laws of Magic Mirrors" that the windows of the scrying room be veiled in "violet drapes" and that its illumination be from "crystal" lamps.

The H. B. of L. versions of Randolph's work also smack of midnight oil and the antiquary, and deliberately omit his driving vision. Compare the following from Randolph's manuscript "Mysteries of Eulis" with the same reworked passage as presented in the "Mysteries of Eros" (see page 230):

> That there are hierarchies—armies of them!—Potencies, Powers, vast Intelligences—not of human or material genesis, before whose awful grasp of mental powers, before whose amazing sweep of mind, the grandest intellect earth ever did or can produce, is as a pebble to a mountain range: a tiny dewdrop to the almighty rush of ocean's waters;—a gentle shower to a tempest of rain; a zephyr to the raging typhoon or its devastating march over lands and seas! These beings may be the arbiters of the destinies of worlds; and I believe that they are the originators of many a drama fruitful of good. But how do you know that such things exist? Because 1st. In the sleep of Sialam I and others have seen them; and we know they were not of this or similar earths, because they are organically different, and look no more like a human apparition than a negro does like a Kalmuc Tarter.[82]

The purely doctrinal and cosmological works of the H. B. of L. similarly lack originality. The Hebrew etymologies and the

---

[82] This is an unacknowledged reference by Randolph to Edward Bulwer-Lytton's Rosicrucian novel *Zanoni*, Book IV, Chapter 4, where Lytton comments on the myriads of beings in the universes: "these races and tribes differ more widely each from the other than the Calmuch from the Greek..."

description of the "Wheel of Ezechiel" that forms the centerpiece of Davidson's "Symbolical Notes to the First Degree" are derived from Blavatsky's *Isis Unveiled* and from the works of Emma Hardinge Britten and Hargrave Jennings. The striking presentation of the cyclical revolution of the earth's pole around its axis, similarly, is derived from the work of the obscure shoemaker of Norwich, Samson Arnold Mackey (1824), with elaborations on the Hindu *yugas* derived from Sinnett's *Esoteric Buddhism* (1883).

To point out these sources, however, is not to disparage the value of the final works or to accuse the H. B. of L. of impropriety, as the enemies of the Order repeatedly tried to do [see B.8.d]. In the H. B. of L.'s own myth of origins laid out in Davidson's "Origin and Object of the H. B. of L." [A.1.c], the Order had existed throughout history under one name or another, and was the real source of everything that was authentic and valuable in the Western occult tradition. Specifically with regard to the sources mentioned above, the H. B. of L. claimed Mackey as an initiate of the Order (Burgoyne promoted him in *The Light of Egypt* to "adept") and regarded Emma Hardinge Britten's mysterious Chevalier Louis de B_____ (see Section 13, on p. 56) as a member of the H. B. of L.'s Interior Circle, and her own works as propaedeutic of the revival of the H. B. of L. in the 1880s. Both Randolph and Blavatsky were seen as true initiates of the Order who had fallen aside from their obligations. On crucial issues, moreover, the H. B. of L. was willing to depart from its sources. The strongest example of this is the Order's explicit rejection, obviously for principled reasons, of Randolph's use of sexual magic for "selfish" ends and its caution on the the dangers of trying to implant the seeds of celestial Powers in one's own soul rather than in the human embryo [see "A Brief Key," Chapter IV of "Mysteries of Eros," A.3.c].

The most salient omissions in all of the H. B. of L. manuscripts, especially in the light of the supposed role of the Hindu, Hurrychund Chintamon as a motivating principal of the Order [see B.6.g], and the undoubted role of Max Theon as the contact between its Interior and Exterior Circles, are the paucity of Indian (Buddhist or Hindu) and of Philosophie Cosmique material. The only allusions to the former are the references in the "Hermetic Key" to various Indian theories of cosmic cycles, which are derived from Sinnett and were in any case part of the *koiné*. The Hebrew homologies expounded in "Symbolical Notes," similarly, were commonplaces of Western occult antiquarianism since the Renaissance, rather than truly Kabbalistic teachings.

11. METAPHYSICS OF THE H.B. OF L.

The impression left by a reading of the manuscript teachings is one of incompleteness. Tantalizing references abound to unexplained things that obviously were conceived of as part of some larger system or pattern. What exactly was the nature of the "monad" said to descend into incarnation? What were the "Potencies, Powers and Intelligences" that populated the universes of creation? What is humanity and what is its destiny? Why was sex and sexual differentiation central to its progress and development? The questions were clear, and were expected to be answered by the neophytes seeking to advance in the degrees of the Order [see A.1.d].

The answers are nowhere stated in the manuscript teachings, and were set forth systematically only in *The Light of Egypt*. The neophyte in the early years, however, was not left totally without help, because he or she was credited with at least an elementary familiarity with the tradition of Western occultism as it had been affected by spiritualism since mid-century. The reader was specifically referred to the works of Emma Hardinge Britten and P. B. Randolph, while Blavatsky's early works (including *Isis Unveiled*) were held out as supplements to the secret manuscript teachings. From these sources and from hints and references in the manuscripts, the neophyte—before reaching the exalted state of intuition and clairvoyance that would enable him to receive occult knowledge directly from the members of the Interior Circle—could derive the beautiful and harmoniously developed system of cosmology and anthropology that was the foundation of the H. B. of L.'s practical efforts.

One element that is often ignored in discussions of the H. B. of L. is found in the very name of the Order—the *Hermetic* Brotherhood of Luxor. It was certainly no accident that the first appearance of the Order was in connection with an edition of *The Divine Pymander of Hermes Mercurius Trismegistus* [see B.3.b]. The Corpus Hermeticum provided a cosmology and anthropology with very striking similarities to the teachings of the H. B. of L.— the Primordial Light (*Phos*) that gives birth to the immortal and androgynous part of man (*Nous*), which is sundered in its descent into matter and after death either reascends to take its proper place among the Choir of the Powers in the Eighth

Sphere, or else lapses into perpetual oblivion. The Hermetic writings constituted the essential background of the wave of "Western" occultism that found expression in the H. B. of L.

In the cosmogony of *The Light of Egypt*, the origin of all things lies in the primordial, divine Central Sun that centrifugally spun off and generated the universes of creation. In contradistinction to the standard spiritualist doctrine that the universe of spirits was limited to the souls of the dead, this Western tradition taught that humanity was not alone in the creative outpouring, and that the universes were populated with myriads of entities, both disembodied and never embodied on this earth, who ascended in vast hierarchies back to the divine origin. These beings intermingled themselves in human affairs and, properly contacted, taught the truths of occultism. The human being was a trinity of spirit, soul, and body (though the same elements were sometimes subdivided, as in the later Theosophical teaching, to make seven principles). Of these, the spirit was divine and immortal. The soul, which was the individual, originated as the divine bisexual monad.

As in Plato's *Symposium*, this was sundered at the beginning, and its male and female halves, forgetful of their origin, thereafter transmigrated through the worlds of material creation, always seeking reunion with their separated soul mates and finally incarnating in this world as men and women. Birth in this world is the critical step in the process, because it is here that a person either unites the individuality with the divine element, thus achieving conscious and individualized immortality (a key concept in the Philosophie Cosmique), or else chooses materiality over the spirit, thus losing forever the chance for individualization and immortality, and descends after death into the "elementary" world and eventual dissolution. After death (or, for the initiate, during life) the immortal individual continues on a pilgrimage through the spheres, finally reuniting permanently with his or her sundered half and becoming a "god" or "angel" that henceforth perpetually progresses, asymptotically approaching the divine origin.

This mythology lay at the foundation of the Order's conflict with its nemesis, the Theosophical Society, and also provided the theoretical basis for the practical, magical efforts of the H. B. of L.

12. THE H.B. OF L. AND THEOSOPHICAL DOCTRINE

The relationship of the H. B. of L. to the T. S. (Theosophical Society) was of universal interest among the neophytes of the H. B. of L., not least because most of them were simultaneously members—and in fact prominent members—of the T. S. For example, Barlet wrote in 1888 to Arthur Arnould (who became the head of the new Hermès branch of the T. S. in France even as he was joining the H. B. of L.) that the situation was proper and that Peter Davidson himself was a member of the Council of the T. S. He wrote that: "It seems particularly fortunate that the President of the French branch of the T. S. is at the same time going to receive from the Mother Society everything it offers to make known. . . ."[83]

Nonetheless, the relationship between the groups was a precarious one for the much smaller H. B. of L., and when serious differences arose, the Order tried hard to avoid an open breach. On the one hand, the H. B. of L. could present itself as the *real* T. S., since it had been behind the latter's foundation, and since its teachings represented the pure, unadulterated doctrines of its founders. On a more practical level, the public posture of the H. B. of L. was that no conflict could exist between the groups, because the T. S. was avowedly theoretical and against practical occultism, whereas (to quote Barlet again) the "specialty of our H. B. of L is to make occultism practical, and to teach it systematically . . . ." (See also B.7.d.)

Underlying these niceties, however, was Davidson's conviction that Madame Blavatsky, in falling away from her original control by the H. B. of L., had fallen into the clutches not merely of the "Sacerdotalists" but of "a greatly inferior Order, belonging to the Budhist [sic] Cult" [A.1.c]. It was these inferior cultists—so the theory ran—who had introduced into Theosophy the dogmas of reincarnation and non-personal immortality and the obsession of the T. S. with celibacy. Central to the proof of this thesis were the letters to which Davidson refers in which Mme. Blavatsky supposedly "confessed"to Otho Alexander the truth

---

[83] Letter of F.-Ch. Barlet to A. Arnould, September 5, 1888, in Fonds Papus.

of the allegations about Buddhist control. These were the *pièce de résistance* in the argument, but unfortunately they have not survived.[84]

Leaving aside the claim of the H. B. of L. that Madame Blavatsky had originally been an initiate of the Order, the fact remains that her early ideas bear a striking resemblance to the cosmology of the H. B. of L. Blavatsky had originally taught a view of humanity and its destiny that was decidedly "Western." The human being was composed of three principles, body, soul, and spirit, the last of which contained the possibility of immortality. The goal of occultism (and of life itself) was individualization—the permanent joinder of the soul to the spirit which produced a conscious, immortal entity that thereafter could progress perpetually through the universes of creation. As necessary corollaries of these views, Blavatsky in the early years rejected, with certain curious exceptions shared with Randolph and the H. B. of L., the notion that the kernel of this entity ever reincarnated on this earth as a human.

After her move to India early in 1879, these ideas began to change. The new doctrines began to appear progressively in 1881 as the famous "Fragments of Occult Truth," published anonymously in *The Theosophist* from October onwards, against which the H. B. of L. railed [B.8.d,e]. The new revelation centered upon the sevenfold constitution of the human being (which the H. B. of L. adopted), the idea of non-personal immortality, and the reincarnation of the sixth and seventh principles. When the conglomerate dissolved at death, according to this teaching, in the usual case of a person with some degree of spiritual development,[85] the sixth and seventh

---

[84] Excerpts from the letters were widely distributed. When Elliott B. Page, a member of the H. B. of L.'s Central Council and also a member of the American Board of Control of the T. S., wrote a letter to *The Occultist* in 1885 to remonstrate with it for the tone of its attacks on the T. S. [B.5.e], Davidson had copies of the letters sent to him.

[85] Of course, if the deceased had totally turned his mind to material things and ignored his higher sixth and seventh principles, he could at death entirely lose access to these and become a "Pisacha," a sort of dis-spirited fifth principle with some elements of the deceased's memories and mind. This was precisely the thing, according to Blavatsky and the H. B. of L., that appeared at most spiritualist seances.

immortal and non-individual principles, together with "some of the more abstract and pure of the mortal attributes of the fifth principle or animal Soul, its manas [mind] and memory," pass into "Devachan."[86] This is a state of "sweet dream" where the "eternal imperishable but also *unconscious* 'Monad'" of the sixth and seventh principles rests, self-absorbed in the purest delights of the few remaining elements of personality taken over from the fifth principle.[87] Finally, after the Devachanic interlude, even the remnants of the fifth (personal) principle are burned away, and only the immortal and absolutely non-personal sixth and seventh principles go on to be reborn in a fresh set of principles 1-5 on earth. The goal was therefore not individualization, immortality, and progress, but impersonal "final absorption into the *One All.*"[88]

There is no doubt that all of this was a departure from Blavatsky's earlier views, as Colonel Olcott frankly confessed in his memoirs of the early days of the Theosophical Society,[89] and the change in position gave credence to the H. B. of L.'s myth that the Theosophical Society had been started under the Order's own aegis, and had then departed from its original purposes and teachings.

The rub of the later Theosophical position, of course, as the spiritualists[90] and the H. B. of L. were very quick to point out, was the denial of any real communication with the dead. The entity in Devachan was only in some very remote sense "individual" or "personal" in our sense of the terms, only remotely identical with the one who lately walked the earth. The entity

---

[86] See, for example, T. Subbha Row, "The Aryan-Arhat Esoteric Tenets on the Sevenfold Principle in Man," with notes by Madame Blavatsky, in *The Theosophist* III (January 1882) [*BCW*, III, 400-424]. Compare also *ML*, 103 (Letter XVI).

[87] *ML*, 101, 104 (Letter XVI); 184 (Letter XXIVB).

[88] H. P. Blavatsky, "Seeming Discrepancies," in *The Theosophist* III (June 1882); *BCW*, IV, 119-121.

[89] *ODL*, I, 277ss., 280-281, 288. See also *ML* 324 (Letter LVII), in which the Master Koot Hoomi reminded his correspondent that it was only in July 1881 that Sinnett had begun to be instructed in the differences between Allan Kardec's "reincarnation" (personal rebirth) and the impersonal rebirth of the "Spiritual Monad." For the chronology, see Conger, 13.

[90] See H. P. Blavatsky, "Is it Idle to Argue Further?" in reply to "M. A. (Oxon.)" in *The Theosophist* III (January 1882); *BCW*, III, 391-395, etc.

surviving death could not be communicated with by the living by being dragged back to the seance room from Devachan. Possibly the "astral ego" of a properly sensitive medium could rise or ascend to the entity in Devachan and to some unsatisfactory extent "blend" with it or "become" it, partaking in its self-absorption. But the personality could progress no further and was annihilated at the rebirth of the sixth and seventh principles (the "Spiritual Ego") after the Devachanic interlude, leaving only a variety of shells and detritus that, while they may have had some of the person's memories and pieces of his or her character, were in fact so much garbage left behind by the departing true Ego and unworthy of being communicated with.[91]

All of this was eminently unsatisfactory to the spiritualists—and to the H. B. of L.—for whom communication with higher entities, including the "spirits" of the dead, was of central importance. And it did not begin to approach the Theons' concept of the ultimate goal of humanity, which was nothing less than physical immortality.

---

[91] See, for example, ML, 101 (Letter XVI); Blavatsky's notes on William Oxley's "Hierosophy and Theosophy," in The Theosophist IV (July 1883); BCW, IV, 557-560; and her notes to M. A. (Oxon.)'s article, "Spirit Identity and Recent Speculations," in The Theosophist IV (July 1883); BCW, IV, 583-598.

13. EMMA HARDINGE BRITTEN
AND THE "HIDDEN HAND"

Setting aside these later differences in doctrine, it is possible, and illuminating, to see the H. B. of L. in the context of a large-scale movement within Western esotericism, of which the early Theosophical Society was also a part. Its driving idea, that of a Universal Tradition of Wisdom descending in unbroken order from the Golden Age before the Deluge, had become a cornerstone of occultism by the mid-century. The ultimate source of information was usually Godfrey Higgins' *Anacalypsis* (1836), or, for the French-speaking world, the works of Fabre d'Olivet, Creuzer, de Rougement, Jacolliot and Frédéric Portal (see Laurant 1975, 29-37). It was obvious to all concerned that some ancient wisdom must lie hidden in the fragments of ancient mythology and in the obscure oriental texts that were beginning to appear in the 19th century, and it was hoped that living schools of adepts—probably in the East—still preserved this wisdom intact and could impart it in a practical way to the seeker.

In his essay "Origin and Object of the H. B. of L." [A.1.b], Davidson sketches this sweeping picture of universal history, beginning with the mysterious "Lost Isle of the West," the origin of the Tradition in this cycle and the source of both Indian and Egyptian wisdom, as well as of the various attempts to reawaken that wisdom, such as Hermeticism, Buddhism, Pythagoreanism, Freemasonry, and the Rosicrucians. Thus far, the history is commonplace, a mere variation on the theme of the *prisca theologia* that had emerged in the Renaissance. The unusual feature of Davidson's version is the idea of schools of initiates with real differences between them and with conflicting approaches to the practical realization of occult truth. All were true initiates, but the Eastern branch (identified with Thebes and India) had rigidified into "sacerdotalism," useless theorizing, and the quest for a monopoly of power, while the Western branch (identified with Luxor and the Hermetic tradition) had continued to teach "practical occultism" to all those found worthy. This idea of a power struggle on Olympus was to have a long history, with definite repercussions on the conspiracy theories that grew up around the forces thought to lie behind the H. B. of L. and the Theosophical Society (see, e.g., Harrison; Godwin 1990-1991; Spierenburg).

Randolph, Blavatsky, and the English spiritualist and medium Emma Hardinge Britten (1823-1899) had been unanimous in seeing spiritualism as a planned intervention by some of these initiates; as a phenomenon created by superior forces to combat the rising tide of materialism and to prepare the way for "occultism." The H. B. of L. added to this the notion of itself as the motivating force behind Modern Spiritualism, and the claim that its adepts had also prompted the foundation of the Theosophical Society in a first attempt to correct the misguided path that spiritualism had taken in its exclusive attention to dead men and women.

Like Randolph, Emma Hardinge Britten started as an unconscious trance medium. We give her reminiscences of how she was employed as such in the 1830s and 1840s by the "Orphic Society" [B.1.a]. By the late 1850s her mediumship, like his, had completely changed, and she was lecturing in a conscious state that resembles Randolph's "blending."[92] In this state she gave out doctrines far deeper than the trivialities about the "Summer Land" that occupied most spiritualists.[93] She went so far as to claim that it was she who had started the occult movement in 1872, with her magazine *The Western Star*. It was here that the autobiographical sketches began to appear, first attributed to "Austria" and later to "Chevalier Louis de B——," that would be published complete as *Ghost Land*. "Louis," who has so far eluded every attempt at identification, was also credited with a treatise, *Art Magic*.[94] Both books were edited and published by Emma, who claimed to have known Louis for years, and her husband Dr. William Britten. Woven among the anecdotes and novelistic episodes is a cogent doctrine of occultism, both speculative and practical.

A detailed comparison of Louis's doctrines with those of Randolph is beyond our scope here.[95] For present purposes, the most important doctrines held in common are the universal evolution of monads (including humans) towards divinity; the dismissal of

---

[92] Britten, 50-51.

[93] See Emma Hardinge [Britten], *Six Lectures on Theology and Nature* (Chicago: Hitt, 1860).

[94] In the copy of *Ghost Land* in the New York Public Library, someone has scribbled in a pencil note that "Louis" was Burgoyne!

[95] Mr. Deveney's forthcoming study of Randolph will provide full documentation.

reincarnation as not being a part of this scheme; and the possibility of conscious self-development, directed by the will. Louis plays down the role of the spirits of the mundane human dead, so beloved of the spiritualists, in favor of a universe full of supermundane spirits (angelic beings, planetary spirits, etc.) and submundane ones (spirits of the elements, called variously elementals or "elementaries"). In *Ghost Land* he describes the blending of his own personality with that of his teacher, Professor Marx, and evokes an Order of living adepts whose hidden hand works behind the scenes of history for the good of humanity.

True "Spiritism," according to Louis, is the communication with higher beings, whether these be the living adepts or members of the earthly and celestial hierarchies. The "Art Magic" of his title is the practical science of Spiritism: an active science of summoning spirits by method and controlling them by will, in contrast to the passivity of common spiritualism. The most powerful means of achieving power and communicating with the hierarchies are magnetism and drugs (especially hashish, opium, and nitrous oxide), while magic mirrors and crystals are helpful in the process. The goal is a complete liberation of the soul from matter, and the free exercise of its spiritual senses. In that state it can ascend to the highest heavens, wander the earth, see the past and the future, and in short enjoy its birthright as a spark of Divinity.

To this glorious prospect, *Ghost Land* adds the sobering notions that there are competing secret brotherhoods, of similar power but with differing goals and theories; that all that appears in vision and that controls mediumship is not necessarily good, and that magical power (including power over the elementaries) can be used for evil purposes; and that the spiritualist movement itself is a front, a deception practiced to prepare mankind for the real Spiritism.

Randolph could have subscribed to all of this, with the possible exception of Louis' stress on "elementaries," a topic which is undeveloped in Randolph's writings. The H. B. of L. would have agreed with them all.

Emma and Louis seem at first sight to neglect the subject of sex; indeed, when writing as "Sirius" [B.1.a] Emma insists on absolute continence as a condition of practical occultism. Given

her position as one of the most eminent mediums of the spiritualist movement, and as its quasi-official historian,[96] Emma was
at pains to dissociate herself from the "Free Love" movement
that had infiltrated American spiritualism and given it a bad reputation [see Introduction to Part 2, and B.8.d]. Nevertheless, in
her writings she shows that she was fully in accord with the doctrine of "soul affinity" between man and woman that is the highest justification for sexual magic. Even in the 1850s she spoke to
her audiences of woman, "the half of which must complete the
angel; the dual principle which makes our God, our father and
our mother."[97] In this purest form of affinity the partners' souls
are complements of each other, halves of an original whole, and
eventually reunite to form but one angel. The Theons concurred,
with their notion of beings as dual, while the H. B. of L. taught
exactly the same idea. Randolph, while he believed in the creation of soul monads in pairs and the progress of the soul
through the soul worlds in company with a partner of the opposite sex, rejected—perhaps from his own unhappy experiences
with marriage—any notion that this affinity was always for the
same partner.

It is a very short step from these ideas to the logical consequence: that the sexual union of the eternal affinities itself plays
a role in the progress of the soul. Whether or not Emma ever took
that step as a practical matter, the idea cannot have been alien to
her. She certainly believed, in some sense, that the means
whereby the rudimentary soul becomes incarnated to begin its
ascent was also the means of progress.

Lastly, it is important, especially in the light of the claim of
the H. B. of L. that its own adepts were at the source of Blavatsky's
original work, to recognize the degree to which the teachings of
Blavatsky's pre-Indian period resembled those of Emma Hardinge Britten, P. B. Randolph, and the H. B. of L. Leaving aside sexual practice, Blavatsky's early writings (especially *Isis Unveiled*,
1877) agree with Randolph and with Emma on the crucial points

---

[96] See her histories, *Modern American Spiritualism* (New York, 1870) and *Nineteenth Century Miracles* (New York, 1884).

[97] Emma Hardinge [Britten], *The Place and Mission of Woman* (Boston: Swett, 1859), quoted in Owen, 13-14.

named above: the goal of human evolution into divinity;[98] the rule of no reincarnation, with exactly the same three exceptions as Randolph;[99] and the encouragement of practical occultism, as opposed to passive spiritualism, in order to realize the goal of adeptship here and now.[100]

The Western occultists had fair reason to claim, after Blavatsky's move to India, that she had deserted their cause, especially when she proclaimed that occult practices of the type taught by the H. B. of L. were dangerous and, for most people, inadvisable.[101] They could not be expected to welcome her running down of Western esotericism in favor of her Buddhist masters. Ayton regarded her *volte-face* as a betrayal of her initiatic oath, writing as follows:

> Nevertheless, I know now, from authority, that [Blavatsky], equally with Randolph, was really initiated in a remote branch of our Order in India. Hence, she has considerable knowledge, having gone further than Randolph. She goes as far as she dare in making revelations without incurring the penalty of her obligation [...] Like Randolph she has perverted [occultism] to her own evil purposes, but unlike Randolph, has contrived to steer clear of the penalty of her obligation.[102]

The higher spiritualism of Emma Hardinge Britten and Randolph, the early Theosophical Society with its "Brotherhood of Luxor," Max Theon, and the H. B. of L., were engaged in a common effort to rescue Western civilization from the twin threats of scientific materialism and its contrary, an infantile religiosity, whether of the churches or of common spiritualism. Already in the mid-1870s there was a nucleus of doctrinal and practical teachings embodied in Randolph and Emma's works, with echoes (usually without

---

[98] See, for example, Blavatsky 1877, I, 290.

[99] Blavatsky 1877, I, 351.

[100] Blavatsky 1877, II, 588.

[101] See especially H. P. Blavatsky, "Le Phare de l'inconnu," in *La Revue Théosophique* I (1889), reprinted with English translation in *BCW*, XI, 212-283.

[102] Ayton to an unnamed American neophyte, 25 December 1884.

the practical side) in other Westerners such as Hargrave Jennings. These broke out once again in the 1880s specifically to oppose the new ideas that had begun to come from the Theosophical Society in 1881. Seen from this viewpoint, the H. B. of L. was part of a continuity of Western occultism, having its origin in the unknown source (unknown to us, because not physical) to which all these adepts gained access.

Whether or not this was Theon's specific intention, the primary result of the Order was to introduce occultists to the practical methods of P. B. Randolph. All the theoretical writings on astrology, cycles, symbolism, the Hermetic tradition, etc., were subsidiary. The aspirants of the 1880s could find such things in a dozen places, but detailed instructions in self-training were not easy to come by.

14. INFLUENCE OF THE H. B. OF L.

The Order fared somewhat differently in the three countries where its activity was greatest: Britain, France, and the U.S.A. In Britain, the use of the magic mirror or crystal was already widespread, having been cultivated with no particular secrecy by Frederick Hockley, by Zadkiel the astrologer (Captain Richard J. Morrison), and by Kenneth R. H. Mackenzie.[103] But they all used seeresses, being unable to see anything in the mirror themselves. Randolph, on the contrary, encouraged people not to give up under the conviction that they were incapable of clairvoyance, but to make the effort in this as in any other difficult and rewarding art. Somewhat analogously, Britain had seen a spate of writings in the 1860s and 1870s on sexual symbolism in religion, but nothing that linked it with sexual practice.

The scandal of 1886 following the discovery of Burgoyne's conviction and prison sentence, gloatingly publicized by the Theosophists, killed the H. B. of L.'s recruitment in Britain, though it did not necessarily prevent neophytes from continuing in their studies and practice. To those hungry for experience, two new doors opened in 1888. One was the Esoteric Section of the Theosophical Society, in which a chosen few would be permitted to sit with Madame Blavatsky in a circular chamber with a blue glass roof, constructed on the Society's property in Avenue Road, St. John's Wood. What they did there, we shall probably never know, for none of the members ever broke their oath of secrecy. But as we have said, Blavatsky would not have started this without the pressure from those who were imbibing practical occultism from another, and, as she thought, a polluted stream.

The other portal was that of the Hermetic Order of the Golden Dawn in the Outer, to give it its full title which implies, just as in the H. B. of L.'s nomenclature, the existence of an "Inner." The Golden Dawn had a glamor entirely lacking in both the H. B. of L. and the Theosophical Society, for it conducted impressive operations of ceremonial magic, with temples, costumes, swords, coffins, and other properties borrowed from

---

[103] On Hockley, see Hamill 1986. On Morrison, see Curry, 61-108. On Mackenzie's crystal experiments, Godwin 1994, 185-186.

Freemasonry [see Introduction to Part 2 and A.1.e,f]. Nevertheless, the neophytes had to study theoretical teachings on Kabbalah, Hermeticism, astrology, the Tarot, etc., and they were
taught to cultivate both clairvoyance and the magical will. The
Golden Dawn, exactly like the H. B. of L., opposed the unconscious clairvoyance of the naturally gifted, mediumistic person,
in favor of the conscious and disciplined development of a gift
latent in nearly everybody. While mirrors were sometimes used,
the favored method was a refinement of Randolph's card exercise, in which the cards to be gazed at were painted in complementary colors. The goal was to be able to travel freely in the
astral, and to encounter the entities one meets there.[104]

The H. B. of L.'s principle of making one's own contact with
the Interior Circle also reappeared in the Golden Dawn, when
S. L. Macgregor Mathers revived the "sacred magic of Abramelin
the Mage," whose purpose was to communicate with one's "holy
guardian angel." Once this contact was established, the neophyte
could speak as an adept and become a channel for new revelations. The signal example of the latter was Aleister Crowley's
inauguration of the "Aeon of Horus" in 1904, with the *Book of the
Law* as its bible. And although the Golden Dawn itself had nothing to do with sex or drugs, Crowley had the equivocal distinction
of being the greatest sex-magician and the most drug-addicted
occultist of the 20th century. His life's work amplified and intensified the current of the H. B. of L. to the point of distortion.

In France, the H. B. of L. succeeded in enrolling a number of
the most influential occultists, Hermetists, esotericists, and Theosophists (many of whom qualified under more than one of
these headings). The national representative was F.-Ch. Barlet
(pseudonym of Albert Faucheux), who is probably to be identified with the "Glyndon" who wrote for *The Occult Magazine*.[105]

---

[104] See "Clairvoyance" and "On Scrying and Travelling in the Spirit-Vision," in Regardie, IV, 11-42.

[105] Glyndon's article "The Astral or Sidereal Body" in *The Occult Magazine* II/13 (February 1886), 11-13, and II/14 (March 1886), 22-23 repeats the themes of "Le corps astral ou sidéral" signed by F.-Ch. Barlet in *L'Anti-Matérialiste*, 20 March 1885. The latter journal is also mentioned in a message that seems to be from Peter Davidson to Barlet ("F. Bar sur Seine, France"): see "To Correspondents," *The Occult Magazine* II/21-23 (Oct.-Nov.-Dec. 1886), 80.

The driving force behind the occult movement of the late 19th century was Papus: physician, publicist, lecturer, organizer of secret societies, writer of encyclopedic treatises, and editor for a time of both the monthly journal *L'Initiation* and the weekly magazine *Le Voile d'Isis*. Papus openly acknowledged three masters: his *maître en pratique* (practical master) was Peter Davidson [B.9.d], his *maître spirituel* (spiritual master) the psychic healer Maître Philippe, and his *maître intellectuel* (intellectual master) the Christian Hermetist Saint-Yves d'Alveydre. The H. B. of L.'s teachings had served Papus himself, they served his numerous friends, and they remained as the esoteric core to which his more public groups, such as the Martinist Order, gave access [B.7.f].

We cannot mention Papus's *maître intellectuel* without noting the remarkable and synchronistic parallel to the H. B. of L.'s methods in the story of Saint-Yves d'Alveydre (1842-1909).[106] Between June 1885 and January 1886, Saint-Yves was given a link with another "interior circle" of adepts ruling the world, this time from the underground kingdom of "Agarttha." The person who initiated him was his Sanskrit teacher, an Indian named Hadji Sharif. Using the power of *dédoublement* or astral travel, Saint-Yves immediately took off on his own to explore this realm, and wrote his own eyewitness description of it in *Mission de l'Inde* (Saint-Yves 1981), a book so uninhibited in its revelations that he suppressed it the moment it was printed. Saint-Yves never seems to have joined any secret society, but his own doctrines are extremely close to those of the H. B. of L., especially in his allegiance to the Western tradition and his later "blending" with the soul of his deceased wife; while his act of first establishing a link with the inner plane or circle, then using clairvoyance to cultivate it, is of the very essence of the H. B. of L.'s own origins and procedures.

The French members of the Order included the early leaders of the Theosophical Society: Arthur Arnould [B.7.d], Louis Dramard, and Papus himself. Others were Barlet, Paul Sédir, René Philipon, René Caillié, Augustin Chaboseau [B.7.g], and possibly Marc Haven.[107] There were probably a number of others,

---

[106] See Godwin 1993, 83; and, in more detail, Godwin 1986.

[107] Sédir, Chaboseau, and Haven (= Maître Philippe's son-in-law, Dr. Lalande) are mentioned as members in Mariel.

recruited through the Martinist Order. As the 1880s passed, the general disenchantment with Blavatsky and her masters only served to strengthen the Western occultism of Papus and his associates, especially Barlet and Guaita [B.9.e], and their respect for Saint-Yves' independent authority (not shared by Davidson— see A.1.c).

In the final years of the 19th century, while the occultist movement was at its height, the H. B. of L. became extinct in France in preparation for the Mouvement Cosmique. We know this from a statement of Barlet's. Early in 1908, in the course of defending himself against Albert de Sarâk's accusation that he had passed through all the forms of occultism only in order to destroy them, Barlet wrote that it was he alone who for years had sustained the only society that had disappeared thus: the H. B. of L. With the words "it only ceased in order to pass on the succession to another perfectly vital form," he clearly implied a filiation with the Mouvement Cosmique, by then in its fullest flowering.[108]

Although fascinated by Sarâk, Barlet was in touch at this period not only with the Theons (Madame Theon lived until September 1908) but also with René Guénon, who was then heading the ephemeral Ordre du Temple Rénové. It was from Barlet that Guénon received a considerable part of his knowledge of the H. B. of L. and its teachings. Its influence on the younger man is evident in his *Théosophisme* (1921), but was present in the earliest developments of his thought. If Guénon was not a formal initiate of the H. B. of L., its teachings were by then circulating so widely that he would have had no difficulty in discovering them.

In the United States, the H. B. of L. had a formidable success among the Theosophists. They had reason to feel rather bereft when the founders of the Society decamped to India, where Olcott stayed on, while Blavatsky returned to spend her last years in London. They were ready for the new Order's teachings, which offered the practical occultism that they most wanted. In the 1880s, a group of American members of the H. B. of L., largely Theosophists, were constituted into the American Central Council. They called themselves a "Committee of Seven,"

---

[108] F.-Ch. Barlet, "Au Fondateur du Centre Esotérique Oriental de Paris, Dr. Albert de Sarâk," in *L'Etoile d'Orient*, 24 March 1908, p. 94.

perhaps in imitation of the similarly-named group that had taken responsibility for the "Brotherhood of Luxor" of the 1870s, hence indirectly for the foundation of the Society. The most prominent among them was Thomas Moore Johnson [B.7.c], who was President of the Council, while Henry Wagner was Secretary. For all practical purposes, the operation of the Council seems to have died with the revelations of Burgoyne's past.

The various strains of the H. B. of L.'s thought continued to exert a strong influence through the end of the century, both independently and in recombination with occultists who ultimately traced their origins back to P. B. Randolph himself. Freeman B. Dowd, a quondam follower of Randolph and member of the H. B. of L. under Peter Davidson, was the most prominent. In the mid-1880s he was a frequent contributor to *The Gnostic*, a New Thought Spiritualist journal published in San Francisco by W. J. Colville, George Chainey, and Dr. Anna Kimball—the last two of whom achieved some brief fame for their having been expelled from the Theosophical Society for their sexual teachings.[109] Dowd went on to re-found the Temple of the Rosy Cross in Philadelphia in 1895 and to contribute to Paul Tyner's journal *The Temple*, published in Denver, Colorado. Dr. W. P. Phelon and his wife, both of whom were prominent Theosophists and members of the H. B. of L., founded and ran the curiously named "Hermetic Brotherhood of Atlantis, Luxor and Elephantae," first in Chicago and then in San Francisco (see introduction to A.1.a), and published a variety of "Hermetic Manuscripts" and a *Hermetic Journal*. Sylvester Clark Gould, a member of the H. B. of L. and an inveterate joiner after the manner of Papus in France, continued to seek the synthesis of sexuality and occultism in a variety of organizations. He was one of the founders of the *Societas Rosicruciana in America* in 1908 and published a short-lived but fascinating journal, *The Rosicrucian Brotherhood*, in 1907-1908, which reprinted material from John Yarker, Robert H. Fryar, Alexander Wilder, and others on the Western occult and phallic tradition.

---

[109] *The Gnostic, Organ of the Delsarte Conservatory of Esthetic Gymnastics and Gnostic School of Psychic and Physical Culture*, Oakland, California, 1885-1888.

The chief heir to all of these was Reuben Swinburne Clymer (1878-1966), who reunited under his Rosicrucian organization at Quakertown, Pennsylvania, most of the strains of the Randolph/ H. B. of L. tradition. He continued the work of the movement in a bewildering jumble of organizations and publications and through the distribution of secret lessons that taught the Mysteries of Eulis.

Finally, there was the Hermetic Brotherhood of Light, founded or reorganized in Chicago [see B.9.c] or in Boston in 1895, whose teachings fed the streams of sexual practice flowing into the *Ordo Templi Orientis* of Theodor Reuss and eventually into the works of Aleister Crowley. Once the secret was out of linking occultism with sex, it was impossible to ignore, and in consequence, practically every occult order after the 1880s has some debt to the H. B. of L.

15. THE PRACTICAL MAGIC OF THE H. B. OF L.

As a transition to the secret documents themselves, we now give an analysis of the practical magic which they teach, and of the grades and degrees through which the members of the H.B. of L. passed, all undergirded by the metaphysical system outlined in Section 11, above.

The terms "Exterior" and "Interior" Circles of the H. B. of L. had clearly defined meanings within the Order that corresponded to the degrees of adeptship or initiation and to the practical training offered to the neophytes.

The H. B. of L. divided all humans into three Grades, which represented the natural possibilities of progress of the human entity pre- and post-mortem, and also corresponded with the stages of progress possible during life on earth to those seeking "adeptship." Each Grade, in turn, was subdivided into three states or degrees (*LOE*, I, 163-164), so that there were nine degrees in all (as in the Ordre Kabbalistique de la Rose-Croix). The First Grade of the H.B. of L. was probably originally called the Grade of Eulis, but in the teaching manuscripts this becomes the Grade of Eros. The names of the three Degrees of this Grade are unknown, but to judge from the section headings in "Mysteries of Eros," the Second Degree may have been called "The Ansairetic Arcanum" and the Third "The Mystery of Isis."

The First Grade of Adeptship corresponded to the possibilities taught in the Exterior Circle of the H. B. of L., that part of the Order to which neophytes were admitted. All of the surviving manuscript material deals with progress in this Grade. The powers to be obtained therein encompassed the "elemental spheres" of earth and the "astro-magnetic currents" that controlled them, all conceived as strictly limited in spatial terms. The possibilities of this Grade were those of the present, embodied men on earth. When the adept exhausted them, he or she usually underwent a process of physical dissolution and passed on to the level of the Second Grade, although in exceptional cases a still-embodied adept could progress to the Second and Third Grades.

The goal of the First Grade was thus the development of Perfect Humanity: an entity who had exhausted the sevenfold possibilities of the human state and developed the full array of human potentialities: intuition, thought transference, clairvoyance, and the power to "converse with spiritual intelligences" at will (*LOE*, I, 166). Readers of René Guénon's metaphysical works, especially *The Multiple States of Being* and *Man and His Becoming According to the Vedanta*, will readily recognize this concept, and perhaps be led to wonder how much Guénon was indebted to *The Light of Egypt* and its lowly author.

The Second Grade of Adeptship represented the Interior Circle of the H. B. of L., whose adepts had power over the "spiritual and ethereal forces" of earth, from the "magnetic zones of the astral world up to the ethereal and spiritual spheres of disembodied humanity." It is the adepts of this Grade—the Interior Circle—who communicated with, controlled, and taught the members of the Exterior Circle. "These spiritual adepts cannot descend to earth (as we understand the term) and manifest their power externally, without the aid of a properly trained instrument whose odylic sphere they can temporarily occupy. Their chief means of communication with the external world are the adepts of the exterior grade, through whom they transmit such portions of spiritual truth as the world has need of." (*LOE*, I, 164)

As we have pointed out in Section 9, above, the method by which the Interior Circle communicated with the members of the Exterior Circle was carefully distinguished by the H. B. of L. from mere passive "mediumship."

The H. B. of L.'s descriptions of the Third Grade, comprising the Seventh, Eighth, and Ninth Degrees, are still less specific. They were thought of as deific, angelic, purely celestial, and beyond human comprehension.

Because of the H. B. of L.'s peculiar ideas on the original bisexual nature of the primordial divine monad, the interface between the Second and Third Grades (between the Sixth and Seventh Degrees) had a particular importance. It was only there that the human being becomes truly immortal and "that the two halves of the divine soul [become] permanently and eternally united. The twin souls, male and female, then constitute the complete whole of the divine Ego. This mystical union is 'the marriage of the Lamb' of Saint John, wherein the man becomes the angel—the Deific life. He is the grand angelic hierophant of celestial mysteries, the nature, power, and functions of which are too transcendent for the comprehension of the embodied mortal." (*LOE*, I, 165)

The three degrees of the First Grade, through which those "born but not made" potential adepts must progress, correspond to the practices set forth in the teachings of the H. B. of L., particularly the "Mysteries of Eros," the sections of which are assigned to the different degrees.[110] All of these practices were intended to evolve the entire human being harmoniously—including, most importantly, the sexual nature, which the H. B. of L. regarded as the essential pivot of development because of our original bisexuality and our fundamental quest to be rejoined to our other halves. Without this reunion of the original divine monad, the potential adept could only know "self" and would never achieve true angelhood.

The H. B. of L. contrasted its teachings in this regard with the "fearful practices in the East, of asceticism, celibacy, self-mutilations, etc., [which] simply starve and chain the animal into subjection, instead of developing it into a useful, obedient and most highly important factor of the perfect man's seven-fold nature." The implied criticism of the Theosophical Society is obvious.

The goal of the progress through the H. B. of L.'s degree work was to develop clairvoyance and clairaudience, to enable the neophyte to perceive the real, occult nature of things, and to be able to contact and be further instructed by the adepts of the Interior Circle and other entities of the celestial hierarchies. The "truth will be realized within, it will not require one single shadow of external phenomena to convince that soul which is fully prepared for the master's reception, neither will the student

---

[110] The assignment appears to have been somewhat tentative and fluid. For example, the manuscripts of the "Key to Eulis" that circulated separately state that it was the teaching for the First Degree, while the systematized "Mysteries of Eros" assigns "Eulis" itself to the First Degree and the "Key" to the Second. There are similar differences in other manuscripts that were consolidated in the "Mysteries of Eros." The sequence in which Barlet sent the teaching manuscripts to Arnould (Elementals, Eulis, Reincarnation, Laws of Magic Mirrors, Psychical Culture) appears haphazard, perhaps because of the problems of translation. The "Symbolical Notes to the First Degree," as its title indicates, was to be the general preparation for all the subsequent teachings.

have long to wait in expectation. 'At the very hour when the soul is ready behold its guide will appear.'" (*LOE*, I, 170)

Here lies the ultimate reason for the primacy of practice over theory in the H. B. of L. Theory was necessary to ensure that the neophyte's steps were on the correct path, but the practice enabled contact with the *real* teachers of the Order.

In all of this, sex was central. It was the fundamental reality of all progress and development, and not, as the Theosophists taught, a mere accidental and external characteristic that might change in each reincarnation. In H. B. of L. doctrine, the entirety of creation flows from the differentiation of the unmanifested divine into male and female. As a consequence, it is sex that propels evolution, and it is again sex, consciously employed by the potential adept, that leads to the reunion of the divine Ego and to angelhood. In the pre-angelic state of the neophyte, celibacy, though it may enable a forced development of certain powers, is an absolute evil. The "vital secretions" or "seminal fluids" of sexual intercourse are precisely the components—if properly used—that go to build up the spiritual body, and "love" (the attraction of the other) is precisely the antidote to the selfishness which fatally limits development to the purely material sphere (*LOE*, I, 169). Finally, it is sex that places the neophyte in contact with the Spheres, Potentialities, and Powers of the celestial hierarchy, all of which are themselves sexually differentiated.

In its creation myth, the H. B. of L. taught the existence of the sundered bisexual monad or "duad" whose reunification made it an immortal "god" or "angel." On the more practical level faced by the neophytes of the First Degree of Grade One, however, the myth created immediate problems. How could the neophyte be sure that his or her spouse, with whom the mysteries were to be practiced, was in fact the incarnation of the sundered primordial monad? The problem was coeval with the revival of the myth of the original androgyne in the 19th century, and it haunted the Swedenborgian and Free Love camps of the spiritualist movement in the 1850s and 1860s.

The answer of the H. B. of L, inserted in the Notes to the "Mysteries of Eros," was a practical one. On this earthly level, even if the spouse was not the sundered soul mate, so long as he or she was from the same "plane of development," the sexual union of male and female enabled the soul to progress [see Appendix to A.3.c.]. The H. B. of L. always encouraged both spouses to join the Order, and the practice was common. Both the Rev. Ayton and his wife, for example, were members. To determine the suitability of the match, Davidson or Burgoyne compared the horoscopes of the partners, as when Arthur Arnould was reassured that the horoscopes of him and his wife "unmistakably shew that *both* parties have emanated from the same *spiritual plane* of planetary existence."[111]

The importance of sex persisted even after the soul mates had progressed beyond this earthly level. Love and sex (though without procreation) continued to be the motive power of spiritual progress.[112] It is apparent from the letters of Davidson and Barlet to Arnould that the sexual union of neophyte and soul mate could continue even when one of the pair had died [B.7.e]. Arnould was haunted (in every sense of the word) by the visions of his lately deceased wife and the sense of her presence. Davidson consoled him with the value of the experiences, and stressed the necessity of rising up in union to the beloved one rather than dragging her spirit down to earth.

The practical consequences—and inherent dangers—of all of this are easy to envision, but they were never explicitly worked out by the H. B. of L. Among contemporary sexual mages, Thomas Lake Harris ended up in a strange sexual union with his discarnate "Lily Queen," and was even accused of begetting children with her on the astral level.[113] The bizarre Abbé Boullan, whose ideas so divided French occultists at the very time that the H. B. of L. was spreading there, taught his disciples to perform sexual "unions of life" with superior celestial beings and the souls of the dead, so as to "celestialize" themselves; and with "Elementals" so as to "celestialize" them (see Bricaud 1927, 51ss.). This aspect of the doctrine of the H. B. of L.

---

[111] Review of horoscopes, dated, 20 November 1888, in letters of Barlet to Arnould in the Fonds Papus.

[112] See *LOE*, I, 33-34.

[113] See Blavatsky, "Lodges of Magic," reprinted here as B.6.m; also Ida C., *Heavenly Bridegrooms. An Unintentional Contribution to the Erotic Interpretation of Religion*, with an Introduction by Theodore Schroeder (New York, 1918).

probably connects with the fascination of Robert Fryar with the *Comte de Gabalis*, which he reprinted, and with his publication of sections from Father Sinistrari's work on Incubi and Succubi.[114]

The second part of the practical teachings of the H. B. of L. centered on the development of clairvoyance through the use of the magic mirror, following the example of P. B. Randolph, who taught that the operator or magician should cultivate this without the intermediary of a scryer. The immediate goal was not the specific content of any given revelation or vision, but the development of the faculty of intuition or clairvoyance itself. Peter Davidson, in a letter to one of his American neophytes, clearly outlines the role of the mirror:

> As to your Initiation in the 2nd Degree, I presume Mr.
> A. will have sent you some [ ] Mss., even in the 3rd
> Degree, the Cycles & such like. But of course you know
> I suppose that you must develop the 3 Occl. powers ere
> you can possibly be Initiated into the Inner Lodge, and
> no doubt you are fully aware what those powers are,
> viz., Clairvoyance, Clairaudience & Intuition, by the
> use of the Mirror.[115]

Related to clairvoyance, and probably viewed as a preliminary to it, was the ability to separate the "astral double" from the body. The H. B. of L. encouraged its newcomers with tales of the success of members of the Order. In response to a letter asking whether young members were "capable of projecting their Astral Double," the Editor of *The Occult Magazine* replied:

> Yes, undoubtedly so. Amidst a mass of correspondence
> upon this subject, we quote the following extract from a
> letter we have just received from a Continental Lady
> Member:—". . . I looked and saw through the shell that

---

[114] R. H. Fryar, ed., *Sub-Mundanes or the Elementaries of the Cabala. Unabridged. An esoteric work. Physio-Astro-Mystic. Annotated from the suppressed work of Father Sinistrari on "Incubi and Succubi."* Bath: Fryar, 1886. One of the prayers to the Elementals used in the H .B. of L. initiations is from *Comte de Gabalis* [see A.1.e].

[115] Letter from Davidson to an unnamed American neophyte, 8 July 1885.

covered me, the light of my lamp shining, whilst I also saw the shadow of a moving form. . . . *I felt free from my body*, and was flying through the rooms. . . . This was the first time I was able to soar with ease and comfort, and by degrees it became a pleasure. . . . I went on until I came to an arched window, and looking through it, the atmosphere became intensely clear. . . . At last *I returned to my wearied body*. . . . I well know this is the result of my *mirror-training*," etc. An English member also recently developed this faculty.[116]

The pinnacle of clairvoyant experience in the H. B. of L. system was the Sleep of Sialam, the exalted conscious trance state in which the initiate communed with the Powers, Potencies, and Intelligences of the celestial hierarchies. The term itself first appeared in Colonel Stephen Fraser's old-soldier's tale of pre-mutiny India, *Twelve Years in India*, in which the author uses it to describe the trance into which the Indian users of the sexually consecrated magic mirrors fell while telling fortunes. Randolph, in *Ravalette* (1863), used the term "Sleep of Sialam Boaghiee" for the prophetic trance, occurring only once in a hundred years, that the mysterious adept Ravalette sought to make the hero undergo. In Randolph's later writings, the term came to mean the higher sort of clairvoyance in general—the elevated, conscious perception of and intercourse with the aerial states and beings of the universal hierarchy—that resulted from the application of his magical laws to mirror use. The Sleep of Sialam as he finally expressed it was not the mere vision of a celestial thing, but the "mental crystallic, ascensive, penetrative, and comprehensive grasp of it."[117]

The final part of the occult practice of the H. B. of L. involved the use of drugs. This is nowhere mentioned in the

---

[116] *Occult Magazine* I/5 (June 1885), 40. It is perhaps significant that Colonel Olcott, in his first report on the progress of the Theosophical Society, chose precisely this aspect of occult development to boast of. See Gomes, 98; H. S. Olcott, "The First Leaf of T. S. History," in *The Theosophist* XII/2 (November 1890), 68.

[117] Randolph 1874, 124-125. Blavatsky also took up the term and explicitly connected it with the use of drugs. See Blavatsky 1877, I, 357-358; "The Esoteric Character of the Gospels" (*BCW* VIII, 204n); Blavatsky 1888, II, 558.

surviving materials, though there are hints to be found in Peter Davidson's writings,[118] but it is at least probable that drug use formed a regular part of the H. B. of L.'s work. In the *Revue Cosmique*, a passage from a novel attributable to Theon alludes vaguely to techniques that allow opium to be smoked without danger.[119] Both opium and hashish were legal and in common use among the European Mesmerists of the 1850s and 1860s. Randolph stressed the ritual use and importance of hashish in developing clairvoyance; it certainly played a role in the initiations of the H. B. of L. The Rev. Ayton, in writing to an American neophyte, explained the circumstances of his own initiation:

> Now, take these two facts into account. First, any Initiate in the East may initiate others, & secondly that he will be dependent on perhaps very imperfect instruments to help him with the details. P. D. told me he had met with an Oriental Adept or some such person who had appeared to him in Astral form &c. & that he was about to revive or add to an Ancient Order, & asked me, to join it. I am an adventurous spirit & I joined it in the hopes of gaining a little more light perhaps. The form of it was much better than that of Portman.[120] An Altar had to be extemporised, lamps burning, flowers on it, incense burning, an invocation of the elements, what purported to be the real Soma juice drunk at a certain stage. The Adepts were supposed to be present in Astral form. I hesitated very much to drink this drug sent me by a perfect stranger, & I thought of omitting it.

---

[118] In Davidson's book on Mistletoe (Davidson 1892), he describes the mysteries of that plant and of vervain that he learned from an "Aryan priestess of Scotland," and "a mystical potion" made from mistletoe that effaced all impurities from the soul and united soul and body, inducing clairvoyance. He was also familiar with the powers of aconite, opium, hashish, and various oriental drugs homologized to "Soma" in separating the "astral body." The work was translated into French by Paul Sédir (Yvon Le Loup), a Christian Hermetist and H. B. of L. member.

[119] "L'Aurisée," in *Revue Cosmique*, VI/7, 437.

[120] Maurice Vidal Portman (see Howe 1972, 273), whose Order of Light Ayton had also joined, as he subsequently joined the Golden Dawn and the Theosophical Society's Esoteric Section.

Ayton's letter describing his initiation.

However, I opened the bottle & smelt of it. All my life, I have been used to drugs, & I at once recognised this. I knew its effects were most powerful, but I decided to take it. Whether it was hallucination produced by this drug I know not, but I was conscious of another presence, tho' I cannot say I absolutely saw any form. I was fully 3 hours at it from midnight. When over, I felt my pulse, & found just what I expected, that it was intermittent, which was what I knew to be the effect of the drug I thought it was. Altogether, I recognized the work of some one who, at least, had been in the East, & initiated there. Still, the results were not all that had been promised, & I had vague suspicions. On mentioning my doubts, I was assured that all was right. This increased my suspicions with regard, at least, to the agents who had to carry out the details, but I placed it all to the account of the impossibility of finding fitting instruments to carry out those details.[121]

Such rituals and practical aids served, in a way, to make good the innate deficiencies of the H. B. of L.'s neophytes. But if one takes the society's doctrines in their integrity, this would only have been a stop-gap measure. For the H. B. of L. taught the same principle as is found in the *Zohar* (as Max Theon well knew): that the aspirations of the man at the moment of conception can cause a child to be born who possesses from the start the magical powers that define adeptship. The logical conclusion, if one believes in the spiritual ascent of humanity, is that eventually every person will thus be an adept from birth.

---

[121] Letter from Ayton to an American neophyte, dated 30 March 1887. To guarantee the authenticity of these letters, whose owner desires complete anonymity, we give here a facsimile of the passage describing Ayton's taking the Soma initiation.

Part II

The Secret Manuscripts

INTRODUCTION TO THE SECRET MANUSCRIPTS OF THE H. B. OF L.

The H. B. of L. documents have been arranged here in three categories (initiatic and administrative, symbolical and cosmological, and practical) to reflect their function within the Order. However, these categories do not reflect either the historical sequence in which the documents were generated, or the order in which they were provided to the neophyte.

Leaving aside manuscripts that have survived in private collections, there are three main public caches of H. B. of L. documents. The Houghton Library at Harvard University in Cambridge, Massachusetts, has a complete manuscript copy of the most important of the H. B. of L. teachings, the "Mysteries of Eros." This is the systematized compilation of the Brotherhood's practical teachings on sex and sexual magic, and it is reproduced here as A.3.b. The component parts of the "Mysteries of Eros" were arranged by Thomas Henry Burgoyne in 1886 and 1887 from manuscripts that had previously been circulated separately to the neophytes of the Order. Most notable among these are slightly altered versions of parts of Paschal Beverly Randolph's manuscript works on sexual magic, the "Mysteries of Eulis" and the "Ansairetic Mystery." (The distribution of Randolph's works in the H. B. of L.'s documents is shown in A.3.b.) These, together with the H. B. of L.'s own "Brief Key to the Eulian Mysteries," which was provided as a corrective and antidote to Randolph's teachings, constitute the essential part of the H. B. of L.'s instructions on sexual practice. The "Mysteries of Eros" also contains the Order's brief treatises on "Psychical Culture," the "Mysteries of Isis," the "Rules for Occult Training," and a variety of small works on various corollaries to the central sexual doctrine.

The Theosophical Society Library at Adyar, India, has a variety of papers relating to the H. B. of L. that were filed by Colonel Olcott together with his brief description of their contents. Most of these documents are the residue of the controversies between the H. B. of L. and the Theosophical Society in the period from 1885 to 1890—most notably Gorham Blake's history of the H. B. of L. [B.6.k]— which have been reproduced in Part 3.

The Adyar materials also include a copy of the "Brief Key" which is essentially identical to the version reproduced in Chapter IV of the "Mysteries of Eros," copies of "The Ancient and Noble Order," and "To Whom It May Concern," and copies of correspondence from principals of the Order.

The Municipal Library of Lyon, France, in its Papus Collection (Bibliothèque Municipale de Lyon, Fonds Papus, Mss. 5.486-5.493), has a fairly complete set of the manuscript teachings of the H. B. of L. These include the manuscripts systematized by Burgoyne as the "Mysteries of Eros," translated into French in the late 1880s by F.-Ch. Barlet, Louis Dramard, and others for the neophytes who could not read English [see B.7.d, B.9.c,e]. Barlet, in his letters to Arthur Arnould in late 1888 and early 1889, enclosed and translated the Pledge and Rules, the Prospectus for the Colony Scheme (now unfortunately lost), the grades and names of the Order, the complete manuscript of "Eulis," the manuscripts on "Reincarnation," "Magic Mirrors," "Psychical Culture," and a lost manuscript on "Elementals." At the beginning of 1890, in soliciting Augustin Chaboseau to join the Order [see B.7.g], Barlet mentions that he has so far received from Peter Davidson seven or eight manuscripts, and that there are many more that he has not yet received because Davidson has fallen on hard times. Most of this material found its way into the Lyon collection, occasionally in multiple, separately translated copies, which indicates the interest aroused by these teachings in France. Of the material published here, only the second part of the "Laws of Magic Mirrors" (the English original of which has been lost) has had to be retranslated from the Lyon manuscripts.

A final public source for the H. B. of L. teaching manuscripts is the augmented edition of Burgoyne's *Light of Egypt*, mentioned in Part 1.

From these sources and from documents in private collections an almost complete set of the teaching manuscripts of the H. B. of L. can be reconstructed. The only manuscripts known to have been circulated that have not been traced or reconstructed are the one on "Elementals" by Davidson, which Barlet translated, and possibly a practical guide to mirror magic to accompany "Laws of Magic Mirrors." With these exceptions, the documents presented here give a complete picture of the inner teachings of this magical order. All versions of the documents have been compared. Substantial variants in the text have been shown in notes, or inserted in the text in square brackets. Otherwise, and with the exception of very minor corrections of obvious errors in spelling and copying, the material presented here is a faithful reproduction of the original texts.

"To Whom It May Concern" (A.1.a)

The permutations worked on this little broadside reveal the changing fortunes of the propagandists of the H. B. of L. as the Order waxed and waned. In its first appearance [B.3.b], the text explicitly appealed to disgruntled Theosophists and requested correspondents to write "Theosi," or "Theon" in care of Robert H. Fryar, Bath. This questionnaire was translated and published, with an article note, in the French review *La Lumière*, 28 February 1886, 281-282. In the copy of the advertisement preserved in the archives of the Theosophical Society at Adyar, M. Theon's name has been crossed out and Davidson's name and address in Loudsville, White County, Georgia added. Finally, in the version printed here, all thought of keeping up with the changing public contact for the Order has been abandoned and the name of the contact is left blank. This version, from a private collection, also adds a request for the biographical information necessary to cast the nativity of the neophyte, and omits the gratuitous slap at the disappointing Hindoo Mahatmas.

To Whom it May Concern:

STUDENTS of the Occult Science, Searchers after Truth, and Theosophists are hereby informed that by sending in an application containing answers, etc., etc., to the subjoined queries, they can, if found suitable after a short probationary term, be admitted as members of an Occult Brotherhood who do not boast of their knowledge, but teach freely and without reserve all they find worthy to receive.

QUERY I.—Are you a member of any Society, either Occult or Spiritualistic? If so, name them.

QUERY II.—Are you a member of, or in sympathy with, any Religious Denomination? If so, name them.

QUERY III.—Are you prepared to keep sacred and inviolable all information, teachings, etc., etc , you may from time to time receive, and always under any circumstances conceal the identity of all Brothers, Neophytes, etc., connected with the Order?

QUERY IV.—Name, Profession or Occupation, Age, Married or Single?

In addition to the above, enclose data for horoscope, viz.: place, country and exact time of birth. If *exact* time is not known send photograph (which will be returned) *and* personal description. The horoscope fee is $1.00.

N. B.—All communications should be addressed—

"THE ANCIENT AND NOBLE ORDER" (A.1.b)

This flyer, preserved in a private collection, was the first introduction to the H. B. of L. for many who aspired to practical realization of the truths of occultism. It is also one of the few
documents to bear Max Theon's name. Its general declarations
were never enlarged on, except concerning the "great Cycle of
Necessity." This was presented in *The Occult Magazine* as the
cycle at the end of which the human race would return to the
point from which it had emanated.[1] The idea—also present in
the Philosophie Cosmique—is typical of the wave of Western
"occultism" that sought in the 1870s and 1880s to complete and
deepen the work begun by spiritualism (see Part 1, Section 11).

The rejection of equality goes against the generally egalitar-
ian (feminist, socialist) tendencies of popular spiritualism. The
social doctrine of the Philosophie Cosmique is based on liberty,
but holds that "There is no such thing in the entire Cosmos as
equality."[2] There is instead a hierarchy, not as something tyran-
nical, and especially not as based on birth, riches, or the power of
the stronger, but as a "sacred authority" sanctioned by the
nature of things. "There is only one royalty, one aristocracy: that
of intelligence," states the 17th axiom of the "Base de la Philosophie Cosmique.[3] This alone can lead to cosmic equilibrium and
happiness.

The reference in the pledge attached to the flyer to the
"American Central Council H. B. of L." seems to indicate that the
document was written at some point after the creation of that
body in late 1885, and the organization of the Order described in
the flyer reflects the organization at that time. When the Order
first comes to light in Great Britain in 1884, T. H. Burgoyne's letters bear the caption "Central Council of the Exterior Circle,
Grand Master, M. Theon," of which Burgoyne is listed as Private
Secretary. The function and membership of this council are
unknown, and it appears to have been largely a paper creation.

---

[1] "To Correspondents," *Occult Magazine* I/11 (December 1885), 87-88.

[2] "Etude inédite de source ancienne," *Revue Cosmique*, III/10, 585-586; see also "L' Eter-
nelle jeunesse," *Revue Cosmique*, VI/8, 484.

[3] On hierarchy, see "Errata. L' aliénation mentale," in *Revue Cosmique*, III/12, 759.

Effective control was, of course, vested in Peter Davidson and Burgoyne, but the administrative work was divided between Peter Davidson, "Provincial Grand Master of the North," and William Alexander Ayton, "Provincial Grand Master of the South." After the burgeoning of the Order in the United States, the American Central Council was set up with Thomas M. Johnson, the noted Platonist, as President, and two lodges were formed, one under Johnson in Osceola, Missouri and one under Mrs. Josephine Cables of Rochester, New York. All of this changed in mid-1886 with the revelation of Burgoyne's past. The version of this flyer circulated in Europe after the debacle reflects the situation and notes parenthetically, that "this organization no longer exists" (*H. B. of L.*, 11).

The degree structure announced in the flyer (four initiations and nine degrees before the initiate enters the first degree of "actual Adeptship") appears different from that laid out in *Light of Egypt*, where the nine degrees in three grades encompass the entirety of human potentialities, and the "Adepts of the Inner Circle" of the Order constitute the second grade. The contradiction between the accounts, if there is one, was probably academic for most members: Burgoyne himself only claimed to be an initiate of the second degree.[4]

---

[4] Letter of W. W. Allen to unnamed "Sir and Brother," dated December 8, 1887 (private collection).

The Ancient and Noble Order
the
H. B. of L.

WE ACKNOWLEDGE the eternal existence of the Great First Cause, the Divine, invisible, central, Spiritual Sun, from whose gloriously radiant Throbbing Soul pulsates the living breath—the life-principle of all that is, or ever shall be. From this Divine Vortex proceeds the invisible power which binds the vast Universe in one Harmonious Whole.

We teach that from this incomprehensible centre of Divinity emanate the divine scintillations of eternal Spirit, which having completed their *orbit*—the great Cycle of Necessity—constitute THE ONLY IMMORTAL PORTION OF THE HUMAN SOUL. But while thus accepting the universal sonship of mankind, we reject *in toto* the doctrine of *Universal Equality*.

The brotherhood is divided into three Grades; each Grade is again subdivided into three Degrees; the Names of the different Grades being communicated privately to each separate Member. After the preliminary Initiation there are also three other Initiations before an Initiate can pass the Ninth Degree, and become eligible for the first degree of actual Adeptship. After the preliminary Initiation each Member must *earn* by his own individual effort, in conjunction with the instructions of his Teacher, the right to admittance to any higher Degree! A Task is given each to accomplish—we are no respecters of persons—and none can progress in the order unless the task before them is completed; it is the test of their fitness for higher Initiation. Remember, *we teach freely and without reserve all we find worthy to receive.* The following are the seven principal Rules to be observed by all, both Teachers and Pupils alike:

I.—This order devotes its energies and means at command towards discovering, gauging, applying, and subjecting the hidden laws, and *latent*, or active Forces in every department of Nature, to the *Imperial Will of the Human Soul*, whose powers and attributes it alone seeks to evolve, in order to establish that immortal individuality which enables the perfected Spirit to say, I AM.

II.—The Members pledge themselves to endeavor to the best of their abilities to live the life of moral purity and brotherly love, and to abstain, under all circumstances, from the use of intoxicants, except under special medical advice; and also to help forward all social Reforms for the benefit of mankind generally.

III.—Members are divided into Circles, each of which has a special and separate Teacher appointed, who has full power to appoint any officers and Assistants that he may deem necessary; each Circle forms within itself its own Lodge, of which the Teacher is always President.[1]

IV.—The Members of each Circle further pledge themselves to obey the commands and follow the instructions of their Teacher *in all pertaining to their Occult Studies*, to the utmost limit compatible with their surrounding circumstances, and to do all within their power for the mutual benefit and assistance of each other.

V.—The Members solemnly pledge their sacred Word of Honor not to reveal any knowledge, teachings, or transactions of the Order with which they are entrusted, without the special permission of their duly appointed Teachers; and further, to conceal under all legal circumstances the name and identity of all persons who, to their knowledge, are connected with the Order, *unless they receive* in Writing the special permission of the person whose name they may desire to divulge.

---

[1] The Archè text (*H.B. of L.*, 11), which is not preserved in the Fonds Papus at Lyon, adds in a parenthesis that "this organization no longer exists." The note reflects the situation existing after the flight of Davidson and Burgoyne to America in the spring of 1886. The text given here is from a printed leaflet circulated in the United States in 1885. The Archè text also lacks the Pledge at the end of these Rules.—Editors

VI.—The Fee for Admission and Initiation as a Probationary Candidate is $5.00[2], and the Annual subscription of Membership is $1.25, which must be paid by the Members (in America) to the Treasurer of the Central Council. There is no further charge except for further Initiation, which can only take place at long intervals—in no case is any Initiation-Fee more than $5.00. All instruction, teaching, and other information must be given by either Teachers, or Members Free of Charge.

VII.—The Members of the order have full liberty to the free and full exercise of their reason and judgment in forming all their opinions. In no case has one Member the right to show disrespect to, or *intrude* his opinions upon, the religious belief of another; and lastly, each individual Member of our ancient and noble Order should endeavor to sustain its dignity and character, by himself or herself becoming a living example of purity, justice, and benevolence; for no matter what your circumstances in life may be, you may, if you will, become living centres of goodness from which radiate all that is virtuous, noble, and true.

By Order   M. THEON
Grand Master *pro tem.* of the Exterior Circle

---

[2] The Archè text has one guinea or 25 francs 25 centimes as the cost of initiation.—Editors

PLEDGE

I_____,
residing at _____, prom-
ise most faithfully, upon my sacred word of Honor, to hold
sacred and inviolable, all teachings, rules, signs, and symbols, with their various explanations, received from my
Occult Teachers, belonging to the ancient and noble
Order—the H. B. of L.; and I further promise to fulfill all the
commands of my duly appointed Guru (Teacher), relating
to Occultism (so far as my convenience and circumstances
permit); and lastly, I promise to conceal under all LEGAL
circumstances the Name and Identity of Members, and
other persons, to my knowledge connected with the Brotherhood.

Dated at _____ this _____ day

of _____ 1888

ACKNOWLEDGED, OR WITNESSED,
AND RECEIVED,

_____
Pres. Amer. Central Council H. B. of L.

"ORIGIN AND OBJECT OF THE H. B. OF L." (A.1.c)

This text is one of the most fascinating of all the H. B. of L. documents. Unlike most of the rest of the teaching material presented in this part, the "Origin and Object" was originally not a teaching manuscript intended for circulation among the neophytes. Rather it appears to have been a private letter of July 1887 from Peter Davidson to F.-Ch. Barlet, in which Davidson expounded the primordial tradition embodied in the H. B. of L.'s teachings and at the same time sought to educate Barlet about the Order's relationship with Madame Blavatsky's Theosophical Society.

The "Origin and Object" makes it clear that the revival of true occultism embodied in the formation of the Exterior Circle of the H. B. of L. was a cyclical phenomenon, and in this respect it should be read in conjunction with "The Key" to Trithemius [A.2.c]. The period from 1879 to 1881, as many occultists of the time believed, marked the entry into a new cycle favorable to occultism for humanity.

The text of the "Origin and Object" survives in a single bilingual manuscript, which preserves Davidson's original text alongside Barlet's very inaccurate French translation. The latter was circulated among French members, and can be found in *H. B. of L.* 1988. An English re-translation from the French was circulated in typescript, containing omissions and further errors. It is thanks to Mr. Pascal Thémanlys, and indirectly to Max Théon, who sent the bilingual copy to Mr. Thémanlys's father, that we are able to present Davidson's hitherto lost original.

The most important thing that emerges from the restored text is that the "adept" who sought a neophyte in England in the early 1870s was not Theon, as we formerly thought was implied (incredibly as it may have been). Theon was instead the neophyte, who in turn became an adept. Moreover, since there is mention here of the original adept being "now" (1887) in Tibet, we are able to identify him with the adept whom Davidson told Ayton he had met in astral form (see Part 1, Section 6). Most important of all, we know that Theon gave his approval to this version of the story by sending it to his pupil. The identification of the adept remains open, with the caveat that we are told explicitly that such people never reveal themselves to non-initiates!

Origin and Object of the HBL Formation, teachings, objects of the Exterior circle of the HBL.

The interior Circle of the H. B. of L. was formed into a distinct and Hermetic Order in Consequence of a division that took place in the ranks of the Hermetic Initiates 4320 years prior to the year 1881 of our present era.

This division was the outcome of the natural difference between the Initiates belonging to the *Sacerdotal Caste,* and those who earnestly toiled and graduated in the Schools or Seminaries of Occultism for the sheer love of Truth, who could not consent to the growing demand for popular power and place amongst their sacerdotal Brethren.

The initiated sacerdotal Pontiffs, then, became the actual Leaders of the mystical orders connected with Sacerdotalism and the rites of the Temple.

The *real Adepts* were the masters of those who from that period were looked upon as *Hermits,* Philosophers, Wise men etc., *but of no particular religion,* and who gradually incurred the displeasure of their priestly brothers, becoming wanderers, through their necessity.

Thebes was the head-quarters of the Sacerdotal Caste, and *Luxor,* the landing-place of the famous city, became the humble chief-center of the true followers of the Divine Grand-Master Hermes Trismegistus.

From these *two Orders,* the complete Occultism of the West, and the religious pagan rites of the ancient Western nations have been derived.

Hermetic Initiates, *have borrowed nothing from India,* and the apparent similiarity between many of the Hindu and Egyptian names, doctrines, etc., instead of indicating that Egypt obtained its doctrines from India, only plainly shews that the main features of their respective teachings were derived from the same parent stock, and this original source was *neither India, nor Egypt but the lost Isle of the West.*

Let it be therein remembered that I do not here allude to the origin of the sacred Knowledge, but only to the *last decade,* and to the center from which *our* present system has been derived, for this period does not embrace the many thousands of years, that some suppose.

I mention all this simply to show you that we do not in any manner look to India, or the Orient, as the Sacred Birth-Place of esoteric science (note also the Mis [sions] of S$^{t.}$ Yves writing as to this).

The Hindu Initiates, as a body, always excelled in metaphysical studies, but they never could approach even to the Egyptians *as practical occultists.* That which Egyptian initiates have gained in abstruse and metaphysical conceptions from India, they have more than a thousand times repaid in the transmission of valuable Knowledge pertaining to practical Magic, the domain of Alchemy, Astrology, Mathematics, and the other ramifications of the Sacred Wisdom, as a *practical Science* which they imparted.

There is one particular era in which is formulated the life-lines of the Occult Orders, of both the Orient and the Occident, and this period is about 600 B.C., the era of[1] Gautama in India, and Pythagoras in Europe. Each of these exalted persons founded an *Exterior Circle.* Pythagoras formed an exterior section of the H. B. of L., and left it to time to show its developments, of which the most important one is Freemasonry, now a lost child, a corporation like the Church, whose knowledge and truth have vanished.

Gautama established an exterior circle of Initiates in India, but it became so degenerate from the interior section that it had to be reorganized. Their faculty of vision, their metaphysical meditations, and a passive life of indolence were the causes of their intellectual inertia, which needed to be galvanized by an active vitality.

But I consider it absolutely superfluous as well as unnecessary for me to retrace the wanderings of the H. B. of L. across long ages of the past, or to show you that

---

[1] Here a page of the bilingual Ms. is lacking, and we are obliged to give the text from the English typescript.—Editors

the groups of its members have often attempted to promulgate the truth through instituting a secret order, of which, among others, incomparably the most notable of modern times were the *Rosicrucians*.

After the establishment of these Orders, the new members founded entirely new orders, which gradually split off from the parent trunk and followed whither their inclinations led them.

Note well what I now say: in 1870 (and not 1884, as the January number of the *Theosophist* says), an adept of the serene, ever-existent and ancient Order of the original H. B. of L., after having obtained the consent of his Brother Initiates, resolved to choose a neophyte in Great Britain who would answer to his intentions.

After having fulfilled an important and secret mission on the *European Continent*, he landed in England in 1873 and discovered by chance a neophyte who satisfied what he had in mind, and after having truly tested him and had the authenticity of his credentials verified, he gradually instructed this neophyte.

You are doubtless aware that there are very strong and valid reasons that an adept *must not* make himself known[2] to many who are *non-initiates*.

One of the chief occult reasons for this is that the concentration of the thoughts of those uninitiated individuals upon the Masters would keep them constantly opposing the streams of active force generated in the *Aska* towards themselves, which would otherwise almost paralyse their efforts for accomplishing our own special mission. It was therefore imperative to observe *Secrecy*.

This Neophyte in question, then, having obtained permission to establish an exterior Circle of the H. B. of L. and thus prepare all *who are deserving* amongst the Members, for that form of Initiation which they were qualified to receive, as also to teach them the vast difference between unsullied

---

[2] From this point, the bilingual Ms. resumes.—Editors

truth and apparent verity, is thus carrying the result of which you are so far aware.

As the time arrived for the diffusion of Knowledge amongst the rising nations of the West, and because of the attempt that is being made, under the garb of *Esoteric Buddhism* to vitiate the Western mind, and fetter it under the dominion of Oriental thought, you can easily realise the object that *Mr. Theon* had in view—I may herein just add that the Adept alluded to is at the present time (1887) in Thibet (not Theon, remember).

We know perfectly, with whom we have to treat, and the Hindou Initiates of oriental occultism will not dare to deny the Truth of what I say. The veritable and *real Adepts* of the Himalayan Brothers neither teach those doctrines of *Karma*, nor *Reincarnation*, which have been brought forward by the authors of Esoteric Budhism [sic] and other Theosophical works.

The principles of Karma and Reincarnation, as taught in such volumes are only the *exterior* teachings of the exoteric church, or sacerdotal order of Budhism. Neither in the above mentioned books, nor in the pages of the Theosophist even, so far as I am aware, has the real or esoteric meaning of the important doctrines, been made known.

One of the main objects of the H. B. of L. is to reveal to those Members who have proved themselves *worthy*, the whole mystery of these momentous subjects.

Mr. Theon who is an adept of the veritable H. B. of L. is nominally the Grand Master of the Circle, and all teaching emanates from an unpolluted and pure fountain, viz: from the ACTUAL HERMETIC BROTHERS.

I may as well observe that the T. S. (Theosophic Society) is *not* at present (nor has it been since Mad^e. B. and Col. O. landed in India) under the control, or supervision of the *authentic*, or real Brotherhood of the Himalayas, but upon the contrary, under a greatly inferior Order, belonging to the Budhist Cult. I speak from *what I know* from indisputable authority.—

But keep all those matters in *Silence* amongst yourselves and Brothers.

The H. B. of L. has a large body of Members scattered throughout the World, and its *Aims* and *Object* may be briefly stated as follows:

—The universal Brotherhood of Humanity.

—The diffusion of the principles of Occult Science, and the ancient Wisdom-Religion, amongst the People.

—The diffusion of the sacred Esoteric Doctrines amongst the Members.

—And last (but not least) the establishment of External Centers throughout the West for the revivification of the Rites of the *Ancient Initiations.*

Trusting that the foregoing details may be sufficient to convince you of our integrity, and noting also that I furnish you such in *strict Confidence*

I remain

very faithfully

Yours:

P21 6 21 8 D 25 4 17 22 7 11 12

(July 1887)

"List of Questions to be put to Neophytes" (A.1.d)

This questionnaire was sent by Burgoyne to his students in the Denver branch of the H. B. of L. in January 1887. Its exact purpose is unknown, but it may be related to the "task" that neophytes were expected to complete before advancing in the Order [see A.1.b.] In any case, correct answers to these questions would certainly have been required before further initiation, because the ideas covered by the questions were fundamental to the H. B. of L. system: sex and the role of sex both cosmically and personally, the "astral light," and the benefits and dangers of practical occultism. To respond appropriately, the neophyte would have to have read and understood all of the hints in the material later embodied in the "Mysteries of Eros."

Unfortunately, none of the neophytes' responses has been preserved. Similar questionnaires were not unknown in other groups at the time, however, and W.W. Westcott's responses to Madame Blavatsky's Examination Paper for entry into the Esoteric Section still exist (see Gilbert 1987b, 9-10). In responding to a question on the role of practical occultism, Westcott gave an answer (inappropriate, in Mme Blavatsky's opinion) that would probably have satisfied Burgoyne—though the role of sexuality is ignored:

> "The successful Practical Occultist may gain the power of purification and elevation of himself and so fit himself to commune with higher beings, and so may assist in raising others: his intuition is extended by training, his senses are rendered so acute as to perceive presences and gain information, beyond the reach of the selfish and sensual man of the common standard. . . .
> He may obtain the art of performing many acts which are impossible to the general public, but is beyond the temptation of using those powers for private ambition or for cajolery of others."

Private Secretary's Office

January 16, 1887

List of Questions to be put to Neophytes in Grade I

I. What is the Astral Light and its Nature etc.

II. What can a Man do with his sexual organism from a Psychical standpoint? Describe its real dangers.

III. What is Sex? Of what does it consist and why?

IV. Are the sexes fairly represented? Are men always men & Vice Versa?

V. What are the *Causes* producing the above.

VI. What are the *Animating* principles of Human Monsters? Describe their proper sphere and destiny.

VII. Describe the Various formulas of soul power, its germs of potentialities and their proper realm or state.

T. H. Burgoyne
Private Sec.

Original questionnaire sent by Burgoyne to his students.

"HERMETIC RITUAL FOR PRIVATE INITIATION" (A.1.e)

One of the proposed goals of the H. B. of L. was the re-institution of the ancient initiations. Obtaining land for temples of initiation and for preparation for initiation was in fact one of the principal reasons advanced for the Colony Scheme that eventually proved the downfall of the Order (see B.4.a). The actual rituals, however, are disappointing.

The "Ancient and Noble Order" [A.1.b] held out for the neophyte a regular progression to adeptship through four initiations, but the scheme probably existed only on paper. Early members, such as the Rev. Ayton, apparently were initiated shortly after joining the Order in a ceremony that included the presence of the members of the Inner Circle in "astral form" and the drinking of "Soma juice." (See Part 1, Section 15.) Later members, especially those in America, were not so fortunate, and had to wait, sometimes for years, before their first initiation.

The text of the "Hermetic Ritual" given here survives only in a copy of a manuscript in a private collection. Accompanying it is a typed copy of a letter from T.H. Burgoyne (Swastika) to ☉ (the Sun), who may have been Thomas M. Johnson, since his Presidency of the American Central Council of the H. B. of L. could have been indicated by the sigil for the sun. The letter and the ritual are undated, but Burgoyne's statement that the prayers to the Elementals could be found in A. E. Waite's digest of Eliphas Lévi's works (published 1886), and his references to the Rev. Ayton indicate that the ritual was first sent out to the American neophytes in early 1886.

Burgoyne's cover letter makes it very clear that the ritual did not work *ex opere operato* and was not viewed as a rite of traditional ceremonial magic in which formalistic adherence to exact detail was necessary for the effect of the rite. Rather, the form and content of the ritual appear to have been *ad hoc* and largely accidental. If one prayer could not be found in Waite or Lévi, another from Barrett would do, or the prayer could even be omitted altogether. Also, unlike the intricate and creative rituals of other magical orders such as the Order of the Golden Dawn in which every detail of the rite was carefully fitted into a pattern of universal correspondences specific to the degree or goal, the

H. B. of L. ritual is surprisingly non-descript and generic. It is serviceable, not elegant or eloquent.

The reason for this nonchalant attitude toward the rituals (but not toward initiation itself) is provided in the lodge ritual [A.1.f], which instructed the neophyte that

> "Our revered Masters and the Adepts do not use nor is it necessary for them to use any such things as ceremonies or instruments and symbolic figures, but for the young aspirant these are absolutely necessary in order to afford the mind something thereon to concentrate itself. . . ."

The Masters themselves, in other words, were the efficient cause of real initiation, and the forms were merely outward show to impress the neophytes and to allow them to concentrate their minds on the Masters.

The notes to the text are those found in the original manuscript.

THE HERMETIC RITUAL
FOR PRIVATE INITIATION OF NEOPHYTES

I

"For 7 days prior to the Ceremony, the Neophyte must abstain from all meats, fish or fowl, as likewise all wines and spiritous [*sic*] liquors. Also Complete Continence during the same period. Further, the Neophyte must also keep himself free from all Contact with the world to the utmost limits compatible with his Circumstances in life.

II

"The room which must have previously been purified of all Contaminating influences (*external to the Neophyte*) by the gradual formation of a magnetic Wall, must be duly ordered as follows: a small temporary Altar must be erected; any article of furniture will do for this, but a small shapely table is best. This altar must be Covered with a white table cloth (new) and the three Crystal lamps Containing Cotton wicks and pure olive oil must be placed thereon in the form of a triangle or pyramid. The lamp which forms the apex must be *elevated* above the others, so as to form a triangular pyramid 9 inches in diameter between the two Lamps forming the base, and the lamp at the apex must not exceed 9 inches in height, but less if possible. This depends upon the size of the *Vase* Containing the Water. The bottom of the lamp must stand on a level with the top of the Vase *behind it*. Thus

A White Cloth (a sheet will do) must be spread upon the floor in front of the Table and a Censor of inscence [sic] must be lighted upon the floor immediately in front of the Table (dhoop will do). The room should be Comfortably warm; and no light used. After the reading of the ritual is over, [no light] must be used except that given by the Lamp on the table.

III

All things being ready, the Neophyte must enter the Room *alone* at the appointed time. Attired in perfectly clean underwear, and his *usual dress*, he must magnetize the room of air with his Wand. Light the Crystal lamps and set them in order. Start the inscence burning, and light up the room in the usual way, and place a Comfortable Chair about 6 feet from the Altar.[1] The Neophyte must sit facing the Altar and must then read & *re-read*

The Third Book of Hermes in the Pymander Called
"The Holy Sermon"

The Neophyte must let his soul expand to the spiritual Surroundings and the mind must follow the truths of this Book. —After this is finished (the Sermon must be read *twice, not audibly* unless the Neophyte can better Concentrate his Thoughts by reading aloud).

IV

After reading Hermes, the Neophyte must earnestly but Calmly repeat the well known elemental evocation. This evocation is given by Eliphas Levi and is published upon pages 122, 123, 124 and 125 of the Mysteries of Magic by A. E. Waite, but note.—

---

[1] I omitted to say that the Altar must be either in the east or north end of the Room, the latter if convenient.

No Notice is to be taken of the Magical formula.—Recite the prayer of the Sylphs. Ditto of the Undines, ditto of the Salamanders and Gnomes.—These prayers *alone* are to be used. All the time this is being done the Neophyte must stand *facing* the Altar, nor turn either to the right or the left.

V

When the above is accomplished the Neophyte must seat himself in the Chair aforsaid [*sic*] and Calmly read and reflect upon what he is reading, Viz., the 4th Book of the Pymander of Hermes, Called "THE KEY."

VI

The above must also be read *twice*. Then the books must be laid aside and all lights in the Room extinguished except the Lamps, a fresh supply of inscence lighted and then the Neophyte must set in the most Comfortable position possible in the Chair before the Altar and Concentrate his Mind *upon the Masters, desiring their advice & instruction* and repeating the mantram given in the *Mysteries of Eros,* "My Souls is one," &c. And Keep the eyes fixed Calmly upon the surface of the Vase upon the Altar which must be filled with pure Water. Spring Water or good *well Water* is excellent for this purpose.

VII

And lastly the Neophyte must sit thus thinking for about the space of *one hour.* Longer if he feels IMPRESSED to do so, *but not otherwise.* He must then retire to his room, *lock the door* and sleep *alone,* giving orders if necessary not to be awakened upon any account the next morning.—

The End

Dear ☉,

   I have hunted all over for my Copy of the ritual and Cannot find it high or low. I have therefore written out for you *all* the necessary parts of the same. I was Very pleased when I saw that Eliphas Levi had given the *four prayers* to the four elemental worlds. You have this Book I think as I saw a review of it in Platonist, if not you may find them in "BARRETT" I think. If you have not the Divine Pymander, Mr. A. has [word illegible] and will loan it you. You have with these Books and the above everything that you require except that portion called *"the blessing of the lights"* which you may find either in Barrett or Agrippa, but I don't know since I have not read these books. If you Cannot find it, you must do without as mine is beyond my reach somewhere. It will not however be an omission of any serious importance if you can [not] obtain it. It must be recited immediately upon first lighting the inscence & Crystal Lamps. Another letter with final advice and if possible further information will be sent to you in 2 or 3 day's [*sic*]; also exact time of Commencement. If there is anything you don't quite understand, write at once. There is plenty of time for a reply.—In haste, fraternally

卍

P.S.
   This ritual is different from that used by Mr. Ayton. His was only a preliminary Ceremony of Initiation.

"THE RITES AND CEREMONY
FOR EXTERIOR INITIATION" (A.1.f)

This ritual was obviously intended for use in the lodges that the H. B. of L. began to set up in late 1885 and early 1886 (see A.1.b). It was probably seldom if ever actually used since the lodge structure fell by the wayside in the disruptions that accompanied the Burgoyne scandal in the spring of 1886. Like the "Hermetic Ritual" [A.1.e], this ritual also is largely generic. The central elements (the prayers to the Elementals) were pieced together from A. E. Waite's digest of Eliphas Levi's works and from the *Comte de Gabalis*.[1] The most striking feature is the total absence of borrowings from Freemasonry—the quarry from which almost all occult groups mined their rituals.

The emphasis in both rituals on the Elementals—the "spirits" of the elements—is curious because the conjuring of these creatures appears not to have played a major part in the magic of the Order. Their role in the cosmic scheme had been defined for occultists of the period by H. P. Blavatsky—who quite properly credited P. B. Randolph with introducing them into the impoverished world of American and British Spiritualism.[2] The H. B. of L. insisted on their existence but did not emphasize their part in human development. In the "Rites and Ceremony," it is vaguely taught that control of the Elementals is an essential step in the development of the will, and that Elementals are somehow "aids or instruments" for the development of clairvoyance and astral sight, but the exact procedure is not made clear. A more fundamental explanation is given in *Light of Egypt*, where T. H. Burgoyne adopts the doctrine (universal in late classical antiquity) that the soul, in entering into the world of matter, vests itself with "envelopes" from each of the elements which the neophyte must strive to cast off on seeking re-entry into the celestial realms.[3]

---

[1] Levi 1886, 122ff. A version of the prayer of the Salamanders is given in Villars, 169-171, and in Fryar, 102-103. The prayers were later republished in Levi 1896, 228-230.

[2] H. P. Blavatsky, "Elementaries," Letter to the *Religio-Philosophical Journal* 23 (17 November 1877), reprinted in *BCW*, I, 265-271; citation from 269.

[3] *LOE*, I, 183.

The second part of the "Rites and Ceremony" is an edifying discourse which was obviously intended to be pronounced for the new members of the lodge. It provides the closest approximation in the surviving H. B. of L. manuscript teachings to a summary of the Order's cosmology and anthropology.

The "Rites and Ceremony" survives only in a manuscript in a private collection. At some point it was worked over by an editor—perhaps in preparation for a performance of the ritual in a lodge—and notes have been added to the manuscript in a different hand. These have been included in the text in square brackets. The footnotes to the text are from the original manuscript.

The Rites and Ceremony
For Exterior Initiation

PART I

Erect a temporary Altar at the South end of the room and cover with a white linen cloth. In the centre place a Crystal Ball or sphere and around this, Seven small crystal lamps, in the form of a Seven pointed star, containing cotton wicks and pure olive oil. The Crystal must be placed upon a stand (a small new wine glass will answer this purpose very well) and around it some choice flowers (if possible). Then in front of the Altar upon the floor place a white cloth, & at each side of the Altar (upon the floor) a tripod holding the incense burners. This incense for the preliminary rite may be of the usual kind used by Roman Catholic priests. This is all that is absolutely necessary for the preliminary rite. Any hour of the day will do. Having put the room in order, darken it and light the lamps. Let all Members form (if possible) a horseshoe circle with the Altar between the two poles, thus:

Each one should hold the thumb of his or her left hand Brother or Sister in the palm of the hand. The one to be initiated then advances from the East and kneels upon the cloth in front of the Altar. The President, who acts as priest, then stands in front of the candidate on the other side of the Altar & the ceremony commences thus—[1]

---

[1] N. B. Some sweet sacred melody suited to the occasion if possible, should be sung in a low voice at the close and also at the commencement of the rite. Music when possible adds to it, and should be used.

RITE

Dearly beloved, this man (or woman as the case may be) having entered by the Eastern gate now humbly supplicates, at the foot of the Sacred Altar, to be admitted as a Brother (or Sister) to the ranks of our Ancient & Noble Order The H. B. of L.[2] I therefore strictly command all of you who are now present, if anyone know any just cause or impediment why this (Man or Woman) should not be admitted, that you now openly declare it or forever after hold your peace.

Do any of you know such cause or impediment? Answer (with one voice) No! worthy brother there is no charge against him (or her).[3]

TO THE CANDIDATE. I now ask & charge you to answer most truly upon your sacred word of honor, in the presence of this lodge, if you are prepared to hold sacred & inviolate all teachings, secrets & other matters referred to in our Seven Rules.

Answer!—

Priest.—You have declared your vow!

Members present.—And we are witnesses [   ] obligation!

Priest.—Rise, brave Soul & henceforth let Veritas be your life's motto!

The candidate then rises & sits in front of the Altar. The Members sitting in the usual form round him, in the position they stood in before.

---

[2] If there *is* cause, the members must declare it.
[3] The name must be repeated in full.

The different Degrees & names are here revealed to the accepted candidate. And the Priest then takes the Hazel Wand and repeats the following Ritual.

THE CONJURATION OF THE FOUR ELEMENTS

The four Elementarys [*in another hand* "forms"] separate & specify by a sort of rough outline the created spirits which the universal movement disengages from the central fire, everywhere the spirit works & fertilizes matter by life; all matter is animated,—thought & Soul are everywhere. In making oneself master of a thought which produces the different forms, one becomes the master of the forms and makes them serviceable to our [*stricken out in a different hand and* "his" *added*] use.

The Astral Light is saturated with Souls which it disengages from the incessant generation of beings; the souls have imperfect wills which can be dominated and employed by more powerful wills; they then form grand invisible chains and can occasion or determine great Elementary commotions.

The phenomena of all magical rites and of the physical seance room of modern Spiritualism have no other cause. Elemental Spirits are as infants; they torment more those who occupy themselves with them unless we govern them with a lofty reason with great severity. These are the Spirits which we designate under the name of Occult Elements. They are the Elementals or Nature Spirits. It is they who often determine for us disquieting dreams. It is they who produce the movements of the Divining Rod and knocks against the walls and furniture, but they can never manifest any other thought than our own, and if we do not speak [*in another hand* "think"], they communicate with all the incoherence of dreams. They reproduce good or evil indifferently because they are without free will and consequently have no responsibility. They manifest themselves to ecstatics and somnambulists under incomplete and fugitive forms. They are neither damned nor culpable, they are inquisitive and innocent. We may use or abuse them as we may animals or infants. [*In another hand* "For this reason"] Also the Magian who avails himself of their assistance takes upon himself a terrible responsibility for he must expiate in his own person all the evils which he causes them to do. The greatness of his torments will be in exact proportion to the extent of power which he has exercised by their agency.

To govern elemental spirits and thus become King of the Occult elements, we must first have undergone the four trials of the ancient initiations. When we have acquired by boldness and exercise this incontestable power of the Human Soul, we must impose upon the Elements the Word of our Will, by special consecrations of the Air, the Fire, the Earth and the Water, and here is the *indispensable commencement of all magical operations.*

We exorcise the Air by blowing towards the four cardinal points and in magical operations with the spirits of the Air, we chant [*in another hand* "recite"] the Orison of the Sylphs, which is as follows:

ORISON OF THE SYLPHS

Spirit of light, spirit of Wisdom, whose breath gives and takes again the form of everything. Thou before whom the life of beings is but a shadow, which flits and a vapour which passes away. Thou who ridest upon the clouds— walkest upon the wings of the winds. Thou who breathest, and the spaces without end are peopled. Thou who inspirest, and all which comes from you returns unto you again. Movement without end in the eternal stability. Be thou eternally blessed, we praise thee and bless thee in the changing empire of the created light, of the shadows, of the reflections and of the images and we aspire without ceasing to your unchangeable and imperishable brightness. Permit to penetrate to us the ray of thine intelligence and the warmth of thy love, then that which is movable will be fixed, the shadow will become a body, the Spirit of the Air will become a Soul, the dream will become a thought and we shall no more be carried away by the tempest, but we shall hold the reins of the Winged horses of the morning and direct the course of the winds of the evening and fly to thy presence. O Spirit of spirits, O eternal soul of souls, O! imperishable breath of Life, O! creative sigh, O! mouth which inspires and breathes out the existence of all beings in the ebb and flow of thine eternal word, who art [*in another hand* "which is"] the divine Ocean of movement and truth. Amen.

•••••••••••••

Interlude [*crossed out in another hand*]. We exorcise the Element of Water by the Sacred Goblet and by sprinkling it with the hand towards the four points of heaven, and in magical operations with the spirits of the Waters we chant the Orison of the Undines which is as follows:

ORISON OF THE UNDINES

Terrible king of the Sea, you who hold the Keys of the cataracts of Heaven and who confinest the subterranean waters in the caverns of the Earth. King of the floods and of the rains of spring, you who open the sources of the rivers & fountains, you who command humidity, which is as the blood of the Earth, to become the sap of plants, you we adore and you we invoke. To us, your variable and changing creatures, speak, in the grand commotions of the Sea, and we will tremble before you, speak to us in the murmurs of the limpid waters and we will desire your love. O! immensity in which all the waves of the being are going, to lose themselves. O! ocean of infinite perfections. O! altitude which sees yourself reflected in the depth. O! profundity which exhales yourself in the altitude: bring us to the true life by intelligence and love, bring us to immortality by sacrifice, to the end that we may be found worthy to offer you one day Water, Blood and Tears for the remission of errors. Amen.

●●●●●●●●●●●●●

We exorcise the fire by throwing into it Salt, Incense, White resin, camphor and sulphur, and in pronouncing three times the three names of the Genii of the fire. Michael, King of the Sun and of lightning. Samael King of volcanoes, and Anael, Prince of the Astral Light, then recite the orison of the Salamanders.

ORISON OF THE SALAMANDERS

Immortal, ineffable, eternal and uncreated Father of all things, who art carried without ceasing upon the rolling chariot of the worlds which eternally revolve, ruler of the etherial immensities where is elevated the throne of thy power, from the height of which your redoubtable eyes pierce thro' everything and your beautiful and holy ears hear all things. Hearken to your children, whom you have loved since the birth of the ages, for thy golden and grand and eternal majesty is resplendent above the world and the heaven and the stars. Thou art elevated above them, O! gleaming light. There thou enkindlest and sustainest thyself by thine own splendor and there proceed from thine essence inexhaustible streams of Light, which nourish thine infinite spirit—thy infinite spirit nourishes all things and makes this inexhaustible treasure of substance always ready for the generation which labors it and which appropriates to itself the forms [*in another hand* "with"] which you have impregnated [*in another hand* "it"] from the beginning. From the spirit draw also their origin these 3 Kings who are around thy throne and who compose thy court O! universal father, O! unique father of the blessed mortals and immortals. Thou hast created in particular the powers which are marvelously like to thine eternal thought and thine adorable essence. You have established them superior to the Angels who announce to the world thy Will. Lastly thou hast created us in the 3rd rank in our elementary empire. There our continual exercise is to prove [*in a different hand* "praise"] thee and to adore thy wishes, there we learn without ceasing in aspiring to *possess thee*. O! father, O! mother, the most tender of mothers, O! most admirable archetype of maternity and of pure love. O! Son, the flower of sons. O! form of all forms, soul, spirit, harmony and number of all things. Amen.

•••••••••••••

We exorcise the Earth by the sprinkling of water, by breathing and by the fire with the proper perfumes for each day and we say the Orison of the Gnomes.

ORISON OF THE GNOMES

King invisible who hast taken the earth for thy footstool and hast hallowed out the abysses of it to fill them with thine omnipotence, thou whose name maketh the vaults of the world to tremble, thou who maketh the seven metals to flow in the veins of the Stones, monarch of the seven lights, rewarder of the subterranean workmen, bring us to the wished for Air and to the Kingdom of brightness. We watch and work without rest, we search, and we hope by the twelve stones of the holy city, by the talismans which are buried, by the diamond nail [*in another hand* "magnet in form of nail"] which traverses the centre of the world. Lord! Lord!! Lord!!! have pity on those who suffer, enlarge our busts [*in another hand* "breasts"], disengage and elevate our

heads [*in another hand* "make us larger"], dignify us. O stability and movement. O! day enveloped in the night. O!
obscurity veiled in the light. O! master who never keepest
back to thyself the wages of thy workmen, O! silver witness
[*in another hand* "Silvery Whiteness"]. O! Golden splendor.
O! crown of living and melodious diamonds, thou who car-
riest the heaven on thy finger as a ring of sapphire, thou
who concealest under the earth in the Kingdom of precious
stones, the marvelous seed of the stars, live, reign and be
the eternal dispenser of the riches of which you have made
us the guardians. Amen

•••••••••••••

We must observe that the special Kingdom of the
Gnomes is to the North, that of the Salamanders is the
South, that of the Sylphs to the east, and that of the Undines
to the West. They influence the four temperaments [*sic*] of
man, viz.—the Gnomes over the melancholic, the Salamanders over the Sanguine, the Undines over the phleg-
matic, and the Sylphs over the bilious. Their Signs are, the
symbols of the Bull for the Gnomes and we command them
with the sword—of the Lion for the Salamanders and we
command them with the forked rod or the magic trident—
of the Eagle for the Sylphs and we command them with the
holy pentacles and finally an Aquarius for the Undines and
we evoke them with the cup of the libations. Their respective rulers or sovereigns are—Gob of the Gnomes, Djin of
the Salamanders, Toroldo of the Sylphs, and Nicksa of the
Undines.

•••••••••••••

In order to govern the Elemental spirits and make them
serve us we must never abandon ourselves to the defects
which characterice [*sic*] them. Thus never will a light capri-
cious spirit govern the Sylphs, never will a nature effeminate,

cold and changeable be master of the Undines, anger irritates the Salamanders, while covetousness and coarseness renders one quite [*in a different hand* "the sport"] powerless in the realms of the Gnomes; but we must be prompt and active as the Sylphs, flexible and attentive to resemblances as the Undines, energetic and strong as the Salamanders, laborious and patient as the Gnomes, or, in other words we must possess all the good qualities and virtues of the four Elementals and thus be able to conquer them in their own realms with their own force, without ever allowing ourselves to give way to their weaknesses. When we are well established in this disposition, the entire realm of Nature will be at the service of the wise initiate. He will pass during a storm and the rain will not touch his head, the wind will not derange a fold of his clothing, he will pass thro' fire even without being burnt.

For it is indubitable that we can by virtue of the Imperial human will, control and direct the [semi?]-intelligent forces of Nature and change or arrest their effects.

The metals which correspond to the four elements are Gold and Silver for the Air, Mercury for the Water, Iron and Copper for fire and Lead for the Earth. We compose of them Talismans relative to the forces they represent and to the effects we propose to ourselves to obtain from them.

And lastly the four elements are used and are really only aids or instruments to aid clairvoyance or the faculty of seeing or perceiving in the Astral light and are used as their various natures suggest. And here it is necessary for you to bear in mind that no incantation, prayer or charm can have the least effect upon the realms of either super or sub-mundane being, of and by itself alone, but only thro' the magnetic impulse given to it by the imperial Will of Man.

Our revered Masters and the Adepts do not use nor is it necessary for them to use any such things as ceremonies or instruments and symbolic figures, but for the young aspirant these are absolutely necessary in order to afford the mind something thereon to concentrate itself and thus effect its purpose, hence all magical ceremonials are useless to an adept of the Sacred science, but are great assistance to the Neophyte.

● ● ● ● ● ● ● ● ● ● ● ● ●

And now dearly beloved we will in a few brief outlines describe in familiar terms the origin and progress of the spirit atom which ultimates in the material Universe as Man, and point out the path of its immortal destiny.

PART II

As declared in our printed rules, our Noble Order acknowledges the eternal existence of the great first cause, the divine, invisible, central, spiritual sun, from whose gloriously radiant, Throbbing Soul pulsates the living breath; the life principle of all that is or ever shall be. From this Divine Vortex proceeds the invisible power which binds the vast Universe in one harmonious whole.

We teach that from this incomprehensible centre of Divinity emanate the divine scintillations of the eternal spirit, which when having completed their orbit—*the great cycle of necessity*—constitute *The only Immortal Portion of the Human Soul.*

That the Soul is an emanation from the central spiritual Sun of the infinite Universe is an eternal verity which has been transmitted from generation to generation of the Initiates of our Order as a divine revelation; down thro' the long vistas of the prehistoric past to the present times. Know then that there are spheres or realms of pure unmanifested being that the uninitiated know not of. In these paradises of purity and love, souls spring up like blossoms of divine beauty in the infinite gardens of Eden that inhere within the chaste womb of the heavenly Bride, the celestial Virgin of light, Queen Isis. It is the tendency of the Divine Nature, whose chief attributes are Love and Wisdom, Heat and Light; to repeat itself eternally and mirror forth its own perfections in scintillations from itself. The sparks of divine fire become Souls, and as the effect must share the nature of the cause, the fire which warms into life also illuminates into light; hence the Soul emanations from deity are all love and heat, whilst the illumination of light, which is ever radiating from the great central Sun of being, irradiates all with corresponding beams of light.

Born of love which corresponds to the divine fire and heat and illuminated with light which is Divine Wisdom and truth, the first and most powerful emanations repeat the action of their originator and give off emanations of their own being, some higher, some lower, the highest tending upward into spiritual essences, the lowest, form particled Matter (which is the Primordial earth or first Matter of the Kabbalist). These denser emanations following out the creative law (the impulse of which is the eternal principle within) aggregate into Suns, Satellites and worlds; each repeating the story of creation, the glorious Soul of Deity, the central Spiritual Sun, projected from within its divine centre, the bright radiant centres of divine energy. From these in turn emanated and for ever emanate, all souls and Suns. Suns gave birth to systems and every member of a system becomes the material Matrix of subordinate states of spiritual and material existence.

This dearly beloved, is the mystery of the glorious En Soph and its emanations, called in the Kabbala, the Ten Sephiroth.

When material earths have arrived at that point of their evolution which gives them the capacity to support organic life, their own interior natures attract it and the embryonic Soul world supplies it in response to the yearning magnetic attraction for such forms of life as are suited to existing conditions; and when at last the young worlds—*pregnant with the Holy Ghost,* cry forth in their travail for the birth of their Lord and Master, the Son of God to rule over them, then the spirits in their distant Edens, hear the whisper of the tempting serpent—the Animal principle; the urgent intellect which is beginning to bud forth within them appeals to the innocent Souls even in their heavenly paradises and fills them with indescribable longings for change, for broader vistas of knowledge, for mightier powers; they aspire to be as Gods and know good and evil. At last the Souls give way to temptation and eat of the forbidden fruit—the union is effected—and the Spirit is precipitated into the realms of Matter, and from their garden of delights, they are expelled by the Divine fiat, to work their way back again only by laboring amid toils and sorrow in the rugged path of material incarnation around the great cycle of necessity. When these pure Souls basked in their innocence, in the sunlight of God's paradise, as spiritual emanations from the deific source, they knew no sex nor reproduced their kind. When they fell, behold! they saw they were naked and were ashamed, for the Earth like a magnetic tractor, drew them within the vortex of its grosser elements, and they became what earthly conditions compelled them to be.

This is the mystery of the fall of Man. So be it. Amen.

• • • • • • • • • • • •

Then approaching the candidate, shake him by the hand and give him the grip, saying: Thrice welcome, worthy Brother. Arise and may the Eternal guardians of our race aid thy steps amid the intricate paths of our Sacred science and Hermes, the thrice illumined great Hermes, the Arch Hierophant and Messenger of the Gods, shall grant thee such light as thy soul merits. Amen.

• • • • • • • • • • • •

Hymn and music if possible.

Finis

The *Pass Word* will be sent privately.

"SYMBOLICAL NOTES TO FIRST DEGREE" (A.2.a)

This teaching is undoubtedly the work of Peter Davidson, presented as a learned and antiquarian disquisition on the phallic mysteries, replete with the usual learned asides in Hebrew and Greek. As such it is but one of a long series of such efforts throughout the 19th century. Its gist is the Hermetic myth of the descent of the soul into matter and its subsequent reascent to the heavens, but in a fashion typical of the times the author draws out the parallels with the Biblical Fall and with classical mythology, and emphasizes the primacy of sex in the human pilgrimage.

Edouard Blitz wrote to Papus that Davidson was ignorant of Hebrew, and that his "erudition" was hollow. The work scarcely pretends to originality, as the references to Hargrave Jennings, Eliphas Levi and Thomas Inman as suitable authors for further reading make clear, and in fact most of the piece is taken over wholesale from Jennings, Madame Blavatsky and Emma Hardinge Britten.

What is original in the treatise and still fresh today is the material inserted at the end of the piece, after the display of quaint antiquarian learning. This is a personal exortation by Davidson to the neophytes that is notable for its sincerity and for the scope of its vision. The student is told to remember that we are "Immortal Spirits. . . infinite in capacity, boundless in power" and is cautioned that patience and time are necessary to accomplish the work. The neophyte is assured that eventually he or she will achieve direct and personal communication with the Adepts of the Inner Circle and with the transcendental Celestial Powers. Whatever else Davidson may have been and whatever other motives he may have had in spreading the word of the H. B. of L., these passages clearly show him to have been sincerely convinced of the reality of the mysterious forces behind the H. B. of L.

The text presented here is from a manuscript in a private collection with additional matter from the version in the Fonds Papus added as footnotes.

SYMBOLICAL NOTES TO FIRST DEGREE

The Student must thoroughly realise that the following is only a very brief and limited outline of a few explanatory Symbols, in connection with the former M.S.S., for the subject is of so vast a nature, as to details, that many volumes might be written explanatory thereunto. This is not for the present, however, required, but as the aspirant begins to fully understand the thorough meanings, interspersed throughout this brief outline, he will the more easily be enabled to continue such studies, and for this purpose he ought, if desirous of prosecuting the subject in its deeper details, to go carefully through Jenning's "Rosicrucians and Phallicism," the works of Inman, Levi, and others.

As a mere matter of probation, however, the following in connexion with the former M.S.S. will be quite sufficient for the purpose in view, towards further advancement and Initiation.

The sexual emblems everywhere conspicuous in the Sculptures of the Ancient Temples, would seem impure in description, but no clean and thoughtful mind could so regard them, whilst recognising the obvious simplicity, solemnity and meaning which such subjects typify. When Science effectually and unerringly demonstrates to us the origin of matter, and proves the fallacy of the Occultists, and of the revered old Sages who held (as their descendents now hold) that Matter is but one of the correlations of Spirit, then will the world of prejudiced and vain skeptics have a right to reject the grand Old Wisdom of the Sacred Science, or throw the charge of obscurity in the teeth of the old religions—but not until then—which will be—Never!

The famous Mysteries of Eleusis, the Bacchic rites, the feasts in honour of Ceres, the orgies of Cybele, and other mythic personages of the Greek Pantheon; Ancient Masonry, speculative and operative, and its degraded and imbecile descendent, modern Freemasonry, have all their origin founded upon the basic principles of these old sex symbols. Every one of these symbols is an embodied idea, combining the conception of the Divine Invisible with the earthly and visible. Nearly all Scriptural names have a direct bearing upon Sexual ideas. The syllables El, Om, On, Di, Mi &c., as well as Adonai, Elyah, Bael, Bel, Belus, Jehovah, Jah, Abraham, Sampson, Jachin, Boaz, Adam, Eve, Mary, Esau, Edom, Zeus, Jupiter, Thor, Odin, Helios, Dyoni, Dionysius, &c., &c., are all names significant of sexual ideas, and the names of the 12 Tribes bear a direct reference to generative functions.

In connexion with this Phallic symbolism, it may herein be observed that Arets, earth; Adam, man; and h-Adam-h, earth, are cognate to each other, have a like signification, and are personified under one form. The two latter of those words are founded on the radical ם ד, dm for blood. From this comes ם ד א, Adam, and this as a verbal means to be red, or blood-covered. Again the Egyptian God-name for Mars was Artes (Αρτησ) Ertosi (Ερτ͞οσι), and the word is but the Chaldean, or Hebrew from Arets, or Earth, and the words are the same for Arts, Hebrew, and Arts, Egyptian, as in Adam for man, Mars, and Earth. Here there is Arets for earth and Mars. The shedding of blood was as much the type of Conception, as of Death. The pictured symbol of this power was "Membrum virile Martis generatoris" Testis and Yoni. Truly the female pudenda is sacred to Mars, for he held the house of Venus, and that of the Scorpion, and, of course his astro-symbol is ♂. Without the shedding of blood, there is no remission of sin.[1]

The nonsensical rendering of Genesis III, 15, must be apparent to any thoughtful student of sexual Symbolism. "I will put enmity between thee and the woman, and between

---

[1] One of the Lyon manuscripts has a note by the translator, "L.D." (Louis Dramard): "The Scorpion has the sign of the Virgin, (♍), joined to that of Mars, (♂); thus ♏. See The Occult Magazine, on the Zodiac." The reference is to an article by "Mejnour" (Peter Davidson), "The signs of the Zodiac," *Occult Magazine* II/17 (June-September 1886), 42-46. —Editors

thy seed and her seed; it shall bruise thy head, and thou shalt bruise his heel." The word ע ק ב which is translated heel, is a euphemism as are the feet in Isaiah VII, 20; see also Jerem. XIII, 22, Nahum III, 5, &c., &c. The part intended to be signified by the word is *pudenda muliebra*, See Dr. Donaldson's dissertation and many others.[2] It will also be seen that in the very ancient Hindu pictures, the heel is placed before, as touching the mouth of the female sexual organ. The circumcision or the bloody circle, performed on the Sacr, was but a Symbol of those significant sex-mysteries, and just as the word Zacr or Sacr—or carrier of the germ, the special word for the male reproductive organ, is translated by male, so is the word sanctified, wrested from its proper meaning. The custom was to make the memorial before the Lord with Sacr. hence the Latin Sacr-factum of the Roman Priest, and the Sacrifio, the English Sacrifice. Just as Sacr related to man's higher existence with another and better realm of life, shadowed forth as Sacr-ment in the body and blood, bread and wine, symbolised the germ of that existence, and that like the Sacr, the bread and wine were vehicles of its formation.

Again, Cain is represented as the first murderer, and every fifth man, in his descent, is also a murderer, mythically expressive of the sexual mysteries. Cain in the Hebrew ק י ן, means a Smith, Artificer, &c., from whence we have Vul-Cain, who is the personification of the art of iron-work. Tubal-Cain was an instructor of every artificer in brass and iron, &c., &c. Astrologically speaking, the planet Mars (♂) rules over such, as well as iron &c. Cain (or Mars) pierces Abel, and the Roman Soldier (son of Mars) pierces Jesus on the Cross. The Nazarene is pierced in the Sinister, or left side, just as when the woman is taken from the man's side, in the allegorical story of the Garden of Eden. Horus is also

---

[2] The reference is cribbed from Jennings 1888, 346.—Editors

represented standing in his boat, piercing the head of the dragon Typhon, or Aphophis. The Scandinavian Thor bruises the head of the Serpent with his cruciform mace; Apollo kills the Python, and St. George and St. Michael pierce the Dragon—all unequivocally symbolizing the same ideas which exist in every country and in every clime.

Esau and Jacob are the allegorical twins, symbols of the ever present dual principle in Nature. In the beginning, God—the Elohim—created man in their own image, male and female, Father and Mother, two in One, for both exist in Deity. Jacob is Israel, who is the left-hand pillar, the feminine principle of Esau, the red, who is the right Pillar, and male principle. The name of Israel is derived from Isaral, or Asar, the Sun-God, also known as Suryad[3], Surya, and Sur and Isra-el mean "strong with God." Jacob's thigh is dislocated in the wrestling with the Angel in the dark, and his name is changed to Isra-el. The Sun rising upon Jacob-Israel symbolises the fecundation of Matter, or earth, represented by the female Jacob, changed to the Male Israel. All these symbols speak plainly for themselves, for Jehovah, Osiris &c., &c. are the symbols of the active principle in Nature par excellence, or the forces which preside at the formation, or regeneration of matter, and its dissolution, the two types of Life and Death, ever fecundating and ever changing, under the ever-existing influx of the Astral Light, which is behind the correlation of the blind forces.

---

[3] The Lyon manuscript reads "Suryal." This entire passage is derived from Blavatsky 1877, II, 402.—Editors

The word[4] Jehovah makes the original idea of male-female as the birth originator, for the ' (Je) is the male emblem, and Hovah is Eve.[5]

The books of Hermes beautifully observe: "The number (1) One is born from the Spirit, and the number 10 (ten) from matter. The Unity has made the Ten, the Ten the Unity." (Book of Numbers, or Book of the Keys) The Phallus I and the Yoni O, form the number 10, which includes all the figures in Mathematics. The number 10 is also symbolised in the Roman Numerals, by the X or Cross, and the upright with the oval placed sidewise, forms again the +.[6] This is also the mundane cross of heaven, repeated on earth by plants and dual man. The physical man supersedes the Spiritual at this junction point, of which, astronomically, stands the Mythical[7] Libra ♎ Hermes, Enoch, for the faithful ♎ (Balana-Libra)—Man is placed between, as the heavenly rescuing shield:—

---

[4] The Archè edition incorrectly reads "mort" for "mot."—Editors

[5] The translator of the Lyon manuscript provides an interesting note on the meaning of Jehovah:

"In Hebrew, the word Jehovah is composed of four letters: yod, he, vau, he, יהוה—literally Jeve. The Yod, ' (i or y) has, since the most ancient times, been the emblem of the spiritual, active or male principle. At least it is so in the most primitive sacred traditions of India. The letter ה, he, in the Kabbalah, represents the plastie element, passive and female. The ו, vau, signifies lying down, copulation. In the sacred divine tetragrammaton the final repetition of the h represents the product. In sum, the yod ', symbolizes the spiritual principle, [illegible] and active; the three letters הוה = Eve, represent the passive, multiple substance—triplicate—whence comes emanation, and which must re-enter into the original unity. Note edited after the works of St. Yves d'Alveydre and Eliphas Levy by the translator of the present work. L.M."—Editors

[6] The Lyon manuscript's figure more correctly shows the oval: ✖ —Editors

[7] "Mystical" in the Lyon manuscript.—Editors

See the Wheel of Ezekiel,[8] thus:—

♈ ♉ ♊ ♋ ♌ ♍
♎
♏ ♐ ♑ ♒ ♓

When Woman issues from the left rib of Adam, the pure ♍ (Virgo) is separated, falls into generation, or the downward cycle, and becomes ♏ (Scorpio), emblem of sin and matter, and astrologically, the sign ♏ (Scorpio) rules over the generative organs.

In like manner, the Sacred Name IAO, etymologically considered means the Breath of Life, generated or springing forth between an upright male, and an egg-shaped female Principle of Nature, for the Sanskrit As means to breathe, and the Hebrew Ah, and Jah, mean Life. Hence, the efficacy of the letter H, which Abram took from his wife's name Sarah and placed in the middle of his own name, Abraham, becomes clear and evident.

The letter I, Iota in Greek has other names in other languages, and is, as was among the Gnostics of Ancient times,

---

[8] The figure in the Lyon manuscript shows the meaning more clearly by the addition of the horizontal and upright, thus:

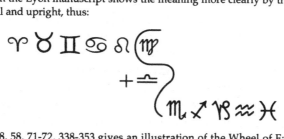

Jennings 1888, 58, 71-72, 338-353 gives an illustration of the Wheel of Ezechiel and a veiled exposition of the same doctrines. The wheel as illustrated here is also found (with the same doctrinal interpretation) in *Art Magic*, 43ff., and in Blavatsky, 1877, II, 461ff. Blavatsky also gives an "esoteric" illustration of the wheel as inscribed within the circle of a zodiac.—Editors a pass-word, meaning the Father's Sceptre, as in Eastern Brotherhoods existing at this very day.

Upon the altar we also find the letter I, with the feminine letter H interlaced with the S or SS, the Holy Spirit, for it's the height of absurdity to assume that the symbol I H S began with the Crucifixion of Jesus of Nazareth, as Iesus Hominum Salvator, whereas IHΣ is one of the most Ancient Names of Bacchus. This is something like the very old Rosicrucian motto "Igne Natura Renovatur Integro"—Nature renovated by the fire, or matter of Spirit, which borrowed inscription is made to be accepted to the present day as "Iesus Nazarenus Rex Judaeorum." Herein let the Neophyte also note that the word Mater means Mother in almost every language, and, in like manner, we have the terms Madra, Mat, Mod, Mud, Matter &c, &c.

The Thyrsus, or pine-cone, carried in the Ancient processions, was also emblematical of the male principle. The erect oval window, containing the picture of the Virgin, the Female principle of Nature, becomes the Vesica Piscis, and frame for Divine things. The Crux Ansata, sign of Venus, testifies the union of the Male and Female principles in the most obvious manner, ♀ or ⚥, the Circle (Yoni) and the Cross. All our Christian Churches contain the Symbol of the Phallus, in their obelisks or Spires, angularly pointing to the heavens, equally so with the Druids, in their Ancient Circles. David performs his Phallic dance before the Ark, emblem of the female principle, whilst the Hindu Vishnavit bears the same emblem upon his forehead, for the sexual element is marked throughout every religion on earth. The Fleurs de Lis of France signify the same. All Architecture is derived from the two mathematical lines, the I and the —, which united and intersecting, form the "Cross." The first is the origin of the upright Tower, pyramid, Steeple or male Phallic emblem, which aspires against the force of gravity— Spirit. The second, the horizontal mark, is the Symbol of the Tabernacle, Chest, Ark, or base-line, matter, the expression of all Ancient Egyptian, Grecian, and Jewish Templar

Architecture. The union of the two lines gives the Cross, the blending of the two Dispensations, Law and Gospel. The Argha is Ark or Arche, is the Navis bifrora, and has the form of the female Crescent ☽, the Woman Deity. This is also the Argha of the Hindus, and the Arghe was also an oblong vessel used by the High Priests, as a sacrificial Chalice, in the worship of Isis, Astarte, and Venus-Aphrodite, the Goddess of matter, or the generative powers of Nature, symbol of the Ark containing the germs of all vitality. From such of course has our present-day Chalice or sacrificial, or Communion Cup descended. Aρχα is the Ship, navis. From thence come nave and navel &c., in which animated Nature is saved, symbol again of the sex mysteries. The Ancients placed the Astral Soul of Man, the ψυχη, psyche, in the pit of the stomach. In like manner, the Patera (or Cup) was a Mystic feminine of Pater, the Father. It indicated a lotus-shaped Cup, or Matrix. The Patera is a Cognate of Pater, Patricius, who wore a lunar, or crescent-shaped shoe. The Chief of the Sacred college was called Pater Patratus, contracted from Paterata, &c., &c. Pater and the Spirit are symbolised by the word Patri-Arche, Patriarch. The word פתר, Peter in Phoenician and Chaldaic, or P.T.R., literally the old Aramaic and Hebrew "Patar"—the Interpreter is Hierophant—can also be traced to a similar Symbolism. SS in the noble Order of the Garter includes the same Symbols, and the very motto, interpreted correctly is:—"Yoni soit qui" &c., and not as erroneously interpreted "Honi."

The origin of the Order of the Garter is very different to that which is usually assigned to it. It is an Imperial and feminine Order, having its origin in the Rose, and of a certain and periodical and physiological fact connected with Woman's life. The garters are double, red and white. The 26 Knights represent the double 13 lunations, or the thrice twenty-six mythic "dark" and "light" changes in the year. The Round Table of King Arthur, the symbolical female discus in certain mythical aspects, is a perfect display of the same subject, and King Edward III chose the octave of the

"Purification" for the inauguration of his Order. (See E. Ashmole's writings, Jenning's Rosicrucians &c.)[9]

As previously remarked, Mars is the Red Planet. Purple or red is the Ancient mark of Initiation. Hence the setting aside of this colour for the robes of Kings and Emperors, of Popes and Cardinals, or British Royalty, as well as of University Degrees. From the same dual principle so often referred to, originated the White and Red Roses of English history. As well as the White and Red banners of the Sons of Mars, the Army.

The presiding Deity of Ireland is the Mystic "Woman" born from the "Great Deep" or the fecundity of Nature. This is she who is impaled or crucified upon the "Tree of Life," the Irish Harp, and her hair is entwined into the Mystical Seven strings. We have also the Venus (♀) day, or Woman's day, or Friday, of the seven-fold weekly period, the unlucky marriage day.

The two tables of stone with rounded top, placed side by side as a united stone, upon the Altars of our Churches, typify the same ideas. They contain the five commandments of the Law, or Man, to the right, the pillar of Jachin, and the five of the Gospel to the left, Woman, or the pillar of Boaz, the right stone being masculine, the left feminine. The first was delivered by I, the second came through —, and united, form the +. The Crescent Moon and Star of the Orientals ☆☽, having the star issuing from between the two horns, emblem of Ali amongst the Muhammedans, is also the symbol of the same ideas in Egypt, and Persia, as well as in the house of Plantagenet. But we must also strictly bear in mind that there is a higher meaning veiled in those Crescent Symbols or the ⊙ (Sun) and (☽) (Moon) in (♂) (conjunction), for they represent the union of the triad with the Unit, and the horns of the Cow on the head of Isis, have precisely the same signification.

---

[9] The reference is to Jennings, 1888, 321ff.—Editors

The Phrygian cap, sanguine in its colour, with the bonnet rouge, or cap of liberty, is of precisely a similar origin, which has descended to us from the Mystic rite of the "circumcisio praeputii." The Cardinal's "red hat" follows the same idea. It is a chapeau discus, a Mystic feminine "Rose." We have also the Pall, pallium, pelisse, (from pellis, skin) coat, a full reminder of the very remote cover of shame of Adam and Eve, and of Noah and Ham. In the Maypole, we again have the Phallus and Yoni, with the former wreathed with the Seven prismatic colours. In the same connexion, it may be stated, that water represents the duality of the Macrocosm and Microcosm, in conjunction with the vivifying Spirit, and the evolution of the little world from the universal Cosmos. In Christian Theosophy, it also signifies the mysterious Symbol of Soul, by the interaction of which, with the Divine Spirit, man regenerate is born again.

"To the pure all things are pure." We are all steps in the ladder of progress, and we must commence our ascent from the bottom. The sexual and love nature are the foundation of our existence, for it is so ordered that Man's greatest physical happiness, as well as his greatest woes, all spring from this source. If there is something of Impurity about it, it is in the mind of him, or her who so estimates it, and of all acts, the sexual is the most potent, for herein Man approaches the nearest to the very portals of Divine Creative Energy. Here, in the Uterus, the veiled Temple of Woman's body, God baptises matter with Spirit, and lo! it becomes an Immortal Being, having in embryo all the powers of the Godhead. Far is it then from there being anything degrading in this, for God has made nothing of which man may be ashamed, for in this relation, soul meets soul in an ecstatic blending of Spirit, and an ever-watchful Deity, bending low from on high, "broods over the Holy of Holies," in the Temple, and accepts the sacrifice consumed with fires of love, and entering in is born of Woman, for the "Immaculate Conception" is the result of elevated souls, and a perfect union of such. The resulting child, this truly

Love-child, must of necessity be superior to the parents, for such is the "Christ," the Son of the living God, not of a dead one, for dead Gods produce demi-men and women, devils in human form. A Virgin typifies purity of Soul, and the Holy Ghost is the "Holy Spirit," or a pure Spirit. Now, the union of such produces "the only-begotten Son of God," for God cannot be incarnated in impurity, save as a progressive being. The vague legend, or tradition, of the "Fall of Man" has a sure foundation in truth, for it belongs to every race, and every nation. For the present, it is of little import to recognise wherein the fall consists. Our Ancient Sages wrote allegorically, parables for the multitude, but explanatory keys for the Initiates. The fall of man was the fall of the Soul from its perfect Spherical form to a diffused atomic state. Man, before he was encased in matter, had no use for limbs, but was a pure Spiritual Entity. As his enveloping shell became heavier, there came the necessity for limbs, and such limbs sprouted.

The Soul, like the perfection of the Spiritual Sun, was a globe; for all organic forms are sections of the perfect sphere, and man is necessarily a complex assemblage of lines and circles, having within his own being all the details in mathematical ratio, and the first means of its evolution, or the capability of producing and reproducing it. This earthly state of existence is of necessity, just as sacred and paramount a theme, as that of the formation of worlds themselves. As the mysterious function of Creation is the highest and most wonderful with which the mind can invest Deity, so the imitative law must become the noblest and most sacred function of God's creatures, but in process of time the instinctive appetites of man's depraved Nature stimulated sex-worship into excess, and thus degraded the noble theme into the grossest licentiousness. Physical generation is the gate by which the Soul enters the stupendous pathway of eternal progress, but, like all other sacred ideas, if abused, the law of such comes to be regarded as mere physical enjoyment, gross sensuality. Hence the necessity which the wise philosophic sages of old perceived of veiling all such teachings on the Mysteries, in obscure Symbolism.

In our Ancient Biblical records and other writings, childless women were branded with the bitterest reproach. Eunuchs and persons afflicted with sexual blemishes, were forbidden to hold sacred offices, a law which descended even to the Roman Catholic Popes.

A perfect Soul has the emotions perfectly subject to the Will and any part of his system may be affected in any manner desired, without the provocation of *contact* with such objects. Prior to the fall, woman was a subjective or Spiritual [being], but intercourse prevented her, a materialized spirit, from returning to her subjective condition.

As the Hermetists say: — Woman is the offspring of man's own impure fancy, for created by an unclean thought, she sprang into existence, at the *evil* "seventh hour," when the supernatural, or real worlds had passed away, and the Natural or *delusive* worlds began evolving along the descending Microcosm, or the arc of the great cycle. But man had unwittingly endowed her with his own share of Spirituality, and she became his "Savior."

When the Soul fell to its atomic state, *subjective* things became *objective*, and *contact* of things became necessary to produce emotions of pleasure and pain. Adam required no contact in sexual intercourse to produce ecstasy. Such could be produced by Will with no loss of virility. Hence the command was that he should not copulate, for, diseases, pain, and death itself, spring from an abnormal or unnatural action of love, or the sexual nature, for, the "fall of Man" is a fall of blood, but virility for the Occultist must be turned *upward* and *inward*, instead of allowing it to flow *outward* and *downward* in the commission of what St. John terms *sin*. See 1st Epis. John III, 9. For, loss of virility is sin, and this was the sin which "lay at the door (or place of egress) of Onan (Genesis XXXVIII, 11). Again we find "Sin lieth as a *Copulatrix*, at thy door" or opening , for צ ב ר, r b ts, is the same א ב ר, r b a, and is not only to lie down, to couch, but also to copulate. A plant or tree grows up out of the mud, but the *flowers* and *fruits descend*. There is a *descent*, as well as *ascent*, and at the point of union there is generation, for this is Nature's Copulation, and plants, flowers, fruits, living things &c., do not in reality ascend out of the ground, any more than the Sunlight does, and we die that others may have being.

As the Kabbalists truly say "the lost Man," Adam should never have yielded to the irresistible fascinations of Eve, but should have contented himself—speaking meta-phorically—with his "enjoined, other impersonated delight," which he outraged in this preference, winning "Death," but to the outside world, this is obscure, because it is a part of the secret, unwritten Kabbalah, which can be explained only to the Initiates.

Man thus evolved out of himself, the woman, as a spir-itual entity. He can create no more by his *Will* or *Spirituality*. He is now only a physical Creator, and he can only gain his former condition by a long imprisonment in the bonds of Matter. In the Hebrew text, we have the union of "Sons of God" with the "daughters of men," who were fair, viz., one race of purely physical creatures, another purely spiritual, for the union of those who produced a third, the Adamite race, which shared the nature of both its parents.

"I will greatly multiply thy sorrow and thy *Conception*, was a sexual penalty. Through woman came the *Fall*, and through the *Virgin Soul* must come Immortality, for Salva-tion is Woman's work. As a Virgin, no birth, nor Conception can take place without, first, the shedding of blood. This was the fruit of that forbidden tree, which brought Death, as well as Life into the World. Conception was as already said, a sexual penalty, a fall of blood, for in full corroboration of this, Nature sheds tears of blood periodically, from the inner and mysterious recesses of Woman's body, and Woman, of all God's creatures, is the only one so accursed, for the Atonement is of blood and of love. In the future grand cycle, under Anael Prince of the Astral Light, Woman will become

Man's just and lawful equal, and Intuition will shew itself the superior of mere Intellect, for Woman *truly is a Mystery* Jesus was never anointed but once; then by a woman of [to] whom he replied: — *"She did it for my Burial."*

True indeed, and significant it is, that the races of animated being, turn their eyes *downward* in sexual intercourse, but the human family is the exception, for man— frail child of matter, turns his looks towards matter, with which he has for a time imprisoned himself, but Woman looks upwards towards the Celestial Canopy, for she is "saved by child-bearing, for, an immortal being is launched upon the infinite universe of Deity."

The Onanist sees in his imagination, the object of his lust, and thus acting upon his emotions, pollutes himself; but this wasted virility though lost to the Man, is not lost to Nature, for it is a protoplasm from which spring infusoria, worms, reptiles &c., which are a curse to the earth and mankind. To keep your heart young, tender, and full of love for your companion, think of her as when you wooed and won her, and a passionless man is an infernal monster, not only in this, but in all the starry worlds of space. In order to destroy physical, or sensual love, think of it in connection with something disgusting and low, and it will speedily die. To gaze at a human body, the creature of nine month's gestation, with repulsive worms crawling in and out of its nine gates, or orifices; to think that this is the end of all flesh, that you will be so soon, that filthy matter now frosts the lips which once could so proudly curl, disgusts one very much with the follies of life, and tames the passions of any man who can think. Thus to destroy any feeling you may create its opposite.

Our Theologians and men of Science see—but truly they only see through a glass darkly— for, they do not comprehend those mysterious and ever-present, secret-cyphered, symbolic characters, traced no less by the Divine finger of the Infinite, upon the multi-coloured shell from the aqueous bed of the ocean's deep; than upon the verdant leaf, that glittering with the dew-drop of heaven, trembles in the balmy breeze; or in the fiery blossoms of Night which jewel the canopy of the Celestial firmament, the trembling stars whose stellar lines are in their sight, nothing more or less luminous than a few lines of Hydrogen.

But above all let the young Neophyte develop within himself, that latent but Divine faculty of the Soul,— Intuition, which is infinitely more vast than hazy book-learning, for this Intuitional power is the crown and ultimatum of his existence, and to it alone are the Hindus indebted for their Vedas, the Jews for their Bible, and what the Nazarene has given to the world, was the fruit of such, altho' now-a-days so sadly disfigured and dogmatically represented.

Studiously bear in mind, then, aspiring Neophyte, that we as Immortal Spirits are infinite in capacity, boundless in power; and the only horizon, which limits such, is not so much the enthrallment and fetters of our Material body, as the want of knowledge how to control and subdue it, for, the moment the sway of passions, or even of the mental emotions, compels the soul to yield to the impulses of the body, the Spiritual reign is exhausted, and henceforth the Soul only exercises a temporary, broken and spasmodic rule over its own grand and transcendental faculties or attributes. Such efforts must be made, ere the lofty and laborious steps of Adeptship are scaled.

Seek not then to encompass Eternity in a brief moment of time. Be patient, and all shall be revealed to thee, as thou wilt deserve, for such philosophic wisdom is now leavening the *worthy* minds of civilised Society, and is taught in isolated fragments by man a solitary pioneer of the "Wisdom Temple," that *shall* be. Our exalted Psychic Ruler—venerated and Noble Masters—are not only Adepts in the mental force necessary for their stupendous office, but practical "Magicians," whose knowledge and experience of the Occult in Nature place her mysterious elements of power at their command, and our teachings are not only derived from the cumulative wisdom of the Ages, but also from the inspiration of far higher realms of Being than those of common mortality, for, researches into these transcendental realms are accomplished by the aids which Man's Spiritual endowments supply him with.

Practice and Theory are deemed equally essential for the formation of true opinions, and from the profoundest depths of earth's centre itself, to the sublimest and loftiest heights of Astral systems, fretted and galaxied in starry blossoms throughout the blue of Heaven's infinitude, from the force which crystallises the dazzling diamond, and rounds the glittering dew, and tear-drop to that which rarefies the finest realms of æther, those Sages have explored the Universe in search of Absolute Truth itself. They are not ashamed of aspirational worship, neither do they ever feel their manhood degraded by the act of meditation, but know and realise fully the efficacy of sacred places and consecrated things, and deem that Spiritual, must ever be the complement to Material Science.

As the infantile *Foetus* develops itself from the *Liquor Amnii*, in the womb of the Mother, so the earths germinate from the Universal Æther, or Astral Fluid, in the womb of the Universe. Those Cosmic children, like the pigmy inhabitants, are first nuclei, then ovules, then mature; become Mothers in turn, and gradually develope mineral, vegetable, animal, and human forms. From centre to circumference, from the imperceptible and microscopic vesicle to the uttermost conceivable limits of the Cosmos, those glorious and stupendous thinkers trace Cycle merging into Cycle, containing and contained in an unbroken series—the Boundless and the Infinite—for, *End there is None.*

"THE HERMETIC KEY" (A.2.b)

The Hermetic Key, which for some unknown reason was always circulated under its French title, "La Clef Hermétique," is one of the major doctrinal teaching manuscripts of the H. B. of L. Burgoyne attributes the "preparation" of the work to H. B. Corinni, the Private Secretary of Max Theon—whoever he may have been, if indeed he existed at all.[1] Whatever the truth about Corinni, the "Hermetic Key" as it exists now strongly shows Burgoyne's own interests and style and must have been reworked, at least, by him. Theon seems to have not believed in the theory of cycles, as he writes in the *Revue Cosmique* of the "so-called" ages which succeeded one another." His system was less rigid and mechanical.

The "Hermetic Key" attempts—not quite coherently—to correlate the four ages of Hindu doctrine with the Biblical seven days of creation, Abbot Trithemius's scheme of the seven angels who govern the world in succession, and Sampson Arnold Mackey's vision of the cyclical revolution of the earth's axis. The crucial framework of the Hindu *yugas* and the rotation of root races through the "rounds" of the cosmic dance is provided by A. P. Sinnett's *Esoteric Buddhism,* published in 1883, which is in turn derived from Sinnett's correspondence with the "Mahatmas," so despised by the H. B. of L. The anomaly of relying on the Mahatmas was explained by Burgoyne as plagiarism by Sinnett (and the Mahatmas), but the borrowing appears to have been in the other direction.[2]

Mackey (1765-1843), whose *The Mythological Astronomy of the Ancients Demonstrated by Restoring to Their Fables & Symbols Their*

---

[1] *Occult Magazine* II/14 (March 1886), 24. See B.6.g.

[2] In his introduction to the "Hermetic Key" in *LOE,* I, 86-88, Burgoyne is at great pains to state that the H. B. of L. work was written in 1880 and "issued to several in the month of January, 1881, before 'Esoteric Buddhism' ever saw the light, and that the supposed 'marvelous and original doctrines,' issued by A. P. Sinnet, Esq., as from India, were all in black and white in England at the time." The choice of dates appears to have been made to avoid criticism like that of G. R. S. Mead (see B.8.d), who noted that the substance of *Esoteric Buddhism* had been published in the famous "Fragments of Occult Truth" in *The Theosophist,* beginning in October 1881. Burgoyne's claim about activity of the Order in 1880 and 1881, if true, would be of great importance for the pre-history of the H. B. of L., but it is unsubstantiated.

Original Meaning (1822-1823) supplied the vision of the rotation of the poles, was variously claimed by the H. B. of L. as an initiate and the disciple of an initiate of the Order.[3] His affiliation with the Brotherhood aside, he was a destitute shoemaker in Norwich, an autodidact, who, like others of his contemporaries, believed he had found in astrology the key to universal mythology. His solution was illustrated with concentric cardboard disks (the "Sphinxiad" and the "Cyclob'thiad") that could be rotated on a plate marked to show the horizons and the zenith and nadir, to demonstrate the rotation of the poles around their midpoint and the corresponding changes in the zodiac. In the H. B. of L.'s version, as in Mackey's, the polar movement, with its regular succession of cataclysms, is pressed into the service of proving the pre-eminence of Egypt and the source of universal, antediluvian Tradition.[4]

The "Hermetic Key" also touches briefly on the truly mysterious "eighth orb" or "Dark Satellite," the realm of Ob and the center of power of the opposing "Brethren of the Shadow," which plays such an important role in the works of P. B. Randolph, Mme. Blavatsky, and Rudolf Steiner.

The version of the "Hermetic Key" given here is from the augmented *Light of Egypt*, with significant variations from the manuscript in the *Fonds Papus* noted. The preface appended to the work is not found in either the French or English version, but is taken from the letter supposedly written by H. B. Corinni which Burgoyne says he adapted for a Preface to the work. The material prefaced by "NOTE" is added from *Light of Egypt*.

---

[3] The "Hermetic Key" calls Mackey "an initiate of our Noble Order," while *The Occult Magazine*, in serializing *Mythological Astronomy*, more modestly appropriates him as a disciple of an initiate. (*Occult Magazine* II/15 [April 1886], 31). Peter Davidson had been offering Mackey's book for sale at least as early as November 1877. See the letters of Davidson to F. G. Irwin that have been discovered in the archives of the Grand Lodge of England by Mr. David Board.

[4] The reprint of the *Mythological Astronomy* and its second part, *The Key of Urania* (Mackey 1973) contains valuable bibliographical information. On Mackey's life and works, see the Bio-Bibliography appended to *BCW*, xiv, 545ff, and Godwin 1994, 67-76. For a review of polar mythologies in general and of Mackey in particular, see Godwin 1993.

Preface to The Hermetic Key

Esteemed Brother,—In attempting an explanation of the Esoteric Numbers of the Universe, there is a formidable difficulty to be encountered, viz., that of being Esoterically understood. Those students who are unable to comprehend the sublime import of the mighty system of Cycles and Periods, which we are about to reveal, would be preferably occupied in eschewing Occult studies for the adoption of others adapted to their sphere of thought, for their souls are insufficiently etherealised for those humanly-Divine attributes to awake into activity, and notwithstanding all merely ephemeral curiosity towards mystical researches, yet their advancement will only reach the portals of the Outer Temple. The fearful "Dweller on the Threshold" will debar their feeble footsteps, they will be unable to enter the inner "Holy of Holies," and they must remain contented, until the time arrives when conditions are evolved in the scale of the succeeding human races, conditions which will permit of the expansive budding and blossoming of their soul's now latent attributes.

But there are also numerous students who, although being in a condition suitable for the perception of truth, and for the true significance of Nature's grand Mysteries, are yet totally unqualified for the perception of this knowledge, owing to their natural but terrible *Elemental Affinity*. The result of this fearful Psychical condition is, as you are well aware, that the Occult powers which they might develop, would be used for purposes of a purely selfish and worldly nature, and it is needless to remark that such individuals would become a pestilent scourge to mankind. But even in this case, my worthy Brother, we know well that happily it is quite a minority of this class who can grasp any actual *power*, for upon the contrary they frequently become the very dupes and slaves of the powers they so ardently seek to control. *To all such we FERVENTLY and SOLEMNLY say*: 'Abandon all thoughts of spirit-intercourse, flee from Occultism, and Spiritualism, as you would from a pestilence, and may the Divine Guardians of the Human Race preserve your souls from the bottomless abyss, upon the brink of which you may possibly have been unconsciously reposing.'

To those people who simply pry into the Occult from mere curiosity, we have nothing to say. They will obtain just *as much as they deserve*, and nothing more. 'Ask and ye shall receive, seek and ye shall find, knock and it shall be opened unto you' is equally as true to-day—in relation to Esoteric knowledge—as it was nineteen hundred years ago, but it invariably presupposes that the supplicator and the knocker are in real earnest, and that they seek only to satisfy the deep yearnings of the immortal soul. The Doorkeeper, or Guardian of the Temple of Truth is as mute as a granite rock to all others, they may supplicate, they may shout and bawl until they are hoarse, they may knock and buffet the door until they rouse a nation with their clamour, and if they approach in any other spirit than that we have already represented, it is all to no purpose. We can never take the Kingdom of Heaven by storm. In the Scriptures it is fabled that Satan at one time attempted this method of obtaining power, but that he along with his assistants were hurled into the flames of Hell for their daring presumption. Instead of acquiring the Kingdom of Heaven, he obtained the Bottomless Pit as an apposite reward for his misdirected ambition and labour, and there is, as you know, my Brother, more real verity in this religious fable than Spiritualists even, dream of.

But to the true student of Nature's inner law, we say:— 'Rest assured that you will receive a full measure of reward for each and every earnest endeavour, for Urania's dazzling lamp will ultimately illumine your dark and difficult path, and you shall indeed perceive the 'Living Light of the World,' which will enable you to draw aside the Veil of the mystic Isis, and behind her magic curtain, read the ever-burning truths of Nature, inscribed upon the unfading scrolls of time.'

To you, then, my faithful and eternal Brother, I present those Esoteric Cycles, along with the Golden Key and Silver Locks that guard our Island Universe. In your possession I well know they will not only be valued at their true worth, but will also be utilised for their proper purpose. Trusting then that our Members and Neophytes may ever use their Psychic powers wisely, worthily, and well, and wishing you and them GOD-SPEED, upon the upward path of the soul's eternal destiny, with fraternal sympathy, and Brotherly regard,—

I remain, very faithfully yours,

H. B. C.

(Private Secy. of M. Theon).

SECTION I

THE CYCLES AND FORCES OF CREATIVE LIFE

In attempting to explain the sublime system of Esoteric Cycles, as taught in the Occult schools of the Egyptian Magi, we shall notice their great Cycles first, which relate to Human and Planetary Evolution, then compare, or rather introduce, for the student's comparison, the Sacred Cycles of Hindoo Initiates, and show some of their striking relationships to the well known facts of geological research, and, lastly, attempt to show how these natural periods of action and reaction of the Cosmic life forces have formed the truthful foundation upon which the Astrological Mystics have elaborated their planetary periods and sub-cycles of celestial influence over nations, and which is further and more fully elaborated by Kabbalistical lore, in the rule of the

Seven Arch Angels as the seven Governors of the world, which they say "after God actuate the Universe."[1]

NATURE'S TRIUNE INDEX

Nature has furnished her students with the means of reaching her mysteries, in the dual form of intuition and intellect, and of measuring her mighty forces in the forms of time and space. The first index of time is the rotation of the Earth upon her axis, the second by her annual motion about the Sun. These are broadly converted into days, months and years. The third index is that of the motion of the Earth's center (the Sun) through space, around a still greater center; this is broadly divided into two measures, viz.: first, through one sign of the Zodiac, a period of 2,160 years, and secondly, through the entire twelve signs, which complete this grand revolution, or great Solar Year, in 25,920 years of Earthly time. The third and last face of the triune index is our Earth's Pole. This magnetic point is the great finger of Nature's Cyclic Timepiece, which governs and registers all the great Cosmic cycles of our planet and its circuit.

Remember this significant fact, then, that the motions of the Earth's Pole is the motion of her Evolutionary forces, both Human and Physical.

POLAR MOTION

When this beautiful motion of the Earth's Pole has become familiar, the student will begin to see the divine harmony of Nature's grandest law, which law causes every portion of our Earth's surface to become alternately a fruitful plain or barren waste; dry land or ocean bed. The Earth's Pole moves in one uniform direction, with a slow, imperceptible motion that forms a spiral path in the heavens, consisting of a number of small spiral orbits, or circles, one overlapping

[1] The reference is to the treatise by Trithemius. See the introduction to "The Key."—Editors

the other. These small spiral circles are termed Volutes, their true value in space being three degrees, thirty-six minutes, no seconds (3° 36' 00").

The motion of inclination of the Pole is at the rate of fifty seconds of space per century, or one second in every two years. At this rate, it requires 7,200 years to move over one degree, and as there are 360 degrees in a circle, or the Pole's orbit, it takes 360 times 7,200 years, equal to 2,592,000 years, to make a complete revolution of its orbit, or one hundred Solar Years. Each Volute being three degrees, thirty-six minutes, no seconds in true value, 25,920 years are required for the Pole to complete one small spiral orbit, and as there are exactly one hundred of these Spiral Orbits in the complete orbit, therefore 100 times 25,920 years equals 2,592,000 years, which period is termed, by Initiates, one Polar Day. One Polar Day equals one hundred Solar Years. We will now give a few brief examples of Polar Motion.

If the student will, for a moment, imagine our Earth's Pole to be perpendicular to the plane of its orbit, and consequently coinciding with the Pole of the ecliptic; then the signs of the zodiac, and the apparent yearly path of the Sun will always be vertical at our Earth's equator; hence universal spring will reign in the Temperate Zones and a gentle, continuous summer in all sub-tropical latitudes; it will cause the equatorial regions of the Earth to become blazing, scorching deserts. The great plains will be unfit for habitation, owing to the fierce rays of a vertical Sun, continuing for long ages. Only the mountainous portions will be the seat of human life. This condition will also cause equal day and night all over the globe, but as we recede from the Equator, north or south, the sunlight becomes less and less, owing to the Sun['s] attaining a lesser degree of altitude with every degree of latitude; until, at the Poles, the Sun will only appear as a dull red ball of fire, moving along the horizon, from east to west, in the twelve hours from 6 A.M. to 6 P.M., hence, darkness and universal winter reign supreme; and the Arctic Circle is an ever-lasting belt of ice and snow, whose frozen breath forms a complete barrier against the existence of human life.

Again, imagine the Earth's Pole, after a lapse of 648,000 years, and we shall now find that it is inclined at an angle of exactly 90 degrees, for, during this Period, it has been slowly, but imperceptibly to the Earth's inhabitants, moving or inclining away from the pole of the ecliptic. The twelve signs of the zodiac and the apparent yearly path of the Sun, are now vertical to the Pole of the Earth. What will be the fearful geological results? Why, that our polar regions will have a tropical summer. Each year the Sun will be vertical on the 21st of June to the North Pole, and on the 21st of December to the South Pole, and also that every portion of the globe, with the Sun and Earth's Pole in this position, will witness a tropical summer and an Arctic winter. This accounts for and fully explains the existence of fossil remains of the seal, walrus and polar bear in the burning plains of Africa and Hindustan, and of the tropical remains now being discovered in the Arctic regions. No human being now living can conceive the fearful natural phenomena yearly transpiring during this period. For instance, all latitudes below the Poles had two midsummers each year; namely, when the Sun ascended north, and when it returned south again. The rapid rate at which the Sun rose into the polar circles, and the terrific heat of a vertical Sun upon the ice and snow, must have caused the most frightful inundations upon all the plains and lowlands. No wonder that it was called the Age of Horror by the Hindoos and Egyptian Magi.[2]

The walls of the mighty Babylon and the eight-volved Tower of Babel or cloud-encompassed Bel were never constructed to resist any mortal foe. NO. Those city walls, which were 60 miles in circumference, 200 feet high, 578 feet thick, were not made to defy the strength of armies, but to resist the fearful forces of Nature, the floods that swept the

---

[2] The term "Age of Horror" was in fact coined by Mackey.—Editors

plains of Shinar, from the mountains of Armenia, every spring during this Age of Horror. The tremendous embankments and river walls constructed by the Ancients are monuments of human skill and enterprise belonging to an epoch that antedates by thousands of years the Age of their supposed builders.

These mighty monuments of old are indeed the sacred relics of our early forefathers; but modern historians are so nosebound by Biblical chronology that they cannot yet see the light. Like young puppets, their eyes will not open to the light until they are nine days old. The student is here requested to notice that all the great solar and lunar observatories were constructed for a two-fold purpose. Their religion, unlike that of their degenerated descendants, was a pure, scientific theology, or "the Wisdom Religion." Those nations and peoples whom our historians denominate "ancient" were but degenerated castes, and, in comparison with the nations who built "the cloud-encompassed Bel," are quite modern. The grand, scientific Temples of the Sun and Moon, then, were erected at a period when the Sun was vertical to the latitude of the place, and their ages can be easily computed by the following simple formula. Our Earth's equator is the zero, or starting point, of all computations; and was taken into consideration by the ancient artists, who always built with some significant occult purpose. Each zone was constituted by the Great Solar Cycle of 25,920 years, during which period the Poles moved over one volute, which they, in round numbers, reckoned at 4 degrees; and all those buildings will be found, when constructed on this plan, to point exactly to the time they were built, if their latitude corresponds with their symbol. For instance, the Tower of Babel was eight-volved; that is, with a spiral staircase winding eight times round it. This means that it was built when the sun was vertical in the latitude of 32 degrees; 4 times 8 are 32, or, as an initiate of our Noble Order, 63 years ago (1822), speaking of the awful Iron Age, says:

In this dread time Chimera had her birth;
In this dread time the Cyclops cursed the
   earth.
And Giants huge, of horrid, monstrous form,
Who ravaged Earth, and strove e'en Heaven
   to storm.
This was the Iron Age; 'twas Python's reign,
When Polar-suns burnt up the golden grain,
And sudden thaws inundate every plain.
Hence Towers and Walls and Pyramids arose
Whose ponderous bulk might all their rage
   oppose.

Assyrian chiefs bade Babel's tower arise
On Shinar's plain, aspiring to the skies,
Whose eight-volved dragon, turning round
   the whole
Shows that eight cycles round the northern
   pole
At four degrees asunder, closed their view
Which proves latitude was thirty-two.
And still in thirty-two, beneath the starry
   host,
The eight-coiled Dragon moulders in the dust,
By Cyrus overthrown, who raised the pile
Round which the Stars and Dragon used to
   coil;
But still its form, its history declares
An hoary age of twice two hundred thousand
   years.

It may be noted that the very ancient sacred towers in the
Pagodas of China always (unless they are of modern construction) faithfully indicate their latitude and date of their
first foundation by the number of stories or terraces. Of
course it is not supposed that these towers, like our ancient
cathedrals, are not periodically restored as they fall into
decay, but always on the same principle. A great deal more

might be said as to the different climates that ensued under different inclinations of our Earth's Pole, but these few illustrations will give the student a few ideas as to the actual cause of the various geological changes that are brought about by Polar Motion.

Remember that the great Polar Day (2,592,000 years, moving once around, like the index of the clock) determines the duration upon our planet of that vital spiritual impulse of evolution, known among students and Initiates as the Great Life Wave. This Life Wave passes around the septenary chain, or circuit, of the seven planets, not in an even, regular, continuous action, but in waves or impulses. For instance, suppose the Life Wave of the mineral evolution commences, upon planet number l; it will here go through its active evolution, and then, having reached its culminating point, it commences to flow, or pass on to planet number 2, and the vegetable, or next life impulse, begins upon planet number 1, and so on with the rest. [Upon this point we would refer the student to Mr. Sinnett's valuable book, *Esoteric Buddhism*, but reminding you that, although there are many outlines in the work similar to these teachings, they are, in reality, widely different, as will be seen when you read his conclusions and those of this revelation.]

In order to better illustrate the evolution of matter and the involution of spirit, we will briefly describe in outline the systematic and harmonious process followed by Nature in the complete evolution of a planet, similar in construction to our earth.

In the first place, it must be borne in mind that there are Seven Kingdoms, Seven Principles and Seven Ruling Powers in Nature, a trinity of sevens, and also that matter, so called, is but the most remote expression of spirit. The further a state is removed from its source, the more dense it becomes, until spirit can express itself in metallic form and become materialized as veins and lodes of mineral ore in the body of a planet, and tower itself upon that planet's surface in granite mountains, limestone hills or chalky dells;

and that the boundless space is filled with a fine, invisible form of condensed spirit, known to scientists as cosmic dust; and, lastly, that Nature's operations are performed in an endless series of waves, which, in their motion, form graceful curves, the rise and fall of the arc of the curve forming its cycle of duration. The Seven Kingdoms are the Three Elemental and invisible, and the Four Objective and visible planes of Nature, while the order of the Seven Principles, or forms of evolution, is as follows; 1, the Spiritual; 2, the Astral; 3, the Gaseous; 4, the Mineral; 5, the Vegetable; 6, the Animal; 7, the Human. The Seven Governors, or Powers ruling a planet, are the Seven Angelic States, [mentioned more fully in La Clef.] Having explained the rudiments, it will better express our meaning to use a Biblical illustration, so we will now esoterically explain.

THE SIX DAYS OF CREATION

Mentioned in Genesis, each Day being one Polar Day, as before stated, or 2,592,000 years of Earthly time. The words "the evening and the morning" signify the two halves of the Polar Cycle. You will notice that "the evening" is mentioned first, and "the morning" last. This is correct. The dark or undeveloped portion of each wave is the first half, and signifies, symbolically, Night, and vice versa. Further, it must be remembered that the spiritual impulse, or wave, must of necessity pass round the orbit that has ultimately to be traversed by the future planet before anything can transpire. It is the Divine Will sent forth by the spirit-state that is equivalent to the Word or Divine Idea of certain ancient writers. This Fiat attracts within its orbit the latent cosmic matter of space, and transforms it into the embryonic, nebulous light, the star dust or radiant fire mist, which is the form, or primitive matter, of all creation. The student must strictly remember that there is no specific duration of this state. It may last for millions of ages before the actual evolution of a planet, and that previous to the symbolical Six Days of Creation this planet exists for untold cycles in a nebulous condition, the exact size of its orbital ring. This being understood, we will describe

The First Day of Creation

The Supreme Angelic Governors project into active evolution the astral tide-wave, viz., the currents of astral light, and the nebulous matter is, at once, transformed into a rapidly revolving globe of fire, which solidifies and cools under the intense concentration of the Deific Will of the Governors in a wonderfully less space of time than any of our transcendental or spiritual writers can imagine. Fire was dominant for the first half of the Polar Day;—when its surface had become so far cooled as to allow the heated vapors of its immense atmosphere to condense and form water, which element was rapidly produced during the next half of the cycle. Thus, we see, that a rude globe was formed during the first day of creation; the first half, the evening, was given to the dominion of fire alone, and the latter half, or morning, was one ceaseless war between those opposing elements, fire and water. "And the evening and the morning were the first day." These two periods of the Polar Cycle are each 1,296,000 years, and were called by the Hindoos the Treta Yug.

The Second Day of Creation

The Supreme Angelic Governors now caused the first evolution of the gaseous or chemical tide-wave, and the evolution of a complete but dense atmosphere was the result. That is to say, the various constituents of the atmosphere were, by this wave, adjusted, and our planet's chemical affinities duly balanced. This caused the whole of the super-abundant gross matter, such as carbon, etc., to condense and fall to the surface of the planet. During this day, also, our planet's surface was the scene of a continual conflict between heat and water; all was the scene of mighty volcanic action; mountain ranges continually rose and fell, and the ocean beds were always shifting.

The Third Day of Creation

After the gaseous, the great mineral tide-wave commenced, and the spirit atoms of future egos became incarnated in dense matter for the first time, namely, in the stratas of rocks and mineral lodes which constitute the stony ribs and metallic veins of our planet. Mountains, valleys, islands and continents were formed; the land above the ocean level sank, and the bed of the ocean became dry land. Now, for the first time, the seas and oceans occupy their proper beds. "And the evening and the morning were the third day." It must be added that during this period, also, the planet's surface was the scene of continual volcanic action; as was each and every period. At the close of this, the third Polar Cycle, we see that the evolution of the astral, chemical and mineral waves have now prepared our Earth for the first vegetable forms of life. And here, be it noted, that the first forms of all things were born (that is, had their origin) in water.

The Fourth Day of Creation

The vegetable tide-wave now reaches the barren shores of our planet, and produces the first rudimental forms of vegetable life, which develop into the most gross, gigantic shapes, rude and imperfect as the earth upon which they grow. But, as time progresses, so does the vegetable kingdom; each age giving more perfect forms. "And the evening and the morning were the fourth day."

The Fifth Day of Creation

The previous tide-waves having run their course, the animal life-wave now sets in, and from the lowest rudimental forms of life successively evolve the various orders of animal life, race after race appearing, running its course and becoming extinct, giving place to more complete organisms. "And the evening and the morning were the fifth day."

The Sixth Day of Creation

The preceding five tide-waves of evolution have now prepared our Earth for Nature's grandest climax; the evolution of the human form, Man, for at this age we read: "And the Lord made man out of the dust of the ground, and breathed into his nostrils the breath of life, and he became a living soul; and the Lord created man in His own image, male and female created He them."

During the five days of creation the vegetable and animal have been evolved, and, when man appears upon the scene, everything is in a vastly improved and highly developed condition, compared with the condition of the early monstrous forms. "And the evening and the morning were the sixth day." And here we must digress.

Some students of the occult imagine (for certainly they are not properly initiated and trained in the schools of occultism) that the missing link, or first human form, the connection between the animal and human, was caused by a spiritual impulse union, which, acting upon the highest form of animal, an ape, for example, produced an entirely different species, quite human in their organism, but hairy, etc., and that from this missing link the human race, as at present, has been evolved. But this is erroneous, and void of truth. While the spirit atoms have been evolving upward from the mineral, the spiritual form has been involving downward until it became tangible and objective, possessing at first a vast but loosely organized body. Each age saw it smaller and more compact, until, at the end of the Third Race of the First Human Round, the spiritual man had a compact, well-organized body, and the commencement of the Fourth Race, (the center of the seven) was the first point of contact, the focus of the spirit downwards and the apex of the material upwards. (See note below.) Matter and spirit met and formed the first real physical man of the human race. This is the great mystery;—the lowest point in the arc of spiritual involution impinges upon the highest arc, or culminating point, of material evolution, and forms the origin of man. The evolution of the remaining root races having taken place, the life impulse begins to ebb and slowly quits our shores, and our Earth for the first time enjoys a rest. The six days of creation are at an end, and the seventh is The Day of Rest.

[*LOE* adds here the following text]:

NOTE: This needs a little explanation. The first race of human beings who existed upon this planet were really spiritual. Their bodies were quite ethereal, when compared with our gross organisms, but were sufficiently material to be objective and tangible. They were pure and innocent, true Adams and Eves, and their country was indeed a garden of Paradise. They were natural born adepts of the highest order. They played with the Akasa and the magnetic currents of our globe as the boys in Bulwer Lytton's "Coming Race" played with the tremendous Vril. The elementals and nature spirits were, by their art, rendered objective, and performed the duties of servants to them. This was the true Golden Age. It was the first spiritual race of human beings; the progenitors of humanity upon our Earth. The race which followed them was termed the Silver Age in the arcane doctrine of the occult. Their descendants, although pure and able to control the psychic currents, and Gods in comparison to ourselves, were far inferior to their forefathers of the Golden Age. Both these races, and also the third, viz., the people of the Copper Age, when they wished to die passed peacefully away, and their bodies were immediately disintegrated by the currents of Vril. There were neither shades, shells nor phantoms in our atmosphere in those days. The third, or Copper Age, people were as inferior to those of the Silver Age as were the Silver to the Golden. Mankind was on the downward cycle; lies, deceit and selfishness began to be engendered and consequently there arose a school of Black Magic. In this age the first elements of that curse, Caste, arose.

This, the Copper Age, was the last remnant of those who inherited the Divine Wisdom of the Gods of the Golden Age. The spiritual races had now reached the lowest possible point in the arc of spiritual involution, and the Fourth race, or Iron Age people, were the first of the gross physical races, who became mighty hunters, and ate flesh meat, and whose animal passions alone ruled their enjoyments. From this date the nations became migratory nomads, and soon lost all traces of that high civilization which belonged to the early Copper Age races. This is, then, the esoteric explanation of the Four Ages of antiquity, and refers only to the first round of mankind upon any newly created planet, and also to the highest and two succeeding races previous to the life-wave leaving the planet, viz., the three highest states possible in any given round. The other cycles of years, termed Golden, Silver, etc., refer solely to polar motion and the change of our Earth's climate.

The Day of Rest. The Sabbath of the Lord. The Earth slumbers and enjoys the peace of Nirvana. After this Sabbath, the first day of a new week commences, for the gaseous tide-wave, having gone the circuit of the planetary chain, once more reaches our globe.[3] The atmosphere is again reorganized, purified, and galvanized with new life to make it fit to receive and sustain a higher phase of evolution. It breathes the breath of a new life upon our awakening planet. The life impulse that has been passive during the Sabbath of the Lord becomes again active.

After the expiration of the gaseous wave, and another Polar Day, the beds of the oceans have risen and become dry land, and the old continents are now at the bottom of the ocean, and, as this takes place slowly, the leading types of flora, fauna and surviving types of the seven human families retreat from the sinking continents and occupy the new-made land and mountains which are waiting to liberate their long-imprisoned spirit atoms, and this is affected [sic], directly the mineral wave arrives, at the commencement of the Second Polar Day. The old mineral elements are now liberated, and the incoming mineral wave becomes incarnated in their place. By the time this tide has attained its climax the newly liberated spirit atoms of this planet form a new mineral wave, which, seeking reincarnation,[4] begins to flow on to the next planet, which has already been prepared for it by the preceding gaseous wave. Then, in succession, comes the vegetable, animal, etc., to prepare a "New Heaven and a New Earth" for the incoming life-wave that shall evolve the Second Round of humanity, which, having again evolved its seven root races and their innumerable sub and offshoot races, again passes on its journey round the chain, leaving only a remnant of its seven leading types to survive the long ages of slumber, to give the struggling monads that Nature has left behind a chance of incarnating themselves to form the connecting links for the next round. And so does evolution proceed until each planet of the chain has evolved seven complete rounds of humanity, and then the Great Jubilee of the Earth takes place. Seven

---

[3] N. B., the second week of Creation commences with the second principle.—Editors

[4] This must be an interpolation by H. O. Wagner in his augmented editions of *Light of Egypt*. The Lyon Ms. has, more properly, "seeking to be manifested."—Editors

times 7 rounds equal 49; and 7 races of human beings on 7 planets is also 49; and the 50th is the year of Jubilee, symbolized by the Jews every 50th year, when no work was done and the land rested. "As it is below, so it is above, as on earth, so in the sky." Remember this.

And now, as a conclusion to this part of La Clef Hermétique, we give the Cycles and Periods in full, tabulated, so as to enable the student to comprehend them at a glance. It only remains to say that at the end of every Great Period, of 1,016,064,000 years, the Sun of our system passes into a passive state of sleep, and remains so for 127,008,000 years.[5] It is, in fact, the Solar Nirvana (just as the Earth enters Nirvana at the end of every complete evolution). All the planetary chains of the solar system are disintegrated during the great solar Nirvana, and recreated upon the awakening of our Sun from its cycle of rest. The alternate states of activity and rest are by the Hindoo Initiates termed the days and nights of Brahma.

THE CYCLE PERIODS OF THE GREAT LIFE-WAVE OF MATERIAL AND SPIRITUAL EVOLUTION

One Polar Day, which is also the cycle of duration of any life-wave on our planet, is, when measured by the common years of our Earth's time, exactly 2,592,000 years.

And, although the 7 planets of our chain vary in the length of their respective life-waves, some a few thousand years more and some a few thousand less, they are, on the average, all of the same duration. Hence the great period of the life-wave, traveling once round our septenary chain of worlds, is 2,592,000 multiplied by 7, or 18,144,000 years. This is for the complete circuit of 7 orbs, but the cycle, or

---

[5] The Lyon Ms. differs in an unexplained way from the text in *LOE* at this point. The former states: "It only remains to say that at the end of each period of 1,088,064,000 years the sun of a system passes into a passive state of repose, and remains so during 136,008,000 years." The Ms. subsequently states (correctly by the premises given here) that "the Grand Cycle of 1,016,064,000 is the exact term of our planet."—Editors

period, of the life-wave, from its leaving the Earth to its reappearance or commencement is 2,592,000 less than the above, or, in other words, exactly 15,552,000 years.

The period of evolution of the 7 great rounds of humanity, and producing 7 times 7, equaling 49, root races of immortal beings (for each race contains its own immortals), is the period of the life-wave passing seven times round the chain, or 127,008,000 years.

There are now say seven great planetary families, each family containing within itself seven root races, and each root race containing within itself, its numerous offshoot races. The perfected humanity, then, rests in the enjoyment of a blissful Nirvana, or "The peace of God, which passeth all understanding," for the 50th Period, that is to say, the 7 planetary families of our Earth have occupied 7 complete circuits of the life-wave round the chain, or 49 Polar Days. The 50th day is the day when those purified souls enter Nirvana, as a family, and this Nirvana lasts until the human life-wave has passed round the chain in a passive state and reached the shores of our planet again, or 18,144,000 years.

After the Jubilee of Nirvana, this vast, and now exalted, host of the 7 planetary families' perfected souls become, in their turn, the originators and guardians of a new and fresh race of humanity, each planetary family, or state, becoming the especial rulers of their own sphere, while their own late Angelic Guardians, the 7 spirits (families of spirits) that stand before the Lord, termed Dhyan Chohans in Esoteric Buddhism, ascend still higher into more perfect spheres of creation. You will take note that each family, or new angelic planetary state of lately exalted human souls, rules the corresponding family upon Earth. Thus the first family, or that which formed the first 7 root races after their cycle, rules the first seven root races of their new creation, and so on with the others. These new races of human beings evolve and pass through the same harmonious process of evolution, from spirit to matter and back again to spirit, thus completing the great cycle of necessity. The planet itself is not recreated after each earthly Nirvana, but re-awakened into activity and life to pass through 7 times 7 races, or circuits of the life wave, or 127,008,000 years.

After the period has again expired, this race of guardians also ascend to higher planes, and the second planetary family enjoys Nirvana for 18,144,000 years, and then in their turn become guardians of the third's 7 families (termed one planetary family). Then the third family originate, rule and guard the fourth, the fourth the fifth, and so on until our Earth (and the planetary chain in its turn) has evolved 7 great planetary families, each family consisting of 7 rounds, and each round of 7 root races, and has also enjoyed 7 Nirvanas. This makes up the grand period of 8 times 127,008,000 years, which, in its grand and complete total, equals 1,016,064,000 years of earthly time.

This period is obtained as follows: 7 periods of 127,008,000 for the 7 great planetary families, and 7 Nirvanas of 18,144,000, which make the eighth; the total eight. This great cycle, 1,016,064,000 years, is the exact term of our planet's physical existence.

The 7 great cycles and the 7 Nirvanas together constitute the eighth, and produce the sleep of death. Our sphere will then have completed the period of child-bearing; old age has gradually settled upon her; she has borne seven sons, and now sinks into the eighth period—sleep—the sleep of death and complete annihilation. Cohesion loosens its hold upon the molecules, and atom by atom the planet's particles are disintegrated and dispersed in space. The great solar sleep, or Nirvana, takes place, and our Sun ceases to be active for a period of 127,008,000 years, viz., a complete evolutionary cycle; and it is only when the first warm breath of new spiritual life pulsates through the spaces of Æth that a recreation of the planetary chains commences anew. The disintegrated atoms of former worlds are reconstructed with new cosmic matter, and once more evolution; but upon a higher plane; begins its almost ceaseless round.

Note the terrible significance of the figure 8. The eighth sphere of our chain is not a visible orb, but a lifeless, dark, semi-spiritual one. It is the sphere of death, and the temporary abode of those souls, or shades, who have, through their depraved lives, lost their connection with the Divine Parent, the spiritual ego that gave them birth. Yet they have bartered a glorious, divine birthright for a mess of pottage, and now must sink unconsciously into the sleep of oblivion, while the enfranchised souls of their nobler brethren are urging their resistless course through the sapphire vaults and starlit realms of the Milky Way. And yet, O most esteemed and eternal brother, in the face of our eternal progress, these vast Cycles and most awful, incomprehensible Periods are but a few fast-fleeting moments of planetary existence. The whole eras of past eternity cannot bring one second more near the end of our immortal, deathless reign. [*LOE* adds the following]:

NOTE: This eighth orb is known to Initiates of the highest interior degree as "the Dark Satellite," whose ruling spiritual hierophant is known by the name of Ob. From this name came that of Oberon, and so evil and infernal is the power of this sphere that all cases of demonia, enchantment or possession came to be termed Obsession. The buried cities of the Gobi desert belong to races who were the devotees of this Ob. (This was after the Gobi had become a portion of the continent of old India and does not refer to the "Golden isle" of the sea, when the Gobi was a tropical ocean.) Hence its name, Gobi, that is, the followers of Ob, or the country of Ob. This is the reason for the awful traditions mentioned in "Isis Unveiled" as to the hidden treasures being guarded by a legion of infernal spirits. It is from this evil orb that the powers possessed by the Black Magi are derived, and, in fact, it is the Spiritual correspondence of those brothers on Earth. For, remember, there is not a class of people, or a society devoted to any subject on Earth, but what has a spiritual correspondence in the realm of spirit. The Hermetic Law is one grand truth, viz., "As it is above, so it is below, as on the Earth, so in the Sky." St. Paul mentions, or rather refers, to this "Dark Satellite" when he publicly declares: "We wrestle not against flesh and blood, but against powers and principalities, princes of the air," etc.

LA CLEF HERMETIQUE

SECTION II

THE SACRED CYCLES AND
NUMBERS OF THE ANCIENT HINDOOS

"'Tis but a moment from its first
evolution to its bier and shroud;
Then, O why should the spirit
of mortal be proud?"

It would be a waste of time upon our part, and a greater
waste of the time of the student of esoteric science, if we
were to wade through and enumerate the whole system of
these sacred cycles and numbers, or were he to attempt the
task of remembering them. We shall supply the key to these
numbers. This sacred mystical key will fit every cyclic lock,
and only requires to be turned with a wise hand to enable
the student to open every portal in the Oriental system of
numbers.

The Five Great Yugas

Satya Yug	1,728,000	years, 4 periods	— units equal 18 and 9
Treta Yug	1,296,000	years, 3 periods	— units equal 18 and 9
Dvapara Yug	864,000	years, 2 periods	— units equal 18 and 9
Cali Yug	432,000	years, 1 period	— units equal 9
Maha Yug	4,320,000	years, 10 periods	— units equal 9

If the student goes over the above numbers, he will notice
that they are all parts of the Divine Age, the Maha Yug, and
that each is composed of the Cali Yug. For instance, Satya
Yug, or 4 periods, is just 4 Cali Yugs, and so on; and the Cali
Yug is the period of the Earth's Pole passing over 60 degrees
of its orbit, and thus forming the sextile to its own true
place. The Dvapara Yug is the period of the Earth's Pole
forming the trine aspect to its true place, and passing over

120 degrees of its orbit. The Treta Yug is the period of the Earth's Pole passing over 180 degrees of its orbit, and forming the opposition to its own place. It is the Cycle that rules the day and the night, the evening and the morning of one Polar Day of Creation. The Satya Yug is the period of the Earth's Pole passing over 240 degrees of its orbit. It is the double trine, or twice 120 degrees. It is also the Cycle that rules the great turning point of the life-wave of the planetary chain; that is, when the Earth has passed through a Satya Yug, the culminating point has been passed, and the life impulse begins to pass to the next planet. Again, you must observe the regular, harmonious progression of the terminating units of each Yug, 2, 4, 6, 8, and of the periods (Cali Yugs), 1, 2, 3, 4. These are the locks, and each one points esoterically to the mysterious, hidden number so carefully veiled from the rude gaze of the profane mind. This sacred, guarded number constitutes the Golden Key. It is the magical 9, the highest unit. It is a triune, or three times three, equal 333 (3 times 3 equals 9); this is 360, less 3 times 9, equals 27 degrees, and in its second aspect shows the magical number of Abracadabra, or 666 (18 equals 9). This sacred number is the perfect symbol of Deity. Multiply it as you like by any number and it resolves itself into 9; and just as all the different aspects of the Eternal and Divine Essence eventually return into the one primordial source, so does this number. No matter to what power it is raised, its ultimate is 9. Hence it is the Divine Figure that can alone unlock the Cycles of the Great First Cause.

[*LOE* adds the following]:

NOTE: The Pole passing over 60 degrees of its orbit is, in the occult, symbolized by the Sun within a six-Pointed star; or Draco, the Serpent, enfolding a six pointed star in its coils. The trine aspect is likewise a trine, but also as a three pointed star; i.e., having three rays.

The Pole in opposition, or passing 180 degrees, is in one of the aspects of the eight-pointed star, in which each ray is opposite another. The period of 240 degrees polar motion is symbolized by the Sun being enclosed in Solomon's Seal or the double trine, viz., 120 degrees added to 120 degrees is 240 degrees.

Having explained the preliminary details of the Hindoo system, we must now enter upon a more beautiful series of calculations of esoteric cycles; and it is necessary, in order to comprehend this, to reveal the Secret Period of the Hindoos, termed a Divine Year. This Divine Year consists of exactly 360 (9) common years, or the number of degrees in the Zodiac. With this year the ancients used to veil their more treasured Cycles.

We will now compare, side by side, the Five Great Yugas, with their esoteric periods when expressed by Divine Years.

Common Years   Divine Years

Satya Yug	1,728,000, equals 4 periods,	equals 4,800
Treta Yug	1,296,000, equals 3 periods,	equals 3,600
Dvapara Yug	864,000, equals 2 periods,	equals 2,400
Cali Yug	432,000, equals 1 period,	equals 1,200
Maha Yug	4,320,000, equals 10 periods,	equals 12,000

In the first place, we see that the Divine Maha Yug is composed of 12,000 Divine Years, which constitute the 10 Great Ages, (see note below) or Cali Yugs, and, in the second, place, that the Divine Years run thus; 4, 3, 2, 1 and 8, 6, 4, 2, and taken by themselves are 1,200 or 1 and 2 equal 3; and 2,400 or 2 and 4 equal 6; and 3,600 or 3 and 6 equal 9; and lastly, 4,800 or 4 and 8 equal 12; which are briefly 3, 6, 9, 12. We explain all these simple matters to show that all the sacred numbers of the Hindoos are one complete and harmonious progression of the 9 units. The student may, if he chooses, go into the Manwatares and Yugs at his leisure and as his inclination prompts. The Manwatares are portions of the Great Kalpa, which is 1,000 Maha Yugs of 4,320,000 common years. This is almost too much for human comprehension, and so we leave it, retiring content with the knowledge that it was but a method adopted by the ancient sages to express their ideas of the sublime majesty of Aum, and to show the utter fallacy of the finite ever being able to comprehend the Infinite, Divine, First Cause or the extent of His attributes.

[LOE adds the following]:

NOTE: The Ten Ages, or Cali Yugs, are also, in the East, shown under the symbol of the Ten Avaters; the Goddess Cali, of the old Hindoos, being a kind of geological Isis, or Queen of geological formations. And lastly, while the whole of this is strictly true, so far as this; the physical or material plane is concerned yet it must, by the laws of correspondence, be considered in its truly occult sense. The four ages are the four Great Cycles of human evolution; First, the Golden, the classical, Saturnian age, then the less spiritual or Silver Age, then the Copper; and lastly the Iron Age; the dense or material barbarian age or state, spirit in its descent, becoming more and more gross, until the lowest point of the age of Earth, or the Iron Age, was reached, and man entered upon the first human cycle. This, of course, teaches that our first progenitors were truly spiritual, or angelic, and that each age in the scale of involution made them more material and directly the lowest point of the arc was reached, then material evolution commenced. But, of course, all these spiritual verities will open out to your mind as you carefully think over this brief paper.

We will now turn from the theoretical to the practical Cycles of the old Hindoos and esoterically explain

THE FOUR CELEBRATED AGES OF ANTIQUITY

In the first place, we have taught that the Hindoos' esoteric, or Divine, year consisted of 360 common years, and that the whole of their cycles bear a direct relation to arithmetical progression and proportion, such as 1, 2, 3, 4 and 4, 3, 2, 1; also 2, 4, 6, 8 etc. We have thoroughly explained Polar Motion, etc., therefore, if we calculate the motion of the North Pole from the period of its being perpendicular to, and coinciding with, the North Pole of the Ecliptic, over a distance of 90 degrees, when it would be horizontal, or in the plane of its orbit, we shall obtain four distinct periods, bearing the mystical relation of 4, 3, 2, 1, which will be found to have a remarkable character in the country round Benares, or latitude 27 degrees North (2 and 7 equal 9). Benares is the ancient seat of learning in India, and at one time was the center of their occult schools; but their sacred place, or temple of observation,was termed the Mountain of Light in latitude 27 degrees. By using the Divine Year as a Key, we find themeaning of the following periods or ages:

Common Years	Polar Motion	Divine Years
Golden Age 259,200,	4 times 9 equals 36 degrees and	720
Silver Age 194,400,	3 times 9 equals 27 degrees and	540
Copper Age 129,600,	2 times 9 equals 18 degrees and	360
Iron Age 64,800,	1 times 9 equals 9 degrees and	180
648,000,	10 times 9 equals 90 degrees and	1,800

Thus, during the passage of the Pole from one point of the quadrant to the other, occurred the mystical ages, which also correspond to fire, air, water and earth. These Periods will be found to differ by 64,800 years, or 180 Divine Years, from one another, and each portion of the angle moved over consists of the mysterious number 9, multiplied by 4, 3, 2, 1; thus, 4×9 degrees equals 36 degrees; 3×9 degrees equals 27 degrees; 2×9 degrees equals 18 degrees; and 1×9 degrees equals 9 degrees; and bearing in mind that our place of observation is Benares, or 27 degrees North latitude, we find that during 720 Divine Years the Tropics passed from the equator to 36 degrees latitude, North and South; and from this point during 540 more the Tropics passed up to 63 degrees latitude, North and South; and also from this position, during a further 360 Divine Years, it reached up to 81 degrees North latitude; and lastly, during a period of 180 Divine Years from this era, the Tropics reached the Pole, when every portion of the globe had a Tropical summer and an Arctic winter. But, to better express our meaning, we will briefly describe these four ages.

The first is the Golden Age, which began with a most delightful climate, a gentle, fruitful, universal summer. This ancient seat of science was indeed divinely favored by the laws of Nature throughout long ages, and no wonder it was christened the Golden Age, which corresponds to Fire. But the Poles gradually moved on, though at no time during this age was the meridian altitude of the Sun, on the shortest day, less than 27 degrees; the latitude of the observatory. Then came the Silver Age, which corresponds to the element of Air. This period lasted for 540 Divine Years, and was a variable period. The summers were hot and the days long; the winters were cold and the days short, but the Sun was always visible above the horizon at noon on the shortest day, and the Tropics reached an angle of 63 degrees. Next in rotation we have the Copper Age, corresponding to the element of Water, which lasted for 360 Divine Years.

It was indeed a dull, watery, lifeless period. A Tropical summer and an Arctic winter, the spring deluging the plains and lowlands with frightful floods, etc. The Tropics moved another 18 degrees nearer the Pole, and on the shortest day at noon the Sun never rose, but was 18 degrees below the horizon. As, however, 18 degrees is within the angle of twilight, they had no absolute darkness. Lastly comes the Iron Age, corresponding to the Earth; the Age of Horror, which lasted 180 Divine Years, and at noon on the shortest day the Sun was 27 degrees below the horizon, and never rose for weeks together in midwinter. It was cold, dark, frozen and death-like, and a period when the extremes of heat and cold waged incessant war, neither obtaining the victory.

In closing this chapter, we will reproduce, for notice, that the Pole passed over 90 degrees, or one-fourth of the circle, in 1,800 Divine Years, or 648,000 common years. Therefore, it passed its complete orbit of 360 degrees in 7,200 Divine Years, or 2,592,000 common years, from which take the Prajanatha Yug of 2,160,000 common years, and the remainder is the Cali Yug of 432,000 common years, or the Age of Heat. The Cali Yug is one-sixth of the polar orbit, and five Cali Yugs make the Prajanatha Yug. The 70 Elders initiated by Moses and Aaron were symbolical of the 72 Divine Years; that is, 70 Elders and Moses and Aaron, making the total 72, or the magic 9; which is the period of the Sun passing the 12 signs of the Zodiac, or 25,920 years. It states in the Holy Writ that they (the 70 Elders and Moses and Aaron) saw the God of Israel, which, of course, was the Sun; and the 72 Elders represented its Great Cycle, or 72 times 360 common years equals 25,920 years.

A COMPARISON OF THE HARMONY OF ESOTERIC NUMBERS AND ESOTERIC CYCLES IN REFERENCE TO TIME AND MOTION

The Earth's Pole moves 1 degree in 7,200 common years;
And also moves once round in 7,200 Divine years;
The Sun moves thro' space at rate of 108,000 Miles per hour.

In one hour the Earth, by its revolution on its axis, causes 15 degrees of the Zodiac to rise, culminate and set, while the Pole moves 15 degrees of its orbit in 108,000 common years.

The Earth, by its diurnal motion, causes the 360 degrees of the Zodiac to rise and set in 24 hours, and in this time the Sun travels thro' space 2,592,000 Miles;

While a Polar Day of 360 degrees is 2,592,000 Years;

And the Sun moves round its orbit in 25,920 Years.

Note that the sum of the digits in each number is the magic 9.

"THE KEY" (A.2.c)

The document presented here as "The Key" is the H. B. of L.'s commentary on the curious treatise by the Abbot Johannes Trithemius, *On the Seven Secondary Causes, that is, the Intelligences or Spirits who, after God, Move the Worlds* (1515). The work itself appears never to have been given to the neophytes, though Ayton had probably translated it earlier and a French translation was published in the 1890s by a member of the circle of occultists around Papus and Barlet.[1] The omission of the original was probably never noticed by the neophytes because the idea expounded is basically simple: the seven planetary gods or angels set over the earth govern it in turn for identical segments of the cosmic cycle, and each of these imparts to his age the tincture of his "personality."

Trithemius (1462-1516) was Abbot of Spanheim and had set his ideas in a Christian and Biblical context. In his original scheme, the cycles of governors began at the creation of the world (which by his calculations occurred in 5206 B.C.) with Orifiel, the angel of Saturn, and progressed in equal periods of 354 years, four months, through Anael, Zachariel and the rest, in the inverse order of the planets assigned to the days of the week. For unexplained reasons, Trithemius cuts short his exposition with the end of the twentieth reign in 1879 or 1880, without completing the third cycle of seven governors and without discussing the reign of Michael which was to have begun in that year.[2]

The author of "The Key" thought in far grander periods of time than had Trithemius, and determined that each of the seven

---

[1] Mme. Blavatsky notes in her diary for October 9, 1878 that she had received a translation of Trithemius's "prophecies" from the Rev. W. A. Ayton (*BCW*, I, 410). If this was a translation of the *De septem secundeis* treatise to which "The Key" is a commentary, it is conceivable that Ayton's translation made its way to his "chelas," although no mention is ever made of the fact and Ayton, after the debacle of the H. B. of L. was always grateful that he had never supplied any material for Davidson and Burgoyne to use. The French version is Johannes Trithemius, *Traité des causes secondes*, Paris, 1897, translated by "Jean Tabris." Mr. J.-P. Brach has kindly informed us that this is a pseudonym of René Philipon, who also was the translator of several of Burgoyne's works into French.

[2] On the whole scheme, see Chacornac, 171ff.

angels would rule 12 times during one Great Solar Period of 25,920 years. In other words, each would govern the world in turn for about 308 years and 208-1/2 days (one eighty-fourth of the cycle), and the seven together would complete one round of governance in 2,160 years, the time it takes the sun to pass through one sign of the zodiac. As is made clear in the companion work "The Hermetic Key" even these large numbers are only the beginning, and the succession of cycles is never-ending.

The significance of the exercise given in "The Key"—presumably obtained by adjusting the starting points—was to demonstrate the uniqueness of the year 1881 and the strength of the cosmic forces behind the revival of the Exterior Circle of the Order. The "Origin and Object of the H. B. of L." [A.1.c] traced the formation of the Interior Circle of the Order to 2,438 B.C.—4,320 years before 1881, a period precisely equal to the time it took the sun to pass through Aries and Pisces and enter Aquarius.[3] The H. B. of L. dated the transition to Aquarius to December 1880 or February 1881 and taught that at that time the Iron Age of Samael, the Angel of Mars, gave way to the enlightened age of Michael, the Sun God. Michael had presided at the initial formation of the Interior Circle and at the Birth of Christ, and in 1881 would usher in the age of the renewal of occultism and the destruction of sacerdotalism and tyranny. "The Key" provides a good example of the anti-clericalism of the H. B. of L. (a leading trait of the Order, shared with Blavatsky and Emma Hardinge Britten) and of the astrological and cyclical reasons brought forward to justify it.

While the H. B. of L.'s method of arriving at the special significance of the years surrounding 1880 was novel, the result was a commonplace of the time. Eliphas Levi, in a treatise published in *The Theosophist* after his death, had dated the transition to

---

[3] This period of 4320 years is one-thousandth the length of a *Manvantara*, and is the starting point for much occult speculation on cycles. See, e.g., Guénon 1970, 13ff. For unexplained reasons the H. B. of L. has not preserved Trithemius' sequence of the angel-governors. Guénon 1982, 207, n.1, says that "these dates refer to the symbolism of 'cyclic numbers.'"

1879. Marie, Countess of Caithness and Duchesse de Pomár, like the H. B. of L., dated it to 1881.[4]

The text of "The Key" given here is from the augmented *Light of Egypt*, which is essentially identical with the manuscript in the Fonds Papus. Burgoyne's significant additions appear as "Notes".

---

[4] See Lady Caithness's "1881," *The Theosophist* III/6 (March 1882), 149-150; also her "La célèbre prophétie de Trithème," *L'Aurore du Jour* II (January 1888), 271, for her exposition of Trithemius. The Theosophists dissented, asserting that 1881 was a year of particularly bad omen; see "Stars and Numbers," *The Theosophist* II/9 (June 1881), 199-201. For a more recent attempt to rectify Trithemius, see M. Clavelle, "Les Rose-Croix et L'Eglise Intérieure," *Le Voile d'Isis*, May 1931, 285ff., who takes Trithemius's "year" to be a "lunar sidereal" year.

A Key to the Work of Abbot Trithemius, entitled—
"The Secondaries, or Ruling Intelligences Who,
After God, Actuate the Universe."

The periods of the ruling Principles, or Intelligences, and
their order of succession in the government of the world is
incorrectly stated by the Abbot Trithemius, although there
is every reason to believe that this wise and truly learned
Abbot knew perfectly well what the true period and order
of succession was.

And it was doubtless from reasons of policy that he
thought well to conceal this knowledge from the ignorant
and profane; knowing, as he must have done, that all worthy and accepted Neophytes would be taught the actual
truth during the process of their Initiation.

The correct Cycle, or Period, during which each of the
Seven Intelligences has chief rule over all worldly concerns,
is an 84th part of the Great Solar Period of 25,920 years, or a
seventh part of the Sub-Solar Period of 2,160 years, and is
equal to about 308 years and 208-1/2 days. It will be seen
that as the Sun's period, or Revolution, round his immense
orbit is 25,920 years, he moves or passes through one Zodiacal Sign in exactly 2,160 years, and that a seventh part of
this gives each of the Seven Principles one term of power in
each of the 12 signs; and in one complete period of 25,920
years each of the Seven Intelligences has 12 times been the
chief governor of this sublunary sphere.

The correct order, or rotation of succession, is the natural
order of planetary application; thus, in the first order of the
Seven Governors, Cassiel, (see note below) the Angel or
Intelligence of Saturn, receives power, and after ruling the
world for 308 years, 208-1/2 days, resigns the reins of government to Zachariel, the Angel of Jupiter, who stands second in the order of the Ruling Powers, and after another term
of 308 years, 208-1/2 days, hands over the control of the
world to Samael, the Angel of Mars, who for the same period
subjects the world and its inhabitants to the influence of

Martial force; then in the fourth order of the Seven Governors comes the Archangel Michael, the center, and also the chief, of the Seven Great Principles, who, having ruled the world for 308 years, 208-1/2 days, retires in favor of the next succession, and fifth in the order, whose name is Anael, Prince of the Astral Light and Chief Angel of the planet Venus, who, after ruling the world for 308 years, 208-1/2 days, retires in favor of Raphael, who receives the scepter of earthly rule. Bright Raphael, the swift messenger of the Gods, and presiding Intelligence of the planet Mercury, rules for 308 years, 208-1/2 days, when Gabriel, the negative, receives the Ruling Powers. This Intelligence, who is the Angel of the Moon, governs the Earth for 308 years, 208-1/2 days, is the Seventh, and last, of the order and this completes the Sub-Solar Cycle of 2,160 years, when Cassiel once more takes command, and so on, Cycle after Cycle, "ad infinitum."

NOTE: Cassiel is the usual name given to the Saturnine principle. The Abbot Trithemius calls it Orifiel, as do several other writers. Hence, it is well to note, that many names are used Kabbalistically; each name expressing the nature, or qualities, symbolically, by the different Hebrew characters of which it is composed, each different name belonging to the same state or intelligence; denoting different aspects of its power or influence. All the active Principles, or positive angelic Intelligences, as a rule terminate with El, while the negative or evil powers terminate with On, one is solar, the other is lunar. This hint will be sufficient for the student of the Occult, who must ever remember that he must not measure good and evil by any modern conception of these terms.

Every power of Nature, whether it be an intelligent, or a non-intelligent power, is ever striving to obtain an equilibrium, that which we call evil is but a more intense expression of that which we call good; for instance, Pride, Love, Ambition, love of Self and Combativeness, are good, when combined in their true proportion, and any human being without any one of these, would be imperfect; but, carry one or two of these, otherwise good qualities, to a great extreme, and we should witness the greatest evil results. Then remember the Hermetic Law; "As it is below, so it is above, as on the Earth, so in the sky."

A brief glance into past History will be instructive to the student of Psychology, and to enable him to do this, and assist his researches, we supply the following correct data terminating a Sub-Solar Cycle with Michael receiving the Government of the world in the beginning of the year 1881 (see note below), when the sub-races of the West reach the Equator of Human progress, and carrying our researches forward from this date up to the culminating point of the arc; from which point Western Races descend the descending Cycle, and once more relapse into ignorance.

NOTE: The student must bear in mind that there are three different kinds of Cycles spoken of in La Clef. The first are Solar Cycles. Thus, 25,920 years form the Great Solar Cycle, and is the period of the Sun passing through the twelve signs of the Zodiac, and, consequently, completing one revolution of his orbit, round his center; but 2,160 years is a sub-cycle, a twelfth part of the Great Cycle, and the period of the Sun passing through one sign of the Zodiac and equal to 30 degrees of space. When the Sun has passed thro one sign he has completed one sub-cycle and the new sub-cycle dates from his entry into a fresh sign. For example, the Sun, at the end of the year A.D. 1880, left the sign Pisces and entered Aquarius. (It must be borne in mind that the Sun's motion thro space is exactly the reverse of the natural order of the Zodiacal signs, as from Aries to Taurus, etc.) From this it will be seen that the Sun in 1881 began a new sub-cycle, and that the order of succession of the Seven Governors is such that Michael governs the first term of each sign, so that by the time Michael's rule works round again the Sun will be entering Capricorn, etc.

The second kind of Cycle is the period of the Seven Governors, which although of exactly the same duration as the Solar sub-cycle of 2,160 years, it is not measured by signs or constellations, and, consequently, neither begins nor terminates with the sub-cycle, but is measured thus; from the commencement of Cassiel's rule to the termination of Gabriel's is one complete period or Cycle.

The third kind of a Cycle is the Arc of Human Progress, Mental and Physical and which alternately carries a race of people or an empire to the summit of power and civilization and down again, in spite of itself, to the greatest depths of ignorance.

The duration of this Cycle varies considerably, according to the kind of race it effects. The greatest period is the duration, or reign, of the Seven root races of each round. The next, the duration of a single root race. Lastly, the duration of each of the numerous offshoot races belonging to the seven branches and their minor sub-races. But, in any case, the Arc moves in the same harmonious order obeying the Divine impulse of the Seven Eternal Principles of Nature, evolving its energies in great, mighty waves, when ruling the earliest root races, and comprising hundreds of thousands of years in a single period, in smaller waves that can be measured by tens of thousands of years when controlling the great branch races, and in gentler ripples of tiny wavelets of cosmic energy when directing the minor sub-races, measuring at the most but a few thousand years of Earth's time.

The year 1881 may appear incorrect to anyone conversant with modern astronomy, which maintains that our Sun will not enter the Sign Aquarius until the year A.D. 1897. This is a difference of sixteen years, but modern astronomers are wrong. The Sun entered Aquarius in February of 1881. This is not the only mistake they have to discover.

The present Great Western Race is one of the seven branches of the Fifth root race, belonging to the fourth round of evolution, and the sub-races mentioned in La Clef, when speaking of the future glory and fall, do not by any means comprise or include the whole of the Great Western Race. It will be sufficient to say that France, England (Great Britain) and the United States may be taken as typical examples of the sub-races therein referred to. Several other European races are also included.

In carrying our investigations into the past ages, it will suffice if we begin in the year 1200 B.C., when Cassiel, the Angel of Saturn, resumed the Government of the world.

From the year 1200 B.C. to the year 897 B.C. the earth was under the melancholy influence of Cassiel's Rule; and in the very first year of his reign, Troy, the famous Trojan City was taken and destroyed by the Greeks, and many other events faithfully indicate the nature and power of Saturine influence. It will well repay those who will study Ancient History.

After Cassiel, the benevolent Zachariel, Chief Agent of Jupiter, became Regent of the world, and here we note the remarkable difference between the two Governors. In the beginning of this Angel's reign, Rome, the Mistress of the world, was built, and the foundation of a mighty Empire substantially laid. All Nations began to progress rapidly into a more advanced state of civilization, and to cultivate the Arts and Sciences, and lastly, but by no means the least of the benefits conferred by Zachariel, was the production, toward the close of his reign, of two of the most extraordinary men our era has ever seen, viz., Gautama Buddha in India and Pythagoras in Europe.

The Angel Zachariel, was in power from the year 897 B.C. to the year 588 B.C. Then came Samael, the Angel of Mars, who reigned from the year 588 B.C. to the year 280 B.C. This period is one of war, Martial Heroes and brilliant achievements on the field of battle. A glance at the history of Greece and Rome will suffice to show how true this is.

After Samael, came Michael, the Sun God, the shining chief of the Seven Intelligences, and ruled the world from the year 280 B.C. to the year 29 A.D. During this period most Nations attained the Climax of power and civilization. Toward the close of his reign, this bright Angel presented the Nations of the West with a teacher, who rivaled, in moral teachings and excelled in practical benevolence, Gautama Buddha, the greatest moral reformer the East has ever seen. This Teacher was styled by His followers, the Son of God, and was called by name Jesus, the son of Joseph and Mary.

He was called the Son of God astrologically, because He was born into the world during the reign of Michael, the Sun God. And esoterically because he was at-one with the Universal Father.

And it is remarkably strange, that, no sooner did Michael's Rule end, than the numerous priestly enemies of this noble reformer became triumphant, and brutally murdered Him, as they have done thousands of others in all ages of the world.

The great religious symbol of all exoteric religious systems and dogmatic sacerdotal castes has been the Cross; inverted, it is a bloody weapon, the sword, and past history can prove how well its devoted priesthood knew its fearful use.

After Michael comes Anael, "Prince of the Astral Light," the Angel of Venus and Love, who ruled from the year A.D. 29 to the year A.D. 337. These were the days of religious persecution; the days, also, of faith and love among the Christians for the doctrine of their noble Chief. It was in these days when it was said, "How these Christians love one another"; but, alas, it was also a time of great licentiousness in Rome, when women, love, lust and debauchery were the order of the day. This period will show the occult student the two opposite powers or forces of Anael's influence. When exerted for evil, it is all that is obscene and disgusting, but, when exerted for good, it evolves that which is noble, elegant and true.

After Anael's rule terminated, the Angel of Mercury, or Raphael, commenced to rule, and was Governor from the year A.D. 337 to the year A.D. 646. It was during this period that the Gospels of the New Testament were forged. Christianity, under the rule of the Brain instead of simple faith and brotherly love, became proud. From being persecuted, she became the persecutor. The church became dogmatic, cunning, and thoroughly determined to succeed at all hazards. The most transparent forgeries were accepted as absolute truth. The mutilation of the works of the contemporary authors of the Apostles and the earliest Christian Fathers, and interpolating suitable passages of their own, were considered meritorious actions. It was during this reign that the celebrated Council of Nice was held, and the divinity of Jesus established—by vote.

At the end of the year A.D. 646 Gabriel, the Angel of the Moon, became the Supreme Ruler, and reigned until the year A.D. 954.

This period, like all Lunar periods, was one of intellectual slumber. The Dark Ages had set in, and gradually increased until Cassiel, the Angel of Saturn, took command, and governed from the year A.D. 954 to the year A.D. 1263, and made things worse.

Pagan darkness and gross superstition held the sway, and reigned supreme, until the year A.D. 1263. The lowest point in the mental arc was reached, and Western nations were in the most dense condition. But a change was at hand, for the benevolent Zachariel, the genius of Jupiter, again resumed the management of the world, and reigned until the year A.D. 1572. This period is one of almost uninterrupted intellectual progress. During this Rule of Power, the despotic power of Rome received its death-blow.

Parliaments were instituted for the people, the days of Good Queen Bess came to an end. Protestantism flourished, and so prepared the way for Free Thought.

After the good reign of Zachariel, Samael, the Angel of Mars, came into power and reigned from the year A.D. 1572 to the year A.D. 1880 (until December 21 1880, when the Sun reached the Tropic of Capricorn. Michael began to reign on December 23).[1] This rule was the Age of Iron, and just as

---

[1] See note, in text, *supra*, on February 1881 as the point of entry into Aquarius, and, consequently, as the start of Michael's reign.—Editors

Rome conquered all before her over 2,000 years before, and achieved imperial greatness, so did Great Britain, the second Rome. It was again a period of war, mechanical inventions and martial glory, and, at times, the whole of Europe was one great battlefield, and resounded with the din of arms "and all the circumstances of war." In the future this will be called the age of warlike inventions, and noted for its huge ironclads, great guns, and other fearful engines of destruction.

Mars rules iron and all martial arts and sciences; hence the wonderful inventions of this age—steam engines, iron ships, and elaborate machinery.

At the end of the year A.D. 1880, the Great Archangel Michael comes into power and once more has the government of the world until the year A.D. 2188. This will be a period of Imperial Greatness. Empires will shine full of glory, the Human intellect will have full play and all Churches, Religious Creeds and Ecclesiastical Dogmas will fall to the ground and become things of the past. Parsons, Vicars and Bishops will have to work in different fields if they mean to obtain an honest livelihood. Yes, I repeat this prophecy. The Churches and Chapels will fall with a terrible crash, and be destroyed. But from their ashes, Phoenix-like, shall arise a new Religion, whose shining Motto will be; Veritas Excelsior, Truth Above. This era shall proclaim the rights of man. It is essentially the age of reason dreamed of by Bruno and Thomas Paine. During the reign of this Angelic Intelligence, the Masculine Element will receive the Solar influx and obtain its highest development. Intellect and Reason will remove most of our Social disorders and women receive more attention in worldly affairs; but at the same time, it is not a feminine period by any means.

Mankind under this rule, will become physically and intellectually immensely superior to what they are now. Startling discoveries in Chemistry, Electricity and all the physical sciences will be brought to light. Steam will be superseded by Compressed Air (gas), Electro-Magnetism (atomic power)[2] as a motive power. In fact a new era of progress will dawn upon the world, as time and space will be annihilated by new transportation and communication; and, last, but not least, Science and Religion will become blended, spiritual intercourse an acknowledged fact, and Psychology the special study of the greatest Scientists of the day.

After the rule of Michael, Anael, Prince of the Astral Light, will receive the Guardianship of the world, and reign from the year A.D. 2188 to the year A.D. 2497. This is the feminine period, and woman will, during Anael's reign, become man's just and lawful equal, socially and politically. Intuition will show itself the superior of mere intellect, and the human form, physically, attain its greatest degree of perfection. Occultism will be taught in our Universities, Astronomers become Astrologers, and drugs for the treatment of disease be consigned to the limbo of oblivion, to keep company with the Religious Dogmas and Scientific Noodleisms of today. It is at this point that I would warn all Western Nations. Remember that this is the period of feminine force and love. Therefore, see to it that you form not those magnetic conditions that would attract into your midst the dark legionaries of Anael. If you do, Woe be unto you; as pride and luxury, licentiousness and debauchery will result, and the fate of Nineveh, Babylon and Rome will be yours; but if, on the other hand, virtue, morality and pure affectional love, stand paramount amongst you; then, all that is noble, elegant and true shall reign in your midst. Then shall Nations abolish fleets and standing armies, kings lay aside their scepters, and a Universal Human Brotherhood begin to comprehend their common origin and Divine relationship with the GREAT FIRST CAUSE.

After Anael, in the order of the seven Governors, Raphael will receive the Scepter of earthly rule—Bright Raphael, the swift messenger of the gods and presiding

---

[2] The interpretations in parentheses were clearly added by H. O. Wagner in preparing the re-editions of *Light of Egypt*.—Editors

Intelligence of the Planet Mercury. This will be the grand era of the mind, the age of the Genius of Humanity, to assimilate all the stores of knowledge, treasured up by the past ages. This is the culminating point (see note below) of this sub-cycle of the sub-Western races. Raphael will govern from the year A.D. 2497 to the year A.D. 2806. During this period, the attainment of Adeptship will be the highest ambition of the noblest minds, though but few will attain unto this ideal height in any race of the present round. Science and the Arts will attain unto a degree of perfection unknown to any past age, and thus will close the Intellectual genius of the Western Race.

From the summit we begin to retrograde, for Gabriel, the seventh Governor, now takes up the reins of power, and rules from the year A.D. 2806 to the year A.D. 3114. This rule is again the stagnation of mind, and once more Humanity having attained the greatest height possible in this cycle, begins to travel on the downward arc and the nations again relapse gradually into ignorance, and spiritual truth will materialize itself into concrete sacerdotalism, nor will mankind of the West again reach its climax of civilization until about the year A.D. 7300.

NOTE: The culminating point of this Cycle is about the year A.D. 2800, or six years before the expiration of Raphael's Rule. The Sub-Western Races, then at their climax of development, will gradually decline, while certain other races of the West will be rapidly rising on their ascending arc, as will the nations of the Orient who will culminate about the time of the Sub-Western Races reaching the lowest arc of the Cycle. Flint glass can be made with a temper equal to that sustained by the finest steel, but the secret of its production is in the hands of the Adepts, and like all other secrets, will be accidentally discovered when the proper time arrives.

"Naronia" (A.2.d)

This treatise is undoubtedly by Burgoyne, and was probably circulated to his students only after his falling out with Davidson in late 1886. Writing as "Zanoni," he had already published some light on the subject of the Naros cycle (the Veil of Isis," *Occult Magazine* I/5, June 1885, 38-39). Since no manuscript survives either in English or in French, the text given here is reprinted from *The Light of Egypt*.[1] The work is reproduced because it complements the H. B. of L. teachings on cosmic cycles given in "The Key" [A.2.c] and because it hints obscurely at the Order's central teaching on the cyclical sexual laws governing the development of Powers from the Spaces of Æth.

The Naros or Neros is the luni-solar period in which the moon completes a whole number of lunations in precisely 600 Gregorian years. Godfrey Higgins in his monumental *Anacalypsis*, published in 1836, had made the Naros the centerpiece of his investigations, using it to prove the antediluvian wisdom of the ancients (who must have known the real length of the solar year) and to show the origin of the vast cyclical periods of classical and Hindu mythology.[2] As the references in "Naronia" show, the Naros then became a commonplace, figuring prominently in the works of Madame Blavatsky and other occult expositors of mythological history. In the H. B. of L.'s discussion, the Naros is superimposed (rather uncomfortably) on the cycles of the angelic governors described by the Abbot Trithemius (see "The Key," A.2.c.) to show a regular cycle of "Messianic" incarnations or irruptions in history every six hundred years: Buddha, Apollonius of Tyana, Mohammed and the Reformation (said to have begun in the 13th century). The latest example of this, of course, was the revival of true occultism in 1881 by the foundation of the Exterior Circle of the H. B. of L.

All of Burgoyne's learned discourse on the Naros, however, is in reality incidental to his true purpose, which is to hint at the greater mysteries of "Naronia."

---

[1] "Naronia" was not included in the original editions of *LOE*, but it appears as Section 2, Chapter VII in the augmented versions published by H. O. Wagner beginning in 1963.

[2] Higgins, I, 4, 6, 30, 166, 177ff., etc.

At various places in his works, P. B. Randolph had promised to reveal the great secret of the Ansaireh Priesthood of Syria, the recurring period when magical sexual intercourse was most powerful as a means to commune with the celestial hierarchies.

> There is a moment, frequently recurring, wherein men and women can call down to them celestial—almost awful—powers from the Spaces, thereby being wholly able to reach the souls of others, and hold them fast in the bonds of a love unknown as yet in this cold land of ours. Would to God every husband and wife on earth would use it; then, indeed, were this a far more blessed life to lead.[3]

Randolph's explicit revelation of the secret has not been preserved, but there is no doubt that the mystery centered on the precise point in a woman's catamenial period when sexual magic was most powerful. Robert H. Fryar, who was the agent for the sale of Randolph's works in the early 1880s and who was also the one who first announced the H. B. of L. to the world [B.3.b], obviously was privy to the teaching and touts it in advertising the line of books he published (see Fryar 1888).

In "Naronia" Burgoyne very obliquely hints at the same mystery. At birth a person is endowed with the "germs of new forces"—"Virtues, Powers, Potencies and Deific attributes." These are in some way renewed annually when the sun again enters the sign and degree of the Zodiac it had at the person's birth. More importantly (and more vaguely), when the moon in its monthly course arrives at a certain (unspecified) place it "impregnates" and vivifies these germs and enables one to actually acquire the full powers inherent in the human constitution.

Farther than this Burgoyne states he cannot go without leading the neophyte out of the "safe path," but he invites the student to meditate on the mystery and be "guided by your own intuitions in the matter." The reader of "Naronia" is similarly left to his or her own intuitions.

---

[1] Randolph 1873, 17-18.

NARONIA

THE MYSTICAL CYCLE OF THE SUN

The real secrets and the inner mysteries of the sacred "Naros" appear to have been entirely unknown to either medieval or modern writers. In fact, the most prominent writers upon occult and theosophical subjects generally avoid all mention of it; or, if they do express their ideas, it is only upon its cosmic, or external aspects, as it applies to the Macrocosm, of the sidereal heavens. But of its spiritual and mystical importance, as it applies to the human soul of the Microcosm, they are universally silent. Briefly stated, the "Naros," in its astronomical and physical aspects, is a Luni-Solar Cycle of the period of the Sun and Moon, and is completed in six hundred years; and, strangely enough, such a period also coincides with some remarkable revolution in the mental and theological affairs of humanity; hence a few extracts from prominent writers will not be out of place to prepare the student for that which is to follow.

Madam Blavatsky, speaking of the Naros in "Isis Unveiled," Vol. I, pages 31-33, remarks "that he (G. Higgins) fails to decipher it (the Cycle) is made apparent; for, as it pertains to the mysteries of creation, this Cycle was the most inviolable of all. It was repeated in symbolic figures only in the Chaldean Book of Numbers, the original book, which, if now extant, is not to be found in libraries."

To the foregoing we may also add, neither will this Chaldean Book be found in the crypts of Thibet, Madam B. to the contrary notwithstanding. She very pointedly tells her readers where they cannot find such a book, but very wisely maintains a discreet silence as to where this rare work can be found.

The learned Countess of Caithness, in her recent volume, "The Mystery of the Ages," mentions the Naros on page 361, viz.: "To the Christian Theosophist, Jesus is a manifestation of 'Adonai,' the Christ, or Christ Spirit, of whom there have been many incarnations on this Earth, and He the fullest and most perfect. They believe Him to be the guiding guardian protector of this planet during His particular cycle, and that in coming to it, He comes to His own, not only to instruct, but to give a fresh impulse at the end of certain periods of six hundred years, called Naroses, or Naronic Cycles, and if, therefore, it could be proven by those who assert that Jesus is only a mythical, and not an historical personality, the whole theory of the Naronic Cycles, founded on astronomical science, which is to be found in the doctrines of every ancient country, all over the civilised world, would fall to the ground, and prove after a million of ages to be but a vain delusion."

It is scarcely necessary for us to point out that, if the Naros is as the authoress asserts, "founded upon astronomical science," then the Cycle is an astronomical fact, and as such is capable of mathematical demonstration; consequently is, and always must be, totally independent of the existence of individuals. In fact, an astronomical cycle, if true, possesses no real relationship with any personality, human or Divine, and this being the case, the Naronic Cycle will remain just the same truth, upon the plane to which it naturally belongs, whether the Christian Jesus is proven to be either Myth, Man or God. Neither does the genuine student of Occultism care, very much, in which position the supposed Redeemer is placed by the masses.

Therefore, the statement of the authoress that without the actual physical incarnation of the personal Jesus this theory of "millions of ages" would prove to be a vain delusion is the very height of mystical absurdity, and the self-evident inanity of such an illogical argument must surely become apparent to all reflective minds.

The learned Dr. Kennealy, Q. C., etc., in his book "Book of God," makes mention of the Naros upon pages 52, 53 where, viewing the period as a Messianic Cycle, he remarks: "This Naros is the Luni-Solar Naros, or Sibylline year. It is composed of 31 periods of 19 years each and one of 11, and is the most perfect of astronomical cycles, and, although no chronologer has mentioned it at length, it is the most ancient of all. It consists of six hundred years, or 7200 Solar months, or 219,146 1/2 days, and this same number of days, 219,146 1/2 gives 600 years, consisting each of 365 days, 5 hours, 51 minutes and 36 seconds, which differs less than 3 minutes from what the length is observed to be at this day." "If on the first of January, at noon, a new Moon took place in any part of the heavens, it would take place again in exactly six hundred years, at the same moment and under the same physical circumstances. The Sun, stars and planets would all be in the same relative position." And in corroboration of what this learned doctor says, Prof. Cassini, one of the great modern astronomers, declares "this Naros to be the most perfect of all periods."

From this, then, we see the utter nonsense of modern theosophical mystics trying to twist and warp the harmonies of natural laws to suit their dreamy, sentimental speculations. The Naros exists in spite of each and every attempt of hallucinated mystics to make it conform to their erroneous doctrines.

The Luni-Solar Cycle of 600 years is the absolute measurement of mental development, and the Luni-Solar conjunction, which commences and terminates this Cycle, evolves forth the embryonic conditions which shall, during its rule, become manifested in the physical world. It is not true, from an occult stand-point, that the Naros specially refers to the birth of some great Saviour or Reformer. It is only true, that the conditions which this Naronic conjunction evolve prepare the way and call forth the man or men, who shall act as the pioneers in the world's need of a higher and a more liberal teaching. At the same time it will always be found that some very prominent teacher or reformer is born into the world at about the same time, not definitely to any nation or country, or exactly on time, within a generation or two, but always near to the period of the Cycle; but such teachers and law-givers are not the cause of the Naros, neither do they become incarnated to fulfill the Cycle, as the

Countess of Caithness very foolishly imagines, but they appear simply as the result of increased mental energies, or in the downward arc of the race they appear to crystallize the existing truths and veil those things which have ceased to be of use and which may become a source of evil.

A brief outline of this thread of mental evolution can be traced, by noting that Gautama Buddha appeared in 600 B.C. or thereabouts, and that 600 years later the Jewish reformer, Apollonius of Tyana, appeared upon the scene of the world's history; then in another 600 years Mahomet, with his warlike issues came upon the planes of human existence. Another Naros passes away when we have a complete host of inspired reformers, and the Reformation began, viz., 1200 A.D. to 1300 A.D. And lastly, we bridge yet another cycle of the Sun and Lo! we have 1881 A.D. and naturally all eyes are looking for another Saviour. The Adventists speak of the second coming of Christ. The Shakers claim that He has already come in the form of Mother Ann Lee. On the other hand the Mormons say that Joseph Smith is the modern Messiah.

It is not of course necessary to say that all of these earnest, and doubtless well meaning sects, are wrong, outrageously in error, because no such Messiah will appear, at least not to them. He will move in the world quite unsuspected as to His true and real greatness; He will do His work comparatively unknown to the world at large; He will be looked upon as an ordinary individual by those who know Him; He will suffer the vilest kind of persecution at the hands of the Inversive element who dread the force of the principles He will leave behind him. His greatest friends, though mystified as to His real nature, will never grasp His real reality until He is beyond their purview. The Messianic Messenger of the ages will not be fully known until He has passed through the valley of the shadow of death, and is beyond the power of the world to flatter or condemn.

The Jews were looking for a Monarch, and a sign from heaven; the sign came, but the Monarch materialized under a very different form from what they expected. He came as the Son of a carpenter. So the Christians of today are looking for the pomp and glory of a Celestial King. They, too, are looking for a sign from heaven; the sign came with the great perihelion of the planet in 1880 and 1881, and we may depend upon it that the teacher was there, ready and willing, but the world knows Him not, nor will it; the time has passed and He can only be known by the generations which are to follow. Hope, Faith and Charity were the symbols of the Nazarene. They were needed in His day and time, but Life, Light and Love are the great requirements of today; they are the pressing needs of the hour.

Having given our students some brief insight into the purely material aspect of the Naros we will not speak of its infinite ramifications upon the physical plane, but reveal a hidden mystery, a mystery that many occult students have hinted at, spoken of, and even attempted to define, but so far they have failed to grasp either its philosophy, basis, or its potency.

The esoteric aspect of the Naros is known to the occult Initiates as the Mystery of Naronia, and refers to the expansion and contraction of the human constitution. As a sort of illustration let us take the motion of the tides, the ebb and the flow. When the Sun and the Moon occupy the same plane in reference to the Earth, we have the high spring tides, etc. It is the same upon the mental plane, with the human brain. The brain of man, magnetically, expands and becomes illuminated by the Luni-Solar influx, from the new to the full Moon, at which time this magnetic force is at its maximum. It is high tide, so to say, and those who have the care and experience of lunatics will verify the fact, that they become perfect astronomical calendars of the Moon's increase and decrease of light.

Let us take a step further, and we then come to the real dominions of Naronia. SHE is the CYCLE of the SOUL and enacts upon the spiritual plane of human existence, a similar series of events to those of the Naros upon the mundane sphere of life. Hence, we can trace a perfect analogy between the motions of the luminaries in space and the revolution of purely psychic entities within the odylic sphere of man.

Each year of life, the Earth, in her orbit, transits the point in space which she occupied at a person's birth, or in other words, the Sun returns to the same sign and degree of the Zodiac that he occupied in the horoscope. In this transit, the Solar force renews the life energies of the Soul and regalvanizes them with additional force (we are speaking spiritually, understand). These germs of new forces are Virtues, Powers, Potencies and Deific attributes of the great Solar Orb. They are spiritual ovums, or seeds of human possibilities, and if consciously nourished and cherished will evolve powers and states within the Human Soul, which correspond in their action to our hidden spiritual attributes. If unnoticed, uncared for, they remain until other forces polarize them, and then pass onward down their cycle.

When the Moon, in the course of her motion, arrives at the same place during each month, she impregnates these seeds and endows them with magnetic life; therefore, in an occult sense, she confers upon humanity the powers and possibilities of magical forces. It is this Luni-Solar influx of Naronia within the human constitution, then, that controls the real foundation and basis of spiritual development and occult power.

Remember these most important facts, then, and, guided by your own spiritual intuitions in the matter, use this knowledge according to the light which Nature has already given you, or which you shall hereafter receive. We have revealed to you the mystery of Naronia; have given you an outline sketch of its basis in Nature, and its philosophy in human evolution, as near as it is possible without leading you out of your safe path, or bringing you nigh unto dangerous ground.

For those who are ready to utilize this mystery, what we have here said will be plain and easy of comprehension. For those who are not yet ready, rest assured, it is wiser to wait until your spiritual nature is more highly developed.

"REINCARNATION" (A.2.e)

In the letters of Barlet to Arnould in the Fonds Papus at Lyon, Barlet mentions in his letter of April 11, 1888 a "little manuscript on Reincarnation" (almost surely by Davidson) that he had translated, was sending to Arnould, and wanted returned so that he could circulate it to the other neophytes of the Order. No manuscript of this, either French or English, has been preserved, but Guénon, who inherited all of Barlet's H. B. of L. material, several times quotes the H. B. of L. teachings on reincarnation from unspecified *cahiers d'enseignement* of the Order.[1] The material quoted by Guénon, in turn, appears with significant omissions and several additions in the original *Light of Egypt*.[2] The additional material found in Guénon indicates that Guénon is quoting from the manuscript on reincarnation translated by Barlet rather than from *Light of Egypt* or Philipon's French translation.

One of the hallmarks of the H. B. of L. school of occultism is the denial of "reincarnation," the rebirth of the same individual on Earth. For Randolph, Britten, the early Blavatsky, and the H. B. of L., once the monad had successfully become incarnate, its destiny after death lay elsewhere, either in perpetual progress as an immortalized individual through the spheres of the universe or in dissolution and annihilation if the person had not managed to join the soul with the immortal spirit during life. This work clearly sets out the H. B. of L. position and its opposition to the later position of the Theosophical Society.

Three exceptions to the non-reincarnation rule are mentioned in *LOE*, and taken up by Guénon to show the influence of the H. B. of L. on Blavatsky's *Isis Unveiled*.[3] They are: infants dead at birth or shortly after; congenital "idiots"; and "messianic" incarnations. Max Theon apparently did not agree. The Philosophie Cosmique rejects the first two instances,[4] and *La Tradition Cosmique* explains what may have caused the confusion.

---

[1] T Palingenius (Guénon), "Les Néo-Spiritualistes," *La Gnose* II/11 (November 1911), 295-297, reprinted in Guénon 1976, 194-197; Guénon 1952, 217-219, 228.

[2] *LOE*, I, 48-53.

[3] *LOE*, I, 50; Guénon 1982, 99.

[4] *Revue Cosmique*, VI/7, 385. See Chanel 1994a.

Among the four modes of human conception that it describes, very different from the usual views of the subject, it mentions an extremely rare mode in which the embryo produced by a human father is also permeated by a "rarefied being." A struggle for mastery of the being ensues, leading it to become either mentally incapacitated or a genius.[5]

However, the Philosophie Cosmique is less dogmatic on the subject than *LOE*. It states that:

> According to the Doctrine Cosmique, reincarnation is an exception. The common fate after death is either disintegration or else rest until the day of reintegration, the day on which the soul re-acquires a physical body. Reincarnation is impossible except for extremely powerful mentalities (or intelligences) that are already cosmic, i.e., that have already conquered their immortality, and which are recalled to earth by the ardent and *legitimate* desire to complete a mission interrupted by death. This reincarnation, very painful in itself, is always voluntary. It is most rare and almost impossible for it to follow closely on death. It needs to be preceded by a period of rest, of slumber in which the soul rebuilds its energies exhausted by the struggle of its previous life. Its duration depends altogether on the personality of the soul to be reincarnated and on its will; it thus has no fixed length or determinable average.[6]

The Theons' position may have been affected by the current climate. In 1885, when the H. B. of L. came out dogmatically against reincarnation, the theory was predominant both in French spiritualism and in the orientalized occultism of the Theosophical Society. Perhaps the Theons thought it better to oversimplify the matter. They themselves envisaged these rare reincarnations as often being those of ancestors, uniting themselves with an entity at the moment of birth: hence the cult of ancestors in the East,

---

[5] *La Tradition Cosmique*, V, 40-42.

[6] "Questions" in *Revue Cosmique*, I/8, 505.

which made Orientals less susceptible than Westerners to the idea of progress.[7] By the end of the century, the Theons regarded the threat to Western dynamism on the part of pseudo-oriental philosophy as less of a danger than the naïve faith in progress on the part of the reincarnationists.

Max Theon had a more subtle concept of reincarnation, as something not restricted to the personality:

> There are those who reincarnate individuals of the past. Others reincarnate only great gifts, more or less individualized, which is very different. Others again reincarnate only vital and other energies.[8]

He also hints that reincarnation might fluctuate over time. One of the entities quoted in *La Tradition Cosmique* says that long ago, "as the influence of the Enemy [*l'Hostile*] increase[d] in the nervous degree of the physical state, the reincarnation of mental and psychic entities [became] rarer and rarer."[9] The tendency had reversed itself by 1899, when Theon believed that the Enemy was less powerful than in the distant past. Now, he writes: "most of mankind are formations; very, very rarely are they Incarnations. But we may expect that before long, incarnations will become more frequent on earth than in the past."[10] Eventually, according to the Philosophie Cosmique, humanity would regain its birthright and achieve physical immortality.

The text given here reproduces all of the material quoted by Guénon, together with some of the material from *Light of Egypt* that Guénon omits between his quoted passages. The beginning of the chapter in *Light of Egypt*, which may have formed part of the original manuscript, is omitted because it consists largely of a generic attack on Theosophical teachings on reincarnation. Omissions by Guénon from the *Light of Egypt* text are indicated by brackets; variants in Guénon's text are given in notes.

---

[7] See "La Philosophie Védique," in *Revue Cosmique* VII/8, 451; *La Tradition Cosmique*, IV, 21.

[8] Thémanlys 1931, 49.

[9] *La Tradition Cosmique*, II, 238.

[10] Théon 1899b, 297.

REINCARNATION

In the descent of life into external conditions, we must not omit to note the fact that in its descent the monad has had to pass through every state in the soul-world,[1] through the four realms of the Astral Kingdom,[2] and, lastly, re-appear upon the external plane at the lowest point possible, viz.: the mineral. From this point we see it enter successively the mineral, vegetable and animal life waves of the planet. In obedience to the higher and more interior laws of its own especial round, the divine attributes are ever seeking to unfold their involved [*i.e.*, involuted] potentialities. No sooner is one form dispensed with, or its capabilities exhausted,[3] than a new and still higher form is brought into requisition, each in its turn becoming more complex in its structure and diversified in its functions. Thus we see the atom of life commencing at the mineral in the external world. The grand spiral of its evolutionary life is carried forward slowly, imperceptibly, but always progressively.[4] There is no form too simple, no organism too complex, for the inconceivably marvelous adaptability of the human soul in its divine struggles of progressive life.

Yet, throughout the entire cycle of necessity, the character of its genius, the degree of its spiritual emanation, and the state of life to which it originally belonged, are preserved with mathematical exactitude.[5]

---

[1] Guénon's text has "spiritual world."—Editors

[2] Guénon adds: "That is to say, the different states of subtle manifestation, distributed in accordance with their correspondence with the elements."—Editors

[3] Guénon adds: "That is to say, that it has completely developed the entire series of modifications of which it is susceptible."—Editors

[4] Guénon adds: "From the *exterior* point of view, of course."—Editors

[5] Guénon adds: "Which implies the *coexistence* of all the vital modalities." At this point Guénon omits two-and-a-half pages of the *LOE* text including a long footnote in which the author of *LOE*, while stressing that the entity is incarnated once and only once on earth, allows for three exceptions, (1) abortions and still-birth; (2) idiots; and (3) "Messianic" incarnations at the end of the Naros periods. Guénon denies these exceptions as metaphysical impossibilities (Guénon 1952, 219). The theory of *LOE*, with the possible exception of the Messianic incarnation at the end of the Naros, is identical with that espoused in Blavatsky 1877, I, 351ff. —Editors

During the process of the soul's involution, the monad is not actually incarnated in any form whatever. [The soul descends into earthly conditions down the subjective arc of the spiral, and re-ascends upon the objective. Rebirth commences, as before stated, when the objective mineral state is reached.][6] The process of the monad's descent through the various realms, is accomplished by a gradual polarization of its Deific powers, caused by its contact with the gradually externalizing conditions of the downward cycle.[7] [At each step the soul becomes more and more involved within the material. The sphere of the reincarnation, embracing the birth of an external form, its transient life, then death, and the same soul's rebirth in a higher and more perfect form of life, is really comprised between the Mineral and Man. Between these two planes the soul must pass through countless forms and phases.][8]

It is an absolute truth[9] that, as an impersonal being, "man lives on many earths before he reaches this. Myriads of worlds swarm in space where the soul in rudimental states performs its pilgrimages until its cyclic progress enables it to reach[10] the magnificently organized planet, whose glorious function it is to confer upon the soul self-consciousness." At this point alone does it become man. At every other step of the wild, cosmic journey it is but an embryonic being, a fleeting, temporary shape of matter, an impersonal creature in which a part, but only a part, of the imprisoned soul[11] shines forth; [a rudimental form with

---

[6] Omitted in Guénon's text.—Editors

[7] Guénon's text has: "the descending and subjective arc of the spiral cycle."—Editors

[8] Omitted in Guénon's text.—Editors

[9] Guénon's text adds: "which the adept author of Ghost-land expresses when he says ..." Compare Ghost Land, 237-240. The use of the pronoun "he" indicates the belief of the author of the reincarnation manuscript (and possibly of Guénon as well) that the Adept Louis, and not Emma Hardinge Britten, was the author of Ghost Land. Guénon 1952, 217, begins quoting from the "cahiers d'enseignment" of the H. B. of L. at this point in the text.—Editors

[10] Guénon adds: "by the gradual extension of this development until it has attained a determined zone, corresponding to the special state which is considered here."—Editors

[11] Guénon's text reads: "of the non-individualized human soul."—Editors

rudimental functions, ever living, dying, then sustaining a brief spiritual existence only to be re-born again, and thus to sustain the successive round of births and deaths. With each change new organs and new functions are acquired to be utilized by the gradually expanding soul as a means of further development. We see it in the fire of the flint, and even as we watch the revolving sparks of the mineral soul, we can see it burst forth to the sunlight in the garb of the lowly lichen. It guards the snow white purity of the lotus, and animates the aromatic glory of the rose. It is the butterfly springing from the chrysalid shell, and the nightingale singing in the grove. "From stage to stage it evolves; new births and new deaths; anon to die, but sure to live again; ever striving and revolving upon the whirling, toilsome, dreadful, rugged path until it awakes for the last time on earth; awakes once more a material shape, a thing of dust, a creature of flesh and blood, but now a man."][12] The grand, self-conscious stage, humanity, is attained, and the climax of earthly incarnation is reached. Never again will it enter the material matrix or suffer the pains of material reincarnation. Henceforth its rebirths are in the realm of spirit.

Those who hold the strangely illogical doctrine of a multiplicity of human births, have certainly never evolved the lucid state of soul consciousness[13] within themselves. Had they done so, the theory of reincarnation as held by a vast number of talented men and women, well versed in worldly wisdom, would not have received the slightest recognition at the present day. We would strongly impress the fact that an external education is comparatively worthless as a means of obtaining a true knowledge of nature.

[One does not find in nature any analogy in favor of reincarnation, but, on the contrary, one finds numerous analogies to the contrary.[14]] Remember, that though the acorn becomes the oak, and the coconut the palm; the oak,

---

[12] The bracketed passage is omitted in Guénon's text.—Editors
[13] Guénon's text has: "the lucid state of spiritual consciousness."—Editors
[14] Added in Guénon 1952, 296.—Editors

though giving birth to myriad others, never again becomes an acorn, nor the palm the juicy nut. So it is with man. When once the soul becomes incarnated in the human organism, and thus attains the consciousness of external life, man becomes a self-responsible being, accountable for his actions.[15] [This accountability constitutes his earth karma, and the reward or punishment as the case may be is consciously and divinely administered in the state which each individual soul has prepared for itself. The soul is not ignorantly ushered again into the world, completely unconscious of its past load of karma. Such a means of redemption, instead of being divine, would be devoid of justice. It would be diabolical. When human laws punish the criminal, he is conscious of the misdeed for which he is suffering. If this were not so the punishment would be horribly unjust. For this reason we do not punish irresponsible children, nor insane men. It is thoroughly useless, however, to deal any further with such a transcendent delusion. We will, therefore, only say that][16] all of the so-called re-awakenings of latent memories, by which certain people profess to remember certain past lives can be explained, and in fact are only really explainable, by the simple laws of affinity and form.

Each race of human beings is immortal in itself; so likewise is each round. The first round never becomes the second, but those belonging to the first round become the parents or originators of the second[17] so that each round constitutes a great planetary family which contains within itself races, sub-races and still minor groups of human souls; each state being formed by the laws of its karma, and

---

[15] Guénon's text adds: "the soul never re-passes through any of its rudimental states. A recent publication affirms that 'those who have led a noble life, worthy of a king (even in the body of a mendicant), in their last terrestrial existence, will live again as nobles, kings, or other persons of high rank.' But we know what kings and nobles have been in the past and are in the present, often the worst specimens of humanity that it is possible to imagine, from the spiritual point of view. Such assertions are only good to show that their authors speak solely under the inspiration of sentimentality, and that they lack knowledge." See Guénon 1952, 228. —Editors

[16] Omitted in Guénon's text. —Editors

[17] Guénon adds in a note: "These are the *pitris* of the Hindu tradition."—Editors

the laws of its form and the laws of its affinity—a trinity of laws.[18] [At the expiration of one round, the polar day of evolution is brought to a close and the life wave leaves the shores of the planet. The second round of humanity—offspring of the first—does not commence until the human life wave, having gone round the whole planetary chain again reaches the planet, a period considerably over 15,000,000 years.][19] Hence man is similar to the acorn and the oak. The embryonic, impersonal soul becomes the man, just as the acorn becomes the oak; and as the oak gives birth to innumerable acorns or embryonic oaks, so does man, in his turn, become the means of giving spiritual birth to innumerable souls. There is a complete correspondence between the two.[20]

---

[18] Guénon's text has: "a great family constituted by the reunion of different groups of human souls, each condition being determined by the laws of its activity, those of its form and those of its affinity . . . a trinity of laws."—Editors

[19] Omitted in Guénon's text. —Editors

[20] Guénon's text adds: "and it is for this reason that the ancient Druids rendered such great honors to this tree, which was honored above all the others by these powerful hierophants." The reference to Druids coincides with Davidson's interests and also with those of Barlet and his circle, and probably reflects the original manuscript.—Editors

"LAWS OF MAGIC MIRRORS" (A.3.a)

No English manuscript of the "Laws of Magic Mirrors" has survived. The French version of the work in the Fonds Papus was translated in 1889 by Barlet, from a manuscript provided by Davidson.[1] Although the translation bears the reference "Peter Davidson, Provincial Grand Master of the Eastern Section," it is clear that Davidson was not the author of the complete work. The First Part of the text is taken almost verbatim from the 28 rules for mirror clairvoyance given by Randolph in *Seership!* published in 1870.[2] Accordingly, Randolph's version of the First Part (the 28 rules) is given here with significant changes indicated by notes, and with the passages in Randolph's work omitted from the Lyon manuscript indicated by square brackets.

The Second Part of the "Laws of Magic Mirrors" is almost certainly by Davidson himself. It clearly grows out of the more antiquarian English crystal-scrying tradition of ceremonial spirit evocations and dismissals, and includes a section on the proper method of determining astrological times and controlling spirits for mirror work. All of this is foreign to P. B. Randolph but could easily have been duplicated from the works of Agrippa, Trithemius, Barrett—and most immediately from Fryar, who in 1870 had written *The History and Mystery of the Magic Crystal* for Emma Hardinge Britten's magazine.[3]

The actual magic mirror ideally to be used by the neophytes of the H. B. of L., however, is decidedly un-English and again

---

[1] Letter of Barlet to Arnould, July 6, 1889. Lyon, Fonds Papus, Ms. 5491—II (6). The version published by Archè (H. B. of L. 1988) reproduces the Lyon version.

[2] Randolph 1870, itself a re-working of part of the lost pamphet *Clairvoyance...* (1860).

[3] Fryar published part of this, together with the substance of Randolph's 28 rules, in his edition of Thomas Welton's *Mental Magic*, which he dedicated to another English scryer, Captain Morrison ("Zadkiel"). Fryar's seer was his wife, whom he called "The British Seeress" and praised widely in the Spiritualist press before the formal appearance of the H. B. of L. He also publicized the traditional ceremonials for calls and dismissals. Fryar offered for sale a variety of mirror ceremonials, including an old manuscript on scrying entitled "Crystallomancy, or the Art of Drawing Spirits into the Crystal." The French members of the H. B. of L. adopted these English ceremonials in their mirror use (see Sédir, 52-53). The sequence of rulers and hours and the adjustments for the different seasons given here by Davidson are the same as those given in Barrett, II, 139ff (originally from Agrippa's *Fourth Book*).

reflects Randolph's practice. English crystal seers in the nineteenth century, following John Dee, appear to have favored simple crystals or polished pieces of stone for scrying, but on Randolph's visits to France in 1855, 1857 and 1861-1862 he had become acquainted with the complex mirrors commonly used by the leading French Mesmerists, such as the Baron Dupotet and Alphonse Cahagnet. These were usually coated with some substance (or contained the substance between plates of glass) designed to retain the "magnetic fluid" thought necessary for the higher sorts of visions.[4] In turn, this substance was "charged" with magnetism by a variety of means. In Randolph's system, the process of charging was sexual. He always kept the details of his process secret, but, as far as can be learned, his process played a role in the workings of the H. B. of L. as well. In his *Eulis* (Randolph 1874), Randolph had quoted at length Colonel Stephen Fraser's description in *Twelve Years in India* of the secret erotic "dance of the Garoonahs" by which a special "parappthaline" substance was sexually charged for coating magic "Bhattah mirrors." Davidson subsequently republished the piece in its entirety in the *Theosophist* for December 1883,[5] and Fryar hinted broadly at the secret processes in his later works (see Fryar 1888). Fryar offered imported "Bhattah mirrors" for sale and Davidson manufactured his own mirrors and in his advertisement in the first number of the *Occult Magazine* was careful to point out that they had the proper "paranaphthaline" surface.[6]

There is reference to another manuscript work circulated by the H. B. of L. entitled "Instructions for Neophytes in Use of Mirrors." This does not appear to be identical with the "Laws of Magic Mirrors" given here, but its precise contents are unknown. It is unlikely in any case, however, that the secret sexual processes of consecration of the mirrors was explicitly stated in the manuscript. The neophyte was probably expected to divine the

---

[4] The method of making these complex mirrors after the manner of A. L. Cahagnet was given in *Art Magic*, in Welton, and in Cahagnet.

[5] Peter Davidson, "The Bhattah Mirrors." *The Theosophist* 5/3 (December 1883), 72-74. See also Sédir, 62ff.

[6] *The Occult Magazine* I/1 (February 1885), 8.

proper method of consecration from "The Mysteries of Eulis," perhaps with oral instruction where possible. In 1885, for example, Davidson sent one of his sons to Rochester, New York, to make magic mirrors for Mrs. Josephine Cables and her circle in the H. B. of L.

The actual practice of developing clairvoyance in the magic mirror is further described in the fifth and sixth "Rules for Occult Training" in the "Mysteries of Eros" [A.3.b].

LAWS OF MAGIC MIRRORS
FIRST PART

I. To have impatience in these things[1] will delay, or totally prevent, success. But unto the true seeking soul cometh ever the real light of the divine magnetic power of true magic. But it cometh in its fullness only to the spirit that is self-possessed and calm. Remember what the Grand Master, himself a genius rare, and, therefore, a true seer,[2] says: "The Rosicrucian, the acolyte, the adept, reaches forth for the infinite, in *Power and goodness*, which are the keys that unlock the gates of glory; and he sees, hears, knows and healeth the mental, physical, social, moral and domestic ills of humankind, by means of his goodness and his mighty secret whereof but few in an age are naturally possessed, and still fewer attain to, for want of WILL and PATIENCE. For only the children of the empyrean, by nature or adoption, are admitted to the treasure-house of the underlying and overflowing real.[3] Such, only, have the true medical and supernal inspiration, and inhale the diviner breath of God. . . . Whosoever hath a strong Will, and purity of purpose, may, if they elect, unbar the doors of mystery, enter her wide and her strange domain, and revel in knowledge denied to baser Souls."

De Novalis[4] says: "The fortuitous is not unfathomable; it, too, hath a regularity of its own. He or she having a *right sense* for the fortuitous, hath already the signet and seal of a royal power, naturally to know then use, not all mystery, but much that lies very, *very* far beyond the ken of mortals

---

[1] Lyon ms.: "in everything relating to the mysteries constituting occult Science." — Editors

[2] Lyon ms.: "The Grand Master of our Order has said." Randolph's reference is to Hargrave Jennings, and the "grand mastership" is taken over, without more ado, by the H. B. of L.—which certainly would not have recognized Hargrave Jennings as Grand Master. —Editors

[3] Lyon ms.: "treasure of the Virgin of the World."—Editors

[4] Unidentified. Surely not Friedrich von Hardenberg (Novalis).—Editors

who are not thus endowed by nature, or have not grown thereto by experience and choice." Such persons can readily determine *truly* that which to others less gifted, or with less COURAGE, WILL, PERSISTENCE, PATIENCE, and quietude must forever remain unknown. For one with these qualities necessarily commands both information and obedience from the viewless intelligences and subordinate powers and agencies of the universe. Such can seek destiny for others, in her own halls; solve her riddles by her own laws; and read, as in an open book, the future—the things that shall befall an inquirer in all that pertaineth to body, soul,[5] health, affections, and possessions; and, still casting forward and upward the Soul's keen glance, can discern the final result and summing up of being, and all by means of the phasoul [?] and phantorama, as revealed to the Searcher's vision onto the surface of [the Symph,] the magic mirror, [the peerless disk of La Trinue.][6]

II. There are glasses of three grades: the mule, or small neuter; the female and the male. The first is small, but fine; more a philosophic toy than of practical use; has two foci, is good for clouds and flame, symbols and shadows; but the magnetic filament is very thin, and the two foci not always mathematically true; they are quite easily warped and broken, cost but little, and are mainly used by fortune-telling, vagrant gypsies of the lowest class, and who are not able to procure a higher and better grade Trinue.[7]

The mirror next in size to the imperfect sort just described, is, in mirrorist's parlance, called well-sexed, or female, because its foci are true, its polish superb, its power great, and sensitiveness most remarkable.[8] [There are magic mirrors in existence really not much superior to these last, valued at fabulous sums. For instance, the one that covers

---

[5] The Lyon ms. mistranslates the English at this point, reading "the soul has its health," etc.—Editors

[6] The derivation of "La Trinue" is unknown. —Editors

[7] Lyon ms.: "mirror."—Editors

[8] Lyon ms. adds "This is the mirror appropriate for men."—Editors

the back of the Sultan's watch, for Abdul Aziz, of Turkey, possesses one of rare beauty, seeing that it consists of a single diamond concaved out; and its value is something over $400,000. The late Maha-raja Dhuleep Singh[9] possessed three: one an immense diamond, the other an enormous ruby, and the third composed of the largest emerald known in the world; and yet, despite the enormous pecuniary difference in value between these and a Trinue of the second order, it is doubtful if the former, for special uses, can ever equal the latter. For a glass of that grade will hold a magnetic film nearly *eight inches* in thickness, flattened on the top, quite as good as a first grade male mirror for seeing all things, and only inferior thereto in not affording a magnetic surface sufficiently extended to admit of the finer and grander phantoramic displays, and not thick enough to enable the seer to readily affect distant persons, or to fix the called-up images or simulacra of distant persons, or the locality of the absent living or dead. But, for all ordinary purposes, it serves admirably, and, in my judgment, is altogether superior to the celebrated crystal glove, belonging to Charles Trinius, of San Francisco, California, for which $3,000 was offered and refused. They are more expensive than the male-glass; more of them are made and imported; and they are the kind generally in use throughout the Western Continent.

Not long ago, a "Reform" paper publisher declared he had no faith in mirrors; and yet, within a month thereafter,

---

[9] Randolph's use of "late" to describe Dalip Singh would appear to be an error, unless he means that Dalip Singh was formerly a Maharajah. Dalip Singh (1838-1893) was Maharaja of the Punjab until deposed by the British in 1849 and exiled to England. Paul Johnson's researches (Johnson 1990, 1994) cast fascinating light on the intricate connections between H. P. Blavatsky and the entourage of Dalip Singh, starting with HPB's assertion that she had first met her Master Morya in Hyde Park in London in 1851, when he had come to London with "the Indian Princes." He draws especial attention to the mysterious figure of a Rajput raja-yogin and magician, Gulab-Lal-Singh, who appears in her *Caves and Jungles of Hindustan,* whom HPB first met in the house of a dethroned native prince —who can be no other than Dalip Singh—in England about 1853. Dalip Singh was resident in England at the times P. B. Randolph visited there, and it is possible Randolph at least met him.—Editors

published column after column to prove the reality of precisely the same thing. For both the principles, rationale, methods and results, are *identical*; namely, spiritual photography. but, in reality, the man only objected to the one, because it did not originate among the faithful of his peculiar household, and commended another form of the same thing, because it *did* thus originate, and was backed up by wealthy lawyers, doctors, judges, and moneyed men, most of whom, judging from their style of argument, possessed more greenbacks than brains. I and my friends are poor, and can't afford to buy up the proprietors of papers, which, you see, makes all the difference in the world; and hence there is a marked contrast in regard to the claims of wealthy Tweedledee, and impecunious Tweedledum, who are, after all, precisely right, because exactly on the same ground. Spiritual and electric photography is, and ever was and will be, true; and crystal seership, and mirror visions, and such photography, are one and the same thing, operated by precisely the same laws and principles, and underlaid and subtended by precisely the same wonderful esoteric chemistry; and the only difference, if any, lies in the fact that but few persons can get spiritual photographs, while a great many can obtain very satisfactory, but evanescent pictures, by means of a differently sensitized plate—a fact I have seen demonstrated hundreds of times, as thousands of others have whom I never saw, heard, or knew.]

The male mirror is superior to either of the others. Its foci are *four inches apart*. The basin over *seven inches* by *five in the clear ovoid*, and of course its *field* is immense. They are better adapted to *professional* use than private experiment, because they are capable of, and frequently do, exhibit *three* separate and distinct *vivoramas*, at one and the same time, to as many distinct on-lookers.[10] [I have often wished I could make these mirrors; but that is impossible, as three conti-

---

[10] Lyon ms. reverses the meaning here, saying that the male "is more suitable for the use of beginners, because . . . ." It adds that this sort of mirror "is specially appropriate for women."—Editors

nents furnish the materials composing them. And even the frames and glasses must be imported from beyond the seas; as must also the strangely sensitive material wherewith the sympathetic rings are filled; concerning which rings and their brightening, when the future is well, and their strange darkening, when evil impends, or friends fall off, and lovers betray, the quadroons of Louisiana, as well as the women of Syria, could tell strangely thrilling tales.[11] And in consequence of the importance attached to these rings and mirrors, counterfeits of them have been, in times past, put forward, albeit the parties who obtained them were themselves to blame, seeing that but one person—Vilmara—ever imported either to this country.]

III. No mirror or ring must be allowed to be handled much, if at all, by other than the owner thereof; because such handling mixes the magnetisms and destroys their sensitiveness. Others may *look* into them, holding by the box in which the frame is kept, but *never* touching either frame or glass.

IV. When the glass surface becomes soiled or dusty, it may be cleaned with fine soap-suds, rinsed well, washed with alcohol, or rubbed with a little fluoric acid, and then polished with soft velvet or chamois leather.

V. A mirror must not be neglected; but should frequently be magnetized by passes with the *right* hand, five minutes at a time.[12] This is calculated to keep it *alive*, and give it *strength* and *power*.

VI. Passes with the *left* hand add to its magnetic *sensitiveness*.[13]

VII. The longer time, and frequency of its use, the better it becomes.

---

[11] In Randolph 1867, 15, 25-26, Randolph explains the practice of lovers or friends exchanging such magnetized sensitive rings; they brighten when the other is well, and darken when ill or suffering misfortune.—Editors

[12] Lyon ms.: "on Sunday, at sunrise."—Editors

[13] Lyon ms.: "to give it sensitiveness, it must be magnetized on Monday at sunrise, with the left hand, facing East, with a prayer to God . . . ."—Editors

VIII. The somnifying or magnetizing power of the glass is obtained to a greater degree than is possible by hand-mesmerism, by looking at its center in perfect quietude. It will magnetize many who defy magnetism.

IX. When used, the mirror's back must always be *toward* the light; but its face *never*. *That* is fatal to its visional power.

X. The position of the glass, held or placed, must be *oblique*; that is to say, its top must lean *from* the on-looker.

[XI. When amateurs, or several, look in at one time, it should be suspended; but must then be touched by nobody at all.]

XII. The proof of the proper focus or position of the glass is when no image or thing whatever is reflected in it. Change its inclination, or move the head, till a clear, plain, whitish-black, deep-watery *volume* is seen, which will not be till the magnetism has time to collect. That surface is the magnetic plane of the mirror; and in and upon it all things seeable in a Trinue[14] are beheld.

XIII. The first things seen are clouds. They appear to be on or in the mirror, but in reality are not so, but on the upper surface of the magnetic field above it. That magnetic plane collects there from the eyes of the onlooker. Persons of a magnetic temperament—brunette, dark-eyed brown-skinned, and with dark hair—charge it *quicker*, but no more *effectually* than those of the opposite temperament—blonde or *blondette*—who are electric in temperament.

XIV. The male[15] is not so *easily* so developed into seership as the female sex; but become exceedingly powerful and correct when they are so. Virgins see best; next to them are widows.

---

[14] Lyon ms.: "mirror."—Editors
[15] Ambiguous. The Lyon ms. reads "male mirror."—Editors

XV. In all cases the boy before puberty, and the girl in her pucilage [virginity], make the quickest and sharpest seers. Their magnetism is pure, unmixed, unsexed; and purity means power in all things magnetic and occult.

XVI. White clouds are favorable; affirmative; good.

XVII. Black clouds are the exact reverse: inauspicious; bad.

XVIII. Violet, green, blue, presage coming joy—are excellent.

XIX. Red, crimson, orange, yellow, mean, danger, trouble, sickness, "beware," deceptions, losses, betrayal, slander, grief, and indicate surprises of a disagreeable character.

XX. To affect a distant person, invoke the image. Hold it by Will, and fix the mind and purpose steadily upon the *person*; and whoever he or she may be—no matter where they are— the telegraph of Soul will find them, somewhere within the spaces. But, observe this law: Nothing is surer than, if the seer's purpose be evil, it will react upon him or herself with terrible effect, sooner or later; wherefore all are strictly cautioned to *be* and *do* good, only; for:

XXI. Remember the aerial spaces are thronged with innumerable intelligences, Celestial and the reverse. The latter have Force; the former possess Power. To reach the good ones, the heart must correspond.[16] In many ways will they respond, when invoked with prayerful feelings; and they will protect and shield from the bad—and there are countless hosts of the bad on the serried confines of the two great worlds—Matter and spirit; myriads of grades of them, [whereof the *puling*, phenomenal spiritualist never yet has even dreamed.] These malign forces are many and terrible, but they can never reach or successfully assault the Soul

---

[16] Lyon ms.: "be in harmony with them."—Editors

that relies on God in perfect faith, and which invokes the Good, the Beautiful and the True.[17]

XXII. The face of the mirror should *never* be exposed to the chemical and actinic influence of direct sunlight, because it ruins the magnetic susceptibility, [just as it does the sensitized plate of the photographer; and no mirror once spoiled can be made good as before, without sending it to Europe to be re-made entirely. Moonlight, on the contrary, benefits them. The back must not be tampered with, or removed, for any light striking it will at once completely ruin all its magnetic properties; hence its careful sealing.] So also are extremes of heat and cold injurious to them, [because either will destroy the parabolic-ovoid shape of the glass, which done, it is thenceforth useless,] for it will no longer retain its hold upon the magnetic effluvium from the eyes—[the sensitive sheet upon which its clouds and other marvels are mirrored;] but it will roll off like water from hot iron [and, in the words of Vilmara, "be good never—no more!"]

XXIII. Whatever appears upon the left hand of the mirror-looker, as he gazes into it, is real; that is to say, is a picture of an actual thing.

XXIV. Whatever appears upon the right hand, as he looks into it, is symbolical.

XXV. Ascending clouds or indistinct shadows are affirmative replies to questions that may be asked—if silently, it makes no difference.

---

[17] The Lyon ms. adds a caution: "It is from these forces that the young, inexperienced neophyte must strictly guard himself. His intimate consciousness will tell him infallibly which powers include the object which he has in view. Remember that *an irreligious occultist is evil.* He is only the unconscious instrument of malignant powers: nothing that he should flatter himself that he can control. [?] At death, his soul falls into the infrahuman spheres of existence; his chance of immortality is lost forever, and in the midst of the Elementaries whom he thinks to have made his slaves, he leads a malicious existence of uncertain duration, until, his vitality being entirely spent, he falls gradually into unconsciousness, a phantom which vanishes, and disintegrates atom by atom into the elements which surround it. Then he disappears finally, leaving not even a shadow after him."—Editors

XXVI. Descending clouds are the negations to all such questions.

XXVII. Clouds or shadows moving toward the seer's right hand are signals from spiritual beings, indicative of their presence and interest.

XXVIII. When they move toward the left hand of the seer, it means, "Done for this time,"[18]—the séance is ended for the present.[19]

SPECIFIC INSTRUCTIONS

When you have been able to procure a good mirror, one you have magnetized yourself as has been explained above, to make it perfectly responsive for you, begin your operations by first of all purifying your body to make it a more appropriate abode for the soul.

Let the period of purification be continued as follows for seven days.

Observe an absolute continence, rise as near the rising of the Sun as circumstances permit, wash your body with cold or warm water and rub it down well with a towel or glove reserved for this use.

After dressing, turn your thoughts towards God, the Great First Cause, and in a spirit of humble devotion raise towards heaven your prayer and your aspirations of the morning.

Next, if circumstances permit, take a two-mile walk and, as you walk, observe everything, especially natural objects; reflect on them and take note of your first impression on

[18] Lyon ms.: "or rather, we cannot accede to your request."—Editors

[19] Lyon ms. adds: "Have a care to liberate all of the intelligences who have been able to manifest themselves (visible or not); never forget in any case this formality, and then put away your mirror."—Editors

each object or each person. After your walk, eat breakfast. If you are then accustomed not to smoke or drink fermented drinks, your best nourishment will be fresh milk, bread made of good wheat, a little butter and fruit; but if you are just beginning to abandon alcohol and the use of alcoholic liquors, drink strong coffee; this will be very effective to counterbalance the former use of tobacco. It must be added here that, in any case, meat must not be eaten. There are, nonetheless, some occasions when a good vegetarian regime is not possible. In those cases, it is necessary at least to reduce the quantity of meat to the least amount possible and to add as many fruits or vegetables as one can.

During the day, keep a mastery as absolute as possible over your intelligence; watch even your small faults and guard against them. Let no one excite your anger; anger dims and obscures the interior light which is awakening.

Remember that it is only when the soul is calm and sheltered from trouble, when the spirit is opened to superior influences, that the scenes of the magical world unfold.

Contrasts cannot subsist together; they have their respective spheres; the eyes of the soul open on an ocean without limits when it becomes free, when earthly objects disappear from view, and the visions of the spiritual world are reflected on its profound, calm bosom.

Finally, see to it that each day marks some progress over the day before; make the resolution of correcting every fault. Take a light meal, like the one in the morning. Meditate seriously on every spiritual thing; desire the progress and the success of all your brothers, and retire to rest at an early hour, without forgetting your evening prayer and thanksgiving for the day which you have just been granted.

Note: These rules naturally apply to the crystal as well as to the mirror.

SECOND PART
RITE OF CONSECRATION OF CRYSTALS
AND OF MIRRORS

Prerequisites:

A special room, employed only for Occult Science.

Windows veiled with violet drapes so that there is no other light except that given by the small crystal lamps (those used in chemistry laboratories will be suitable).

Two small tripods 18 inches in height, the feet of which must be made, one of polished iron, one of polished bronze and the last of copper; the bowl in which perfumes are burned must be of brass.

A small pedestal or table covered with a white linen cloth; and another covering of white linen for the floor.

Fire, incense, pure olive oil, wicks of cotton and a white linen cloth for them to lie on, and finally a white linen surplice.

Place the table covered with its white linen cloth at the far east corner of the room; place the mirror or crystal in the center of the table, and the lamps of crystal around it; on each side of the table, place the tripods with the incense. At the head of the table, put a white linen cloth (a white covering) on the floor. If you are using a mirror, you should incline it at an angle suitable to finding its focal point; if you are using a crystal, you should place it flat. A glass of new wine will be appropriate.

All being made ready, you must enter the room, barefoot, head uncovered, just after you have bathed and dressed, without your clothes—dressed in a white surplice, like a robe, and you proceed as follows:

Light the lamp and place the incense on the tripod to make it burn. This incense must be of the same sort as that used in Buddhist temples; then, on your knees, facing the table and the East, in a pious concentration of spirit, address the following prayer: "O God, all powerful and very merciful, our Father and our Creator, I ask you humbly that it please your majesty to deliver me from all bad and worldly desires; move me so that I keep myself in the presence of the Celestial Beings who, with your permission, respond to my prayer, to my supplication, during the consecration of this mirror (or crystal) to accomplish my operations, by your divine power, for the interest and the good of my brothers and fellow creatures. I beseech you humbly in your name, you, Eternal God, who live and reign without end over the world. Amen!

Then, extend the *left* hand toward the East and lift up your heart and your soul in reciting what follows: "O God, all powerful, you, Grand Author Supreme of all Goodness, of all Mercy, of all Wisdom and of all Justice, I beseech you humbly, deign to permit your Grand and Powerful Servant Saint Michael the Archangel, governor and chief of numerous legions of heavenly Spirits, under the direction of whom humanity is guided through the evils which afflict the earth, that he turn his holy and heavenly influence on this mirror (or, this crystal, as the case may be) so that any celestial intelligence that I may evoke may be permitted to assume his Angelic form, to appear in this mirror and to respond to all questions that I may desire to pose to him in a manner that is appropriate and well-suited [bien seante] to his heavenly nature. I pray thus in the name of the true, always living God, by the grace of the Holy Spirit, and your power, to you who live and reign from infinite centuries to infinite centuries. Amen!"

When afterwards you desire an evocation, ask (Archangel) Michael to send a spirit, by the following formula:

For the Evocation of a Spirit

"O! Infinite Source of Light and of Love. O! You, eternal and all powerful Spirit, hear the voice of your child. O! celestial being who govern the present cycle of the World; Michael, powerful Archangel of the Sun, you who raise yourself daily in the Eastern Heavens, we, your humble disciples of the second order (or of the second rank), we beseech you humbly that our senses may be clarified by the ministry of your Holy messengers; grant me (or, to the seer, as the case may be) permission to see clearly and to evoke spiritual visions in this sacred mirror (or, this crystal). Help me, then, great and powerful Angel of the solar Fire. If it please you, send one of your messengers to guard this consecrated instrument, and instruct me in the sacred Art of pre-Science. I pray you for this humbly, for the honor and glory of the sacred Science. Amen, Amen, Amen!

This is a formula of evocation to call the guardian angel of the mirror (or crystal). After having recited the evocation of the Spirit, recite the following with an intense concentration of spirit.

"In the name of the Eternal and Omnipresent Creator, in whom we move, live and have our being, I beseech the faithful guardian of this mirror to manifest his presence now for me (or, to the eyes of the seer). Hasten, hasten, on the wings of the air, because we await you, and let all honor be rendered to your Master who sends you. Amen!"

When the guardian is present, you can ask him for a particular vision (if you desire it), in the following terms: "And now, angel guardian, I request you to manifest a true and faithful vision of [state the vision desired] and let that which I have omitted not be omitted, you, in granting it to me in the name of this symbol [pentacle or sign of the guardian]. Amen!"

The symbol must be requested when the mirror is dedicated, which is the first use to be made of it.

After the consecration, never omit to dedicate a mirror destined for occult revelations to the *Angels of the Sun* because the *Sun dominates* or governs in the present cycle.

This rite of consecration must be begun on the morning of the first Sunday after June 21st, just at the hour of the rising of the Sun in the location of the operation, and then repeated on each of the six following days, at the rising of the Sun, with the following variations:

After having recited the evocation of the Spirit, add for Monday:

> "And you, brilliant Gabriel, celestial angel, who govern the sphere of the moon, grant us your aid and your power in the exercise of this divine art, and let peace and harmony exist among us always!"

On Tuesday, add:

> "Strong and brilliant Samael, who govern the sphere of Mars, etc."

On Wednesday, add:

> "Brilliant Raphael, sweet messenger of God, who govern the sphere of Mercury, etc."

On Thursday, add:

> "Glorious and benevolent Zachariel, who govern the sphere of Jupiter, etc."

On Friday, add:

> "Angel of Love, brilliant Anael, Prince of the astral light, who govern the sphere of Venus, etc."

On Saturday, add:

> "August Cassiel, mysterious spirit of the hidden Science, who govern the sphere of Saturn, etc."

In using the mirror (or crystal), remember that whatever you request must be governed by the appropriate day; that is, that the question must be posed on the day which governs the subject with which it has to do. In occult matters, the different subjects are governed as follows:

All questions of Esoteric Religion and of Sacred Science are governed by *Michael*.

Those concerning sex, of generation, of animal and vegetable life, by *Gabriel*.

Those concerning fire, courage, will, war, by *Samael*.

Poetry, music, joy, birth, marriage, love, by *Anael*.

Sacerdotalism, the Church, rites and ceremonies, by *Zachariel*.

All questions of profound and hidden mysteries, the world of Elementaries, Death and the dead, sickness, occult troubles, by *Cassiel*.

These brief instructions are given solely to furnish clear instructions for the appropriate direction of the operations.

Once the mirror (or the crystal) has been duly consecrated seven times, it must be placed aside, reserved for use, and no one must be admitted to handle it.

What must be done next is to train a special seer, and for this a young, pure virgin [girl] of about 13 years is the best seer; although she is not essential. Any young person of good and moral soul will do, if she is naturally of a clairvoyant temperament. A boy of pure soul, or a youth, can be selected to be magnetized and patiently trained in the practice of the mirror on Sunday, at the hour of the Sun, and on Wednesday, at the hour of Mercury.

Because each planet governs in its day the following hours, *viz.*, the first, the eighth and the 15th, counting from the rising of the sun.

To find the true planetary hour, divide into 12 parts the time which must elapse between the rising and setting of the Sun. The 12 parts are called the *planetary hours of the day*; and from the setting to the rising of the Sun, these are the *planetary hours of the night*. As a consequence, the planetary hour will sometimes be greater and sometimes less than our ordinary terrestrial hour, according to the houses.

The hours are, in rotation, as follows: Saturn, Jupiter, Mars, the Sun, Venus, Mercury and the Moon.

For example, suppose that the time between the rising and the setting of the Sun is 9 hours: the planetary hour will be only 45 minutes. If now we wish to know the hour of Mercury, for a Sunday, since the Sun governs the first hour, Venus the second and Mercury the third, the two planetary hours for the first two being of 45 minutes each, or a total of an hour and a half, the hour of Mercury will commence one hour and a half after the rising of the Sun and will continue for 45 minutes.

After this will come the hour of the Moon, then that of Saturn, and so on. Each planet governs the first hour of its day, beginning with the rising of the Sun.

The hours of the night are found in continuing the series of planets in the same manner.

To find the length of the planetary hour of a given day, divide by 6 the time (in hours, minutes and seconds) of the setting of the Sun for that day.

To find the length of the planetary hour of the night, divide by 6 the hour of the rising of the Sun, and the result will give the length of the planetary hour during the preceding night.

Peter Davidson
Provincial Grand Master
of the Eastern Section

THE MYSTERIES OF EROS (A.3.B) □ 213

"THE MYSTERIES OF EROS" (A.3.b)

After being circulated separately for several years to the neophytes, the practical instructions comprising the three degrees of
Grade I of the H. B. of L. were compiled and systematized in 1886
or early 1887 by Burgoyne, who was then in Denver, Colorado.
By that time the relationship between Burgoyne and Davidson
had soured considerably, and the "Mysteries of Eros" or "Mysteries of Erosa," as the compilation was called, omitted all reference to Davidson and was circulated primarily to Burgoyne's
own students in the Exterior Circle, first in manuscript, then in
Edison "mimeograph" and finally as a 52-page printed pamphlet, bound in silk, published by Dr. Henry Wagner in Denver.

The text published here is from a manuscript acquired by
the Houghton Library at Harvard University in 1929 (Ms Am
947, Dexter Fund). Its provenance is unknown, but appended to
the "Mysteries of Eros" is a platitudinous text entitled "Esoteric
Development" (omitted here) by Charles H. Mackay who was, in
the late 1880s the managing editor of Hiram Erastus Butler's
magazine *The Esoteric* and who went on to propound New
Thought as the "West Gate Philosophy" in his magazine *The Oracle*. Butler was a sexual mage and astrologer in his own right and
published his ideas under the guise of "Solar Biology" and
founded a curious group called G.N.K.R. (Genii of Nations,
Knowledge and Religions) which he headed under the name
"Adhy-apaka, the Hellenic Ethnomedon." Madame Blavatsky
railed against the sexual magic of Butler's group, stating that the
initials G.N.K.R. actually stood for "Gulls Nabbed by Knaves
and Rascals."[1] Madame Blavatsky consistently equated Butler's
group with the H. B. of L., claiming that "it was a mere repetition—more enlarged and barefaced, and with a wider, bolder
programme, still a repetition—of the now defunct 'H. B. of L.,'
with its mysterious appeals of four years ago to the 'Dissatisfied'
with 'the Theosophical Mahatmas.'" Despite this, however, But-

---

[1] See H. P. Blavatsky, "On Pseudo-Theosophy," *Lucifer* IV (March 1889), 1-12; *BCW* XI, 45-
61; "Second Letter of H. P. Blavatsky to the American Convention held in Chicago,
Illinois, April 28-29th," *BCW* XI, 161-169; "Crows in Peacock Feathers," *The Boston Daily
Globe*, March 8, 1889, 4, reprinted by Michael Gomes in *The Canadian Theosophist*, Novem-
ber-December 1985, 114-117. See also G. R. S. Mead [B.8.d], 63.

ler's sexual doctrines emphasize a different side of the role of sex in occultism from that chosen by the H. B. of L. Sexual abstinence was a prerequisite for joining his fraternity, and total continence in thought and deed was required for progress.[2] The only known connection between the groups lies in the fact that Butler joined the T. S. in Rochester, New York,[3] in the branch controlled by Mrs. Josephine Cables, who was in 1885-1886 the head of one of the lodges of the H. B. of L.

The erotic philosophy of the H. B. of L. bore resemblances to that of the Theons. In the Philosophie Cosmique, woman symbolizes the *force pathétique*, the highest of the four great cosmic energies, as well as the *plasticité* which is the faculty of receiving these energies. (We keep the French terms because the English homonyms are so distant in meaning.) The *union pathétique* of man and woman, essential for their achievement of dynamic balance, is called *dualité d'être* (duality of being).[4] By this the Theons meant—and the alchemical language is intentional—"the fusion of two beings who are in mutual affinity."[5] Ideally this should take place at every level, whereupon each supplies what is wanting in the other. "Such individuals are the pioneers of the Restitution: this equilibrium is the condition that allows for the endless perfection for which man was formed by Brah Elohim in His own image."[6] However, *pathétisme* is most often only partial: e.g., the partners may be in intellectual balance, but not psychic, nervous, or physical, in which case the satisfaction will not be total.[7] The Philosophie Cosmique, in fact, considered that true duality of being was impossible to achieve in the present age of the world.[8]

The practice prescribed in the "Mysteries of Eros" is totally Randolph's, though the H. B. of L. has arranged his rules to cor-

---

[2] See Vallee, 139ff.

[3] Information supplied by Mr. Michael Gomes.

[4] Cf. Axiom IX of the "Base de la Philosophie Cosmique."

[5] "Questions," in *Revue Cosmique*, II/12, pp.759-760.

[6] *La Tradition Cosmique*, II, 356-357.

[7] *La Tradition Cosmique*, II, 357-358.

[8] Such a union seems to have been envisaged only in the case of "ABA" and "AMA," representatives of man and woman in the "sixth epoch of the classification of matter."

respond to the three Degrees of the First Grade of the Order and has added a variety of minor teachings on "Human and Inhuman," "The Mystical Womb," etc.[9] The three great principles of Eulian magic—named here Formulation, Execution and Reception—were called by Randolph Volantia, Decretism and Posism, and are a powerful statement of the mental attitude and training of the magician of any age. The emphasis is on focus, clarity of perception and visualization and on the primacy of the "Imperial Will." Both Randolph and the H. B. of L. are emphatic that power in magic is a product not only of will, but of love and the feminine side of the Soul, rather than of the cold, dispassionate intellect.

Traces of each of these great laws can be found in many Western and Oriental systems, but Eulis as a whole remains uniquely the creation of Randolph. The European Mesmerists, such as the Baron Du Potet, in whose circle Randolph moved in the 1850s and early 1860s, emphasized the role of the will ("Volantia") and the projection of its action ("Decretism") through the universal, all-pervading magnetic fluid which Randolph calls the "Æth." "Posism," the Receptive Principle, Randolph says he deduced from a close reading of Machiavelli's supposed power to divine a person's intent from his body language, but the principle has clear analogues in the Western magical tradition. Agrippa's *Philosophy of Natural Magic* (Book I, Chapter LII) describes the role of the "Countenance and Gesture, the Habit and the Figure of the Body" in magic, but he bases his discussion on the system of universal correspondences rather than on practical experience, as Randolph appears to have done.

Although it is clear from the "Mysteries of Eros" that the three principles of Eulian magic bear some relationship to sexual practice, the precise connection is not explicitly given. The lapse may be supplied, however, from a passage in Randolph's original "Mysteries of Eulis" that was omitted by the H. B. of L.

---

[9] The identity of most of these can be discerned from the table of contents of "Mysteries of Eros" and most of these in turn are reprinted in the augmented version of *LOE*. The H. B. of L. doctrines even in the added material largely correspond with Randolph's own writings.

The entire mystery can be given in very few words, and they are: An upper room; absolute personal, mental and moral cleanliness both of the man and wife. An observance of the law just cited during the entire term of the experiment—49 days. Formulate the desire and keep it in mind during the whole period and especially when making the nuptive prayer, during which no word may be spoken, but the thing desired be strongly thought and the three Principles enforced—*Volantia, Posism, Decretism.* The end sought, the power coveted or the thing desired must be clearly defined in each mind—*then*, and both after and before. These few lines invoke and embrace a mystery of superlative grandeur.

Chapter IV of the Second Degree provides the H. B. of L.'s caveat to Randolph's sexual magic. This originally circulated over Davidson's name as "A Brief Key to the Eulian Mysteries" and contains dire warnings about the use of sexual magic for other than elevated goals, specifically warning of the obsession that must follow from the implanting of "seeds of magical powers" in the soul of the practitioner rather than in the embryo. Randolph, the H. B. of L. and later Max Theon all taught the possibility of creating superior children by magical means. Randolph's own life-long eccentricities and eventual suicide were attributed by the H. B. of L. to his ignoring these precepts.

The point of the entire Eulian magical endeavor is given in the third point of the teachings for the First Degree—"Realization"—by which term the H. B. of L. and Randolph meant conscious contact and communication with the "Centers, Spheres, Potencies, Hierarchies and Brotherhoods" that peopled the universes stretching back to the divine origin. These entities included beings "who were of earth once, and others who have never been ultimated on, nor incarnated within this external plane of objective life," beings who were "the arbiters of the destinies of the worlds and the originators of the grand drama of external life." These beings and the adepts of the Inner Circle were the real teachers of the H. B. of L., and it was contact with them that provided the initiate with the doctrines of the Order.

The
Mysteries of Eros

———

Omnia vincit veritas

———

Expressly arranged
for the
Exterior Circle of the H. B. of L.

———

By T. H. Burgoyne
Private Secretary

Preface

In presenting this revelation of the mysteries of man's inner nature to the neophytes belonging to the exterior circle of our venerated order, I am requested to earnestly and solemnly impress upon each and all, personally and individually, the absolute necessity of studying and thoroughly mastering every detail here laid before you. Carefully study out every law action and principle that may arise in connection with this mighty subject. For it is only by first mastering Nature's alphabet, that you can ultimately become Nature's expert scholar, whose trained, disciplined soul can read the Arcane mysteries of the Cosmos, in the clearly written characters traced by the finger of divinity itself all around you.

Make this Arcanum the subject of long, deep, thoughtful study. Commit it to memory, so as to be able to repeat it at pleasure and when this task is achieved, you will be fully prepared to ascend another step higher in the stairway of

Urania's sacred temple. In conclusion, I must not forget to add that my task throughout has been but that of an amanuensis on one hand and that of a compiler upon the other, for truth is ever the same. "There is nothing new under the sun," saith the wise man; and so it is with the contents of this Arcanum. Its teachings are as old as the very hills. It is, in fact, but a reawakened echo from "The Wisdom of The Ages."

Fraternally yours,
T. H. Burgoyne.

Grade I
The Grade of Eros
[Grade I, First Degree]

The grand object of the mysteries of Eros is to build up the individuality of each Acolyte to the end of evolving the latent powers within the human soul. Each individual is a responsible being, working out the problem of his own redemption from the thralldom inherited from ancestry and the dead ages, and forced upon him by external conditions. These mysteries indicate the way, furnish a chart, and bid him square his sails and depart for the shining shores of immortality.

The Arcana of Eros is divided into three separate grades, and for want of better terms can only be described as Formulation, Vitalization and Realization. The first two are triune qualities and contain three principles each. The last is the sum total of the other two and contains but one definition, thus making up a total of seven, which number is the symbol of action and completion of all mundane affairs. Taking the principles as they stand in the order of their relative importance we first come to the grand doctrine and science of

I. Formulation.

The three sub-principles of formulation are Formation, Execution and Reception. They each deal specifically upon their own special lines with one of the triune attributes of man's internal nature. The formative is the Creative attribute whereby man imitates deity. The second is the controlling attribute whereby man receives, conserves or stores up the deific energies and then imitates the laws of his own creation by radiating and projecting this borrowed energy upon the lines, and in the special forms and angles, of his own formation. The third is the receptive quality of the soul, whereby man receives and again transmits to the planes below him the grosser forms or the finer essences of the great life-force of the Kosmos, in the exact proportion and ratio of his soul-development and the higher laws of his mentality. From this it will be seen that Formulation is not only the first principle of man's being, but, that is at the same time the most vital one with which we have to deal in soul-development.

It is the absolute foundation of all power, knowledge and energy possible to embodied humanity.

Formulation then, in every instance is to be taken absolutely as the first grand principle to be mastered, studied and applied, in the search for knowledge and the endeavor to enlarge the scope and range of individual power, mental and psychological, and to this end the following definitions are presented:

a. The Formative principle is the quiet, steady, calm, non-turbulent, non-muscular exertion of the human Will.

To increase this power and render it practically and magnetically serviceable, a regular daily practice is required. Observe these rules and follow them:

Place a round white card with black centre against the wall, and gaze at it calmly and steadily one minute, willing at the same time to increase the Attention, Concentration and Abstraction; then slowly turn the eyes to the blank wall, the optical effect will be an apparition of the card,—colors reversed,—passing slowly across the line of vision. This may not occur on the first trial, or there may be no more than one or two appear; but after practice the number should and will increase to four, seven or even more. The card may be of any other colors, and the phantoms will be the exact opposite or complementary hue. This exercise is intended to develop the above-named power, and its ultimate end and purpose is to enable the acolyte for fix his mind on anything living or dead and *will* its phantom (in the latter case—itself) to appear. Excellent results may be sooner obtained by using a good magnetic mirror with a white wafer affixed in the centre thereof.

Do not permit the mind to be disturbed or startled if a face or figure appears upon the black-white, magnetic sea of the mirror. If the acolyte does not possess the necessary nerve for this he had better at once abandon the study of High Magic, which requires heart, courage and persistence for its noblest and most successful culture.

After the card has been in daily use for six months or more it may be abandoned either for the wafered mirror, the head of a brass nail, or better still, three nails,—zinc, copper and horseshoe nail,— arranged in a triangle whose sides are one inch in length; one end of a fine copper wire should be wound around the three nails and the other held in the left hand while gazing. The effect is magnetic and serves to render the attention more firm, positive and concentrated. It may and probably will require from two to three years practice before mental conceptions can be successfully substituted for those herein recommended.

One great object for the Neophyte to achieve in this steady practice of formation, is to gradually enable his mind to pierce the Astral light. When the eye is taken from the card, remember that object has become a thing of the *past;* reproducing it again in the phantoms upon the wall is in reality reproducing the past vividly before you. It may be only a few seconds of time, still no matter how brief it is still the past and careful daily practice will enable the Neophyte to become more and more potent in this realm of Psychology and render it possible for him to reproduce instantly any object or person in all its original reality. Therefore, simple as this principle of Formation may seem, it is the first stepping stone in the path of the soul's ultimate state of perfection, which is that of the real Master of Mysteries, the exalted Adept.

b. The Executive is the second principle and is purely volitional. It is the projecting, ordering, commanding and mentally enforcing the behests of Desire and Will,—to say, think, feel and ordain a thing to be or an action to occur, and, as such, is the opposite pole of the first principle—Formation. It is the *must and shall be* idea in action, the positive, executive force of the human soul, without a proper culture and activity of which no great thing whether within or without the path of White Magic, can be accomplished. It is the blessing or cursing energy of the soul and is at once the grandest and most terrible force, alike potent for good or evil. Its action is periodical, its orbit elliptical and its effect magnetic; therefore, what it takes from you it always returns with interest—if good, then good—if evil, added evil.

Great care must be taken that there is no other emotion or action going on in the mind during the executive instant, for this ordaining power (especially after the exercise of the Formative), leaps from the soul like a flash of vivid lightning, traversing space and centering on its object though oceans flow between, or vast spaces divide; yet its period of activity and duration never exceeds three to seven seconds of earthly time.

c. The third or Receptive principle consists in placing one's self in a receptive position, state, frame of body, mind and feeling. It is the most important and difficult of the three great principles, and its results especially in affectional lines correspond. To exert it successfully requires a fair development of attention, concentration and abstraction, in addition to the exercise of the Formative and Executive principles, not merely as regards any special object or power to be sought, but to induce the Receptive condition itself. When we strike or sustain a blow we pose the body, hands, face, eyes, nostrils and mouth; even so is the same rule imperative in the higher or superphysical, metaphysical, mental and ethereal regions of our vast being, and it must be enforced in order to reach the sublimest of all receptive powers. There is no Magic save in Formation, Execution and Reception, and their foundation is *Love*.

To illustrate our meaning, let us say for example air and heat rush in to fill a vacuum, and there can be no vacuum if anything is there. Similarly one cannot wholly either notice, wish for, will, decree, or receive the full measure of anything sought, or power desired, or the entire weight of any mental or metaphysical desideratum, if half or more of the mind is already occupied by something else which receives a proportion of its attention and of the heart's desire. This principle requires the entire devotion, absorption, and concentration of all the inner being. When a thing is to be done, an Energy (individual in both senses),[1] hierarchy or special power is to be invoked and brought down from the aerial kingdoms of the spaces, or evolved and called up from within, the mind must not only be brought to wholly bear upon the reception thereof, but room within the Odyllic sphere must be with withdrawn and vacated, except for that special thing, gift, energy or power then sought through the mysteries of Eros.

---

[1] The Lyon ms. adds this note: "That is to say, of your own energy (individual to you), or of a celestial energy (which is itself an individual)."—Editors

This road is a royal one; the weak minded, blind or credulous can never travel its imperial path, because the higher powers only have an affinity with those capable of appreciating them; they never coalesce with starving souls, and never at all, unless the laws of their evocation, development, operation and evolution, are earnestly, calmly, steadily, persistently followed and implicitly obeyed.

II. Vitalization.

The second of three great principles of the triune soul is Vitalization, which means life giving. Everything is vitalized in exact proportion to the capacity of reception and transmission. Every spirit atom or Divine Ego, is in reality a central point or Focus of Deity for the transmission of life. The soul Monad projected into matter, in order to evolve the latent attributes of the divine spirit, is supplied incessantly from its own state and center with the life force required and it in return transmits it to planes and states still lower than itself.

Everything, from the highest Arch-Angelhood to the cold granite rock and dense veins of mineral, is in a state of reception and transmission. That all human beings in the natural state are mediumistic—some in excess of others—must, to be in accord with the laws herein revealed, appear perfectly plain, especially so, when we comprehend the *relationship* of humanity to Deity. In a similar manner all material substances are mediumistic in this sense of the term, viz: in the degree in which they are capable of receiving and transmitting Force. In this connection, Hermetic Science teaches, that active spirit inheres in every grade of matter as the instigator of life force and motion, being an attendant upon the ethereal forces that permeate all worlds and every atom of space. For in proportion to the refinement of substance is the sphere, vitalized by spirit.

In the brain and nervous system of the human being the Climax of Material Vitalization is reached, hence as the

Neophyte by training gradually builds up his individuality, and refines his physical organism by throwing off the grosser particles and replacing them with more ethereal ones, he becomes capable of receiving, retaining and transmitting the finer and more potential essences of the Astral Light, consequently his will is correspondingly potent within the realms of White Magic. Taken in a general sense Vitalization may be divided into three separate sections, viz: Inspiration, Respiration and Breathing. The latter as the most external embraces the two former. Considered separately, we have first

a. Inspiration.

"The simple senses crowned his Head,
'Omega! thou art Lord,' they said"

_____

"Who forged that other influence
That heat of inward evidence?"
—Tennyson

The discriminating student will not fail to note much significance in the four lines quoted above. The sentiment of the first couplet is declarative, affirmative, positive, assertive, active, or briefly, Male. The second couplet is equally distinctive in its sentiment, but the diametrical opposite, being that of inquiry, solicitation, invitation, negation or Female. Considered relatively they are polar opposites. They also possess a broad generalization, or, more properly, a classification of the world's creeds and doctrines upon inspiration, its sources and rank. One class claiming that inspiration is of the senses and intellect; another, that it is external to the senses and intellect. Hermetic science does not join in alliance with either one of the two doctrines against the other, but teaches that both are the complimentary halves of a complete truth; expressed otherwise, a unity under two modes of action. When the mode of action is considered, duality stands squarely before us. Indeed, consciousness itself is due to the ebb and flow of the energies that pertain to duality. Inspiration means in-breathing. We inspire the essences and forces of the One life, according to our refinement of material structure and adaptation for receiving it.

The Gates of Heaven open inwardly; so does inspiration, and when we have in-breathed and replenished the body, soul and spirit, the action becomes polarized, reaction sets in and we throw off and transmit all that our system is unable to neutralize or assimilate. This brings us to the second section of our subject, namely,

b. Respiration.

Respiration means out-breathing, out-flowing or expulsion of any fluidic substance or essence. It also takes the meaning of loss or extinguishment, and herein stands as the antithesis of inspiration, which is so significant of cumulation and gain. When we further consider that the framers of our linguistic symbols spoke of breath, and air or wind as being or containing the intrinsic Potencies, the inspiration and expiration of this kind, meant flatly, either gain or loss of power. Expiration is the emission, loss or expenditure of power. The loss or absence of power leaves behind it the attribute or correlative state, which we call coldness. It is not mere verbal fancy to speak of the heat and fires of inspiration, for herein we have a veritable truth. Inspiration and Respiration are related as the Vishnu and Siva, preserver and destroyer in oriental religion.

It has been said that no man can serve two masters; but herein is a paradox, for it is plain that we do seventy times every minute transfer our subserviency from one to the other of these two sovereigns; one brings us emancipation and the other takes it away. "Tantalus, thou art living still!" But the philosopher, looking beyond the scope of the present times, sees therein the law of faithful compensation and the equipoise of beneficence, for we are not privileged to reap unless we likewise sow. It is also an exposition of that law, "Give all thou hast of breath or power, or life, in just duty and lawful motive; expire honestly the corrupted or contaminated matter, and you shall instantly be filled with the celestial fire and become refined." Too much inspiration causes levitation, too much respiration, gravitation. We now come to the realization of these two sections, the actuality of both inspiration and respiration, and which may be totalized as Breathing.

c. Breathing

There are two results of breathing—the first is from the inspiration of common atmosphere which sustains the life of matter—sensation. The second result is from the inspiration of the magnetic, electric, more ethereal particles of the air which support the life of soul and emotion; that higher, inner, deeper part of man which concerns itself about infinite and eternal interests. The first gives force, the second generates power. It is possible to fill the lungs—therefore the brain—with this last, sifted from the first, and thus the soul, with ascensive inclination and ability, with the loftier kind of trance-power, known as the "Sacred Sleep of Sialam," in which the soul bids defiance to all barriers which, awake, asleep, or in the mesmeric states, limit and bound it: with that grand flight-power whereby it can reach infinite altitudes and sweep with masterly vision the realm of stellar galaxies; that sleep of Sialam, in which man may gain whatsoever of knowledge, and power he wills, provided it lies within his soul's capacity of comprehending and using.

By slowly, regularly breathing, two things occur: First, a gain of vitality, therefore, physical life; the organs instantly extract the *vif* of the air and discharge their accumulated load. The exhalent movement is always the longer in natural breathing; but, if you wish to gain force and have more ethereal than physical life, the slow breathing must go on from ten to 20 minutes at a time, and to obtain a more harmonious influence, the heaving of the chest should be regular and its inspiration and expirations of equal duration. Fix some desired object in the mind, and the ethereal air will be retained in the lungs, brain and nerves until sufficient reserve force is gained to add new power, enabling the soul to subdue sense and affording the pure intellect ability to take lofty, prolonged, and heaven-sublimed flights into the Empyrean, or, indeed, in any direction fancy or inclination prompts or necessity suggests. This is one of the most potential of all the powers within the human soul. The term Æth signifies that finer essence which the soul breathes; it fills the spaces, cushions the worlds and penetrates the outer air just as odors do. It is inhaled by Æthereal beings precisely as we of earth inhale the influence of matter in its grosser and lower forms. No real divine or celestial energy can be evolved until, by patient and continued effort, the Neophyte learns to inhale the Æther while the mind is firmly fixed upon what is in and of it. Thereby he contacts the essence of power and the denizens of the ethereal and far-off spaces. Thus doing will he breathe the elements which generate power in the Human Soul.[2]

Remember, O Neophyte, that Goodness alone is Power, Silence is Strength, Will regaineth Omnipotence, and Love lieth at the foundation of all. These forces should never be trifled with; should never be brought into action for any mere worldly or temporal motives: because their sphere of action pertains only to the highest and most interior states that it is possible for embodied man to penetrate.

III. Realization.

All centers, Spheres, Potencies, Hierarchies, and Brother-hoods, in fact, all things on earth externalized, have their orbits and periods. In like manner all conceivable powers, qualities and energies in the spaces, have the same. There are times when they are, and are not, contactable, and it is very difficult, if not impossible, for any [person] living in domestic turmoil to contact them at all save through the exercise of a resolute, unbending will, and perfect indifference to the surrounding inharmony; but there are orders of beings, invisible to material eyes, who were of earth once, and others who have never been ultimated on, nor incarnated within this external plane of objective life who understand anything and everything which man can conceive; who possess every species of knowledge, and who respond to the desire and invocation of those who follow the same lines of thought and feeling, who belong to the same state of intelligence, or who voluntarily place themselves under the essential conditions of rapport and contact.

---

[2] NOTE—The student should extend this philosophy of respiration and inspiration to his body griefs and captious irritants of every kind. Expire them all, cast them out, and make room for better company, which will flow in like a festive troop if you will make room and extend them a cordial invitation.

Mean thoughts, passions, and her ideals, have killed thousands. You cannot afford to entertain such guests. Therefore, expire them with your next breath, and bid them an external farewell.   —T. H. B.

The Neophyte must be careful to divest the mind of all but the subject in hand; never seek for two dissimilar objects at the same time, or within seven clear days between the operations, every one of which should be prepared for with a full heart by fastings, ablutions and soul aspiration.

Study these laws thoroughly nor forget this caution; nothing can be done except through Law, Order, Rule and a clear, definite comprehension of the underlying principles set forth herein, and above all, a perfect *formulation* of the objects desired.

But before proceeding further it is advisable to consider one or two points, which, in the end, will be found to be of great service to the thinking student of the Philosophy now taught. There is no accident nor any such thing as *chance* in this life or the worlds beyond; all external things and events are the result of internal causes, and there are rules by which they can be forecasted and anticipated. We do not mean by this that all human events and occurrences are foreseen by those who were once denizens of the world we inhabit, and who for redemptive or other ends may reveal many things to their worthy proteges; but we mean that within this universe, there is a great central source of intelligence, power, presence and energy, which necessarily knows all that was, is, and is to be. This central power must be environed by colossal mental energies, potentialities in knowledge, only second to its Supreme Self; nor do we conceive such potencies to be ascended human beings, who once dwelt in physical bodies, lived, died and rose again.

There are electrical, ethereal, non-material universes, far grander, vaster and more magnificent than this of ours with all its amazing splendors, its myriad galaxies and rain storms of starry systems; with all its inconceivable distances, and stretch of fathomless eternities, than this of ours is superior to an ant-hill. There are Hierarchies, legions of them, Potencies, Powers, and Intelligences, not of human material genesis, before whose amazing sweep of mind the grandest intellect earth ever has or can produce is as a pebble to a mountain range, a tiny dewdrop to the mighty rush of ocean's water, a gentle shower to a tempest of rain, a zephyr to the raging typhoon on its devastating march o'er land and sea.

These beings are the arbiters of the destinies of the worlds and the originators of the grand drama of external life. The capacity of Deity is boundless; that of man is limited, and is either vast, or contracted in strict accordance with the relative ratio of his soul development and independence of mere bodily sense, personal or material bias. Perfect development means perfect at-one-ment; this atonement is the sacrifice of the lower nature upon the cross of purification and the evolution of the true Christ within; the real Christian, beyond all creed, exists only in the truly perfected man. One is developed can place himself en-rapport with the centers of celestial life, traverse the spaces, and penetrate the grand arcana of the universe itself. Man has not omniscience, but has much penetration; he is not omnipotent, yet possesses enormous latent powers; he cannot be omnipresent, but is capable of Ubique: that is, of being mentally and spiritually in many places and scenes at the same time. A million photographic instruments will instantly chain a million shadows or images of such prototypes, given off by everything continually; this is even more true of the soul than of the body, and this fact brings us face to face with the sublime mystery of Projection and that of its opposite, Soul-attraction.

Projection means the sending, forcing, compelling of the astral form, or double and soul symbol to appear wherever the will may command through the three principles of Formulation.

Attraction is the exercise of the same power in opposite direction, to compel the apparition of another. Where-ever the Neophyte has sufficient steady will-force to decree his presence, he may compel the appearance of whatever phantom or intelligence he chooses, and may act with enormous force upon whom he desires.

Observe: Formulation can be excited from two planes; 1st from pure intellect, cold and joyless, which is its negative force or plane; 2nd from the heart, the soul-emotional, or love-plane, which is its positive point of action.

Execution is always masculine, positive, ordering, commanding, electric—of the brain alone. Reception requires, instantaneous transition from the masculine brain to the tender, soft, loving, emotional side of nature. Woman is the receptive and Man the executive force. He imparts, she receives; so also the intellect of man acts on imperative principles, her love on receptive ones; this is the law. All good works begin and end with devout aspirations, and posing to receive the boon craved, while desires of an opposite nature begin with, and end on, opposite principles. In all matters connected with the punishment of wrong, the protection of the weak and imparting power, health and prosperity to others, Execution terminates the formula invariably. In actual practice the Neophyte must first remember that the party or person to be frustrated must be present either in person or apparitional presence, which latter can be achieved by the process of Formulation; this force must be continued until the apparitional image or images stand out clearly defined before the operator; then think that which is required to be done and formulate it just as clearly; at this point the Executive force must be projected on its orbit. But it must never be forgotten or overlooked, that this executive force is to be retained within the grasp of the operator during the climax of the formulative moment, and never projected until the soul is full to overflowing, or it will fail to reach its object, and having traversed its orbit, recoil upon the operator and produce inharmony.

Let us solemnly impress upon each and every Neophyte the fearful dangers that will overtake him should he
ever attempt to use these powers for evil purposes or the
injury of others; therefore, be warned and rather suffer
injustice than retaliate with vengeance.[3]

—T. H. B.

---

[3] NOTE—In repelling any evil influence, that is or may be directed against him, the
Neophyte must use the powers of Execution wisely, not with vengeance, but with
cold, withering, lofty contempt, desiring neither vengeance on the one hand nor
giving mercy on the other. It is that state of mind which is calm, cold, heartless and
indifferent to all save self-protection, it is a state of stern, unbending justice, and
extremely difficult to be obtained.

The Ansairetic Arcanum

[Grade I, Second Degree]

Chapter I

There are three planes of action, or manifestation, of the sexual forces and affinities (each separate and distinct from the other) that are knowable, reachable, and partly controllable by embodied *Man*. Commencing from the center of our being, and consequently the most interior plane or state, we find that it is there alone recognized as pure soul affinity, and may, for the want of a better term, be designated *spiritual love*. The next plane exterior to this sublime center, is that which holds, as it were, the great *via media* of the dimensional spaces. It is the *spirito-natural* plane or state, and can be classified as *mental love* or intellectual affinity, while the theral and most external of all, is that of animal magnetism and Physiological affinity, known by the popular name of *sexual love, per se*.

We will, therefore, for the better understanding of this most important part of the occult principles of our human nature, commence with the most external state, viz: that of the great Procreative passion of the sexes, the *animal nature*, and generally denominated as the love of the sexes. In all these various planes of the action, and interaction, of nature's primal law, we must impress upon each student's mind the absolute necessity of fully comprehending the significant advice of the Ancient sage, "Man, know thyself." Modern sophistical savants have tried to improve upon this, and said, "Man, ignore thyself, and learn to know thy God," little dreaming that this latter is fully embraced within the command of the former. Man is a complete *but finite* epitome of his creator, God! Deity! the Infinite! To fully enter the path of occult science, and eventually become heirs and partakers of the secret doctrine of Hermetic Philosophy, this our first revelation of the sex mysteries, must be carefully studied. It is a part and portion of that animal nature you have to conquer. It is, also, upon the interior planes of Æth, a portion of that divine, celestial nature that will ultimately become your birthright. Consequently, it at once and forever deals with the most sacred powers and functions and forces of your being. You are dual matter and spirit. So is love. It is animal passion and it is soul affinity. Commit this important fact well to memory. It is a well-established axiom that God and nature marry the sexes together, while man, custom and the laws of the State, legally unite individuals. The former unions are never *failures*; hence, those who are thus happily married, being the perfect expressions of the dual laws unto themselves, need but little light to guide them in the Arcana of this mystical subject, seeing that they have already obeyed the laws which form the very quintessence of their existence; and Nature, when so obeyed, *never makes a mistake.* But, of the latter class of marriages, (which lack the interior principle) which the laws of the State and the custom of men have only and merely *legally united*, there is always an overwhelming majority which turn out the most wretched failures. Therefore, it is this class that need all the knowledge that the experienced Occultist can bring to bear upon the subject in order to guide them from the quicksands and hidden rocks upon which, unfortunately, myriads are continually being wrecked.

The true man and the true woman are only such, and can only be termed so, perfectly, when the sexual organism is healthy, sound, vigorous and complete. It is upon this section of human nature alone, that conjugal happiness depends, and we draw special attention to the fact, that all the numerous so-called nervous and sexual diseases originate and are perpetuated from generation to generation by a complete violation of the sexual system. Be it therefore known that the preservation, rejuvenessence and sanctification of Love, between man and woman, primarily and always depends solely upon the perfection of this conjunction. In plainer words: upon the fullness and completeness of the conjugal union, in each case, and *upon both sides*. The vast majority of civilized men have no *endurance* (sexually.) Their love-passion is short and spasmodically ended before the female organism has had time to reciprocate the contact and she is thus deprived of all the finer and more acute sensations which constitute the sum total of Love's Master Passion. Not only so, but the positive magnetic current set in motion by the impulsive spirit of the male cannot react harmoniously when the female principle has not been roused to the same force of action; hence the attractive portion is wanting and the union becomes a mere magnetic poison to both. It is this magnetic poison that contains the germ seeds of so-called sexual disorders. In real truth, they are the unnatural larvae that have been (ignorantly) brought into existence and which possessing only the male positive destructive element, form minute but vicious vampires, that feed upon the life principle of the organs which gave them birth, and disastrous results always follow, of which the female is generally the only direct sufferer and man indirectly, as such states can affect him only by the direct action of the mother upon her unborn offspring. Therefore, in all sexual intercourse there must be a perfect sympathy and *desire* between the male and female. This must be especially so upon the woman's part, as she alone possesses the highly strung organism with the uterus capable of creation.

No mortal man can, for one moment, realize to what intense, exquisite pitch the harmonious, loving, soul of woman can be awakened when nature's laws are allowed to flow undisturbed. Woman is a most delicious, sensitive and magnificent instrument, and when the conjugal act is an harmonious one, she is capable of evolving the keenest energies of our nature, and of attuning our whole sphere with the most exquisite *harmonies of space*. All sexual unions other than such as these are poisonous, a fraud, and do incurable mischief. Remember, then, that to the true and perfect-conjugal union, it is absolutely necessary that the neck of the uterus be bathed in and by the husband's prostatic lymph and *ejected semen every time* they know each other, for, unless their mutual acids and alkalis, generated then and there, meet, mingle and blend and fuse, the electro-magnetic and nervous conditions essential to the perfect union are not present, and as a consequence, the reaction is fatal to health and this will ultimately result in mutual coolness, loathing and repulsion and the measure of soul-fusion, before existing, is most effectually injured if not totally destroyed, and from this state is evolved act I in the drama of matrimonial strife.

The wise man will not go where he is not wanted, nor be so blindly foolish as to attend the funeral of his own joy. He knows the sensitive, delicate value of woman too well. It is only the idiot who is brute enough to intrude his *lust by right* upon an unwilling wife. He cannot realize that she is not ready, and, consequently, is totally unable to respond to the embrace, or give pleasure. He cares not, and, therefore, obtains nothing but a mechanical union, devoid of all magnetic flow. He becomes disgusted with her, whom his lust has turned into a *dead passive instrument,* and, in the end creates a train of diseases that medical skill in vain tries to master. Remember, that of all the varied actions capable of being performed by the physical organism of man, the sexual conjunction must be reserved and considered as the most holy and sacred.

Chapter II.

In the 1st chapter of this Arcana we but briefly outlined the general facts of sexual law. Continuing the same teachings, and holding the same fundamental principles in view, it is here necessary to point out the more important laws and regulations that should be observed by both husband and wife. For, although we speak chiefly of man and hold him up to your view as though he alone were the only one guilty of wrong, this is by no means the case. Therefore, when speaking specially of man, our remarks must be understood to include both sexes, as, when either transgress nature's law, the result is the same. How few are the men who really and truly understand woman's fine, delicately strung nature, or have the manly nobleness to gratify and affectionately sustain it when they do know. If this be true, how much less in number are those who, when they do know, will reveal such priceless knowledge to others? It is one of the missions of our venerated Order to make these sacred mysteries of sex plain, and to bring the light of human reason to bear upon the occult principles which control the very vitals of humanity. Not otherwise should we dare to tread upon the ground that from time immemorial has been consecrated by faithful, loving hearts, and ever held sacred between the sexes as the scene of their bridal union.

To resume: It is far too common in practical everyday life to need extensive comment, for man to demand from *his legal wife* all that a coarse, passionate nature may require to gratify its depraved appetite. He makes by *right* that which he has assumed to be his by *right*, and has not the slightest thought for the more delicate feelings of her whom his brutal nature has outraged. Such considerations to the *animalized man* would be ridiculous to the last degree. *He* has been satisfied, and that is all that his coarse, dull nature can appreciate, while poor *she*, with a painful sigh, turns in disgust from the one whom our civilized law has made her lord, (?) and sobs her miserable life away and doubtless wonders how long it is possible for her to remain in that particular section of domestic limbo. And yet, how all this could be altered, if, instead of stern indifference and probably impatience, her husband would try to be less like a mule and more like a true man, meet his faithful partner with a loving, grateful kiss, a gentle caress, and by various, delicate means, try to change her cold nature into genial warmth, her total indifference into affectional, chaste desire, and when the loving union has become completed, a kind, endearing word and that tender embrace which woman alone can appreciate will sustain the warm, sympathies which have been awakened into life, as forerunners of true domestic bliss. Instead of such course, however, man, as a rule, after satisfying himself, turns away from his partner, and in five minutes is sleeping as sound as a log. Calmly considered, what must woman's secret thoughts about such an husband be?

But there—it is enough. And more than enough, has been said on this subject to make the student remember that a world of power for the bettering of our social life, and the happiness of our homes lies within the realm of continual kindness and affectionate respect for man's superior companion—woman. Never should man be hasty. *It is his duty to wait for her*, no matter how long, until he wins the soul and passions as well as the duty, respect and obedience of the mysterious being he calls wife—God's profoundest miracle and nature's grandest masterpiece of organic beauty. She, the possessor and bearer of the mystical uterus, the mysterious womb from which spring all life-atoms of Divinity itself. The potential power of continual kindness between the sexes, cannot possibly be estimated. It weaves that bond of union, that mystical link in nature, which, as the immortal Shakespeare says "makes the whole world akin." There is a vast difference between *lust* and *love*. Neither must the one be mistaken for the other. This fact alone is the true *"reason why"* our ascetical brethren of the Orient have so loudly proclaimed celibacy as the *sine qua non* of the neophyte's commencement in the path for initiation. The natural passions of all Orientals are infinitely more susceptible and excitable than the races of the West, and consequently, more liable to lead them astray. So, by the well-known rule, they have chosen the least of the two horns of a most perplexing dilemma, and strictly commanded the complete destruction of the sexual nature. This in itself, so far as we of the occident are concerned, is almost as great as a mistake as excessive indulgence. But we are now dealing with a different people; a race sprung from the frozen bosom of the hardy North, and therefore, must completely ignore a code of rules that are so formulated as to be only specially adapted to the more sensitive offspring of warmer skies.

Do not misunderstand this important doctrine and conclude that sexuality is to be encouraged, for, by so doing you will seriously err. The sexual nature must only be exercised in those peculiar intervals when two souls become blended, by their love into an harmonious one. Nature seeks her own time for such intercourse. Therefore, keep complete control of self, patiently wait for her, for the two must, in fact, when mystically considered, be truly husband and wife and this in its highest and most sacred sense. Volumes of writing would be required to fully elaborate this delicate subject, and, even then, much would have to be left for the intuitional faculties of the neophyte to discover. Many minor points are therefore left for his special private researches in the vast domain of sexual law. The chief rule to be always observed in this connection, is to steadily avoid quick, sudden or hasty conclusions, for the greater the heights of occult knowledge attained, the more clearly will you see how very little you really know, and how very simple, after all, are those truths of nature which you, after so much study, have been able to master. The profoundest mysteries of the Cosmos, when discovered, are but laws of the most absolute simplicity. Nature is ever thus.

The real gist of the Phallic mysteries taught by Ansairetic initiates of the Oriental priesthoods can be formulated in twenty-one slokas, or verses. They are a trinity of sevens, viz: a statement of the seven laws, powers and principles; seven rules of instruction, and seven laws of precaution. The whole combined constitutes what is known as *legacy of Aphrodite.*

Chapter III. The Legacy of Aphrodite

Herein are contained the fundamentals of nature and of Human Love between the sexes. Herein are revealed all that is absolutely essential to anyone. For their application is as broad and varied as life itself. The mystery contained within this legacy is that of the sexual principles and interior essential of Eros, as set forth in the previous revelations of the "Ansairetic Arcanum." These principles come into active operation upon the external plane in many ways, but chiefly within the bounds of these seven planes:

I. For purposes of increasing the brain and organic force of an unborn child.

II. For influencing one's wife or husband; directing their internal thoughts, and magnetically controlling them.

III. Regaining youthful beauty, energy, vivacity and the affectional and magnetic powers.

IV. For prolonging the life of either the subject or the operator, or both, at will.

V. For the attainment of supreme command in the realms of white magic and evolving the supreme will.

VI. For the furtherance of financial schemes and worldly prosperity and success.

VII. For the attainment of the loftiest insight of nature's mysteries.

These seven constitute the crowning glory of the "Earthly Soul."

Now the manner and method whereby these seven principles are utilized and turned into real, external living realities, is by duly and loyally conforming to these seven laws, which now follow:

I. Perfect continence, upon the part of both the male and female, for a period of from 21 to 49 days.

II. Absolute cleanliness of person by frequent baths and ablutions.

III. Perfect cleanliness of the brain and mind by philosophical study and meditations upon the grand purposes of Divinity.

IV. A daily formulation of the triune of powers desired, so that they stand out clear and distinct to the mind's eye.

V. Absolute purity of purpose in daily routine life, free from discord, dishonesty or despondency. These last 3 especially.

VI. Perfect loving relationship between the male and female, and domestic peace.

VII. Prayerful devotions morning and evening, with the exercise of pure love and charity to all, and the practice of the executive and receptive powers.

There are, likewise to be considered, causes of failure and possibly disaster in the magical operations of nature's law when evolved through the medium of gender. Therefore, carefully consider the following precautions, likewise 7 in number:

I. Neither the man nor the woman must be virginal or unsexed, but must have previously known and experienced sexual union.

II. An harlot, or lust-woman, is worthless for all such holy and lofty purposes. So is one who accepts pay for her compliance in the ceremony.

III. Success will not attend the debilitated or lustful, nor the passion-driven apology for a man.

IV. Failure will attend all efforts, unless there is an harmonious agreement of thought, temperament and mental balance.

V. Both male and female must be exact and unanimous in their desires, i.e., both must desire and formulate the same powers, or conflict and failure will result.

VI. There must be mutual love, affinity and accord between both operators to succeed.

VII. Complete failure will attend all efforts where self, worldly power or fame, is the real and only motive of using the mysteries of sex.

These, solemn things are never to be imparted to the young and thoughtless, nor to any individual but those who by nature are pure, noble, aspiring and true, and in whose hand they will remain sacred. Fix this first principle firmly in your memory. Its basic form is "Love lieth at the foundation," and Love is convertibly passion, enthusiasm, heat, affection, fire, God. And Master that. Second. The moment wherein a man discharges his seed, his essential self, into a willing or unwilling womb, is the most solemn, energetic and prayerful moment he can ever know on this earth. If under the influence of mere lust it be done, the discharge is suicidal, losing, demoralizing to himself. It is hatred, disease, magnetic abomination to the woman, and, if successful, generates murder, crime and misery in the child. If in love on both sides, then strength and its cognates follow. Thirdly. At the moment the seminal glands open, his nostrils expand, and while the seed is going from his soul to her womb, he breathes one of two atmospheres, either foetid damnation from the border sphere, or Divine energy from the far heavens. Fourthly. Whatsoever he or she shall truly Will and internally pray for, when Love, pure, Divine, natural, passional or volitional is in the ascendant, that moment the prayer's response comes down. If he Will for any power from the moment of passing the outer door, till the womb shall have *expelled* him, that will he reach. It is only when man admires, reveres and loves, that triple law is obeyed and power, not weakness, follows the act of sexual union. He who sexually contacts a woman who has not been previously excited to the passional mood, is a suicidal fool, and will ultimately reap a rich harvest of contempt and remorse.

Chapter IV.

Part 1.

A brief key to the mysteries of sexual law, in their practical application, is now presented for the student's careful attention. In the first place, he must make himself thoroughly acquainted with the laws of the sex, and its exterior symbolism. He must also realize that the great lever of all magical power is centered in the imperial Will of Divinity. The human soul is in possession of the greatest portion of this Divine power on this mundane plane of existence; hence it follows that whatever the soul desires can be accomplished, provided there is sufficient concentration of the Will upon the object sought. This occult truth unfortunately leads those who are imperfectly initiated in the more recondite mysteries of nature, into very serious errors, and even into something worse; because simple error not only implies the bondage of the soul, but it also means becoming the very slave of, and being controlled by, the power which all neophytes seek and strive to master, viz: the real realms of Elemental Being.

In order to avoid such disastrous consequences, the student must ever keep in view the primal law of occult science, viz: That the grand, magical agent of nature cannot produce that which already has no existence; neither can it stimulate into sudden activity any latent germ, or force, which is already completely polarized by antagonistic influences under complete, subjection. From this fundamental law it naturally follows, as already remarked that "whatever the soul desires can be accomplished," if the Will has been sufficiently concentrated upon the object. Still the fact remains that there may be objects which would require such an intense degree of concentration of the Will as to be out of the reach of even of the highest adept. In the Occult, as in Physical Science, that which is true in theory cannot at all times be fully realized in practice. Hence, if the student keeps these primal truths constantly in his mind, he will but seldom fail. But this will not depend so much upon the potency of his Will as upon his knowledge and familiarity with these laws which enable him to concentrate his Will upon the acquirement of those purposes which to him are possible. In all cases, let the Neophyte only seek to assist nature in evolving the attributes of the soul. Stimulate to healthy activity the latent powers of your being, gradually develop your own Spiritual nature and occult possibilities, by *living* the life of the Spirit, and not of the flesh. Never, under any circumstances, attempt to force upon any organism a premature development by unduly stimulating any natural predisposition of the soul, for, assuredly, a fatal reaction will be the result. Keep the foregoing advice constantly in your memory, because thoughtless attempts are the fatal centers around which continually revolve all forms of so-called Mediumship in modern Spiritualism, and this is the reason why so many Mediums, especially those of the physical nature, generally lapse into an immoral and depraved state. This is also the reason why Mediums, possessing the higher grades of clairvoyant and inspirational Mediumship, are the nervous, sickly and feeble apologies for men, or the sensitive females of weakly constitution and passive nature, who are unable to resist any positive influence. To this, however, there are exceptions, as to every other rule.

Part 2.

The whole tenor of the revelation of the Ansairetic Arcanum, and the mysteries of sex in relation to the Occult, are such as to lead the uninitiated to the conclusion that pure sexual intercourse may be made the means of magical power. This conclusion, in its general sense, is a *fearful delusion*, but, at the same time, it is a sublime truth when understood in its proper light. The doctrines of Eulis, as set forth by Randolph,[4] teach that the concentration of the will upon any one, or upon any triune of powers, or attributes, by both the male and female at the supreme moment of seminal emission during sexual intercourse, calls down from within the spaces of Æth the Divine germs of spiritual powers and attributes; or, in other words, the seeds of magical powers, and that these become planted in the souls of those who call them, grow, and in due time, ripen into the grand powers, or gifts, so rarely found existing in the human organism in a natural state. (By natural state we mean the present unnatural state of incarnated humanity; because, when man is in a *natural* state, he is the perfect man, or, in other words, the Adept.)

When taken literally in this light, the teachings of Eulis are an awful and terrible delusion, and mean ruin to all who practice them as a means of obtaining power, since they call down powers into the soul, which fasten upon its vitality and can never confer the remotest power or benefit. Such practices rear and nurse a swarm of vipers which will ultimately sap not only the vitals of the body, but the soul and terminate the physical existence of their victims by suicide, or drive them to the grave as driveling idiots, or as howling maniacs to the madhouse. Not content with this when death puts an end to physical torment, they still cling, like magnetic vampires, to the soul, and cause the complete destruction and disintegration of the spiritual remnant of their prey in the lower planes of the soul-world.

Therefore, be warned, O Neophyte, and rouse not the Furies lest you cannot lay them. This is the magical delusion of Eulis. This is *one* of the dwellers of the household [*sic;* "threshold"], and all those who have become the slave instead of the master of such powers, had better follow the example of Judas Iscariot, and hang themselves before it is *too late to save their immortality.* For, in this life, they will only

---

[4] The Adyar manuscript of "A Brief Key to the Eulian Mysteries" is stronger in its language against P. B. Randolph: "The 'Mysteries of Eulis' as taught by the unfortunate P. B. Randolph, who fell a miserable victim to the fallacies of 'Eulis' by Committing Suicide—constitute the 2nd Degree of Grade I in our Noble Order, and exhibit in the Case of Poor Randolph the calamitous consequences of imperfect Initiation."—Editors

get from bad to worse; in the next, if not *too late, they may* shake off *the power of the fiends.*[5] In the soul union of twin souls, as also in the physical union, there are mighty and potent effects, but they are far too recondite and abstruse to be here explained. Never, therefore, attempt to seek them until spiritual initiation has been attained, then you will know how to use and utilize them in a proper manner.

Part 3.

Having explained the error and delusion of sexual law, we now proceed to explain the sublime truths. In the first place, it must be known that the whole teaching of the Arcanum may be followed in the attainment of the only two legitimate objects of conjugal love, viz: the evolution of powers in the unborn child and the elaboration of social and domestic bliss in the married state. For the perfect attainment of the first named and most important to object, the same preparations are to be observed as before taught, viz: continence for the space of at least twenty-one days, but forty-nine, if possible. When these preparations are observed, both the male and female in the same prepared state, at the close of her *lunar period* the solemn ceremony may be performed, each with the whole nature, for the time being, given to the excitement of sexual love, their thoughts and wills firmly fixed upon the triune of powers desired in conjunction with an ideal personage, they, at the supreme moment of sexual excitement, when their souls expand and the seminal glands open to pour forth their contents of embryonic life, launch and project their whole souls in one effort of Will for the power desired upon the one object of the ceremony; but this object is not for power for any living being, but for the embryo formed by their sexual union.

---

[5] The Adyar manuscript concludes Chapter II at this point, and adds "(Signed) P. Davidson, Provincial Grand Master of the Northern Section." Other English-language manuscripts add two footnotes at this point: "P. S. The next lesson will contain the *truth of Eulis* and how the power of sexual intercourse *can be utilised.* N. B. that P. B. Randolph fell a miserable victim to the delusions of Eulis."—Editors

Hence, the whole mystery, in relation to love and sex, is the procreation of a human soul; and the child so begotten will possess naturally the very powers or gifts which the uninitiated fools imagine and dream they can possess for themselves. It has been said by an eminent sage, that when mankind shall truly understand the mystical laws of sex, they will be able to realize any ideal in their children and bring forth gods instead of men. To this truth we ever hold. Here, then, is the Grand Mystery so long dreamed of—a mystery within the reach of most.

The great difference between the initiated and uninitiated in the sex mystery is, that one drags down powers from elemental realms, and by directing his Will toward himself, fastens them like parasites upon his soul, and thus lays the foundation of ruin. The other directs the spiritual germs into the living seed of the future human organism which, under the mystical spiritual impulse of a woman's nature, are transformed during the period of gestation, into the lovely attributes of the soul.

Remember, that these spiritual germs of life, when drawn down, are pure Paradisiacal units, neither good nor evil in themselves. Nature takes care of them in the healthy womb of a female; but, when they become planted by Magic Will-force in the soul for a matured organism, they are out of their element, and the surrounding influences of human life transform them into demons, or, rather, vile larvae which destroy everything worth possessing in either this world or the next. These embryo powers or soul germs, to be evolved into pure, human soul powers, must be planted in an embryo organism, *not a matured one.*

Never forget the fact that these germs are completely at the mercy of the human Will, so much so, that they are liable to be cramped and warped by any impulse of a mother's mind. This fact is well known. Lastly, remember that these spiritual germs will only plant themselves where the will directs them, so that Neophytes, in becoming the parents of children, need not fear that any of the germs will fasten upon their souls, because the will directs them, along with the seminal fluid, into the vessels of the uterus. It is, however, to be observed, that the soul-germs are, in the general course of nature, attracted during sexual intercourse, and left to general law as to their nature and power, because mankind are unacquainted with this mystery.

The student will now see the great difference between implanting powers in a human foetus and *attempting to plant them within his own matured organism.*

Part 4.

Important Items of the Sex Mysteries

1. An evil desire or wish, during the excitement of sexual intercourse, directed against the male by the female, or vice versa, will magnetically poison and result in innumerable disorders (generally of a sexual nature).

2. A good and benevolent desire expressed in a tender and earnest, loving spirit, will magnetically strengthen the sexual organisms and benefit the person.

3. An evil thought or desire, if projected against any person during the supreme moment of sexual excitement, will have a most evil effect upon the one against whom directed; but, at the same time, remember that every desire, when it has completed its orbit, returns to the source from whence it emanated; consequently, those who are guilty of such diabolical practices, reap with interest all the evil they have sown.

4. A good or benevolent wish projected under the same conditions cannot effect much, because the soul, when excited by any passion, cannot *penetrate* any *very* high *state* of good.

The student may ask why an evil desire may have more effect during the excitement of sexual intercourse, than at any other times. The answer is, because the power and potency of all magical operations of the human Will, below a certain plane of development, depend upon the degree of excitement of the soul *at the moment of projecting the Will*— and we know that the sexual passion is by far the most intensely powerful in the human organism. It is for this very reason that the exciting Phallic dramas in the ancient sex ceremonies were instituted;[1] not because the almost nude female forms, passing through every obscene and suggestive position, pandered to a depraved nature, *but to arouse the Will by passional excitement* to the pitch of magical possibilities. The soul cannot support[2] or contact any powers of a very high grade when the excitement is the result of any passion. Hence, this class of passions is especially potent for evil or a material purpose. (That is to say it cannot direct them; or, in other words, the Will cannot, when excited by any passion, penetrate the more interior state, and thus reach the good or angelic powers. This has nothing to do with, and must not be understood to, apply to the states occupied by the embryonic soul-germs before spoken of, because these are attracted by either force, good, bad, or indifferent, seeing that the germs are neither good nor evil in themselves, and may become either as surrounding circumstances determine.)

As the Neophyte advances up the height of the Occult, all passions will have to be gradually overcome and held in complete subjection, to enable the soul to put forth its highest energies and powers, and so direct the potential Will, without any passional excitement whatever; but this state cannot be attained until all the subordinate degrees have been satisfactorily passed, and full initiation accomplished. Then, and

---

[1] The Lyon manuscript adds a footnote extending the idea to the "orgies of the Sabbaths."—Editors

[2] The correct reading (from "The Key") is "come into rapport, or contact, with."—Editors

not till then, will the Neophyte begin to entertain hopes of final Adeptship.[3]

Chapter V.[4]

Hitherto we have dealt solely with sexual love, as it is manifested upon the external, or Physical plane of our earthly existence. It is absolutely necessary, for the full and complete development, both physical and spiritual, of the complex, duplex human organism, to thoroughly master the lower before the higher can be attained. *The Neophyte must have practically experienced what we have described; must have known the value, beauty and the exquisite enthrallment of love's master passion; and have had the energies of his soul impregnated with the true, unalloyed reciprocity of woman's affectional nature, ere he can hope to penetrate the grand Arcana of the sacred sanctuary, and scan the mysteries concealed beneath the Virgin Veil of Isis.* See note II at the end of this chapter.

The second plane of action, or manifestation of love is that of mentality. This mental state occupies, as before stated, the great via media, or spirito-natural plane, and relates purely to *ideas* and *ideals* insofar as they are comprehensible by the physical senses. It is the action of this plane that binds individuals into sympathetic groups, or classes, and is the true foundation of all harmonious society. The artist will find his greatest pleasure in the society of his fellow artists and those of artistic taste, because they alone can truly appreciate and sympathize with his artistically ideal conceptions; so with all other groups and planes within the mental states of embodied humanity.

It is useless to carry our observations further upon this plane as the student can extend his own experiences and conceptions at pleasure. It is, however, a field of occult research that will yield the student very profitable returns

---

[3] The manuscript "Brief Keys to the Mysteries of Eulis" adds: "(Signed) P. D., Provincial Grand Master of the North [Northern Section]."—Editors

[4] The French manuscripts subtitle this "Intellectual Love."—Editors

for his labors of careful investigation, but in this research, the great objects sought in the equilibrium of his mental plane, must not be lost sight of, seeing that they are the special mission of every true man and woman, viz: "Universal Brotherhood." The sympathy reciprocation and love of one state, order or, society of individuals for another. This ideal conception of Universal Brotherhood has been the highest aspiration of the world's noblest reformers. It was [for] the hoped-for realization of such a state that Guatama [sic] left his imperial throne of power, to follow the life of a beggar. It was for the hoped-for accomplishment of this possibility, that the gentle Nazarene gave up his life upon the Cross, and then prayed for his murderers. And so with many other noble souls who have consecrated this plane with their heart's blood, in order to aid suffering humanity and hasten the millennium of our social joy. One great and fatal mistake will always be made by those who aim to enroll their names on the shining scroll of *the world's crucified saviors*, if they seek to accomplish that which belongs to universals before they have completely mastered that which belongs to particulars; in other words, the instruction of mankind can only be gradually accomplished by commencing with the careful instruction of the individual man. He must be taught to know himself, and when he has completed that task, he will have solved the problem of Divinity, and social science can be left to elaborate itself in a natural, harmonious growth. When this is done, it will be a solid structure. From its deep foundations, amid the ramifications in the animal nature of man, to the exalted philosophical speculations of its summit in the Divinely human spheres of the Angel. Such a system of moral, social and intellectual science, will be worthy of the Divine genius of the perfected man.

Before concluding this chapter, we would briefly draw the student's attention to the fact, that the power, force, and creative genius of intellectual and mental love, upon the grandest plane of its force, belongs by sole right, to woman;

in the formation of the tendencies, moral and spiritual, of the unborn humanity of the future, the very genius, intellect and destiny of future races, are entrusted to her care; therefore, all pregnant females should, as far as possible, cultivate assiduously the ennobling companionship of exalted, noble minds, and ever direct their aspirations to the most exalted conceptions of truth and beauty, and steadily avoid reading, looking at, or thinking about anything immoral, obscene or impure. This done, their offspring will bear the deep impress of their mother's mental love toward them while yet unborn, and the fond mother will have the blissful satisfaction of seeing the purity of her own mental state brought down from its ideal state in the realms of subjective life, and mirrored forth externally in the pure, noble lives of her children. Be it your endeavors then, to read, mark, learn, and inwardly digest, the momentous results that depend entirely upon the proper understanding of these important Ansairetic mysteries, which are the result of long ages of thought, research and skilled observation.

NOTE I.

Upon this vital point we must not be misunderstood. Where we say that all intercourse between *unmatched souls* is a crime, we do not mean that it is only the true soul-mate that can be considered as a *match*. By no means is this so. On the contrary, the *earthly union* of true soul affinities is quite the exception and *not the rule in the present cycle;* but we mean that all unions, to be lawful and harmonious (in an occult sense), must be between those who, by nature, are harmoniously suited to each other in mind, temperament and disposition. This is, in every sense, a *natural union,* because the two so united form the positive and negative, as it were to each other. In all such cases it will be found that these naturally united souls, though not the real spiritual counterparts of each other, emanated from the *same center* of deific life. Again: we must not be [mis]understood, by center, we mean state or sphere. Hence, they belong to the same spiritual race of Angelic life, which is becoming embodied into external conditions.

NOTE II.

The Neophyte, struggling for initiation, must not think that we mean the physical, carnal contact with *his* or *her* kindred mate. No, this is not at all necessary (for initiation). We mean that these souls must meet and blend *somewhere* within the spaces of Æth. There must be a *spiritual union.* This often takes place *unconsciously*, when the body is sound asleep, and of which all recollection (generally) vanishes upon reawakening. Once this union has been found, however, its power is never again lost, though Hell itself at present divides, *they* must ultimately become again united.

Chapter VI.[5]

The majority of students who commence investigating the forbidden realms of our sacred lore, desire to attain mystic powers without treading along its own royal road. They thirst for that grand mental force which will enable them to scan the sublime mysteries and sweep through the vast realms of sidereal and sphereal spaces; *but they are impatient of the methods.* Now let all whom it may concern know, once and for all, that the doors are forever closed against all, save the strictly obedient; and the effort to prematurely obtain mental intensity *need never be attempted*, neither need efforts be made to attain unto any power, force, or state, unless The Law! its Law! be scrupulously observed; because, no real magical or magnetic powers *can* or *will* be evolved from its central embryonic germ-state within the soul except in the mighty movement within the odyllic spaces caused by the soul-union of Both. Remember, that as harmony is absolutely requisite for birth, so is discord the chief factor of death! Not by one alone can these potentialities be evolved. No. But when the music of the soul reverberates through

---

[5] The French manuscripts subtitle this "Spiritual Love."—Editors

the worlds of Æth, and the dual union of the two harmonious natures cause the requisite symphony of the soul to penetrate the interior of the celestial heavens, then, and then only, do the doors of the sacred sanctuary open and admit the seekers within. The adytum of the Holy of Holies—the eternal spark within us—never flashes, except when the pure, loving female brings to her feet the noble, loving man; not in their animal lusts, but in their soul's mutual infiltration of soul, in the *sexive* death of both. Billions of ages ago, far away in the dim, silent vistas of the past, woman proved herself the weakest portion of the dual soul. In that awful, intense moment, their mutual demise was created by Allah. Material incarnation resulted, and thence forward, spirit binds its human body only when the pure sexual union of the soul opens the mystic door of the spaces for it to *re-enter, through woman's faithful heart,* "The True Perfected Man." *Through man, the woman; through her,* the world; *through them* the spaces of celestial life; *through these* Deity Itself; not as a drop, or an atom, in the infinite ocean of mind, but as a Being in the Heavenly Hierarchies! of the Universal Soul!

What doctrines, then, follow from this grand sequence in the harmonies of nature's immutable law? Why? 1st: It teaches that every aspirant to this immortal birthright should never forget his fealty to woman, but remember who and what she really is: *The gem of the Creator's blazing crown.* 2nd: That the grosser man should ever be considerate and *gentle to* and *with* woman; never rude, fierce and brutal; never impatient of her *failure* or *inability* to respond to his passional desire; 3rd: Constantly remember that it is the feminine portion of the spirit alone that contains the potential germs of all true greatness, and that the coy, angelic Isis of the soul, will quickly resent any violation of her virgin rights. The revolving "cycle of necessity" however, is not undertaken by the deification of life to evolve the attributes of these purely feminine qualities, for it possessed them in their celestial perfection and virgin purity in the interior heavens of the embryonic soul-world—*the Garden of Eden.* But the fall of spirit, as it is termed, and the descent of life in reality, into external planes of matter, was necessary and undertaken to gain knowledge and experience, and through knowledge, attain unto perfect wisdom by partaking of the tree of life, and thus round out the latent but positive individuality upon this plane, and the identity in the interior state that will then enable It to say: *I am, that I am!* "As it is above, so it is below, and that which is below is like unto that which is above," or, in other words, this revolving globe of earth, the scene of all our physical pains and joys is but the prototype of heaven. It was thus, in the very dawn of God's creation, and will be the same when our present system is disintegrated and lost within the unborn systems yet to be. But, though lost to us, they are not beyond the ken of that deific mind that propelled them into being. No! but as forming the harmonious portions of other states and centers, they will obey the same immutable laws as we them obey now. When once the fiat of Deity is sent forth, it continues throughout all ages. It exists as the potential attribute of Him who sent it forth throughout that vast unknown Eternity, which none but Deity itself can comprehend. *"Increase, multiply and replenish the earth,"* was one of the commands thus given to spirit, and from the very commencement of material evolution, this fiat of God has been obeyed and the accomplishment of such was the special plane of action for love to manifest itself in her lowest estate. Of that state we have already dealt, and we now come to speak of the love of the spirit.

The pure, unsullied affection of the soul man's inward yearning for the embraces of the long lost Eurydice of his former state, and woman's tender aspirations, *to once more be clasped to the bosom of her own Osiris and share the joyous companionship of her true,* rightful Lord which her quick, sensitive intuitions often tell her is a very different being from the one she now obeys. When the sexes are truly married their life, even amidst its greatest trials, is one continuous round of spiritual joys: but, when otherwise, the very marriage rite itself is an imposition and *the continuance of the sexual relationships* a Fraud. No matter how me may try to disguise these facts in the use of accommodating terms and the artistic sophistries of modern society, they stare us in the face at every turn, and the trained initiate of Urania's mystic law beholds, *too often*, with pitying eye, the soulless, wistful vacancy of those eyes which ought to flash forth in their diamond energies the sparkling, joyous scintillations of an illuminated soul.

The potent indignation of woman's loving nature, when standing forth in defense of the idol of her heart, has been happily expressed by Byron in "The Bride of Abydos":

> "As the thunder-bolt bursts
> From the dark clouds that bound it,
> Flashed the soul of that eye
> From the dark lashes around it."

While it is exceedingly painful to thus penetrate the real cause of so much human suffering, at the same time, it is true pleasure for the initiate to behold the happy harmonious state of those who are, in very truth, *united*. Whether they have conformed to legal customs or not, can make no material difference upon that interior plane of which we are now speaking for spiritual love, in its most interior state, or degree, is totally separate and distinct from all grades of earthly affections and possesses nothing in common with them. It is the soul-fusion of two natures which belong to the same *identical state*, and who sprang forth into existence from the same celestial focus of emanative life. *They are twin souls*, the Isis and Osiris of the Divine Ego, which gave them birth, and as such, it impossible for one soul to appropriate, steal coalesce with, or ensnare the affections which belong to another. "The love of man is constituted by the higher laws which are the genius of his creation, and *the form which this genius has assumed, is the love of man.*" Woman adores

God in the supreme form of her love for man. So does man adore the same Divine power in the angelic form of his love for woman. It is thus, and in obedience to these higher laws of our being, that the true, celestial bride sees God mirrored forth in her husband's form, and the husband's love sees his highest conceptions mirrored forth in the celestial beauty of his bride. Woman is the liberatress of the powers that are involved in the genius and structuality of man. She enters occultly into the very internals of his nature, as the vernal sun of spring enters the germ-seeds of vegetable life. Thus she is the celestial flora of his spirit, and the ambrosial aroma of his soul. Such being the fact, complete harmony requires the *complete union of the two*. Therefore, seeing that complete or true harmony can only result when the notes sounded are in perfect accord, we find, by the principles of our science, that for every masculine spirit-atom there is a corresponding feminine monad. When ultimately united, they form the duad. This union generates the highest music of their internal natures, and *it is* the responsive harmony (which in the sixth state attains the crown), that makes them celestially, the King and Queen of their sphere: This is the mystical at-one-ment of the Christ within; henceforth they possess the triune nature, the scepter of Deity. They are children of God, and inheritors of the Kingdom of Heaven.

We must at this point impress upon the student the true mystical significance of the states with which we are now dealing. Lust, passion, and carnal desires, are here entirely unknown, for they belong to that lower state which has been conquered, and during the process of conquering the lower principles have been gradually *absorbed* and regenerated and transformed into the higher. Therefore, sexual union, as we know it, hath no existence, but, has gradually become blended into the harmonious, responsive reverberation of soul to soul, the glorious, transcendental ecstasy of which the uninitiated man can form no possible conception.

At this point of our revelations we must stop! for the Divine laws and sacred mysteries which lie beyond, are too transcendent for the exterior circle, and pertain to those alone who win the right of admittance to the interior of the temple. We will therefore, in concluding this chapter, take a passing glance down the path which we have so far traversed, and then, for one moment, let the eyes of the spirit rest upon the distant, celestial heights to which this same path will lead us. Looking down the winding uneven road over which we have laboriously traveled, we can now perceive that it is *of a spiral form and ascensive* in its course; that we have *ascended* through the planes of the physical and intellectual worlds, and that now we have arrived within the spaces of pure spirituality. In this most interior state of our being, we have beheld love in its own true, beautiful form pure as the Infinite from which it sprang, chaste as the snow-white leaves of the sacred lotus. Upon this physical plane we have found our virgin Goddess, clothed in *personality*, while, upon the intellectual planes, she has become incarnated within the spheres of *individuality*. But now, in this celestial sphere, such forms are no longer required, for the soul has reached, or rather, *regained* the primal state from which it fell, and is now recognized only in the special form of its identity, no longer bound with earthly ties or compelled to submit to worldly customs. At this point of the arc soul seeks its kindred soul, and, as their harmonious natures throb in grand unison to the music of the spheres, we witness the celestial marriage of the lamb. From this point they are forever united, each supplying the other with the requisite grade of harmony in their upward progress through the ages that makes the purified perfected soul Divinely complete. Cycle after cycle in their journey, and eternity upon eternity, always fulfilling, with Divine completeness, the purposes of creation, within the brilliant radiance of their pure, Angelic spheres.

What a majestic radiance hath Wisdom! What a deific principle, love! But, oh, how incomprehensible to the carnal, human mind, is the celestial glory of the union of these twin, Angelic souls, who, in this deific state, can thus scan the whole scheme and destiny of God's creation! Mind fails to ascend further. *It would be lost.* Such a possibility, O Neophyte, is ours, it is mine, yours. What earthly distinction, or ephemeral greatness, is worth one moment's consideration when it may clash with the possibilities of the above? But away with such a reflection. The thought is insanity itself. Therefore, take up the Cross at once, and forever part companionship with those who would sell such a glorious birthright for a mess of worldly pottage. For when such *inferior beings* are sinking through the states of annihilation in Hades, your soul will be winging its immortal flight amid the sapphire vaults and starlit realms of eternal day.

THE MYSTERY OF ISIS
GRADE I, THIRD DEGREE

Introduction

It will be clearly seen from the two previous Degrees that *sex* is the great fundamental expression of nature. Electricity is *positive* and magnetism negative relatively, and *yet within themselves contain both positive and negative.* Man is positive, woman negative, and yet contain within themselves the same double force, manifested on the plane of the Astral soul as *intuition and intellect.* The Astral soul is negative to the more ethereal attribute or Divine soul, which is positive in reference to all below, but negative to the interior Ego, the Divine Spirit itself, which is dual, expressing itself in *love and wisdom* in the seventh state; intuition and intellect (or reason) in the fifth state; to a vague sense of right and wrong, and parental affection in the third state, while in the first state it is natural sense of self (termed instinct). Love manifests itself first in the sexual organs, in the 1st and 3rd human states. Love has only parental regard and *lust* for its foundation. Passion is supreme chief. Remember that all things, modes and forces, are positive to that which is external, and negative to that which is internal, even unto the first manifestation of the God-head, viz: *the pure realm of unmanifested being* (the garden of Eden), or pure innocent spirit, *which is ever awaiting the tempter, eager to be deceived* (to fall into matter).

Remember all this, especially the terms *above* and *below*, which mean without and within or interior and exterior states of being, it will then be more easy to see the grand object the Ancient sages had in view when expressing these sublime mysteries of nature in Phallic symbols. It was the *sole* and only reason that the lotus was the sacred flower of the gods. The seeds of the lotus contain perfect miniature plantlets within themselves and are self-generating, springing as they do from the water, which is perfect symbol of the universal mother, and when pure, is composed of two gases, oxygen and hydrogen. One is positive, the other negative, and it is not by "a chemical combination of the atoms," as taught by our professors of chemistry, but it is by the positive hydrogen completely polarizing the atoms of the oxygen that the universal (material) solvent is formed. The chemist can separate the components of water and ascertain their proportion, but when he has done all *it is still gas, water or vapor;* but the Alchemist can by polarizing the vaporous gas, separate the two and retain them separately for an experiment, and, what is more, *they will never unite again in the combination known as water,* but this is one of the Rosicrucian secrets of the interior Grade.[6]

To continue our notes upon sex. The human organism is, in its more interior sense, *the mystical uterus of Isis* (that is, the human, organism is the uterus of nature), ever pregnant with the Holy Ghost (the incarnated soul), which, when the period of gestation is completed (the cycle of evolution), shall give birth *to the Son of God,* whose kingdom is not of this earth, but of Heaven (that is, of course, the soul which has attained its immortality, is a Son of God, etc., whose future state of being is the boundless realm of Spirit). I and the Father are one, meaning that the human Ego is but an atom of the Father, is not the same idea as the more interior state of Adeptship or being at one with God. This at-one-ment is the mystical *Atonement of the Christ* (Spirit) within the human soul. These ideas if carried out and meditated upon, will reveal unto you the whole mystery of Christ and the *immaculate conception.* The idea of the human organism being the mystical womb of nature, was the cause of the Ancient Priests of the sanctuary elaborating the magnificent

---

[6] The separate manuscript of this section of the H. B. of L. teachings (in the handwriting of T. H. Burgoyne) reveals Burgoyne's lack of formal education and the editing process that went into the production of the systematized Mysteries of Eros: "No chemist can separate the components of Water. He can only ascertain their proportion, but when he has done all he can it is still water (or vapour), but we can by Polarizing the Vapours, separate the two and retain them separately for any experiment, and what is more they will never again unite in the Combination known as water . . . ."—Editors

funerals, the cremation of the Hindoo, Greek and Roman rites, and embalming of the Egyptians. It was the most important ceremony of Ancient times, because the most mystically important and the most sublime rite that the soul can pass, from matter to spirit, or "back to the Father's home."

The Mystery of Isis

Chapter I.

Advice and Warning. The symbolism of the central Phallic idea having been completely mastered and a full knowledge of sex, as revealed in the Ansairetic teachings, and the mysteries of Eros obtained, the student will be prepared for this third and final revelation of Eros in the exterior circle of our noble Order. From the Phallic symbolism of ancient sex-worship, through the dual power of love and hatred, lust and brutality the same law holds good. Sex is the great primal law of nature, both visible and invisible, objective and subjective. The powers of love and hatred in man are feminine and masculine. Love is the feminine, hatred the masculine force. The man who cannot love is an inhuman monster;[7] there is nothing human about him, except the outward physical form of humanity, which is but the lamb's clothing that ill conceals the ravenous wolf within. It is only the truly human that can truly love, and in loving let their souls transcend all lower passions. Lust is not love. Lust is the animal or passional appetite, with nothing human about it, and woe be to those whose love cannot rise above the plane of lust. The sexual passion, in itself, is pure, but of all the passions it is the most liable to abuse. Therefore, Neophytes, if you are not perfectly confident and certain that your sexual passions are pure and respond only to those (or, rather, *to that one*) whose soul affinity you possess, then at once and

---

[7] Both the English and the Lyon manuscripts add: "The same remark applies to the two sexes."—Editors

forever debar the passion completely and lead a life of celibacy, for the soul cannot evolve healthy powers where the tainted mildew of either lust or an impure life is allowed to remain, and if powers are developed in such a state, they are abnormal and impure, *mere spiritual fungi of the soul*, more tender than hot-house plants, because they are forced and reared under artificial conditions and consequently liable to wither and die up on exposure to the first blighting currents of the Astral light, when disastrous results always follow. Read, mark, learn and inwardly digest these great fundamental truths. There is no middle course for the Neophyte who aims at the practical realization of the occult powers of his soul. It is either heaven and ultimate glories of eternal progression or it is hell and ruination, with the terrible surroundings of the Black Magician and almost a certainty of final extinction in the elementary spheres of the soul-worlds. True it is that so-called spiritual gifts do not depend upon moral purity, but the utility of these attributes do; hence, avoid the curse of (irresponsible) mediumship. Trust to no controlling spirit guide. Always remain the complete master of your own organism at any cost, and remember that the modern spiritualistic seances, or spirit circles, are often, very often, nothing but steaming hot-beds of vice and spiritual impurity. Not that all are such; far from it, but only the sacred circle of the home and family circle of kindred souls, whose blameless lives and moral purity form an impassable barrier to either elemental or elementary, is spiritual intercourse to be encouraged. There, and there only can Spiritualists obtain anything worth having or be free from danger. Every realm of being, either above or below this state, is for the initiated occultist alone to explore. All Neophytes are, therefore, as they value their soul's liberty, forbidden to participate in anything of the spiritualistic kind, except under the superintendence of an experienced and properly initiated teacher.

N. B. It is well to add that while spiritual mediumship is a truth, and intercourse with disembodied spirits a fact yet *pure mediums are so rare* and the spiritual dangers surrounding mediumship *so great* that the *only wise and safe course* for the Neophyte is *to avoid all spiritual surroundings*, until, by occult training, he has placed himself beyond danger, viz: until he has made himself complete master of his own organism.

Chapter II.

The Human and the Inhuman. We now approach a most sacred subject and one of the most vital importance to both man and woman, because it deals with the fundamental principles of their being and explains how through the magical attraction of human passions, they may become the unconscious instrument of untold evil by launching upon an already over-suffering humanity, cruel monsters in human form. There are already too many *wise spiritualistic teachers* who assert that *nothing exists in nature but the human* (to name them), but God forbid that we should accept as human that which is as yet animal. The occultist cannot afford time to moralize upon the mysterious laws of nature. *He* knows that such laws exist and that alone concerns him. *Our conception* of that which constitutes good and evil, morality and immorality is not the standard he (the occultist) can accept for a single moment.

What concerns that practical Neophyte at this stage of his progress is, what beings, and from what states is it possible for mankind to attract beings that may become incarnated in the human organism? Is it possible for any intelligence but the human to incarnate itself in the human form? This is the point at issue. "Impossible, under any circumstances," the Spiritualist would say; "not only our Divine parent but the countless hosts of purified souls of the disembodied humanity would step forward and prevent such a cruel injustice." Not influenced by any such illogical, sentimental ideas, the experienced occultist would reply that it is not only possible but that "under certain conditions (of too frequent occurrence) the probabilities are greatly in favor of the inhuman becoming incarnated in place of the human." What these conditions are and the mystery of inhuman incarnation, we are now about to reveal.

The Neophyte in the 2nd lesson of this grade of Eros, knows how to incarnate the human soul and, though much may be said and written on the mystical conditions that combine the formation of the form of an embryonic child, it is enough to say that the physical form will of itself obey the internal impulse of woman's nature and so far may be left to itself or, if necessary, can be studied out from physiological works bearing specially upon the subject of prenatal conditions. With this brief digression, we resume the subject of our teachings, viz: *the incarnation of inhuman beings.*

In the first place, it must be understood that the offspring of average human beings, under average conditions, will be quite human and accordingly, more or less intellectual according to the accidental conditions that surround their prenatal state. But parents of small spirituality and under the dominant influence of the animal passions, are to be considered as below the average of mankind. It is chiefly of this class we shall speak. In the second place it must be known that there are vast realms and races of beings existing *in, or around our planet* who are neither elementary nor elemental spirits, but aerial beings, possessing a very powerful affinity to man. There are seven grades of them corresponding with the seven planetary states, and, consequently, corresponding with the seven great divisions of the human race. It is this class of beings that *can* and *do* become incarnated in the human organism.

The class of persons who most frequently are the means of incarnating these beings are, as before stated, those of large animal propensity and small spirituality. The conditions are generally sexual intercourse when the male is in state of intoxication. When thus inflamed with drink, lust, and other vile passions, *augmented perhaps by a loathing wife,* who is compelled by *civilized law* to submit to such intercourse, there is no possible chance of anything human. Conception often takes place under these conditions, and an inhuman soul is the result. It is from such sexual unions that the inhuman Neros and Nana Sahibs of history originated. Remember that the social position, or artificial education, cannot alter nature. This class of people are almost as numerous among the upper class, in proportion, as among the very lowest.

The second class of individuals who may be means of such incarnations are nervous, sensitive persons, who *are actually obsessed by elementaries* during the sexual union, and who, by such obsessions, again seem to realize and enjoy the excitement of their lustful passions. In all such cases inhuman incarnation is the result. Should conception take place, the only remedy this class possess is to abstain completely from sexual intercourse, or prevent, by the moral purity of their lives, the possibility of elementary obsessions.

Of course, a female is just as liable, in fact *more liable, to such a state of obsession* than a man. And, lastly, a woman may, during the period of gestation (especially before the foetus quickens) magnetically attach an evil being to her otherwise human child, who will obsess it completely during life, and doubtless lead it to the scaffold or asylum. This magnetic attachment is caused by some sudden exercise of the animal passions to an extreme degree.

Enough has now been said to enable the thoughtful Neophyte to see the great mystery of sex completely. He now knows the use and abuse of sexual intercourse; understands how to become the parent of good, noble, intellectual human souls, and the laws that govern the production of monsters.

Chapter III. The Mystical Womb.

Continuing the same laws we now leave the physical and enter the spiritual or magnetic states of being and find that sex still remains the supreme law. That same principle which manifests itself as parental instinct and ferocious passion in the animal, as affection and lust, jealousy and hatred in the human, blooms out into its own pure states in the Angelic or celestial condition, as Love and Wisdom. This is the most interior state and its attributes in all exterior states of Angelical or spiritual existence are intuition and reason, the feminine and masculine qualities of each human soul. Magnetism is of two kinds, viz: animal and mineral, and from what has been taught, the Neophyte will know that each kind is dual, or male and female, positive and negative. It is the Astral fluid containing the properties of the body it is connected with; hence sex always predominates the very soul force of nature, because it is through the agency of this Astral fluid that all the various phenomena are produced and the actual cause of every effect in both the material and spiritual planes of existence. This force is the indispensable agent of every Adept, Magician or Mesmerizer, and the cause of all magnetic and occult phenomena. It pervades every atom of that vast universe. Not only the human body, but the earth, planets and stars also, are subject to this double law of sex. Attraction and repulsion correspond to the feminine which attracts, and the masculine which repels. It is the sympathy and antipathy of the stellar worlds through space, and, as all bodies are saturated through with the double magnetic influx of this Astral fluid, they must obey the dual law of action and repose. Just as night rests humanity from the day's activity, does this force restore the equilibrium of the spiritual as well as cosmic nature.

The magnetic and Astral fluid then, is androgyne or bisexual (exactly like the human soul), because equilibrium is but the resultant of two forces eternally re-acting upon each other. The result of this is *life*; but, when these two forces expand and remain so long inactive as to equal each other and come to complete rest, the condition is *death*. From this it will be seen that the same soul-force, in the hands of the expert magician, has complete control over life, death and disease; for, if the magician wills a thing and his will is sufficiently potent, *that thing is done.* This, you see, is the exact reverse of Mediumship. One requires the naturally positive and masculine spirit, the other passive and feminine.

And now we come to the last mystery of the circle [or] Grade of Eros, which is the climax of the potential powers of sex, and embraces all the previous teachings in the recognition of the human organism, as the grand mystical uterus of nature. It is the sacred Yoni of the glorious Isis, the universal mother. It is this mystery that explains the immaculate conception of *the Christ,* or Divine human within. It is the immortal soul begotten of the Father enclosed, or incarnated in the flesh. (The human organism.) The *virgin womb* which shall give birth to the immortal Son of God when the period of gestation (human incarnation in or on this material plane) is completed. This period of gestation is, of course, the great cycle of necessity for "except ye be born again ye cannot enter the Kingdom of Heaven." Certainly not. The human soul, while incarnated in the physical organism, is within the womb of nature and it is only when its full time has come, and it has gained its immortality, that it is reborn into the realms of spirit. It has burst the bonds of flesh and blood; escaped from its mother's womb, the uterus of nature. All those who *lose* their immortality are simply the miscarriages of human nature. In short, they are simply looked upon as spiritual abortions.

PSYCHICAL CULTURE

A brief system of Soul Development, with Rules for Practical Occult Training, specially adapted to the Natural Requirements of the Western Members of the Exterior Circle of the Hermetic Brotherhood of Luxor.

Introduction

The primary law to be remembered in all and every species of occult training is that of equilibrium. The scientific evolution of the latent powers of the human soul is just as much the result of methodical procedure and constant application as the training and education of the young. No sudden results can naturally be expected. If there are, they are premature and abnormal, and instead of cultivating them, they must be retarded, since the perfect harmony of equilibrium has been violently disturbed. In the cultivation of psychical powers and attributes of the soul, ever remember that there must be the seed time and the maturing period before the season of reaping arrives when we can expect to gather in the spiritual fruits of our laborious toil and industry. The Neophyte must, first of all, thoroughly understand what he is about, and not set blindly to work. He must have a perfect conception of what spiritual training and discipline is, before he makes any attempt in its actual practice, to enable him to arrive at a fairly correct idea of this extremely important subject.

The following brief but significant hints can be very profitably meditated upon: Occult training or Psychical culture means, primarily, the enfranchisement of the soul. Secondly, it means the cultivation and practical utilization of the spiritual senses of the soul. And lastly, it means the complete subjugation of every animal passion, principle and desire within us, to the undisputed harmonious control of the divine self-hood. Commit these facts well to memory and also remember that vice, habit and passion, or other inharmonious traits of character, must be conquered. Until this is accomplished, we are but the helpless mediums of matter. It is not the actual, external indulgence in any particular practices that constitute the real vice, but it is the power, force and magnetic control which this habit or practice gains over the inner self that constitutes the actual transgression against the higher laws of our being.

Having briefly outlined the broad principle of Psychical culture, it is now only necessary to add a few words of warning. No practice, whether it be that of using tobacco immoderately, drinking intoxicants, or any other petty vice, must be checked immediately, but slowly, gradually, in fact, almost imperceptibly. A sudden suspension means a sudden reaction and above everything else, psychical culture requires quiet repose, equilibrium. No man can take a sudden leap from Hades to Heaven. It is as well he cannot, because he would be out of place and worse off than when in his previously congenial hell. Consequently it is impossible to jump from the planes of selfish sensual desire, into the realm of spiritual growth, —first, the seed time, then the maturing period, lastly, the spiritual harvest of heavenly fruit. Remember this and your spiritual discipline will be conducted wisely, worthily and well.

Rules for Occult Training

1st: The Neophyte must abstain from smoking, the use of intoxicants, flesh eating, etc. The diet must be pure, wholesome, and be strictly vegetarian in nature.

2nd: Each morning, or as often as possible, the Neophyte must take a cold or tepid bath, according as the natural constitution is robust or delicate. When the bath is not convenient, the body must well be rubbed with a coarse, wet towel.

3rd: During the day, whether engaged in business or otherwise, there must be a strong, systematic effort made to check the slightest evil thought, word or deed, and gossip, under all circumstances, must be completely prohibited. In fact, the Neophyte, while pleasantly performing the necessary duties of life, must cultivate a quiet, calm reserved, self-possessed state of mind, and endeavor to his outmost to hold in check, grief, joy, surprise, pleasure or pain; for be it remembered that the passions and sensations of the body are each and all but petty, subordinate states, or, in other words, centers of occult force which ever strive to usurp the imperial rule of the true monarch, the human Will. The vast majority of mankind are but mere slaves of their predispositions and earthly passions, and seem to the true occultist like an empire divided into innumerable small states, each of which has a ruling prince of its own, powerful enough to totally ignore any command of his liege lord whenever it suits his pleasure to object. Until the body is brought under the command of the Will and stands in absolute subjection to the soul, occult progress except in degrees, is simply impossible; and this is the greatest barrier with which the Neophyte has to grapple, viz: Self—"first conquer thyself, and then, but not till then, mayest thou hope to conquer the forces of nature," is the advice of our revered Grand Master M. Theon.

4th: When the Neophyte has advanced a few degrees on the path toward self-control, active training should commence immediately after the morning ablution, and in the evening practice with the mirror, or crystal meditation which follows the card practice.

5th: When convenient obtain some of the dhoop incense such as is used in the Hindu temples. Place the mirror or crystal (prepared according to instructions given in the M. S. entitled "The Laws of the Magic Mirror"), in position, and, sitting in a passive state of mind, gaze into the center, or focus, repeating this incantation every two or three minutes: "My soul is one with the Universe, and my Spirit an emanation from God." Then let the mind meditate upon these mystic words, and at the same time the spiritual soul-sight will slowly but surely penetrate the Astral light collected from the eyes of the Neophyte upon the sensitive, magnetic surface of the mirror. The practice must last for not less than half an hour each morning. The mind should be kept as spiritual as possible during the practice, and all worldly objects banished.

6th: The evening practice is very different from the above. The Neophyte should sit in an easy chair or recline upon a couch in the most easy position, and then gaze upon the card or wafered mirror, (see mysteries of Eros), and commence to formulate mental or metaphysical objects, and then try to project them externally upon the wall or ceiling. He may also find much benefit from a psychic point of view, if he tries to reproduce any of the objects seen during the day. This is the grand secret of penetrating the Astral light of the past. By secret, we mean that this is the commencement of the pathway that leads to the secrets of the Astral light itself. Remember that one can neither make a talisman nor make the powers of a magic spell for good or evil until he becomes the complete master of the phase, viz: "formulation." The best time generally for such practice in the evening, is twilight or near midnight, and at sunrise (just before), for the morning meditation.

7th: And lastly, the moral tone of the Neophyte's life must be pure, spotless and unsullied by selfish desires. Especially must all sexual relations be carefully guarded, and only participated in after due thought and a careful study of the Ansairetic Arcanum. It is this very fatal mistake of sex that has ruined thousands of otherwise promising aspirants for occult initiation.

Concluding Note

The awful list of powers attributes and forces set forth in the works of P. B. Randolph, as attainable by the actual use of the sexual force, is a terrible snare. It was this fatal mistake that ruined the unfortunate, misguided Randolph himself. Therefore, remember, if you value your soul's immortality, that evil powers can be so gained, but those who gain them are forever lost. It is the true way to Voudooism and Black Magic. So beware how you play with the infernal laws which rule the realms of animal nature and outer darkness.[8]

APPENDIX
THE ANSAIRETIC ARCANUM

Note I. The student will naturally ask, after reading the Ansairetic Arcanum, and its companion work, the Mysteries of Eros, how the principles of nature, as therein set forth, can be practically utilized, seeing that in the great majority of cases, the true marriage of the twin souls cannot be brought about, owing to the fact that the two individuals may be born in different states, and probably in different countries; also, that they may never meet on earth, or be within a thousand miles of each other. All this is very true; but it must be borne in mind that these laws must not be considered as absolute, from which there can be no departure, because harmonious marriages, with all the requisite attendants of true, earthly affection and sympathy, may be found without attaining this ideal height of true, soul union. In this case, it is only necessary to marry or become united to one from the *same state* from which you emanated.

Spiritual states are very similar to races of people. By *races* we *do not* mean mere *nationalities*. These races are further divisible into states, groups, or families. Call them what you will, a thoroughly happy union requires the marriage to be between those of the same race, the male and the female of which form the true positive and negative of the

---

[8] The Lyon manuscript adds: "Peter Davidson, Grand Master of the Oriental [!] Section, Loudsville, White Co., Georgia, United States, July 14, 1887."—Editors

mental and physical states. A martial man, for instance, will find his real love in the female who is his opposite; that is to say, who is gentle and dovelike in temperament, but whose mental state *glories in martial actions.* The meek, gentle-natured man, will, in the contrary, love the quick, sharp, active female, whose mental state is *kind* and benevolent. These two states mentioned, are the opposite poles of each other, and the student can figure out the other varieties for himself at leisure, always bearing in mind that the temperament and mental state are two different planes, and may be called temperament and *disposition,* (which are generally of opposite natures). Unite a truly martial man with a thoroughly *positive* martial woman, then you have the flint and steel in perfection. They will clash and strike fire before they have been married a month. On the contrary, unite a truly *saturnine man* with a truly *saturnine woman,* and you will evolve the miserly spleen of satan in less than a week.

With these considerations before you, it is easy to see that these mysteries point to a thorough revision of the present matrimonial code. The time of birth should always be carefully noted; and it is to be hoped that the day will come when the registration of this important date will be enforced by law, just as the registration of birth and death is now enforced in Europe, so that it will always be possible to ascertain correctly the natal data. From this data an Horoscope should be calculated and the true temperament and disposition carefully delineated. This will always infallibly indicate the real spiritual state from which the soul emanated; because it is impossible, (except through *disease or injury*), for a child to be born until its *magnetic,* as well as physical period of gestation is completed, and these are always in complete harmony with the stella[r] influx. *Nature, when natural,* always works in cycles. *Unnatural,* nature *is the convulsion of nature.* With this information to guide them, man and woman will always know *who* and *when* to marry.

Note II. Remember that the deliberate use of so-called "checks" against conception, is a fearful crime, and should never, *under any circumstances*, be resorted to; for the vital germ-seeds so wasted *will not leave you*, but, like famished vampires, they will germinate within the odyllic soul-sphere. *Your cruel act* has separated the Divine spark from them; only the animal portion remains, and they become the spiritual elementaries of your own creation.

When children *are not* desirable, those *natural periods*, when *pregnancy*, or, rather, *conception* is *impossible*, should be selected for conjugal union, if the female can be brought to the passional mood (not otherwise). It must also be added that those who have not the true, moral courage to battle for their offspring should at least have the physical will to refrain from sexual union. That man or woman who is *too mean* to pay the Piper for his music, should never be permitted to dance. Be it remembered that during the natural periods when conception is impossible upon the part of a healthy woman (and unless healthy they are not fit to become mothers), there is no ovum to become impregnated, consequently there can be no germination of life; hence, under these circumstances, *no elementals are evolved* into being. This natural course, then, alone, is safe, certain, and strictly honorable.

Note III. It has often been asked in reference to these sex mysteries, what must be done in the event of *one* of the pair not knowing or understanding these mystic laws? The answer is simple enough: The one who understands *must teach the one who does not*. If this is, from any cause, impossible, why, *then do your share of the work*, and you will be measurably successful. Nothing like so complete as "the dual exertion"; but still you will succeed to a far greater extent than you would think possible. Mankind are slow to learn, and educating them is a difficult task. We must, therefore, work by degrees, and be truly and devoutly thankful for small mercies.

Note IV. We have been asked to specify the teachings of our Order upon the subject of marriage. We take this opportunity of doing so. There are three classes of marriage, only two of which our order will recognize. The first is pre-eminently that of true, soul union. This is spiritual marriage in truth, and the happiest state when so united on earth. The second is *the natural union* of two, who, by nature, are suited to each other, as belonging to the same plane, state or center of emanative life.[9] These two classes, we hold to be sacred and inviolable, and consider all infidelity on either side, as one of the greatest crimes. We teach real purity in married life; but only when united as above. The third class are legal unions; they are marriages in name, and *frauds in nature.* By legal unions we mean *union by law* of two individuals unsuited to each other. This class of marriages, we teach, are unnatural to begin with, and we do not recognize such unions, but consider them as mere social expedients only. It is this kind of marriage that is alone responsible for the fearfully long catalogue of crimes specified in our divorce courts, and the petitions for judicial separation. When a man or woman, so united, becomes tired of the bondage, they have a natural right to be liberated from the load, and if the arm of the law refuses to untie the gordian knot, they are perfectly justified in *cutting that knot themselves* and setting such unjust laws at defiance.

Briefly stated, the above are the teachings in reference to marriage and its laws.

Concluding Note

It must not be forgotten, that the ideal state and the true, mystical soul-union, that we have expounded, is, in this generation, *the exception and not the rule,* and therefore, cannot be realized except by the few who may be called

---

[9] The letters of Barlet to Arthur Arnould, when the latter was applying to the H. B. of L. for membership, indicate that Burgoyne judged not only the horoscope but also the relative planes or states of the postulant and his wife. Note IV, as a whole, reflects quite closely the Theon's ideas as they would later be expressed.—Editors

fortunate individuals. Nevertheless, by a thorough study of these laws and the mysteries that they involve, an infinite amount of good will result, and *perfect unions* become more frequent.

We have given the laws of sex and revealed its hidden mysteries, not to gratify an idle or morbid curiosity, but to enable you to become true benefactors to your race by teaching others how to become happy themselves, and how to transmit such human blessings to their own posterity. We have spoken plainly and to the point. The student of nature's inner law cannot find room in his soul to store up any such useless stock as *mock modesty*. We look at nature as she really is. If God is not ashamed of his own creation, why should man entertain such feelings? *True men and true women do not.* With the remainder we have nothing in common. *They are but counterfeits,* and degrade the dignity of humanity. Therefore, dear readers, "Honi soit qui mal y pense."

—T. H. B.

PART III

THE HISTORY OF THE
H. B. OF L. IN DOCUMENTS

PRECURSORS OF THE H. B. OF L. (B.1)

Occultism Defined by
Emma Hardinge Britten (B.1.a)

Source: *The Two Worlds*, 18 November 1887, 3-5.

Although written in 1887, this account by Emma Hardinge Britten (1823-1899) is the single strongest clue to the precursors of the H. B. of L. If Emma was not even thirteen when she was discovered by what she elsewhere calls the "Orphic Society" (Britten 1900, 4), that dates its activities to the 1830s, and her departure from it to 1848 or shortly after, when "Modern Spiritualism" began.

As early as 1865, in an address given at the Winter Soirees, London, on "Ancient Magic and Modern Spiritualism," Emma had compared the new movement to the occult sciences of antiquity and, without yet using the term "occultism," had given a description of its main features. In her *Nineteenth Century Miracles* (Britten 1884, 436-437), she takes credit for having introduced the Western world to occultism in her magazine of 1872, *The Western Star*. She was very much more than the spiritualist medium and historian that she later appeared to be.

The world of the Orphic Society and its members is investigated in Godwin 1994, 205-212. Among the members whom Emma names, "Zadkiel" (Richard C. Morrison) was the dedicatee of Welton and Fryar's *Mental Magic* (see A.3.a, B.3.b), and the Fourth Earl of Stanhope was a patron of the French magnetizers, especially Baron Dupotet on his visit to London in 1837-1838. Dupotet is said to have been responsible for introducing Randolph, as a medium, to high society in France. The theme of secret manipulations of public opinion by the occultists of the 1830s recurs in Harrison, 78-86.

The description of the state requisite for practical occultism resembles that of the adept Mejnour, in Bulwer-Lytton's novel *Zanoni:* a man whose occult powers (notably that of eternal life in his earthly body) have removed him from every human emotion.

The main theme of that novel is the decision of Mejnour's pupil Zanoni to renounce such emotional sterility and the avoidance of death that goes with it, and to allow himself both to fall in love with a woman, and to die. Bulwer-Lytton makes it plain to the reader that Zanoni has thereby chosen the better path. Neither did Emma Hardinge Britten display these symptoms of the practical adept, for her writing is passionate, sentimental, and filled with strong affections and dislikes. We cannot guess her motive in printing this article in her spiritualist magazine, unless it was to set a standard of perfection that the Theosophists were incapable of meeting, and thus, as hinted in her last sentence, to debunk their claims.

OCCULTISM DEFINED
(by one who knows)

MY own claims to be considered as an exponent of true Occultism are founded upon the following grounds: When quite young, in fact, before I became acquainted with certain parties who sought me out and professed a desire to observe the somnambulic faculties for which I was then remarkable. I found my new associates to be ladies and gentlemen, mostly persons of noble rank, and during a period of several years, I, and many other young persons, assisted at their sessions in the quality of somnambulists, or mesmeric subjects. The persons I thus came into contact with were representative of many other countries than Great Britain. They formed one of a number of secret societies, and all that I am privileged to relate of them is, that they were students of the two branches of Occultism hereafter to be described; that they claimed an affiliation with societies derived from the ancient mysteries of Egypt, Greece, and Judaea; that their beliefs and practices had been concealed from the vulgar by cabalistic methods, and that though their real origin and the purpose of their association had at times been almost lost, it had revived, and been restored under many aspects. They claimed that alchemy, mediaeval Rosicrucianism, and modern Freemasonry were offshoots of the original Cabala, and that during the past 150 years new associations had been formed, and the parties who had introduced me into their arcanum were a society in affiliation with many others then in existence in different countries. These persons, deeming that the intrusion into their ranks of unprepared minds would be injurious to the harmony necessary for their studies, carefully avoided assuming any position of prominence in reference to the society, so that they might never be solicited to admit those whose presence might be prejudicial. Indeed it was one of their leading regulations never to permit the existence of the society to be known or the members thereof named, until they passed from earth to the higher life. It is in virtue of this last clause that I am at liberty to say that Lord Lytton, the Earl of Stanhope, and Lieut. Morrison (better known as "Zadkiel"), and the author of "Art Magic," belonged to this society.

I should have known but little of its principles and practices, as I was simply what I should now call a clairvoyant, sought out by the society for my gifts in this direction, had I not, in later years, been instructed in the fundamentals of the society by the author of "Art Magic." When modern spiritualism dawned upon the world, for special reasons of my own, the fellows of my society gave me an honorary release from every obligation I had entered into with them except in the matter of secrecy. On that point I can never be released and never seek to be; but in respect to the statements I am about to make, my former associates—deeming their publication might serve to correct some of the erroneous opinions that are put into circulation by individuals who arrogate to themselves a knowledge, of which they have not the slightest iota—not only sanction, but command me to present to the candid enquirer the following brief definitions of genuine practical OCCULTISM— ANCIENTLY WRITTEN IN "CABALA"

OCCULTISM is a study and application of the occult, or hidden principles and forces of the Universe, or, in its more limited sense, of Nature.

The study of occultism, called speculative. The application of that study is practical occultism.

Speculative occultism includes opinions and teachings, often so widely at variance with commonly received beliefs that it would be extremely unwise to subject it to the criticism of persons generically called the world. Speculative occultism of course might be regarded as *speculative only*, were it not possible by the aid of practical occultism to demonstrate its truths.

The subjects which engage the attention of the speculative occultist are THE CREATOR, or creative power; WORLD BUILDING, and the order and design of the earth and its spirit spheres; MAN, and his relations to the Creator, the earth, and his fellow-man.

DESCENT OF SPIRIT into matter, and its growth through embryotic stages, during which period it is first *elemental,* then *animal,* then *man.*

ASCENT OF SPIRIT into matter, and its progress through future stages of growth as planetary and solar spirits.

Besides these purely theoretical subjects are suggestions concerning the best methods of communing with spiritual existences, and or receiving information from lower and higher states than man. These, together with *some mental exercises and practices,* form the main themes of consideration in the colleges of speculative occultism. Spirit Communion, together with Astronomy, Astrology, Mathematics, Geometry, Music, Anatomy, Physiology, Psychology, and Psychometry, are all kindred branches of study which must engage the attention of the true occultist.

PRACTICAL OCCULTISM

PRACTICAL OCCULTISM consists, first, of a perfect mastery of the individual's *own spirit.* No advance whatever can be made in acquiring power over other spirits, such as controlling the lower or supplicating the higher, until the spirit within, has acquired such perfect mastery of itself, that it can never be moved to anger or emotion—realises no pleasure, cares for no pain; experiences no mortification at insult, loss, or disappointment—in a word, subdues every emotion that stirs common men's minds.

To arrive at this state, severe and painful as well as long continued discipline is necessary. Having acquired this perfect *equilibrium,* the next step is *power.* The individual must be able to wake when he pleases and sleep when he pleases; go in spirit during bodily sleep where he will, and visit—as well as remember when awake—distant scenes.

He must be enabled by practice, to telegraph, mentally, with his fellow associates, and present himself, spiritually, in their minds.

He must, by practice, acquire psychological control over the minds of any persons—not his associates—*beneath* his own calibre of mind. He must be able to still a crying infant, subdue fierce animals or angry men, and by will, transfer his thought without speech or outward sign to any persons of a mental calibre below himself; he must be enabled to summon to his presence elementary spirits, and if he desires to do so (knowing the penalties attached), to make them serve him in the special departments of Nature to which they belong.

He must, by virtue of complete subjugation of his earthly nature, be able to invoke Planetary and even Solar Spirits, and commune with them to a certain degree.

To attain these degrees of power the processes are so difficult that a thorough practical occultist can scarcely become one and yet continue his relations with his fellow-men.

He must continue from the first to the last degree, a long series of exercises, each one of which must be perfected before another is undertaken.

A practical occultist may be of either sex, but must observe as the first law inviolable chastity—and that with a view of conserving all the virile powers of the organism. No aged person, especially one who has not lived the life of strict chastity, can acquire the full sum of the powers above named. It is better to commence practice in early youth, for after the meridian of life, when the processes of waste prevail over repair, few of the powers above described can be attained; the full sum never.

Strict abstinence from animal food and all stimulants is necessary. Frequent ablutions and long periods of silent contemplation are essential. Codes of exercises for the attainment of these powers can be prescribed, but few, if any, of the self-indulgent livers of modern times can perform their routine.

The arts necessary for study to the practical occultist are, in addition to those prescribed in speculative occultism, a knowledge of the qualities of drugs, vapours, minerals, electricity, perfumes, fumigations, and all kinds of anaesthetics.

And now, having given in brief as much as is consistent with my position—as the former associate of a secret society—I have simply to add, that, whilst there are, as in Masonry, certain preliminary degrees to pass through, there are numerous others to which a thoroughly well organised and faithful association might advance. In each degree there are some valuable elements of practical occultism demanded, whilst the teachings conveyed are essential preliminaries. In a word, speculative occultism must precede practical occultism; the former is love and wisdom, the latter, simply power.

In future papers I propose to describe the two Ancient Cabalas, and the present attempts to incarnate their philosophy in modern—so-called—Theosophy.

—SIRIUS.

Olcott Discovers the
Brotherhood of Luxor (B.1.b)

Source: *The Theosophist* XIII (August 1892), 651-652, reprinted in Henry S. Olcott, *Old Diary Leaves*, First Series, second edition (Adyar: TPH, 1941), 74-76.

Henry Olcott published his memoirs first in *The Theosophist*, and then in book form as *Old Diary Leaves*. This comes from his account of the first months of 1875, when he considered himself under the tutelage of the African Section of the Occult Brotherhood, before he was "transferred" to the Indian Section following Blavatsky's own reorientation. Here he describes his writing of a circular designed to attract spiritualists to the new movement of occultism. Its interest lies in the evidence that the term "Brotherhood of Luxor" originated with Blavatsky. While Olcott was still inclined to follow Blavatsky's example in *Isis Unveiled* [B.1.d] and to identify this group with the "Brotherhood of Luxor" mentioned by Mackenzie [B.1.c], she herself was at pains to dissociate the two [B.6.m]. H. B. of L. members such as S. C. Gould persisted in identifying their Order with the earlier one [B.9.a], a view from which Olcott angrily dissented [B.6.n].

I wrote every word of this circular myself, alone corrected the printer's proofs, and paid for the printing. That is to say, nobody dictated a word that I should say, nor interpolated any words or sentences, nor controlled my action in any visible way. I wrote it to carry out the expressed wishes of the Masters that we—H. P. B. and I—should help the Editor of the *Scientist* at what was, to him, a difficult crisis, and used my best judgment as to the language most suitable for the purpose. When the Circular was in type at the printer's, and I had corrected the proofs, and changed the arrangement of the matter into its final paragraphs, I enquired of H. P. B. (by letter) if she thought I had better issue it anonymously or append my name. She replied that it was the wish of the Masters that it should be signed thus: *"For the Committee of Seven, BROTHERHOOD OF LUXOR."* And so it was signed and published. She subsequently explained that our work, and much more of the same kind, was being supervised by a Committee of seven Adepts belonging to the Egyptian group of the Universal Mystic Brotherhood.[1] Up to this time she had not even seen the Circular, but now I took one to her myself and she began to read it attentively. Presently she laughed, and told me to read the acrostic made by the initials of the six paragraphs. To my amazement, I found that they spelt the name under which I knew the (Egyptian) adept under whose orders I was then studying and working. Later, I received a certificate, written in gold ink on a thick green paper, to the effect that I was attached to this "Observatory," and that three (named) Masters had me under their scrutiny. This title, Brotherhood of Luxor, was pilfered by the schemers who started, several years later, the gudgeon-trap called "The H. B. of L." The existence of the real Lodge is mentioned in Kenneth Mackenzie's *Royal Masonic Cyclopaedia* (p.461).

---

[1] It has been already explained that I first worked under the Egyptian part of the African section and later under the Indian.

Mackenzie's Definitions (B.1.c)

Source: Kenneth R. H. Mackenzie, *The Royal Masonic Cyclopaedia* (London, 1877; reprinted Wellingborough: Aquarian, 1987), 309, 453, 461.

Mackenzie (1833-1886) had already referred to the Hermetic Brothers of Egypt in *The Rosicrucian* of April 1874. According to Howe 1972, 260, Mackenzie was keen to become a member of the "Fratres Lucis" (meaning Brothers of Light), a very closed group founded by Francis Irwin in 1873 (see Howe 1972), of which he gives a mythologized history here. Irwin was already corresponding with Peter Davidson in the late 1870s. In the third of these entries, for all Blavatsky's denials [B.1.b, B.6.m], Mackenzie seems to be referring to the young Theosophical Society. However, Davidson accounted for it by saying that many members of the Interior Circle of the H. B. of L. lived in America: a statement that might be understood as relating to Randolph.

HERMETIC BROTHERS OF EGYPT—An occult fraternity which has endured from very ancient times, having a hierarchy of officers, secret signs, and passwords, and a peculiar method of instruction in science, moral philosophy, and religion. The body is never very numerous, and if we may believe those who at the present time profess to belong to it, the philosopher's stone, the elixir of life, the art of invisibility, and the power of communication directly with the ultramundane life, are parts of the inheritance they possess. The writer has met with only three persons who maintained the actual existence of this body of religious philosophers, and who hinted that they themselves were actually members. There was no reason to doubt the good faith of these individuals— apparently unknown to each other, and men of moderate competence, blameless lives, austere manners, and almost ascetic in their habits. They all appeared to be men of forty to forty-five years of age, and evidently of vast erudition. Their conversation was simple and unaffected, and their knowledge of languages not to be doubted. They cheerfully answered questions, but appeared not to court enquiries. They never remained long in any one country, but passed away without creating notice, or wishing for undue respect to be paid to them. To their former lives they never referred, and, when speaking of the past, seemed to say whatever they had to say with an air of authority, and an appearance of an intimate personal knowledge of all circumstances. They courted no publicity, and, in any communications with them, uniformly treated the subjects under discussion as very familiar things, although to be treated with a species of reverence not always to be found among occult professors.

LIGHT, BROTHERS OF—A mystic order, *Fratres Lucis*, established in Florence in 1498. Among the members of this Order were Pasqualis, Cagliostro, Swedenborg, St. Martin, Eliphaz Levi, and many other eminent mystics. Its members were much persecuted by the Inquisition. It is a small but compact body, the members being spread all over the world.

LUXOR, BROTHERHOOD OF—A fraternity in America having a Rosicrucian basis, and numbering many members.

Blavatsky Defines the
Brotherhood of Luxor (B.1.d)

Source: H. P. Blavatsky, *Isis Unveiled* (New York: Bouton, 1877), II, 308.

This passage occurs in a footnote just after Blavatsky has quoted Mackenzie on the "Brothers of Egypt," without making any comment. She now seems to be half-confirming the information given by Mackenzie, particularly the numerous membership he attributes to the Brotherhood, and half-confusing it further. Bela and Kech are now in Pakistan, and there is a Lukh-i-Surkh in northwestern Afghanistan, but all were so inaccessible in comparison to Luxor on the Nile—a favorite winter resort for Europeans—that Blavatsky does seem to be drawing a deliberate blind. She returned to this theme in her article "Lodges of Magic" [B.6.m].

What will, perhaps, still more astonish American readers, is the fact that, in the United States, a mystical fraternity now exists, which claims an intimate relationship with one of the oldest and most powerful of Eastern Brotherhoods. It is known as the Brotherhood of Luxor, and its faithful members have the custody of very important secrets of science. Its ramifications extend widely throughout the great Republic of the West. Though this brotherhood has been long and hard at work, the secret of its existence has been jealously guarded. Mackenzie describes it as having "a Rosicrucian basis, and numbering many members" (*Royal Masonic Cyclopaedia*, 461). But, in this, the author is mistaken; it has no Rosicrucian basis. The name Luxor is primarily derived from the ancient Beloochistan city of Looksur, which lies between Bels and Kedgee, and also gave its name to the Egyptian city.

MAX THEON (B.2)

Theon's Marriage Certificate (B.2.a)
Source: General Register Office, London.

There are several errors in Theon's marriage certificate, including the ages of the partners. The registration of Madame Theon's death (10 September 1908, Parish of Saint Martin, Jersey) gives the age of 65 for "Miriam Lin Woodroff, femme de Max Théon." Theon was not a real M.D., but practiced occult medicine [B.2.b], and is reported by Mirra Alfassa and Pascal Thémanlys to have worked as a healer while in Algeria. Augusta Rolfe (born 1845), one of the witnesses, was known as "Sister Teresa." She lived with the Theons and worked as their secretary almost up to Max Theon's death in 1927.

CERTIFIED COPY OF AN ENTRY OF MARRIAGE

GIVEN AT THE GENERAL REGISTER OFFICE, LONDON

Application Number 4740 9

1885. Marriage solemnized at the Marble Office in the District of Westminster in the County of Middlesex

No.	When Married	Name and Surname	Age	Condition	Rank or Profession.	Residence at the time of Marriage.	Father's Name and Surname.	Rank or Profession of Father.
421	Twenty first March 1885	Louis Maximillian Bronstein	28 Years	Bachelor	Doctor of Medicine	4b Dean Street S. Anns	Isaac Leon Bronstein	Rabbi
		Jean Josephine Penelope Morel	27 Years	Spinster	—	41b Grove Road St. Johns Wood Marylebone	Villiam Jersey Morel (Deceased)	Gentleman

Married in the Register Office according to the Rites and Ceremonies of the _____ by License before me,

| | Louis Maximillian Bronstein | | | Augusta Rogers | | F. Whitensand Registrar |
| in the Presence of us, | J. Ib Morel | | | J. Boul | | G. Boul Superintendent Registrar |

CERTIFIED to be a true copy of an entry in the certified copy of a register of Marriages in the Registration District of Westminster
Given at the GENERAL REGISTER OFFICE, LONDON, under the Seal of the said Office, the 9th day of April 1984

Theon Advertised as Psychic Healer (B.2.b)

Source: *The Medium and Daybreak*, 3 July 1885, 431.

The publication of this advertisement in a popular spiritualist magazine prompted the *Occult Magazine* to deny that the Grand Master of the Exterior Circle had anything to do with this "Eastern Psychic Healer" (I/8 [September 1885], 57), without mentioning where the announcement had appeared. However, the fact that the address in Belgrave Road (now Belgrave Gardens, London N8) is the same as the one on Theon's marriage certificate [B.2.a] proves that Max Theon was indeed responsible for this advertisement. We do not know whether Theon consented to the denial, but clearly Burgoyne wanted to protect his master's incognito. The notice still appeared in the magazine a few days after the Theons and Augusta Rolfe (Teresa) had left London on 9 March 1886 (according to Teresa's diary), confirming the sudden nature of their departure [see B.6.j]. On the same page appear advertisements for Robert Fryar's magic mirrors, and for the *Occult Magazine*.

JULY 3, 1885.   THE MEDIUM AND DAYBREAK.   431

F. FUSEDALE,
Tailor and Habit Maker,
Style, Quality and Cheapness combined with Durability.

500 PATTERNS TO CHOOSE FROM.
Made on the Premises at the Shortest Notice. Goods direct from the Manufacturers, all Wool and shrunk.

SUMMER SUITS from £2 2s.

8, SOUTHAMPTON ROW, Opposite "Medium" Office.

TO AMERICANS VISITING EUROPE.
GENTLEMEN,—I am now buying direct from the Manufacturers, and can supply the best goods far cheaper than any other House in London, having everything made at my own Workshops.

SPECIAL PRICE LIST FOR NETT CASH.

Superfine Dress Suits, lined Silk	...£3 18 0	worth	£5 5 0
Beaver Overcoats, lined Tweed	... 2 10 0	,,	3 10 0
All Wool Trousers ...	... 0 16 6	,,	1 1 0
Suit of best Angola ...	... 2 10 0	,,	3 10 0
Black Twill Morning Coat	... 2 10 0	,,	3 10 0
,, ,, ,, Vest			

Soliciting the favour of a trial,—I remain. Gentleman, your obedient servant,

JAMES MALTBY,
8, HANOVER PLACE, UPPER BAKER ST., N.W.

N.B.—Patterns post free on application. City Atlas Bus from the Bank, and Atlas Bus from Charing Cross pass the door.

CALL AND SEE
MALTBY'S SHIRT WITH TRANSFORMATION CUFFS.
Making one equal to two Shirts, lasts clean double the time, a saving in washing, and at same price as ordinary Shirts, 5,6, 6,6, 7/6, a reduction on taking half-a-dozen.

WHAT IS BROWN'S AMERICAN VEGETABLE VITALIZING MIXTURE FOR?
IT is a certain and positive Cure for Nervous Debility, Indigestion, Palpitation of the Heart, and all Affections of the Nervous System. It never fails in giving satisfaction in all cases. Prepared by

W. M. BROWN & SON, 50, STANDISH STREET, BURNLEY,
THE GREAT AMERICAN MEDICAL BOTANISTS,
Members of the Eclectic Medical College of Pennsylvania, U.S.A., also Members of the National Association of Medical Herbalists of Great Britain.
IN BOTTLES AT 2s. 6d. AND 4s. 6d. EACH.

A GOOD BOOK FOR EVERYBODY.
Now ready, in neat cloth, eighty pages, price 1s.

HEALTH HINTS;
SHOWING HOW TO ACQUIRE AND RETAIN BODILY SYMMETRY, HEALTH, VIGOUR, AND BEAUTY.

Contents of Chapters:

I.—Laws of Beauty	VIII.—The Mouth
II.—Hereditary Transmission	IX.—The Eyes, Ears, & Nose
III.—Air, Sunshine, Water, & Food	X.—The Neck, Hands & Feet
IV.—Work and Rest	XI.—Growth, Marks, &c., that
V.—Dress and Ornament	are Enemies to Beauty
VI.—The Hair & its Management	XII.—Cosmetics and Perfumery
VII.—The Skin and Complexion	

WORKS BY R. B. D. WELLS.
GOOD HEALTH, AND HOW TO SECURE IT. With many Engravings. 208 pp., paper wrappers, 2s. ; cloth, 2s. 6d.
HEALTH AND ECONOMY IN THE SELECTION OF FOOD. Price 6d. ; or bound in Cloth with "Good Health," 3s.
WATER, AND HOW TO APPLY IT IN HEALTH AND DISEASE. With Engravings, ::.
WOMAN : Her Diseases and How to Cure them. Paper wrappers, 1s. 6d.
THE SYMBOLICAL HEAD AND PHRENOLOGICAL CHART. A Beautifully Coloured Engraving, and Definition of Organs, suitable for hanging on the Wall. 6d.
THE PHRENOLOGICAL AND PHYSIOLOGICAL REGISTER. For Marking Developments. 6d.
WORKS ON MAN embracing, "The Phrenological and Physiological Register," "Good Health, and How to Secure it," "Health and Economy in the Selection of Food ;" "Water, and How to Apply it in Health and Disease ;" "Vital Force ;" "Marriage, Phrenologically Considered." Bound in One Volume, cloth, 6s. ; half calf, 8s.
WORKS ON HEALTH : embracing, "Good Health, and How to Secure it," "Health and Economy in the Selection of Food," "Water, and How to Apply it in Health and Disease," "Woman ; Her Diseases, and How to Cure Them." Bound in One Volume, cloth, 5s. ; gilt edges and side stamp, 6s.

FOOD REFORM COOKERY BOOK. The Text Book of the Food Reform Association. By Thirza Tarrant. 2d.
HOW TO LIVE ON SIXPENCE-A-DAY, by Dr. T. L. Nichols. 6d.
HOW TO COOK : The Principles and Practice of Scientific, Economic, Hygienic, and Æsthetic Gastronomy ; with Model Recipes in every Department of Cookery, Original and Selected. By Dr. T. L. Nichols. 6d.

LONDON : J. BURNS, 15, Southampton Row, W.C.

Mr. and Mrs. HAWKINS, Magnetic Healers.
At HOME Monday, Tuesday, Thursday and Friday. Free Treatment on Friday, from 12 to 4 o'clock. Patients visited at their own Residence. — 43, Fitzroy Street, Fitzroy Square, W. (Near Portland Road Railway Station. Healing Seance every Sunday morning, from 11 to 1; voluntary contributions.

CURATIVE MESMERISM AND CLAIRVOYANCE
PROFESSOR ADOLPHE DIDIER attends Patients and can be consulted daily from 2 till 5, at 5, Rue du Mont-Dore, Paris. Clairvoyant Consultation by letter for Diseases, their Causes, and Remedies. For any serious cases, Professor Didier would arrange to come and attend personally in England

CURATIVE MESMERISM, by Mr. J. RAPER, Herbalist, also Healer of many years' experience, Daily from 2 till 10 p.m. Free on Saturday evenings from 7.30 till 9.30.—12, Montpellier Street, Walworth.

MR. OMERIN, known for his wonderful CURES of Rheumatism, Gout, Neuralgia, Lumbago, Epilepsy, General Debility, and several affections of the Head, Eyes, Liver, &c., attends Patients from Eleven to One and Two to Five, at 3, Bulstrode Street, Welbeck Street, Cavendish Square, W.

MRS. HAGON, Business Clairvoyant and Magnetic Healer 21, North Street, Pentonville. Patients attended at their own homes.

CAROLINE PAWLEY, Writing, Speaking, Healing Medium. By the desire of her Guides, no money accepted.—Letters sent first, with stamped envelope for reply. 33, Bayston Road, Stoke Newington Road, N.

MRS. KATE BERRY, MAGNETIC HEALER, 23, Ordnance Road, St. John's Wood Terrace, N.W.

MRS. CARRINGTON, 46. Formosa Street, Warwick Road, Paddington, Medical Rubber and Magnetic Healer. At home, 11 to 4 daily, except Friday. Patients attended at their own homes.

MISS GODFREY, MEDICAL RUBBER, and MESMERIST, 31, Robert Street, Hampstead Road, N.W. By appointment only.

NO MESMERIC PRACTITIONERS.—Zinc and Copper Disks for assisting in the production of the mesmeric sleep. Well made and finished, 4s. per dozen, and upwards.—J. BURNS, 15, Southampton Row, W.C.

THEON, THE EASTERN PSYCHIC HEALER, cures all diseases. Consultations by appointment. Free attendance on Saturdays, from 11 a.m. to 5 p.m. 11, Belgrave Road, Abbey Road, St. John's Wood, N.W. Eastern sure preventive of Cholera.

MR. A. MONTGOMERY, Magnetic Healer and Mesmerist, 167, Seymour Place, W. Tuesday, Wednesday, Thursday and Saturday : 10 till 6.

MR. J. J. VANGO, 22, Cordova Road, Grove Road (near G.E.R. Coborn Station), Trance, Test, and Business Clairvoyant. Seance (for Spiritualists only) Sunday evenings, 7.30. A Seance on Wednesday evenings, at 8.

PHYSICAL PHENOMENA.—Spirit-Lights and other evidences of Spirit-Power at an old established private Circle. Earnest Inquirers only admitted, on Sunday at 7.30, and Tuesday and Thursday at 8 p.m. Mrs. Walker, Medium.—Mrs. Ayers, 45, Jubilee Street, Commercial Road, E.

J. HOPCROFT, 3, St. Luke's Terrace, Canterbury Road, Kilburn. Trance and Clairvoyance. At home daily from one till five, and open to engagements.

MR. W. EGLINTON requests that all communications be addressed to him personally, at 6, Nottingham Place, W.

FRANK HERNE, 8, ALBERT ROAD, FOREST LANE, STRATFORD.

J. THOMAS, GENERAL CORRESPONDENT. Address: Kingsley, by Frodsham, Cheshire.

MR. TOWNS, Medical Diagnosis, Test and Business Clairvoyant, is at home daily, and is open to engagements. Address—31, Stibbington Street, Clarendon Square, St. Pancras, N.W.

MISS LOTTIE FOWLER, Trance, Medical, and Business Clairvoyant, 16, Bury Street (entrance in Gilbert Street), opposite the British Museum and off Oxford Street. Hours: 2 till 7 daily. Open to engagements to visit in the evenings.

MRS. CANNON, 3, Rushton Street, New North Road, Hoxton. Trance, Test, and Medical Clairvoyant. Seance for Spiritualists only, on Monday and Saturday evenings, at 8 o'clock. Thursday, developing. At Home daily, from two till five, except Saturday, and open to engagements.

ASTROLOGY.—Map of Nativity, with remarks on Health, Mind, Wealth Marriage, &c. Fee, 4s. Short remarks alone, 2s. 6d. (Stamps.) Time and Place of birth, sex. Letters only.—ZAEL, care of M. Jones, 21, Kingarth Street, East Moors, Cardiff.

ASTROLOGY AND ASTRONOMY.
DR. WILSON may be Consulted on the Past, and Future Events of Life, at 103, Caledonian Road, King's Cross. Time of Birth required. Fee 2s. 6d. Attendance from 2 till 8 p.m. Lessons given.

Personal Consultations only.

PHRENOLOGY & ASTROLOGY.—Delineation of Character, Trade, Health, &c., from photos, 1s. Nativities cast. Questions, and all important events of life answered by letter.—" WALES," 2, Ireton Street, Bradford, Yorks.

NATIVITIES Cast, Yearly Advice Given and Questions Answered. Send Stamp for terms to NEPTUNE, 28, Little Russell Street, London, W.C. Near the British Museum.

ASTROLOGY.—Nativities cast. Advice on Business, Marriage, Health direction of success, &c., by letter.—WALES, 2, Ireton Street, Bradford, Yorks.

A GENERAL SERVANT wanted in a homely family. An experienced person preferred. Write to "A. D.," care of Mr. Burns, 15, Southampton Row London, W.C.

VISITORS to London can be accommodated with Board and Lodging on reasonable terms, at 16, York street, Portman Square, London, W., only two minutes from Baker Street Station, W. Vegetarian diet if required.

A LADY wishes to meet with two Ladies to share a well-appointed home. Earnest inquirers into the truth of Spiritualism preferred. Address, LEX, care of J. BURNS, 15, Southampton Row, W.C.

ISLE OF WIGHT.—Annandale Villa, Sandown.—One or two invalid Ladies will be taken great care of by a Healing Medium, including Board and Lodging, for 30s. per week, for the six winter months at this pretty seaside town, which is known to be particularly salubrious.

ROBT. H. FRYAR, the inventor of the almost human " Automatic Insulator " on Crystal Balls, the Planchette of the future—still supplies the Black, Concave, Ovoid Mirror for developing "Clairvoyant Faculties," (the original speciality) by which untold numbers have been awakened to Lucidity of Soul-sight. See Circulars. "Mental Magic," post free, 2s. 6d.—ROBT. H. FRYAR, Bath.

THE OCCULT MAGAZINE : A Monthly Exponent of Psychical Research and Philosophic Truth. It embraces the Ancient Wisdom-Philosophy, Folk-Lore, Magic, Freemasonry, Crystallomancy, Astrology, Mesmerism, and Occult Spiritualism. Price 1s. 6d., post free.—MAY NISBET & Co., 38, STOCKWELL STREET, GLASGOW.

Theon on the Origins
of the H. B. of L. (B.2.c)

Source: Pascal Thémanlys. Used by kind permission. Translated from French.

This was the covering letter that Theon sent in the year of Peter Davidson's death with the bilingual manuscript of the *Origin and Object of the HBL* [A.1.c]. The poet and writer L. M. Thémanlys (probably a pseudonym of Louis Moyse, 1874-1943) came from a Marrano family of Angoulême. He discovered the Philosophie Cosmique in late 1904 or early 1905, and thereafter devoted himself, with his wife Claire, to promoting the Theons' works by word and writing. He was chosen by Madame Theon to direct the Mouvement Cosmique, and was the principal continuer of the Theons' initiatic line after their death.

The text of the letter is, in parts, so ambiguous and ungrammatical that any translation risks imposing meanings that may not have been intended. Therefore we give also the original French text.

The name "Hermetic Brotherhood of Luxor" was one of the most successfully guarded secrets of the H. B. of L. (see Introduction, Part 1). In 1886 Blavatsky wrote of a "Hindu Brotherhood of Luxor" (Blavatsky 1925, 348; Letter CLXXXII). Others thought that the acronym stood for "Hermetic Brothers of London." As late as the 1930s, the editor of *Etudes Traditionnelles* was still guessing about the name. Theon may here be giving the original form of the Order's name: compare the change of his own name from "Theosi" [B.3.b].

Theon here confirms the continuity, at least of intention, between the Order and his later work, as well as the fact that he was really the chief of the society. Moreover, he seems to acknowledge his own identity as the "neophyte" sought out in Great Britain in 1873 and to conform to the idea that the Theosophical Society was hierarchically inferior. The question remains open as to exactly when he found the H. B. of L. unsuitable for his own purposes: as early as 1884, leaving Burgoyne (as we know) to answer applications in Theon's name, or as late as March 1886, when the Theons left England for good.

The idea of "plasticity" is important in the Philosophie Cosmique. Love, or *pathotisme* (see end of letter) was for the Theons the plastic force *par excellence*, which could eliminate all kinds of fixities, especially moral rigidity. The Theons used the expression "Le Sans Forme" to designate what they also called the Causeless Cause, which alone in their system is not material.

Zarif
31 March 1915

The plenitude of goodness to you. Blessings.

My dear children and friends, we send you a short study. It is not from today.

As you know, or perhaps you do not know, a Society was founded years ago called the H. B. of L, which signified The Holy Brothers of Luxor [*Les Saints Frères de Louxor*]. Their head was Max Théon. Originally the society was destined for the Cosmic Work, but things were such that there were disaffections, and personal ideas or commentaries arose among the members, and they began to formalize different schools deviating from the Cosmic Light, and thus there was beneath it a class of so-called Theosophists. We send you a little copy of the first theme or sketch of the H. B. of L. Society, which we think you probably know. At the time of the dissension, we thought it best to cease active participation in the H. B. of L.

As you will observe, there are sketches there of Cosmosophy, of which we thought it well to give out the Cosmic Work which we have published. As Head, you must know clearly and positively the first effort of this work to which you have devoted yourself so nobly and in so fine a manner, with which we are so contented.

I do not doubt that you will find expressions there that we have perhaps not used in the Cosmic books; naturally, with further development, things change—not fundamentally but in form; thus you can see that the form is always destined to change, because form cannot be without fixity. You use that word in your last letter, saying that we must struggle against fixity and that nevertheless fixity is necessary for form. It is difficult to express in words; intellectually I can understand it more easily; intellectually. That which cannot be expressed can be conceived of. There, you see plasticity intervenes, but in any case we think it right for you to read the study, since it should be thus.

Tell my little cosmic friend Pascal hello from me, and I embrace him tenderly. I wish him the wisdom that begins with obedience, a beginning that is the best foundation. Embrace my dear Claire. I am yours in all pathotism.

Extrait d'une lettre de Théon à Thémanlys (31 mars 1915)

A vous la plénitude du bien. Bénédiction.

Mes chers enfants et amis. Nous vous envoyons une petite étude. Elle n'est pas d'aujourd'hui.

Comme vous savez, ou peut-être vous ne savez pas qu'une Société était établie il y a des années, intitulée le H. B. of L., ce qui signifia Les Saints Frères de Louxor. Leur Chef fut Max Théon. Originairement la société était destinée être l'oeuvre Cosmique mais les choses étaient telles qu'il y avait désaffection et des idées ou commentaires personnelles s'élevèrent parmi les membres et ils commencèrent à formaliser différentes écoles déviant de la Lumière Cosmique et ainsi il y avait là-dessus une classe de soi-disant Théosophes. Le premier thème ou ébauche de la société H. B. of L., nous vous en e[n]voyons un petit exemplaire que nous pensons bien que vous le connaîtriez. A l'époque de la dissension, nous le pensions bien de cesser l'agissement actif dans le H. B. of L.

Comme vous observerez, il s'y trouve des ébauches de la Cosmosophie dont nous le pensons bien de donner l'ouvrage Cosmique que nous avons publié. Comme Chef, vous devez savoir clairement, positivement, la première tentative de cette oeuvre à laquelle vous vous êtes consacré si noblement, d'une si belle manière, ce dont nous sommes si contents.

Je ne doute pas que vous y trouverez des expressions peut-être que nous n'avons pas exprimée dans les ouvrages Cosmiques; naturellement avec plus de développement, les choses changent non pas fondamentalement mais en forme, ainsi vous verrez que la forme est toujours destinée à changer parce que la forme ne peut pas être sans fixité. Dans votre dernière lettre vous vous serviez du mot en disant qu'il nous fallait lutter contre la fixité et cependant la fixité est nécessaire pour la forme. Il est difficile d'exprimer

en mots; intellectuellement je peux comprendre plus facile-
ment intellectuellement. Ce qui ne peut pas être exprimé
peut être conçu. Là vous voyez intervient la plasticité, mais
en tout cas nous le pensons bien que vous lisiez l'étude car
il doit en être ainsi.

Dites à mon petit ami cosmique Pascal bonjour de ma
part et je l'embrasse tendrement. Je le souhaite la sagesse
qui commence par l'obéissance initiative qui est le meilleur
fondement. Embrassez ma chère Claire. Je vous suis uni en
tout pathotisme.

Symbol

THE LAUNCHING OF THE H. B. OF L.
AND THE *OCCULT MAGAZINE* (B.3)

A First Hint (B.3.a)

Source: *The Seer and Celestial Reformer* I/1 (July 1884), 1.

We know nothing about the "British and Foreign Society of Occultists," in which the H. B. of L. appears to have had a part. *The Seer*, which was very lightweight in comparison to the *Occult Magazine*, was edited by John Thomas, who was a medium claiming to heal from a distance (as he advertised in *The Occultist* I/1 [January 1885], 8). Ayton mentions him in his letter to Irwin [B.6.c].

PUBLISHED EVERY MONTH.

POST FREE 1s. 6d., PER ANNUM.

No 1.—Vol 1.　　JULY, 1884.　　One Penny.

THE SEER

AND CELESTIAL REFORMER.

JULY, 1884.

INTRODUCTORY.

It is to the "British and Foreign Society of Occultists" that we dedicate this our little monthly. As it is to the liberality of this grand Brotherhood that our paper owes its existence, it may be briefly stated that the object and aim of this Order is, " Peace on earth and good will towards men, and Glory to God in the Highest." The teachings of this fraternity are of two kinds : Esoteric or secret, and Exoteric or what is for publicity. Hence the principles advocated in this paper may be looked upon, in the main, as the principles of the above Society.

The size of our paper will contrast but poorly with those bulkier penny journals which are issued weekly and monthly by wealthy and enterprising publishers, nevertheless, we indulge ourselves with a hope that we may be able to compensate in quality for what now appears lacking in quantity. In the meantime, we promise a larger edition when subscribers will put us in a position to do so. We have much to bring before our readers which we think cannot fail to be interesting, and in many cases instructive, to a very numerous class. As there are in the present day tens of thousands of thoughtful persons, whose highest pleasures are derived from assurances of the great beyond.

All religions, and every creed, recognizes the being of a God, the immortality of the soul, and a future state. These are also our basic truths, as these contain all the material we shall ever require for present speculation, and for future elaboration. It is not our intention to make or meddle with the conscientious beliefs of any man or sect of men ; but simply give to the world what we may have to impart, leaving results in His hands, to Whom we are accountable.

Instead, therefore, of finding fault with this or that creed or dogmas, let it rather be our endeavour to prove the superiority of our own creed by living better and more useful lives, as such would be more to the point than useless displays of literary dexterity in hair-splitting ; for that is the good tree which brings good fruit, and it is by the fruit the tree is known. " For it is not everyone that saith, Lord, Lord, that shall enter into the reward ; but he that doeth the will of the Father."

THE ETERNITY AND UNIVERSALITY OF IDEAS.

THERE is not an idea, however new its claim, but what antedates its supposed birth. For what is universal must be eternal, and *vice versa*. At least, so far as our powers of comprehension carry us. But the universality of ideas does not imply that such have existed from eternity in their present developed condition. Not at least such as we may now find them in their materialized forms, clothed in the words, works, and deeds of mankind. An idea is a power, but not before it be formed and verified by something greater than itself. This something lies deep down in that nature called human. This something is a divinity. This divinity extracts, it modifies, it manipulates. Yes, and what is greater still, this divinity creates. Thus it is that originally all ideas are devoloped from those mysterious depths, depths that have hitherto been unfathomed, and will prove unfathomable for ever. And it is out of these depths that ideas have been projected in materialized forms, partaking of all the shapes which accost our outer senses. When a man has conceived a new idea, it is

The First Advertisement (B.3.b)

Source: *The Divine Pymander of Hermes Mercurius Trismegistus*
(Bath: Robert H. Fryar, 1884), 112.

This is the first document we know to bear the name of Theon. The name as printed was "Theosi," corrected to "Theon" in a printed errata slip. The announcement was repeated in the review of the work in *The Theosophist* (November 1884, 46-47) and in several other places [see B.5.a, B.6.m].

Fryar was a bookseller in Bath who published the "Bath Occult Reprints," limited editions of occult works. His publications included the first scholarly work of W. Wynn Westcott: editions of *The Isiac Tablet of Bembo* and *Sepher Yetzirah* (both 1887); also *The Virgin of the World* (1885), edited by Anna Kingsford and Edward Maitland, which gave rise to Blavatsky's confusion about "the fair Anna" being involved in the H. B. of L. [B.5.j]. Fryar's booklist included mild and erudite pornography, including the four books of his "Esoteric Physiology Series" (see Jennings 1895, 57). The journal *Miscellaneous Notes and Queries*, published in Manchester, New Hampshire by S. C. Gould [see B.9.a], regularly listed Fryar's publications, including some for which subscriptions were invited but which never materialized.

Fryar also imported the first "Bhattah mirrors" into England and sold other types [B.2.b]. In the early 1880s at least, he was the agent in England for the sale of Randolph's sexual magic manuscripts. By January 1885 his relations with Davidson and Burgoyne were going bad, and by late spring he was expelled, the stated reason being that he was overcharging neophytes for copies of *Eulis*. Fryar wrote to Ayton that he had not, in fact, been paid for his work.

The Preface to this edition of the *Corpus Hermeticum* was contributed by Hargrave Jennings, writer on the Rosicrucians and on phallicism, whose works were adapted for the H. B. of L.'s teaching manuscripts [A.2.a]. Other translations of the Hermetic corpus appeared in *The Occult Magazine*.

At least one copy of the *Pymander* bore the handwritten advise that communications should be to "Theosi, care of R. A. Campbell, Publisher, St. Louis, Mo." Campbell was even more of a fringe figure than Fryar. He was the author and publisher of various potboilers on the phallic element in religion and mythology. His cards reveal his proclivities: "School of Theosophy & Psychic Healing. Teacher & Practitioner of Philosophic & Scientific Mind Cure, No. 418 Olive Street, St. Louis. Consultation & Correspondence solicited." In a letter of 1 December 1885, to an unnamed American neophyte (Private Collection), Ayton warned his American "chelas" that Campbell had applied to the Order and been rejected—as usual, Ayton labeled Campbell a "Jesuit." However, Campbell continued to have some relationship with groups collaterally related to the H. B. of L.

TO WHOM IT MAY CONCERN.

Students of the Occult Science, searchers after truth and Theosophists who may have been disappointed in their expectations of Sublime Wisdom being freely dispensed by HINDOO MAHATMAS, are cordially invited to send in their names to the Editor of this Work, when, if found suitable, [sic] can be admitted, after a short probationary term, as members of an Occult Brotherhood, who do not boast of their knowledge or attainments, but teach freely and without reserve all they find worthy to receive.

N. B. All communications should be addressed 'Theosi' c/o Robt. H. Fryar, Bath.

[Printed erratum] CORRECTION.

"Correspondents" will please read and address "Theosi" as "THEON."

The Seer Becomes The Occultist (B.3.c)

Source: *The Seer and Celestial Reformer* I/6 (December 1884), 1.

An Important Announcement.

The noble brothers of the "Inner Temple" have proposed that the first number of the *Occulist* be a double number. And they have most generously offered to make up deficiencies of a financial character in the first number. They are pushing the sale of our paper most *energetically*, in order to make our enterprize a success to ourselves, and a GREAT BOON to all classes of readers. We therefore urge upon each member of the B.F.S.O. that they do all they can to get subscribers, and that such subscriptions be sent in with as little delay as possible.

THE EDITOR OF THE OCCULIST.

NOTICES.

The first number of *The Occulist* will appear in January, 1855, which will contain an able article, entitled—

THE "VEIL OF ISIS,"
BY "ZANONI."

It is in deference to a very ancient and honourable order of Occulists, the H.B., of L. that THE SEER AND CELESTIAL REFORMER, will, after the current number, be published as THE OCCULIST.

The question of who owned the title *The Occultist* was never clearly resolved, obliging the editor-in-chief (actually Davidson, though he did not appear as such) and Burgoyne to abandon it for the more ambiguous title of *The Occult Magazine* [B.3.d]. *The Occultist* later complained about this state of affairs [B.3.f]. The date 1855 is a misprint for 1885.

The Occultist Becomes *The Occult Magazine* (B.3.d)

Source: *The Occult Magazine* I/1 (February 1885), 1.

This first page of the H. B. of L.'s new magazine (now indepen-dent from John Thomas) shows the essentials of what it would contain during the two full years of its existence (counting no.1 of *The Occultist*): texts from the *Corpus Hermeticum*, and articles mainly by Davidson (under the pseudonym of "Mejnour") and Burgoyne (under that of "Zanoni"). These two names were bor-rowed from Bulwer-Lytton's novel *Zanoni*, as was the later con-tributor "Glyndon," who readers were told was a French occultist. This was almost certainly Barlet, since Glyndon's arti-cles appear under Barlet's name in *L'Antimatérialiste*.

The Occult Magazine:

A MONTHLY JOURNAL OF

Psychical and Philosophical Research.

· "*A Chronicle of Strange, and Secret, and Forgotten Things.*"—SHELLEY.

VOL. I. NO. 1.] GLASGOW, FEBRUARY, 1885. [PRICE ONE PENNY.

TABLE OF CONTENTS.

Omnia vincit Veritas.

TO OUR READERS.

SUBSCRIPTION RATES.—Single Copies, post free, 1½d.; for Twelve Months, 1s. 6d.

SPECIAL NOTICE.—To any one sending us FIVE Subscribers' Names for One Year, we will post *The Occult Magazine* as a premium for that period.

Friends throughout the world will oblige the Editor by forwarding to him Papers or Magazines, issued in their respective localities, that may happen to contain any matter likely to prove interesting, or in which statements may appear of an incorrect character. The paragraphs *should be marked* in order to save trouble.

CORRESPONDENCE.—All Communications, whether of a Literary or Business Character, Books for Review, etc., should be addressed :—

>   *To the Editor of* "THE OCCULT MAGAZINE,"
>   Care of H. NISBET & CO.,
>   38 STOCKWELL STREET, GLASGOW.
> Postal Orders to be left blank.

The Occult Magazine.

FEBRUARY, 1885.

It is our painful duty to herein announce to our readers that the Private Secretary of our Noble Order is in the meantime seriously ill, the overwhelming strain having been too much for his organisation. Those students who are, therefore, specially under his counsel are hereby requested to note this.

Our readers will observe that this, our new monthly, appears under a change of name—*The Occult Magazine*—an entirely separate paper from *The Occultist*, the latter having been Registered as the property of another. Our Title is sufficiently suggestive to anyone slightly acquainted with the multifarious branches included in the arcana of Occultism. Having a mission to fulfil and a duty to perform towards our fellow-students, and from the nature of the subject-matter and the space requisite for the teachings of our Order, we have been compelled to take this independent course. In future *The Occult Magazine* will be issued on the 1st of every Month.

We regret to state that owing to the severe illness of "*Zanoni,*" a continuation of his admirable article, "*The Veil of Isis,*"—the first portion of which appeared in *January* "*Occultist*"—must be postponed until our *March* issue. In order to complete that voluminous portion of "*The Book of the King of Ammon,*" which forms the 1st Chapter, we have been prevented from inserting the continuation of "*Rosicrucia*" (by "*Mejnour*") in our present number. This article will also be continued in our issue for *March*.

The Ancient WISDOM-PHILOSOPHY, FOLK-LORE, MAGIC, CRYSTALLOMANCY, ASTROLOGY, MESMERISM, OCCULT SPIRITUALISM, and other branches of a kindred nature, will always find an appropriate place in our columns, and our policy amounts to a pledge that no facts shall be suppressed, nor tampering permitted with any communications in order to partially serve, or favour, the ends or purposes of any sectarian or biased creed whatsoever.

IMPORTANT ANNOUNCEMENT.

As the valuable works of the ancient Hermetic writers have heretofore been confined to volumes, scarce and difficult to obtain, or to "*Reprints*"—the prices of which are, in most instances, entirely beyond the reach of the masses; to remedy this evil, and to bring those ancient authors into familiar intercourse with the thinking classes, we beg to notify that it is our intention to issue *cheap* translations and reprints of such, should sufficient subscribers come forward to meet the expense of publication.

We, therefore, beg to call the attention of our readers to the advertisement in our last column.

A Page from
The Occult Magazine (B.3.e)

Source: *The Occult Magazine* I/1 (February 1885), 8.

This page is rich in information on many things. Although the H. B. of L.'s practical teachings depended largely on Randolph's sexual magic manuscripts, it distanced itself from the man because of his eccentricities. Therefore it deliberately recorded his suicide, which would be censored or modified by many later writers.

Second, in the correspondence column there appears the notorious Theosophist, Otho Alexander of Corfu, an assiduous correspondent with a fertile imagination (see *Occult Magazine* II/21-23 [Oct.-Nov.-Dec. 1886], 80). The letters of Davidson to Barlet in July 1887 originated from him. René Guénon wrongly identifies him with Alfred Alexander of Madras, who published the (forged?) Blavatsky-Coulomb correspondence (Guénon 1982, 319). The correspondent "X.Y." of Rochester (NY) refers to Mrs. Josephine Cables or one of her circle.

Third, there is an advertisement for magic mirrors, showing that Davidson was now competing in this field with Fryar [B.2.b, B.3.b] and the inheritors of Randolph's business. Later issues give the name "Peter Davidson Junr.," presumably his son. The "Oriental Sensitising Substance" refers to the sexual-magnetic consecration of such mirrors. Davidson published an article, "The Bhattah Mirrors," in *The Theosophist* V/3 (December 1883), 72-74, which reproduced Col. Stephen Fraser's description of the consecration rites from his *Twelve Years in India*. This received a friendly and confirmatory note from Blavatsky (*BCW*, VI, 6-8).

Fourthly, Theon is mentioned in the "Important Notice" about reissues of occult and Hermetic texts after the example of Fryar [B.3.b], which did not appear, perhaps for want of subscribers.

Fifthly, there is reference to the emblem of the H. B. of L., which is found in reissues of *The Light of Egypt* and also on Ayton's and Burgoyne's letterheads [B.6.c, B.7.b]. The two intersecting equilateral triangles were also used by the Martinist Order of Papus, which was intended to be under the H. B. of L.'s authority [B.9.a], while both these and the Uroboros serpent appeared earlier on the Theosophical Society's seal. A similar pantacle used on the cover of the *Revue Cosmique* (1901-1908), all of whose articles are anonymous but mostly written by Theon or his wife, uses right-angled triangles, this being the only difference from the version still used by the Sri Aurobindo Ashram. The four figures of Bull, Eagle, Lion, and Angel correspond to the astrological Fixed Signs of the Four Elements, who are invoked in the initiation rite [see Introduction to Part A, and A.1.e-f].

Lastly, *Ghost Land* is often mentioned in the magazine and even in certain manuscripts [A.2.e]. This work, which began publication in Emma Hardinge Britten's *Western Star* in 1872, tells of how its author, "Chevalier Louis de B—," was employed as a child-medium in Berlin, became a neophyte of the "Orphic Circle" in London, then attained adeptship in the "Ellora Brotherhhood." Barlet believed that Louis was in the Interior Circle of the H. B. of L. [B.7.g]. Every criticism leveled by the H. B. of L. at the new teachings of the Theosophical Society, following the move to India, had already been expressed by Emma Hardinge Britten in her *Nineteenth Century Miracles*.

8   THE OCCULT MAGAZINE.

To Correspondents.

THE LATE DR. RANDOLPH.—In reply to several enquiries, Paschal Beverley Randolph, the author of many remarkable works, for and against Spiritualism, the minor Rosicrucian Mysteries, etc., committed suicide in Toledo, Ohio, July 29th, 1875. He was a mulatto, about fifty years of age, and claimed to be a nephew of the celebrated John Randolph, of Roanoke, Virginia. In a letter to S. S. Jones, of Chicago, dated July 20th, 1875, Dr. Randolph wrote:—"Now that I am on the thither side of the *to-be fated 29th of March*, 1875, I feel that I can work and win new victories, no longer afraid of a lack of greenbacks, friends, or faith in God." "Did he mistake March 29th for July 29th? Had he a premonition of the day," asks Mr. Jones, "with the true month wisely concealed?"

T. L. M., INVERNESS.—Thought-transference is in reality nothing new, and dates not from to-day. Even history, apart from other sources, furnishes abundant evidences relative to the Occult faculties of the human soul. The Astral Light, or Universal Ether, is the repository of the *Spiritual images of all forms, and even of human thoughts.* Apollonius of Tyana, whilst in Asia, described the death of the Emperor Domitian, at the moment of the assassination of the latter in Rome; Plotinus, whilst at a distance from Porphyry, felt the magnetic influence of the latter contemplating suicide, went to his house and reasoned with him; and Swedenborg, whilst residing in Gothenburg, at a distance of 50 miles from Stockholm, saw in his *lucidity* a fire in the latter place, which almost destroyed his house. But history is abundant in such cases.

PROF. JOS. RHODES BUCHANAN, M.D., BOSTON, U.S.—Your valued work, "*Sarcognomy*," to hand, of which due notice will be taken in our next.

O. A., CORFU.—Thanks for your earnest support; we shall endeavour to merit such.

X. Y., ROCHESTER, U.S.—Your suggestions are admirable, and quite in accordance with our own ideas, but we cannot unfold to you our plans in this—an early number.

S. W., ITALY.—*Demon*, or *Dæmon*. Do not make such a foolish mistake as to this word. The early Christians, in order to make the ancient Philosophy odious, were in the habit of attaching the very worst meanings to that of angels and the immortal gods, although philosophers of the Alexandrian School applied it to all kinds of spirits, whether good or bad, human or otherwise. The later translation of *Devils* makes much of the opprobrious meaning. The *dæmonium* of Socrates was simply the *voi*.

The Occult Magazine:

A Monthly Journal of

Psychical and Philosophical Research.

Monthly, Price 1½d., or per annum, 1/6 Post Free.
H. NISBET & Co., 38 Stockwell Street, Glasgow.

To stimulate and satisfy the desire for information upon subjects of a Psychological nature, it is desirable to place "THE OCCULT MAGAZINE" on the Tables of Reading-Rooms, in Clubs, Mechanics' Institutions, etc.; and when such consent is obtained, the Editor will post copies for public use for 1s. annually. We hope that many of our friends will assist in this direction.

IMPORTANT NOTICE.

In order to meet the wishes of the Members and Neophytes of the Exterior Circle of the H.B. of L., and of the many Students of the Occult Sciences, who have hitherto been prevented from procuring Hermetic works, owing to their exorbitant prices, the Proprietors of "THE OCCULT MAGAZINE" beg to announce that, as correct translations and reprints of those writings are now appearing in the columns of that paper, upon the completion of each it is their intention to publish, BY SUBSCRIPTION, *cheap* editions of the following works:—

THE BOOK OF THE KING OF AMMON; THE VIRGIN OF THE WORLD; ASCLEPIUS, or the MYSTICAL DISCOURSES upon INITIATION; the works of the ROSICRUCIAN, PHILALETHES (Thos. Vaughan), viz., LUMEN DE LUMINE, MAGIA ADAMICA, etc.; SECRETS REVEALED by COSMOPOLITA; THE HERMETICAL TRIUMPH, and ANCIENT WAR of the KNIGHTS; BISHOP SYNESIUS on the PHILOSOPHER'S STONE; the COUNT DE GABALIS, or CONVERSATIONS upon the SECRET SCIENCE; the works of ELIPHAS LEVI (*English Translation*), etc., etc.

The cost of each Volume will be such as to be within the reach of the *many*—not of the *jew*—and in no case will the price of any of those Works exceed 3s. 6d. per Volume.

Each Work will contain *explanatory Notes* by the eminent Occultist, M. THEON. It is therefore to be hoped that our Readers will cordially Subscribe, in order to render our efforts self-supporting, and thus justify our intentions.

Meanwhile Subscribers' Names should be sent to—
The EDITOR of the *Occult Magazine*, c/o H. NISBET & Co., 38 Stockwell Street, Glasgow.

BY ORDER of the
SECRETARY.

To MEMBERS AND NEOPHYTES of the H.B.L.

Magnificent WATER-COLOUR EMBLEM of this ancient, noble, and venerated OCCULT FRATERNITY, well adapted for FRAMING. Price 2s. 6d., post free. Address—Editor of *Occult Magazine*, at NISBET & Co.'s, 38 Stockwell Street, Glasgow.

WANTED.—Copy of GHOST-LAND. Must be in Good Condition.—Address, stating price, to EDITOR of *Occult Magazine*, c/o H. NISBET & Co., 38 Stockwell St., Glasgow.

GLASGOW: Printed and Published by HAY NISBET & Co., 38 Stockwell Street.

The Seer Makes its Excuses (B.3.f)

Source: *The Occultist* II/7 (July 1886), 1.

This appears prematurely in our sequence in order to clarify the connection between the two magazines (see the commentaries on B.3.a and B.3.c). It already refers to the Burgoyne scandal. Peter Davidson answered what he called this "vindictive farrago" in *The Occult Magazine* II/21-23 (Oct.-Nov.-Dec. 1886), 80.

The Occultist:

A MONTHLY JOURNAL OF

PSYCHOLOGICAL & MYSTICAL RESEARCH.

[ENTERED AT STATIONERS' HALL.]

No. 7.—Vol. 2.	JULY, 1886.	One Penny.

THE RETROSPECT.

It is now two years since we set our little paper afloat. The first six months it sailed under the title of " The Seer." After being in existence a little over four months, an offer, a tempting offer of considerable support was made us by the Leaders or Masters of a certain " Noble order" known to the uninitiated as the H. B. of L.

The conditions to which we were asked to comply being as follow: First, that we allowed them, the officers of the H. B. of L., a portion of our space for Notices, Reports and Correspondence connected with Society matters.

Secondly, that we changed the name of " Seer " to " Occultist ;" and Thirdly, that we, being considered somewhat deficient in those rare qualities which are requisite in an Editor of an Occult Journal, were strongly urged, and urgently requested, to place all our MSS. in the hands of one of these officials, who being a " Master in Israel " would put such a finish upon our Paper as would make it quite a respectable Monthly, and so attractive as to render it worthy of all acceptation.

Of course we were duly informed that these kind offers were made quite disinterestedly. That it was purely out of kindness to us, as proprietor, that so liberal an offer was made, and that no ulterior or selfish ends were concerned. O dear, no, they were far above that sphere, of course. But, at the same time, we were not so low as to be capable of descending to matters of that kind. Yes, THE OCCULTIST was ours, so far as we were honoured with being responsible for the debts, and would be required to pay all expences, &c. But that the Editing and Management was to be placed in *their* trusty hands. Now we were willing to grant them a portion of our space for their own purposes. We agreed to change the name of the Journal from the " SEER " to the " OCCULTIST." But the third requirement began to awaken our suspicions, we began to feel we were

not quite safe, that is, that our paper was in danger of being "kidnapped," so we protected our publication by copyright. Seeing this, *they* now suspected, that *we* suspected that it was possible after all, that they might not be quite so good as they had represented themselves to be. Finding themselves defeated, they threw up the Sponge with a determination to begin upon a new line of tactics. They started another Journal, the " Occult Magazine." Well, this was not out of place, they had a perfect right to start as many as they chose. And, had this been *all*, we should not have complained, but a secret current of private slander was put in circulation, we were most cruelly treated by false representation. The few friends we once had became alienated from us, and forbidden to correspond with us. Our main support,. on which we relied for our bread was broken. The fact is, we were " Boycotted " as a " Black Magician" and branded as a " Hypocrite."

But the Angel world supplied us with courage. We started our little Paper upon the strength of Divine Promises, and although we have frequently been very low in a worldly sense, yet we have never been forsaken, while our would-be destroyers have been brought to confusion.

Such is an epitome of our past history. Our generous supporters will occasionally get from us back numbers for distribution, and we ask them to circulate to the best of their ability.

——◦◦:◦——

OCCULT TEACHINGS.

THE RELIGION OF THE PYTHONIANS.

In the Religion of the Pythonians we discover simplicity combined with the profoundest philosophy. There was nothing in their outward demeanour calculated to impress beholders with the idea of distance, haughtiness, or superiority. They did not *assume* anything beyond what they *lived*. They had no stereotyped mode of giving expression to their thoughts. They expressed

THE COLONY (B.4)

The Colony Proposed (B.4.a)

Source: *The Occult Magazine* I/9 (October 1885), 70-71.

Burgoyne's letter to the Editor (i.e., to Davidson) outlines the project for an agricultural colony that would eventually bring about the downfall of the H. B. of L. in Britain. The great attraction was the promise to reinstitute the ancient initiations (in "Temple, Grove, and School" as mentioned here—see A.1.e,f). Ayton, already an old man, was so enthusiastic that he was prepared to leave immediately. The Golden Dawn would soon supply this need of his and of other H. B. of L. members.

Theon, during the Mouvement Cosmique period, showed himself sympathetic to the establishment of a retreat-house for "sensitives," though this too came to naught. The initiation that Theon intended to perform on suitable people directly from his residence at Tlemcen underlines the fact that he no longer considered the ritualism of the secret societies to be necessary [see A.1.e, and compare B.2.c].

The eventual choice of Loudsville, Georgia, was due to Gorham Blake, an H. B. of L. member living there. The claim of the colonizers to be "total vegetarians" is at variance with Blake's impression of them [B.6.k].

A PROPOSED COLONY OF THE H.B. of L.

(To the Editor of the Occult Magazine.)

DEAR SIR AND BROTHER,—I am requested to bring under your notice the following particulars relative to a plan for the formation of a select Colony of our rural Brother Occultists. In this division alone there are many who possess a good education, whose lives are exemplary, but whose surroundings are quite uncongenial to that state which is requisite for the more complete evolution of the sublime powers of their souls. Time after time have their simple but urgent requests for brotherly co-operation been made known at Head Quarters, and at length it has been decided to place the scheme before those of our Brothers who are in a position to aid us. It is almost unnecessary herein to observe that the whole plan has met with the hearty approval of our revered Grand Master, M. THEON, whose valuable assistance has been kindly promised to us in the arrangement of all necessary laws, etc., for the government of the Colony, as also his special guardianship over the training of those Neophytes who belong to it.

The scheme—subject to modification—is briefly as follows:

1st. The chief object of this scheme is the formation of special training quarters for the exterior circle of our noble Order in the United States, isolated from untoward surrounding influences, wherein any Member could, upon approval, retire for study and meditation, as also for practical instructions in the Sacred Science, prior to his actual Initiation into the *interior* Circle of the H.B. of L.

2nd. The most practical method for the realisation of this absolute plan would be, to select about one square mile (640 acres) of good land, away amongst the Foothills of either the Coast Range, the Gabilan Mountains, or the Sierra Nevadas, in California, such land to be selected within a reasonable distance of a good market town.

3rd. This land would be cultivated as a farm at first, and in the least expensive manner. Amongst this section of our worthy Brethren are many who are practically familiar with every branch of agriculture, and who are ready and willing to form such a Colony at a month's notice.

4th. In order to put our propositions into practice, we require those, whose position in life enables them to concur with us, to form a small Syndicate to raise the necessary capital. Five per cent. per annum upon the capital advanced would be guaranteed, payable annually. The Title Deeds of the Land, Buildings, Stock, etc., would be held as security by those who advance the money on loan, until the original sum was repaid in full, with interest. It is unnecessary to observe that *such a scheme would be found to be, beyond all possibility of doubt, a sure success.* A goodly portion of the land would gradually be formed into orange groves, vineyards, etc., etc., and these, as capitalists well know, bring in almost fabulous returns ; but until the Share-capital was paid up, the Colony would be worked as one large farm, in order to save the expenses of sub-division, and implements necessary to supply a large number of small farms.

5th. The Colonists would do all the labour, grow everything requisite for food, and from their being total abstainers and vegetarians, the matter of food would be a minimum. During the spare intervals of farm labour, they would cultivate their own gardens and beautify their village.

In conclusion, we would say that it is impossible for our wealthy Brethren to sustain any loss, as improved land in California soon trebles its original value. There are experienced professional gentlemen, Members of our Order, whose private means are small, but quite ample to support them in such an ideal Colony, who would accompany the Colonists, and give their services free, so that we should possess all the elements necessary to form the foundation of a great and grand success. When the farm and village are in full working order, and the debt paid up—which would take about five years—then the Temple, Grove, and School, for the purposes of Initiation, would be built, and all Neophytes, who were strangers, whilst in the Colony, for the purpose of Initiation or Special Instruction, would be supported free of charge.

I shall be happy to give any further information upon this subject, if required.—Yours Fraternally,

T. H. B., *Private Secy. of the Exterior Circle.*

[We have been for some little time expecting to hear of the above propositions, which have now so opportunely reached us, viz., the proposal for the formation of a Colony to unite the scattered, poor, and industrious individuals, who are members of our Brotherhood, and who intend to live entirely for the amelioration of their spiritual, along with their earthly condition. It is intended that this Colony be exclusively confined to the Brethren of our venerated Order. By the formation of such, one great bane of social intercourse would be thoroughly avoided, viz., the strife and bickerings of sectarianism and religious animosities, for those Colonists would be simply devoted to progress, their aim being not merely earthly advantages, but a higher and holier development of humanity, that would carry its effects not only into the present, but into the future sphere of existence. Such an enterprise would embrace no state of cloistered or monastic seclusion, no un-natural and debasing asceticism of Monks, Nuns, Shakers, etc., but be maintained in purity of the family relationship, waging warfare alike with poverty, criminal riches, ignorance, idleness, vice, and sin of every description, until its influence would be felt as a mighty impetus upon the ages. From our being total abstainers and vegetarians, etc., we secure the greatest enjoyment and delight to the progressive mind, as well as the most perfect health of all our intellectual, moral, and physical faculties, thus promoting the growth of our spiritual nature. We shall keep ourselves entirely apart from political strife, or from the overturning or destruction of any social order of the country in which we may be located, but shall render full obedience to its laws as long as they remain the general expression of its inhabitants. We are, then, kindred minds grouped together, having one common object in view, viz., the progressive development of the race, by Members working and co-operating with unity of purpose to attain that grand object. We would therefore say to a few of our Fraternal friends, be up and doing, waste no more time in a life of either sloth or slavery, but feel your own responsibility, get far removed from those slums of moral degradation, where vice and misery shelter themselves in order to reproduce their kind—

> Where brutal Lust and Drunkenness lead the way,
> Where Squalor's sceptre has unquestioned sway,
> Where man—through animal—becomes a ghoul,
> And crawls in tears and hate through vapours foul ;
> Where children, screaming as their mother falls
> By father's fist, who to his Maker calls,
> As, standing o'er his wife in tottering force,
> He bellows curses till his throat is hoarse.

Knowing that it is a well-established fact that there are, amongst the Members of our venerated Order, men of pure benevolence, and of considerable means, who would gladly avail themselves of the opportunity to assist their poorer Brothers in obtaining a position and comfortable existence, in a country where

> The fertile earth for them spontaneously yields
> Abundance of her fruits,

we would observe that no poor, industrious, and true-hearted Member need despair of entering into a superior and better condition. We shall take care that the suitability and efficiency of our few brother Members shall be such as to secure us from the peril of individuals with misdirected minds, pernicious habits, or of false brethren. Of course agricultural progress will form the basis of the Association's first work. In America there are many such Colonies, at Oneida Creek, at Shalam, at Santa Rosa, etc., and indeed there are many other people whose minds are awakened to the need of a better state of things. In 1857, a German Colony purchased 1265 acres of land in the Santa Ana Valley, California, at two dollars per acre. It was divided into fifty lots, and each lot now contains a comfortable homestead, the village having a population of over 400, with Schools, Store, Post Office, etc. There are many other Colonies of an equally thriving nature scattered throughout this Garden of the West, and it is only a few months ago that we read of an orange orchard of ten acres yielding a crop which was sold for $10,000, or, say, £2000. It was only planted in 1875, ten years ago.

It is intended that the Library in connection with such shall contain the best books, so that ignorance, plethoric riches, poverty, and crime may die a natural death, and bright intelligence and sound moral habits reign triumphant. The children being removed from immoral examples, and the contaminating influences of vicious societies, would grow up in wisdom, intelligence, truth, purity, and industry. It is with confidence, then, that we appeal to our Brothers of means, to form a Council for the accomplishment of this, our most earnest desire. Already one gentleman offers his valuable Library of Books, etc., towards this object, which embraces hundreds of volumes upon Scientific as well as Occult subjects, Music, Philosophical instruments, etc., etc. Each owner will have every encouragement for the improvement of his own home, for it will be his own permanently, and with the possession of such a home comes the love, the respect, the industry—the natural consequences of its possession; and as home is the nest of virtue, a progressive moral tone is certain to be developed.

We see with pity some of our Brethren, sober and industrious parents, whose earnings, individually—a few shillings per week—are barely able to support them, and we say, Surely the hour has come for their redemption. Let our thoughtful Brother Members, then, lay those things well to heart, let them speak out by their actions, and welcome to a home in the West, our down-trodden but industrious Brothers —the sons of toil. To our wealthy friends we would remark, Contribute manfully your share of the world's wealth, if you wish to be a disciple in the world's work. Why should a man be a contemptible niggard of that which bestows bliss upon a fellow-creature, yet takes little or nothing from his own means of enjoyment?

Here is an extract from the letter of a Continental Brother. He refers to himself and another Brother Member :—

" Are we not poor and needy, thirsting and ardently wishing to go to such a Colony, and try to the utmost of our abilities to devote our lifetime to such grand pursuits. . . . If we are to be assisted in this matter it is our duty to return any advance made towards our passage expenses, by paying so much percentage yearly of the net proceeds of our income, falling to the share of each of us, and thus repay our debt. . . . This will be the true example of the union and division of labour, under the powerful impulse of loving and thirsting souls, who . . . will give the example for the real life men ought to lead on earth, in order to make not only themselves, but others, happy. Land gives in superabundance all possible necessaries of life, and Nature is bountiful for the sustenance of man, etc."

We are prepared to take immediate action, for now is the suitable time for accomplishing the work we have in hand. The above are only a few scattered thoughts, but we earnestly solicit correspondence from those of our American, and other Brothers, who may be inclined to assist us in our anxious endeavour—this laudable and meritorious undertaking—the accomplishment of which is our soul's earnest desire. We want a few wealthy and humanitarian Brothers, who would unite in the purchase of the land—in this there could be no loss—for the Colonists would pay a certain per centage of such every year, until the debt was cleared up. We earnestly request all those who are able to support the scheme, to correspond with us at once. It is proposed to raise the necessary capital by shares of £10 each, and when we receive a guarantee of support, we shall at once estimate the probable amount of capital required. It cannot but prove a very profitable investment.

Highly virtuous, indeed, therefore is the man who relieves the corporeal wants of others, who wipes away the tear of sorrow, who gives agony repose, and who disseminates wisdom, expelling ignorance from the soul, and thus benefits the mortal and immortal parts of his fellow-creature, for he who is perfectly vanquished by riches can never be just; and truly, what is *Fame?* Fame has been alternately assigned to the hero, the statesman, the philosopher, astronomer, theologian, but fame confines itself not to any rank or pursuit in life, for it can only exist in the breathings of righteousness. Real fame is not the birthright of the hero, for the laurels that decorate his brow have been culled from the cannon's mouth, 'midst the sorrowful music of the widow's moan and the orphan's wail. True fame never draws its immortality from the dying groans of the war-field; it possesses a higher origin than this, for it consists in the lofty aspirations of intellectual and moral truth, in an ever-present desire to HELP THE DESERVING—the humble but industrious sons of toil.

" Then let us pray that come it may,
    As come it will for a' that,
  · That sense and worth, o'er a' the earth,
    May bear the gree, and a' that.
  For a' that, and a' that,
    It's coming yet, for a' that,
  That MAN TO MAN, THE WORLD O'ER,
    SHALL BROTHERS BE for a' that."—ED.]

An Enquiry and an Answer (B.4.b)

Source: *The Occult Magazine* I/11 (November 1885), 85-86.

The communications of the "Philadelphia Brother" and the "San Francisco Brother" quoted in the Editor's reply to this letter, and "Excelsior's" letter [B.4.c], suggest that a few people were willing to subscribe to £10 shares. But formalities for a share issue were never completed [B.4.e], and Gorham Blake [B.6.k] confirms that no funds were raised in this way. A notice that appeared the previous month in Thomas Johnson's *Platonist* magazine supports Guénon's assertion [B.9.e] that the Californian location was quickly abandoned. It states that the colony "will probably be located in Florida" (*The Platonist* II/10 [October 1885], 157), which is much closer to the eventual location in north-eastern Georgia.

THE PROPOSED COLONY.

(To the Editor of the Occult Magazine.)

SIR,—I have read with interest the proposal to form a Colony of the H. B. of L., and locate in California, which appears in a late Magazine. Your selection of California, although so distant from Europe, appears to me a wise one, because it is possible to select a locality in that state, where the climatic influences encourage life in all its manifestations.

I assume that the promoters of the scheme do not intend to attempt a community life, excepting only during the building of the needful houses, but separate households united together in a federal bond, for clearly expressed and well understood purposes, accepted by all before joining. Community life, as such, has failed everywhere and at all times, and I beg the promoters of the H. B. of L. to lay the above to heart, for experience has taught that when the causes of dissatisfaction with their surroundings, which always induce the *majority* of a community, have ceased to operate in the new conditions, another series arises from the bottomless pit of the self-hood, more potent than the first, and these invariably operate inversely to it, and dissolve that appearance of solidarity which the former has set up.

To provide the conditions most favourable to success, it is essential that several commercial principles should govern, in every detail. Every thing undertaken that does not pay must be abandoned. The children of the " *World*" are herein wiser than those of the "*Light*,"·but in the proposed undertaking, the children of the " *Light*" must be as wise as those of the " *World*," for those of the " *World*" follow mother Nature's law, and err only in laying their natural gains upon the altar of *self*. The children of the "*Light*" should not, need not, and *will not* err.

I would suggest to the promoters to induce such of the H. B. of L., as would be willing to form themselves into a Company, with Limited Liability, to purchase an eligible tract of land much larger than required for the purposes of the H. B. of L. The most suitable portion should be appropriated to the purposes of the Colony, and sold to the H. B. of L. settlers at remunerative sums, payable in a series of yearly periodic payments. The portion needed for the educational purposes of the H. B. of L. should be sold at only the necessary advance upon cost to repay all expenses. The remainder of the tract should then be sold at the enhanced value which the settlement by the H. B. of L. would command. From this latter source there would arise sufficient profit to pay upon proper investment a sufficient and permanent dividend upon the original investment, and leave a balance, out of which an endowment for educational purposes could be made. There are yet suitable tracts in California, possessing timber, water, and minerals, to be bought at a price to make commercial success certain, under good management.

The location of indigent but worthy Brethren in the Colony could also be undertaken by the Company, who would add the cost of their journey to the price of the lands and houses, the repayment being spread over a term of years, as with the others; but no one should be allowed to settle on the Colony, unless they could obtain means to keep them, from one source or the other, until their land would support them.

Permit me, in closing to offer a few words of warning to Brethren—if such there be—who think that their location in such a Colony will be an earthly Paradise. To such I say affectionately, do not deceive yourselves, Paradise is evolved from within ; it is not primarily an outward condition. Paradisiacal conditions to a man not prepared for such, will intensify his discontent ; but a man earnestly longing for, and resolutely determined to find, Paradise at any cost to self, will perhaps find it more quickly when he is surrounded by loving and helpful friends, than in an isolated condition. —I am, yours, Experientia Docet.

[It never was our intention to form such an Utopian scheme as that which our respected correspondent seems to imagine. All such systems must of necessity fail—at least, in the present age, and with the future we are not in the meantime concerned. Our duties call us to the *ever-present ;* therefore, it must be clearly understood that our Colony scheme, being planned upon the advice, as well as the experience, of those who have spent a lifetime in the "Far West," it is really unfeasible that failure can arise from a pecuniary point of view. During the first few years, the land required for the Colony will be cultivated as one large farm, simply to save expenses. The homes of the Colonists will be erected in the place, and in such a manner as, that when the division of the land takes place, each home will be found located upon its own allotment of land. Oranges, vines, and olives will form the principal products as the land gradually comes under cultivation, but, until then, all available space will be occupied with that particular kind of produce, which, in the opinion of *those upon the spot*, will bring the best returns. We should only be too glad if a few of our wealthy Brothers would enable us to accomplish that which our correspondent proposes, viz., the purchase of a large plot of land. We already know of a magnificent tract of fine rolling land, well timbered, and with extremely rich soil, that could be purchased for about 2 dollars per acre. This could, when once colonisation was fairly established, be sold for at least 20 or 30 dollars per acre, and this in itself would well repay the shareholders.

We already have received several very encouraging letters from inquirers, as well as their promises of shares. One esteemed American Brother says: —" *Occult Magazine* just received. I have read the article upon the Colony scheme, and I wish it every success. I will take at least one share at £10, but if I were a 'wealthy bondholder,' I should like to multiply it sevenfold—aye, seven times seven. . . . . Such a colony will become as a city set upon a hill."

Another Philadelphia Brother writes :—" The *Occult Magazine* for *October* has just come to hand, and I certainly have enjoyed it. Your scheme for a Colony is a splendid one, and you may depend upon me for one share. I only regret I am unable to do more. . . . . Would that I could only join your grand enterprise."

A San Francisco Brother writes us :—

"To commence with, I should say 20 cows, a few hundred young fowls, several horses, sheep, goats, hay, and sufficient provisions to sustain life, a few houses, tents if wished—even with the latter one could live pleasantly and prepare the land for crops before the rainy season. I am acquainted with most of the nurserymen in this state, and can obtain the best and most profitable kind of trees, implements, etc., some even on credit. . . . . Should some Brother be impatient, and wish to start right away, they can camp on my ranche, until they found a suitable place to colonise on. . . . Allow me to state that the proper time for Colonisation is from July to October, this is the best time to examine land and its possibilities—not from December to May, when all California blooms like a garden. In the valley of the San Joaquin, with rich soil and irrigation, a Caledonian, and many an Englishman, would feel ill at ease—I know it from experience—besides there is the question of chills, fevers, mosquitoes, and gnats, which is important. . . . . My collection of Books and Agricultural Papers are at your disposal. The question is, Can we, the Colonists, raise a Capital of ten or fifteen thousand Dollars?"

Should any of our European Brothers, who have the necessary means, wish to embrace the opportunity offered by our San Francisco correspondent, viz., to go out as a pioneer in advance, we shall be glad to correspond with him, and we would earnestly invite those of our Brothers who wish to assist and further this important enterprise, to correspond with us as early as possible.—ED.]

More Promises (B.4.c)

Source: *The Occult Magazine* II/12 (January 1886), 6.

THE PROPOSED COLONY.

(To the Editor of the Occult Magazine.)

Sir,—Several letters having appeared in your valuable Magazine respecting a proposed Colony of the H. B. of L., which have excited my interest in this really splendid endeavour, I hope that prompt action will be taken to bring about so desirable a result—a result. which cannot but prove eminently harmonious, and very pronounced in its effects. The undertaking being of so much importance—a Colony of kindred and progressive souls—I trust no time will be lost, and I hope ere long we shall see the work commenced and carried to a successful issue. Every Member who really has the welfare of the cause at heart, and who is in a position to do so, cannot fail to support such a benevolent work, not only upon their own account, but for the general welfare of the race. I shall cordially take a few shares.

Yours, &c.,

Dec. 14th, 1885. EXCELSIOR.

[We heartily thank our Brother for his promised support, and we beg to announce that we are at the present time engaged upon the investigation of a portion of land, offered to us on very favourable terms by a landed proprietor, in America. In early Spring one or more of the British Members of our Order will go out to America—where in all probability a few of our American Brothers will join them, in order to form a nucleus of the new Colony. In a short time we shall forward to every Member a provisional Directorate Circular, and in the meantime we shall be glad to correspond with any of our Brother Members, who may be competent and willing to aid us in this grand movement. By the time the next Number of our Magazine is issued, we shall be in a position whereby we can give more decided details.—ED.]

The Principals Move to America (B.4.d)

Source: *The Occult Magazine* II/14 (March 1886), 17.

IMPORTANT NOTICE. — CHANGE OF ADDRESS.

ON and after the *14th of March*, and until further notice, let our American Correspondents address the Editor of this Magazine as follows :—

> *To the Editor of* " THE OCCULT MAGAZINE,"
> *Care of* G. BLAKE, ESQ.,
>   LOUDSVILLE, WHITE CO.,
>   GEORGIA, U.S.A.

Note also that our British, European, and Continental Corres. pondents may address as usual to Glasgow until the *20th instant*, after that to the above address in America. Also, all letters for P. Davidson, Banchory, N.B., are in like manner to be addressed to LOUDSVILLE, WHITE CO., GEORGIA, U.S.A., as above.

Our departure for America will make no difference as regards *The Occult Magazine*, which will be regularly sent out from Glasgow in the usual manner to the subscribers.

WE expected to have had our *Colony Prospectus* in the hands of our readers along with this number of our Magazine, but owing to an unforeseen delay n the *final reply* of the American Proprietor, we have been prevented from completing it. His reply, however, has just reached us as we go to press ; in a few days we shall post a copy of the Prospectus to each of our readers, and we trust that those who are interested in such a highly important undertaking, will cordially assist us in the establishment of this, our first Colony. If the capital can be raised, *we are certain of its being a grand financial success;* therefore we hope that every reader who can afford such, will subscribe for at least *one share.*

This shows that both Davidson and Burgoyne stated their intention to emigrate before Ayton revealed the scandal of Burgoyne's past. Davidson's new address is in care of Gorham Blake, who would later find himself very disillusioned by the man he helped to settle [see B.6.k]. Not surprisingly, the magazine was seriously interrupted by the change, and after April 1886 no longer appeared monthly, but in two oversized issues [see B.4.e].

Some Clarifications (B.4.e)

Source: *The Occult Magazine* II/17-20 (June-Jly.-Aug.-Sept.1886), 41.

The break with Gorham Blake had by now taken place, the chimerical goldmines had vanished, and the idea of soliciting shareholders interested in making a profit had given way to that of inviting persons interested in a spiritually-based community to come and join the colony. Barlet's letter to Chaboseau [B.7.g] fills in the background to these developments.

Davidson did not give up the idea of the colony easily. He enclosed the prospectus in his 1888 letter to Arnould [B.7.e]. We have not discovered a copy of this prospectus, which would have named as sponsors all the prominent people connected with the H. B. of L. in England, and perhaps in France.

ANNOUNCEMENT.

WE must herein apologise to our Readers and Correspondents for the delay caused in the publication of the Magazine, as well as our having up till now been unable to reply to several Letters, which shall have our due attention, as soon as opportunity permits. Several of our MSS. have been lost in transmission from this country to the Printer and Publisher, in Glasgow, which have entailed no end of trouble. Our Readers must also recognise that owing to incidental difficulties in locating here, in Georgia, the Magazine has had to be edited as time would now and again permit, and this literary work has almost all been done "out of doors," our rural and temporary "Home!" being too "confined" for such a purpose. Hence during this year it must be issued as a *Quarterly*, the next Number appearing in *December*. We are much disappointed that this has to be the case, but those difficulties have arisen from circumstances over which we have had no control, and we have endeavoured, under a weight of trouble, to do our best, and to make the Contents as interesting as possible, therefore we trust our Readers will be prepared to make all due allowance for the delay and the anxiety which they have sustained, but which really has been unavoidable, and totally independent of any direct fault of ours. We shall soon however be in a more favorable position, whereby we shall be able to meet all Correspondential demands, as well as carry on the literary work in a more suitable manner. To those childish enemies who have so zealously and maliciously abused and vilified us to their heart's content, whom all charity and benevolence hath fled from, and. who are jealous of the very *praise* their own lips uttered, whose choice epithets towards us are "*Black Magicians,*" "*Rogues and Swindlers,*" &c., &c., we can only say: "*We sincerely wish them well,*" and our desire towards them is that of our poetical countryman, when addressing his dusky Reverence, viz. : that they may

"*Tak a thocht an' men'.*"

————

CONVERSANT as we now are with the prices of Land—since we have become acquainted with this country—we found out that the property intended for a Colony of the Hermetic Brotherhood was, for many reasons, quite unsuitable for such, the contiguous lands being lower in price, and equally, if not better adapted for agricultural and other purposes ; that also owing to an error in the Colony Prospectus, we discovered it could not be carried out strictly according to law, but the Colony will in all probability be established upon a still more favorable and satisfactory footing, than if subject to the interest of Shareholders. This Colony will not be formed however upon any portion of the "*Blake Property*"—in which we have not the slightest interest whatsoever—neither will it have any connection with "Gold Mines"!! or such like risky, or speculating ventures. Intending Members who may be desirous of settling upon a small home in this locality—where the climate is perfection, and Nature so beautiful in her products—the Editor will be glad to correspond with. Let them address us as in next paragraph.

Davidson's Budget (B.4.f)

Source: Notebook of Peter Davidson, by kind permission of Dr. Allen Greenfield.

This list of the cost of basic items for an agricultural life in Georgia gives a good standard of comparison for the admission fees of the H. B. of L. [B.7.a, B.7.c-d], and proves that Davidson was not enriching himself thereby, as his accusers claimed.

Prices &c.

A House of one story say 15 × 24 feet containing 2 Rooms and small Kitchen, chimney in center, with Fire-place in each room will cost about $50.

Very little additional cost would give a 1-1/2 story house & 4 Rooms.

Lumber, that is, deals, cost about $10 delivered.

Wagon $60 to $100

Harness $12 to $20

Farming Tools $15

House Furniture $25 to $50

Cooking Utensils $5 to $20

Horse Feed, & Provisions enough for start say $20 to $50.

Customs Duties &c.

If you send Books & Globes the Duty is 25% on all Books under 20 years old, on Globes 33% of their value. If you *bring* them along with you there is *no* Duty charged *providing* your Name is written in each Book and on every article of that kind. If you desire to bring in Books to form a *Library*, you may bring only *one* of each kind for that purpose free, with this amendment, viz should there be among the number any which are for *Sale here* (US) a Duty will be charged.

Prices &c in Georgia State...

Good Labour is 75 cents per day

Farm Labour, 50 cents

Beef 3d or 4d per lb.

Corn 50 cents per Bushel

Chickens 10 cents each

Good Horse from $80 to $100

Cows from $12 to $20

Sheep $1.50 each

Farm Land $2 to $10 per acre according to Location & Improvements

Adjoining Land $2 to $5 per acre.

The "Colony" Established (B.4.g)

Source: *The Occult Magazine* II/21-23 (Oct.-Nov.-Dec. 1886), 61.

WE have much pleasure in informing our Brother-Members and others who may be interested in our work of reform, that several respected Members of our Fraternity have decided to settle down on small " Homes " in this locality, in order to promote the developement of their psychic faculties, to which the country and climate, etc., are admirably suited, and to live in a congenial spot where Nature adapts itself so much to our daily wants. One of our esteemed friends has already purchased a small farm adjoining us. Any of our foreign Members who may wish to know the prices of land or to learn of the nature of the country, or the easiest and most direct modes of transport, travelling, etc., we shall be happy to correspond with, and give them all the necessary information in our power.

This is the last that is heard of the Colony. One family, at least, appears to have joined the Davidsons in Loudsville.

THE POLEMIC WITH THE
THEOSOPHICAL SOCIETY (B.5)

An Invitation Renewed (B.5.a)

Source: *The Occult Magazine* I/3 (April 1885), 24.

TO WHOM IT MAY CONCERN.

Students in the Occult Sciences, earnest searchers thirsting for Truth, and Theosophists who may have been disappointed in their expectations of Sublime Wisdom being freely granted by the HINDU MAHATMAS, are cordially invited to transmit their names to the *Editor* of this Magazine, on receipt of which, applications will be forwarded to them for signature, etc. If found suitable after a short probationary period, they will be admitted as Members of an Occult Brotherhood, who do not boast of their knowledge, but teach freely and without reserve, all they find worthy to receive.

All communications to be addressed to—

The *Editor* of *Occult Magazine*, c/o H. NISBET & Co., 38 Stockwell Street, Glasgow.

The chief difference from the original announcement [B.3.b] is that postulants are now to address not "Theosi" or "Theon" but the Editor of the magazine, i.e., Peter Davidson [see A.1.a]. When *The Theosophist* (VI [November 1884], 46-47) reviewed *The Pymander*, it included the notice verbatim, commenting only that it "will be 'News' to our fellows of the Theosophical Society; and any one, who now believes that his qualifications have not been duly appreciated by the Himalayan Mahatma, may find a way to redress. But we will leave them to follow their own intuition."

Judge Utters a Warning (B.5.b)

Source: Notebook of Peter Davidson [see B.4.f].

William Quan Judge (1851-1897), sometimes regarded as the third founder of the Theosophical Society, had recently returned from a visit to India and was running the New York Theosophical Society while working as a lawyer. Obviously knowing very little about the H. B. of L., he identifies it with Hargrave Jennings (who never had a magazine), presumably on the grounds of the *Pymander* advertisement [B.3.b]. He cannot have thought it important enough to tell Blavatsky, because it came to her as a complete surprise several months later [B.5.j]. Despite this, Davidson wrote on 7 July 1885 that Judge had contacted the H. B. of L., and been accepted! A long exchange followed about whether he was really in or not. In his *Practical Occultism* (Judge 1957, 47-48; letter of 25 September 1886, to Mrs. Helen L. Sumner), he writes: "The Hindu Brotherhood of Luxor did some good to earnest people but I long ago knew—although I never joined it—that it would not last."

April 7th 1885

My dear Sir: The Society to which you refer is only a *scheme*. It is an effort on the part of Mr. Hargrave Jennings to make a profit by selling his books and Magazine, using the popularity and forum of the T. S. He, or Davidson, have nothing, never had anything, and never will have anything more than you can read in any book. By mysterious pretension and running down "Eastern Sages" they hope to gain adherents, subscribers, and purchasers. Damodar does not belong to them, nor anyone of us, nor countenance him, nor even run him down: But if you or your friends join in the hope of getting more than now, it will not benefit you. They have no connection with anything but themselves, and their Neophyte business is all bosh. Shew this to the others. Give my regards to Mrs. C. and your brother and believe me your friend,

—William Q. Judge

The H. B. of L. Defines Itself (B.5.c)

Source: *The Occult Magazine* I/6 (July 1885), 41-42.

This was a reply to an article in *The Theosophist* of May, 1885, entitled "Sham Societies." The Editor's fourteen years of occultism
are also claimed by the Private Secretary, Burgoyne, in a letter to
The Theosophist [B.5.g]. They correspond with the fabled journey
to England from the Continent of the mysterious adept, dated to
the early 1870s in the H. B. of L.'s own history [A.1.b]. In Burgoyne's Preface to *The Light of Egypt* [B.8.d], the fourteen years
become "nearly twenty," a figure that called forth caustic comments from both Blavatsky [B.6.m] and G. R. S. Mead [B.8.c].

THERE appear to be a few over-zealous Members of the Theosophical Society, in the neighbourhood of New York, who labour under a very erroneous, but dominant impression, viz.: that the H. B. of L. is but a *new* Order, and founded in consequence of the popularity of the Theosophical Society. We observe that the *Banner of Light*, in its notice of our *Monthly*, also makes the same mistake. For the information of all parties concerned, we herein distinctly state that the H. B. of L. is based upon no mushroom existence of yesterday, for its origin is almost lost in the depths of time. The present writer has been a Member of such for upwards of fourteen years. Our noble and exalted Order gives special attention to Practical Occultism, whilst the Theosophical Society has hitherto only presented the great majority of its members with volumes of Theories, and has taken, if we mistake not, but very little trouble to give instructions to those who are naturally adapted for developing in themselves

the only means by which such theories can be tested and verified, as well as thoroughly comprehended. Relative to the article in the *May* "*Theosophist*" —referred to in our last number—the most charitable conclusion at which we can arrive, is, that the writer has been labouring under a gross misapprehension as regards our ancient Order, though otherwise writing perhaps with a perfectly good intention, and upon a generally sound basis, recognising that *all* the Members of the Theosophical Society are *not* adapted for instructions in Practical Occultism. But we would say, in all good faith, that in our humble opinion the Theosophical Society errs in not taking valid means to find out amongst its aspirants those who are really qualified for practical study, and even those few who are eligible for such, have learned quite enough of theory from the Society to make them sadly feel the want of something more. All historical facts pertaining to the ancient Schools of Occultism, plainly demonstrate that self-development is a necessary means for comprehending "cosmic" laws, and the writer of the article in question—as the essay plainly evinces—is well aware of this fact, yet strenuously endeavours to repress it, and again stultifies his doing so by endeavouring to support himself by a quotation from Hermes to the effect that "the way is hard and difficult *for the soul that is in the body.*"

The H. B. of L. Defines the Theosophical Society (B.5.d)

Source: *The Occult Magazine* I/7 (August 1885), 56.

To THE AMERICAN THEOSOPHISTS.—The H. B. of L. is purely and simply the Western Division of the UNIVERSAL BROTHERHOOD OF ADEPTS, for whilst *all Adepts* are by no means Members of this Order, yet *all Adepts are Members* of the ONE SACRED BAND. Our Order does not in any manner interfere with The Theosophical Society, upon the contrary, it greatly aids it. The Theosophical Society does *not* teach Practical Occultism in a form suitable to Western people, in reality it is but a "sect" for the diffusion of "*Buddhism*," and its great aim is to propagate this creed amongst the thinking population. The Adepts of the Theosophical Society have very little indeed to do with it, and are *unknown even to its Members*. Those whom the Theosophists recognise as Adepts are simply the high officials of Buddhism, many of whom have developed Psychic powers. The H. B. of L., upon the contrary, teaches no "creed," but Initiates its Members into the Hermetic Wisdom, or, in other words, into Practical Occultism, and the *exterior* Circle of our Order bears about the same relationship to the *Inner*, or *real* H. B. as the Theosophical Society does to the Hindu Mahatmas, with this difference, however, viz., that we place Rules before each Probationer, and give him special advice, whereas the Theosophical Society does not. When the Probationer has developed the three requisite powers of his Soul, he is then Initiated into the real Lodge. There is not the slightest cause for any disagreement, and if the leaders of the Theosophical Society are jealous over the matter, it plainly shews that they are not yet free from the weaknesses and failings of common humanity, consequently they cannot lay any just claim to Adeptship.

Before Blavatsky and Olcott left the United States at the end of 1878, they were already in correspondence with Swami Day-ananda Saraswati (1825-1888), the head of the neo-Vedic Arya Samaj, and—to Dayananda's subsequent ire—with Unnanse H. Sumangala (1827-1911), chief priest of the Buddhist temple at Adam's Peak, Ceylon. On the Buddhist question, see Elliott Page's letter [B.5.e].

An Apology (B.5.e)

Source: *The Occult Magazine* I/10 (November 1885), 79.

Davidson implies ingenuously that Burgoyne had written the previous answer [B.5.d] without editorial control. In fact, Davidson had caused Ayton, a month earlier, to send Page (a member of the H. B. of L. and soon to be one of the Committee of Seven) the famous Otho Alexander letters (see Part 1, Section 12), to convince him of the truth of the charges against Blavatsky. The reply underlines the fact that the changes in Theosophical policy began with the publication of "Fragments of Occult Truth" in October 1881.

A MISCONCEPTION.

(To the Editor of the Occult Magazine.)

MY DEAR SIR,—Your note "to the American Theosophists" in the *August* number of your Magazine contains at least one statement which the American Board of Control feel called upon to correct. Without going into the question of Adepts or Mahatmas, or the kind of Occultism best adapted to the East and the West, the statement that the Theosophical Society is "but a *sect* for the diffusion of *Buddhism*" is entirely unfounded. The charge has been often made and as often denied and disproved. The fact that in India, where the rivalry between Buddhism and Brahminism is often bitter, far more Brahmanists than Buddhists belong to the Society, at once disproves the statement. Though Colonel Olcott is an avowed Buddhist, he has taken such pains to keep *sect* out of the Society as to satisfy thousands of Brahmanists of his entire sincerity and the non-sectarianism of the T.S.

You are simply mistaken, my good brother, and the necessity for this correction arises from the fact that the statement is offensive to the thousands of other faiths who belong to the Theosophical Society. If the H. B. of L. is to work as you say, hand in hand with the T. S., statements like those referred to, calculated to offend and easily disproved, should not be made, as they certainly will not promote fraternal feeling.

By Order of the Board,

ELLIOTT B. PAGE,

Secretary General for America.

THE THEOSOPHICAL SOCIETY,
American Board of Control,
ST. LOUIS, MO., U.S.,
September 15, 1885.

[We much regret that the paragraph under notice should have inadvertently appeared in the columns of the *Occult Magazine*, and we have much pleasure in inserting the above letter from our respected Brother, Mr. Page, protesting on behalf of the American Board of Control. For several months past our literary work and correspondence have been of such an onerous and overwhelming nature, queries and misapprehensions to answer, and rectify, from all parts of the world, etc., that we have been obliged now and again to intrust the transcription of copies, along with the correction of proof-sheets, to others, and we beg to assure our American friends that the notice referred to was inserted quite unobserved by us. We have, however, called the attention of the writer to the matter alluded to, and we find that the objectionable reply has arisen entirely from a misconception of the subject, his explanation being as follows.

Upon reading up the greater portion of literature published on behalf of the Theosophical Society, the writer of the paragraph found that Buddhism, either in its esoteric or exoteric form, was a prominent feature; that all his acquaintances belonging to the Theosophical Society were teaching Buddhism, pure and simple, as the future creed of Theosophy; that the Founders were Buddhists; that Col. Olcott's "*Buddhist Catechism*"—now printed in different languages, circulated far and wide amongst its Members; and moreover, that the revered Mahatmas and Adepts, who form the Interior Section of the Theosophical Society, are, every one —so far as the writer could learn—Members of the Buddhist cult.

It was with those facts so prominently standing before him, that the writer thought himself justified in using the terms adverted to, in response to a number of American Theosophists, who had written, asking if "we taught any creed, and if so, did it run parallel with Buddhism," but such conclusions, however, were really as *incautious* as they were *incorrect*; but without wishing to enter into any controversy with our respected Brother, we cannot allow his assertion, that there are "more Brahmins than Buddhists" in India "who belong to the Society," to pass unchallenged. Col. Olcott may, and we feel certain does, try to the utmost of his power to carry out the original intentions of the T.S., viz., to keep the idea of Sect entirely in the background, but those Members who are the real energy of the Society, *may not do this*, and in fact we have every reason for believing that such is the case. We base our statement upon the following quotation from the "*Theosophist*," October, 1881.

"'Those Theosophists who deny to disembodied spirits a legitimate share in the marvellous phenomena' are few indeed, for the great majority of Theosophists concern themselves with Spiritualism very little—if at all. Indeed, our members may be divided into five principal classes, and described as follows :—

"1. Men *profoundly concerned in the revival* of their respective religious philosophies in all their pristine purity— *Buddhist devotees outnumbering all others.* These neither know of, nor do they care for, Spiritualism."—*Fragments of Occult Truth.*

It was the above statement (which we have italicised) appearing as it did in the Official Organ of the T.S., that was the primary cause of the writer of the note under dispute, forming such a hasty opinion.

Our American Brothers will now perceive that the objectionable paragraph was written without due consideration, and also that it was printed without our knowing the exact terms employed. We at all times endeavour to render due justice to everyone, and we are vexed that for once, such a mistake should have occurred, but our American friends may rest assured that we shall, for the future, use every vigilance in supervising every article, in order to exonerate ourselves from the great misunderstanding which we are sorry to see has arisen, as to the aims, or objects, of the H.B. of L.— Ed.]

A Peace Offer (B.5.f)

Source: *The Theosophist,* **December 1885, xxiii–xxiv.**

Burgoyne's letter, and this reply, were prompted on a fundamental level by the belief in the ultimate unity of all truly occult
societies, and on a practical level by the desire to avoid an open
split between the H. B. of L. and the Theosophical Society.

THE "H. B. OF L."

We have received a letter, from the Private Secretary of the
Secret Society known as the "H. B. of L.," couched in most
friendly terms and expressing a deep interest in the work of
the Theosophical Society. The writer very calmly and
lucidly shows that the true field of our Society is not so
much the private instruction of individual members, as the
enunciation of the great general principles of Universal
Brotherhood, the Basic Unity of Religions, the importance
of a study of Aryan Philosophy, and the potential development of the latent psychic faculties in man. Hence, that any
feeling of discontent among our members arising from the
failure to take their development in hand as the Guru does
that of his chelas is entirely unreasonable and uncalled-for.
He also avers that the system of psychic education in vogue
throughout the East is ill adapted to Western needs and
temperament, and implies that his fraternity supplies the
better method for occidental students; he disclaims the
remotest intention on their part to show "irreverence for the
Adepts and the Mahatmas of Tibet"; and adds the interesting testimony that the Founders of his society "know personally that such exalted beings do possess an objective
physical existence, and in fact we have known of their personal existence for the past fourteen years." Our readers
will remember the somewhat pretentious and offensive
wording in the advertisement accompanying the reprint of
The Divine Pymander, offering speedy occult advancement

to members of our Society "who may have been disappointed in their expectations of Sublime Wisdom being freely granted by the Hindu Mahatmas," which was noticed in these pages at the time of its appearance. It is now explained that this was not an intentional affront, and the earnest wish is expressed that our two societies may work side by side in mutual harmony and good-fellowship. Needless to say, the Theosophical Society is as ready now as ever before to keep in brotherly relations with every other body whose aim is to promote morality, strengthen the religious sentiment, and foster a spirit of research into the profound and priceless teachings of the ancient sages. The directors of our movement have certainly no wish to dissuade their colleagues from joining other bodies, as far as such bodies have a right to public confidence. And had the letter from the H. B. of L. contained some definite information—given in confidence even, if that were deemed indispensable—as to the conductors and plans of the secret sister society, we should have been happy to have printed it at length. No one likes to deal with masked allies.

The H. B. of L. Beyond
East and West (B.5.g)

Source: *The Occult Magazine* II/12 (January 1886), 6-7.

This is the letter that *The Theosophist* declined to print in full [B.5.f]. The questions of Interior Circle, Mahatmas, and Adepts had already been put before the readers of the magazine [B.5.c]. The idea that Eastern philosophies were ill-adapted to Western mentalities is taken up insistently in *The Light of Egypt*. Probably it came from Theon himself, since the Tradition that he expounded, particularly in the six volumes of *La Tradition Cosmique*, was deliberately framed in a context and a language as familiar as possible to Western readers: the references were to the Hebrew Scriptures and the Gospels, the language free from oriental terms. Its source, however, was given as the same from which all religions and philosophies had issued. Sri Aurobindo and the "Mother," who were very largely inspired by Theon and his wife, found nothing in the Philosophie Cosmique incompatible with the Vedas and with Indian tradition.

A MISCONCEPTION.

We have received a rather lengthy letter from Mr. Babajee Dharbagiri Nath, F.T.S., informing us, that at the present time, there are more Brahmins and Hindus in the Theosophical Society, than Buddhists. It will, however, be of interest to know that the latter term is used in a rather roundabout manner. Mr. Nath says :—

" But a great deal of misconception exists as to the meaning of the words ' Buddhism,' and ' Brahmanism.' *Brahman* and *Buddha* are both Sanskrit words, extensively used in the *Vedas, Vedânta,* and *Purânas* of the Hindus, in the sense of *mukta,* the *liberated.* ' Buddhism ' is therefore used by Theosophists in its peculiar and real sense of ' Wisdom-Religion,' or the Occult Science, or *Yôga-Vidya.* In Theosophic literature, unless the word ' exoteric ' precedes it, the word ' Bud lhism ' is almost invariably used to mean the Esoteric Philosophy, or the Secret Doctrine, accepted and taught by Occultists of every age, including the modern Thibetan Fraternity. . . . When Colonel Olcott and other Theosophists declare that Buddhism is destined to become the *future* religion of Humanity, they only mean that the Occult Philosophy will beccme universally recognised as the essence of every creed, past, present, and future ; and not at all the exterior systems of the Sinhalese and the Buddhists."

The above explanation from our Brother, Mr. Nath, is no doubt all-sufficient for Eastern people, but we of the West never recognise the Sacred Science, or Hermetic Philosophy, under the term "Buddhism," for we might with equal propriety term the Occult Science, *Esoteric Christianity,* or Druidism. It did not originate solely in India, therefore we of the West always prefer to use our own Western designation, neither " Buddhism," " Brahmanism," nor " Christianity," but Occultism pure and simple. And we certainly think it a great error upon the part of Theosophists to give the name of any creed, or sacerdotal caste, to that which appertains purely to Esoteric Science. Such a course can only supply a fruitful source for further misconceptions in the future, with those who are not thoroughly acquainted with the subject. Let us speak of the Wisdom of the Orient, as " Yoga Philosophy," if you will, but drop the "Buddhism," or any other title, intimately associated with either creed or caste.

But those mere minor matters of detail are of very little real import, for we of the East and West are in one bond of brotherhood, and must work amicably together, whatever name or title we may adopt ; our combined work is for the redemption of the race, and may *God speed* it on. But as some of our readers may be apt to misapprehend us even in this matter, we append a few extracts from a letter of the Secretary of our Order, to the *Theosophist ;* and as that letter has only been referred to, but not inserted in that Journal, we perceive it is the more necessary to publish a few extracts herein.

. . . " A large number of Theosophists, to our *certain knowledge,* having been disappointed by the fact that all the information they could obtain was pu'lished alike to every one who became a purchaser of the ' Theosophist ' — whether those purchasers were Members or not—concluded that their Membership was of no real benefit to them *apparently,* although we decidedly admit that the disappointed ones had only themselves to blame. Their expectations of learning valuable secrets in Occult Science originated entirely with themselves, for such a promise had never been given, either in the Prospectus, Rules, Objects, or Aims, publicly declared by the Council of the T.S., but the truth is that a great many completely misunderstood the cosmopolitan Nature of the Order they were joining, and overlooked the fact that *its great and sole object, as a body,* was to unite the various

nations as *One Great Universal Brotherhood,* irrespective of Creed or Caste, and to disseminate the Knowledge that all Religions have but one basis for their formation, as also that individual training, as experts in Occult Science, was quite a minor matter, and lay entirely with themselves. They, in short, either forgot, or were ignorant of the fact, that the so-called secrets of Occultism can never be revealed unto any one, until by soul-culture, the evolution of the latent powers of the candidate has been developed in such a manner, as to enable him, not only to *understand,* but to *use* those powers wisely, worthily, and well. Nevertheless, amongst the number of those disappointed ones, were many really earnest souls, who were ready to devote their life-time, if necessary, to the attainment of the Hidden Wisdom. Fully considering, therefore, the direction in which the T.S. exerted its greatest energies, viz., Universal Brotherhood, and likewise recognising what a heterogeneous assemblage the Society — as a body—represented, we observed that unless great alterations were made, no attention could possibly be paid to the thousands of cases awaiting practical advice, for their personal development, as scarcely any two persons require the same mode of culture.

. . . . "We know personally that such exalted beings (the Adepts and Mahatmas) *do possess an objective physical existence,* and, in fact, we have known of their personal existence for the past fourteen years. It has been stated in the columns of the ' *Theosophist,*' if we mistake not, that whilst 'all Mahatmas *are Adepts,* it is *not all Adepts who are Mahatmas.*' In this we fully concur, since the Adepts who guide the Interior Circle of the H.B. of L.—although Members of the same Sacred Band of the Himalayas — *are not Mahatmas,* neither are they connected with that Section of the Order to which the Mahatmas and Hierophants of the Buddhist culte belong. It is simply impossible, therefore, for the aims of the H.B. of L. to be antagonistic to the T.S. If the T.S. gives a few general outlines of the ' Secret Doctrine,' we give—to those who prove themselves worthy of receiving them — such details as are necessary to complete the interior ' missing links,' but which *cannot be published,* at least not in this age. Whilst the T.S. devotes its great energies for the benefit of mankind *generally,* the H.B. of L. gives the same attention to Humanity *individually.*

. . . "With the Orient, as regards Occult training, we have really nothing to do, for our labour lies amongst the rising Nations of the Occident, and as there are many pathways that may lead to the same mountain summit, so are there many methods of Occult training, exactly suitable to different Nationalities, by which the same soul-powers may be evolved in the best manner. Yoga training, as practised in India, is totally unfitted for Western people residing in our colder climates. European habits of thought, the influence of past generations of Christian sway, and everything belonging to the civilisation of the West, in fact, has powerfully assisted in making European nations the very opposite in 'thought, word, and deed' to those of far-off Hindostan. For this reason alone the Oriental mind—even although it may be that of an Adept—can neither properly *understand* nor *appreciate* the requirements of the Western race, as they should be, but the Adepts who belong by race to the Occident not only can, but do perfectly meet those difficulties. It is quite impossible for a European, unless he has resided many years in India, to fully realise the true significance of abstruse Hindu metaphysical terms ; they are just what he does *not require,* but this style of mental nutriment is no doubt eminently adapted to the subtile mind of the Oriental.

. . . "To those *who know,* we would remind them that a dire and dreadful period surely and swiftly approaches that will put to the stern test all those who, *during the Sunshine,* are basking in the light of their newly-fledged ideal—devotion to the ancient Wisdom-Religion, and the Brotherhood of Man—but ere many years disappear in the lap of time, they will be rudely awakened from their pleasant dream, and may be called upon, perhaps, amidst great sacrifices, to put their pet theory into actual practice. Perceiving, then, the ' signs of the times,' we would earnestly beseech of you, our worthy Brothers,—no matter what Order, Creed, or Caste you may belong to—that although slight differences upon minor points of doctrine may exist amongst you, nevertheless stand loyally and truly together, let UNIVERSAL BROTHERHOOD be always your watchword, and VERITAS your motto, then all will be well, for in these highly critical and dangerous days, neither Occultists especially, nor the humble followers of the True Light, can afford to quarrel, and you, our worthy Brothers, KNOW why such contentions would indeed be attended with very serious consequences."

A Peace Offer Rejected (B.5.h)

Source: *The Occult Magazine* II/13 (February 1886), 15.

"THE THEOSOPHIST" and the H. B. of L.

(To the Editor of the Occult Magazine.)

Sir,—Allow me to say a few words in reply to the curt remarks contained in the Supplement of the December *Theosophist*. I was not aware that any specially private information relative to the Founders of the Exterior Circle of our Order would have been required, naturally thinking that such had been at least by this time *in their possession*, from a *higher source* than the Council of a purely outward ring, as it were, but it seems I am mistaken. As to not liking to have any connection with "masked allies," I think the less said about "mask" matters the better, seeing that perhaps in no other Fraternity, saving the Theosophical Society, has the *real* Directors been more completely "*masked*." The Exterior Circle of the II.B. of L. is purely a secret organisation, and no information can be given except to its *Members*, and NOT EVEN TO THEM, UNTIL THEY HAVE PROVED BY THEIR CONDUCT AND LOYALTY that they *deserve* such, for we only teach *freely* and *without reserve* those whom we find *worthy to receive*. Yours fraternally,

THE PRIVATE SECRETARY.

[The ungenerous paragraphs alluded to are the following:— "The directors of *our* movement have certainly no wish to dissuade their colleagues from joining other bodies, so far as such bodies have a *right to public confidence (!)*. And had the letter from the H.B. of L. contained some definite information—given in confidence even, if that were deemed indispensable—as to the conductors and plans of the secret sister society, we should have been happy to have printed it at length. *No one likes to deal with masked allies.*"— *Theosophist, December.*

The italics are ours, and we must herein remark that, even at the menace of being finally "snuffed out," we are more than surprised at such statements appearing from those whom we imagined would have known that which they apparently do not, however ; *Magna est Veritas, et prevalebit.*—ED.]

HISTORY REPEATS ITSELF.

(To the Editor of the Occult Magazine.)

Dear Sir,—I find that it is necessary to inform all the Members and Neophytes of the Exterior Circle of the H.B. of L., that they will confer upon the venerated Order to which they belong—as well as upon the cause of truth and progress generally—a signal service, by indignantly repelling the vituperative charges against the Order that are now so profusely circulated by parties who *ought* to know better, perceiving as we do, that our grossest calumniators are the very people who *profess* the most to be students of the Ancient Sages. Only about ten years have elapsed since the Founders and Members of the Theosophical Society, at New York, were publicly charged with being evil-minded Jesuits, and teachers of Witchcraft and other forbidden rites in the category of the Black Art. The parties who made those monstrous charges, and who used every means to vilify the reputation of noble Members—men and women who had the moral courage to leave the beaten path of society—those vilifiers were the cowardly and dishonest souls who clog the skirts of respectable communities, waiting and watching for any *unfashionable victim*, upon whom they may vent the malicious spleen of their depraved nature. In their visionary knowledge, and *soi-disant* superior attainments, they spit forth their venomed abuse upon all who chance to belong to the mediocre sphere of the humble, for the most innocent and pure-minded of God's fair creatures are in no greater safety from the assaults of these indiscriminate traducers, than the wild dove is from the talons of the eagle.

The disclosure of the identity of base-minded calumniators is at all times a disagreeable task, but should those grossly false and vile charges be continued against us by those metaphysical aristocrats, hailing from the neighbourhood of Boston, New York and Rochester, &c., we shall publish their names, along with extracts from their letters, in order to prove to our readers the *just necessity* which compels us to insert this letter. I am yours, &c.,

T.H.B.,

Secretary of the Exterior Circle.

Davidson and Burgoyne together answer the *Theosophist's* ambiguous letter. In Burgoyne's letter, "History Repeats Itself," he reminds his Theosophical critics that they, too, were once abused as black magicians.

Blavatsky's Suspicions (B.5.j)

Source: *The Letters of H. P. Blavatsky to A. P. Sinnett,* transcribed and compiled by A. Trevor Barker (New York: Frederick T. Stokes, 1925), 159; Letter LXIII.

Margaret Conger dates this letter, written by Blavatsky in Würzburg to Sinnett in London, to 21 or 22 January 1886 (Conger 1973, 16). Dr. Anna Kingsford (1846-1889) had been President of the London Lodge of the Theosophical Society before leaving to found her own Hermetic Society, and still remained nominally on good terms with Blavatsky and Olcott. It was probably her editing of *The Virgin of the World* for Fryar in an edition uniform with *The Divine Pymander* that suggested her hand behind the Order, together with the determinedly Western slant of her work. Also the Hermetic Society was founded at exactly the same moment as the H. B. of L. made its appearance. The two groups are considered together in Godwin 1994, 333-360.

Dr. Jirah Dewey Buck (1838-1916?) was a physician and writer, whose concern with the H. B. of L. reappears in his covering letter to Gorham Blake's statement [B.6.k]. He had been accepted as a neophyte under Ayton in November 1885, and had been in contact with Davidson for months. He was evidently playing a double game, fishing for information from the other side.

A *third* calamity. A letter from Buck, Cincinnati. Writes a few lines that I copy. "Can you tell me anything about the Society known as 'H. B. of L.'? *For the sake of the cause of the T. S. in this country* send me anything you can on the subject. You can put it in two or three hasty lines, and I particularly desire to know whether Mrs. Kingsford is *'officially or otherwise connected with it.'* P. Davidson is its outside figurehead. Is the Society he repesents old or new? false or true? etc.

Yours sincerely,

J. D. Buck.
136, W. Eighth Street,
Cincinnati, O.,
U. S. America."

Now what do *I* know! Do you? It is evident there's some new treachery emanating from the fair Anna. For mercy sake get information and write him through Mohini if you do not wish to do so yourself. It is *very important.*

Discovery of Burgoyne's
Conviction by the Theosophists (B.6)

Blavatsky Utters a Warning (B.6.a)

Source: Theosophical Society archives, Adyar.

This continues the correspondence initiated by J. D. Buck [B.5.j], and marks the point at which Blavatsky's investigations, aided by her companion Countess Wachtmeister, had revealed the worm at the heart of the H. B. of L.: Burgoyne's felony.

Letter to J. D. Buck U.S.A.
From Md^e Blavatsky, sent from Wurzburg, 1886.

April 16

Two words in a hurry: You have heard no doubt of the speculation schemed by the H. B. of L.—the buying of some land in America; capital of 20,000£ stn., etc. If you get it, or some of our Theosophists, please notice among the names of the Directors that of Rev. A. L. Ayton. He is a Theosophist or was, since he broke with the London Lodge but not with us & is very friendly to me. Well surprised at seeing his name appear, the Countess Wachtmeister who has passed with me the winter, wrote to him to ask the meaning of this. I enclose his answer copied by the Countess. Please keep this (my information) to you secret but notify all the theosophists & warn them, without saying you got the information from me. It is not from me, but on account of Mr. Ayton as his name is still on their advertisements, you might write to him as though you know nothing and address yourself to him as to a gentleman and an ex-member of the London Lodge asking him to give you particulars and save thereby hundreds of American Theosophists. Say you saw his name on that "Hermetic Circular" which I suppose you must have seen by this time as it is sent every-where. I hope this "H. B. of L." will not be identified with our movement, for it would be the last blow. Yet, since the 'prime mover' of it is a 'convicted felon' *only*, and an Englishman, he will, no doubt, never be exposed. It is only I, who am a Russian, who is made a victim in England. Do my dear brother, all you can to save our Theosophists from such an alliance. Thanks for your long letter and Skinner's pamphlet. I see he does not see anything in the Kabala beyond *measure* and *inch*. Funny discovery. And he exalts Masonry thereby. His figures, or most of them correct; but he errs greatly in other things.

Yours ever faithfully,

H. P. Blavatsky.

Rev. Alex Ayton's address is; Chacombe Vicarage, Bronburry [sic], Oxford, England. He would never forgive me if he knew that I gave his name or told you he was an Occultist. Please keep this secret.

Ayton Identifies Burgoyne (B.6.b)

Source: *The Letters of H. P. Blavatsky to A. P. Sinnett*, ed. Trevor Barker (New York: Frederick T. Stokes, 1925), 240; Letter CXIII.

Here Blavatsky supplies the extract from Ayton's letter to Countess Wachtmeister, mentioned in the previous item [B.6.a]. This letter, written from Würzburg to Sinnett in London, is dated by Margaret Conger [see B.5.k] on or after 6 April 1886, but from its content would seem to be earlier. Ayton and Blavatsky shared a paranoia concerning Jesuits, whom they called the "Black Brothers." "Bert and Arch" are Bertram and Archibald Keightley, who were among Blavatsky's staunchest supporters at this period. It was their generosity that enabled her to settle in London the following year.

Letter received by the Countess from a friend concerning the "H. B. of L."

. . ."You will be surprised to hear that my name was put to this Hermetic circular (a purchase in America for £20,000 of a land for Occultists) without my consent and that I have repudiated it and demanded that my name be taken away out of it, at once. I have for some time been sure that there was something wrong in the H. B. of L. and have taken great pains to find the clue. The real fact is, that the Occultism which exists at the back has been made use of by a convicted felon. (?!) I obtained specimens of handwriting and also a photograph which identified the *prime mover* with the *felon under an alias.* There was to be a "London Lodge" opened by him, but I sent a friend to it with a photograph in his pocket to identify him. He did not appear, but all present recognised him as the man who had represented himself as the principal mover in it. It is a gross attempt of [an] unmitigated scoundrel and practicer of Black Magic to engraft a moonshine scheme of colonisation upon Occultism". . . . and to disgrace it finally. It is the work of the Jesuits I spoke to you of. Now the Kingsford is mixed up in it and many others. If you do not protect the L. L. yours—the genuine, from connexion with that lot as they seem determined to so connect it by hook or by crook, then the public will never be convinced if any new scandal comes out that *you* and *we* were not mixed up in it. So take care. Send Bert and Arch for information. Expose them by all means, and the louder the exposure the better. Warn all the theosophists with circular.

Yours ever,

H. P. B.

Frauds and Black Magic (B.6.c.)

Source: Theosophical Society archives, Adyar.

This is a letter from Countess Wachtmeister to J. D. Buck, with a postscript added by Blavatsky in her own hand. The letter also contained a copy of the Colony Prospectus (lost) and this copied extract from a letter by Ayton, telling the Countess what he discovered concerning the Order's leaders.

The enclosed paper has been sent to Md^e. Blavatsky by a gentleman of unimpeachable character. He adds that, having had his name placed on the committee of the colonisation movement without his consent & having his doubts as [to] the integrity of several concerned in the movement he took extreme measures to find out the truth & discovered that the whole was a gigantic fraud. The H. B. of L. had agreed to have an occult Society and Lodge in London, 20,000£ was to be amassed through 5£ shares to enable them to carry their soi-disant plans of colonisation where Occultists were to emigrate to America & Australia & form branches of the H. B. of L. Some of the money had already been subscribed. A first meeting of members had been convened by Burgoyne alias d'Alton, but having an inkling that his fraud was suspected he never made his appearance. At the meeting the photo of d'Alton the convict was shewn and identified with Burgoyne, many members immediately resigned & the H. B. of L. in London virtually came to an end. As d'Alton has now gone together with Peter Davidson to America where he is capable of doing a great deal of harm—it is necessary that all Theosophists should be put on their guard & particularly Mrs. Cables and her friends. Being true Adepts in Black Magic their very presence should be shunned. Should it be necessary perhaps a photo of d'Alton could be obtained signed by the prison authorities where he was incarcerated.

[Blavatsky adds:]

Ponder over the above facts dear brother Buck & please notify all the Theosophists in America. . . . Hurrychund Chintamon as Judge may tell you is the Hindu expelled from the T.S. at Bombay in 1879 for stealing the money we sent to the Arya Samaj—*our greatest enemy*. He robbed also Swami Dayanand of 4,000 rupees and ran away to England where he stopped for over four years working against us. Jesuits are also concerned in the movement.

[Ayton's statement:]

Hurrychund Chintamon constituted in himself the H. B. of L., e.e., without him it could not have existed. The man d'Alton, alias T. H. Burgoyne, made his acquaintance at Bradford, Yorkshire, in 1882 and was learning occultism from him.

At the end of that year d'Alton was convicted of felony in Leeds and sentenced to 12 months imprisonment. [...] On his release from prison at Armley, it has been ascertained that H. C. and his son suddenly disappeared from Bradford and could not be traced. H. C. had swindled people there. The inference is that d'Alton assumed the name of Burgoyne and that these two black magicians mounted the H. B. of L. and settled at Burnly, Lancashire. The identity of Burgoyne with d'Alton is proved. There was another name used as secretary, H. B. Corinni, which I am told is an Indian name, and possibly it may be HC's (Hurrychund Chintamon's) son. The whole scheme was well devised. D'Alton and Peter Davidson sailed for America on the 29th April; P. D. going in company with this convicted felon, although he was acquainted with the true facts which looks very badly for P. D.

The knowledge of occultism shewn and particularly Indian occultism and Black Magic confirms the source from which the information was derived.

Burgoyne's Conviction (B.6.d)

Source: Theosophical Society archives, Adyar.

This is the verbatim report from a Leeds newspaper, typeset and circulated by the Theosophical Society to discredit Burgoyne and, by association, the H. B. of L. Thomas Henry Dalton—his real name—had a number of aliases, including J. W. Seymour (perpetrator of this mail fraud), d'Alton (visitor to Ayton), Thomas H. Burgoyne (as Secretary of the H. B. of L.), R. A. Stella (writer on astrology for *The Occult Magazine*), Zanoni (compiler of *The Light of Egypt*), and probably H. B. Corinni (Private Secretary of M. Theon) [B.5.j].

Extract from a report of the proceedings at the Leeds Borough Sessions in the " Leeds Mercury," of January 10th, 1883.

AN ADVERTISEMENT FRAUD IN LEEDS.

John Thomas Prince (23), mason, and Thomas Henry Dalton (27), grocer, of Livingstone Place, Roundhay Road, Leeds, were charged with having conspired to obtain by false pretences from divers persons, certain sums of money with intent to cheat and defraud on or about October 20th, 1882. The evidence offered by the prosecution showed that on October 19th the following advertisement appeared in the *Leeds Mercury* :—" Grocer's Assistant Wanted ; permanent situation ; good salary given to a steady and energetic young man. Apply in the first instance to L24, *Mercury* Office." This advertisement one of the prisoners ordered to be inserted, whilst the other went to receive letters sent in reply. Letters were found upon one of the prisoners after his arrest which showed that the advertisement was a fraud. The practice pursued by the prisoners was to write a letter to each applicant informing him that he had been selected for a situation and stating that a further remittance of 2s. 6d. was required. About October 21st, the prisoner Prince called at the *Mercury* Office to obtain letters in answer to the advertisement, and was handed a number of letters which had been received. Outside the office Prince was joined by the other prisoner A day or two afterwards when l'rince received more letters a detective officer followed him to his lodgings at 37, Preston Street, Roundhay Road, and there arrested him on a charge of obtaining money by false pretences. In reply he stated that a man named Seymour had been living there but had gone away to Pickering, and he was about to send the letters to him. He added that he had met this man at the railway station, but knew nothing about him. The prisoner Dalton, who was afterwards arrested at Pickering, informed the officer who took him into custody that Prince was his brother-in-law, and that they would not have done it if they had not been hard-up. In Dalton's possession were found a number of memorandum forms bearing the following, " The National Employment Agency and Mercantile Assistants' Bureau. Partnerships negociated, and loans contracted. Northern Branch ; J W. Seymour, manager, Leeds." It was further shown that a grocer's assistant named Henry Oliver, residing in Burley Road, had in reply to an application by him received a letter, and had forwarded thirty penny postage stamps as requested. No situation was at the disposal of the prisoners, and it was clearly proved that there had been a conspiracy on their part to obtain money.—The prisoners were sentenced to seven months' imprisonment.

Burgoyne's Police Record (B.6.e)

Source: Theosophical Society archives, Adyar.

This is the Leeds Constabulary's "mug shot" of Burgoyne, which Ayton obtained and compared with the photograph he had taken of his visitor d'Alton.

Ayton's Experiences (B.6.f)

Source: Library of the United Grand Lodge of England.

Previously published in *The Alchemist of the Golden Dawn*, ed. Ellic Howe (Wellingborough: Aquarian, 1985), pp. 58-59.

The Rev. William Alexander Ayton was Vicar of Chacombe, a village near Banbury in Oxfordshire. As Provincial Grand Master for the South until the Burgoyne scandal, he stamped his writing paper with the seal of the Order [see B.7.b], but only when writing to neophytes on the Order's business. It is odd that he was still using it in 1890, despite his disillusionment.

The addressee of this letter, Captain Francis G. Irwin, was founder of the Fratres Lucis [B.1.c]. John Thomas was the editor of *The Seer* [B.3.a]. The "very big swindle" of which the police were suspicious was the proposed raising of several thousand pounds in £10 shares, and the unauthorised use of Ayton's and perhaps others' names in promoting the scheme. By June 1886, Ayton had become convinced that Davidson was as guilty as Burgoyne.

Chacombe Vicarage
29 December 1890

Dear Sir and Brother [i.e., F.G.Irwin]

It was very good [of] you to think of me this Xmas-tide, and I am very much obliged by your fraternal card of greeting. Please excuse me not answering directly, for Xmas brings me such multifarious duties & interruptions that I am not my own master.

In your letter, I think there is a solution of continuity, in your having omitted one or two words necessary to the full understanding of your meaning. However, you allude to Davidson and Thomas. I assume you mean Peter Davidson of the H[ermetic] B[rotherhood] of L[uxor] & Thomas, of Frodsham, Cheshire, the Spiritualist and Medium. As you did not belong to the H. B. of L. and I did not send you the particulars of the smashing up of the whole wretched affair [sic]. It came to my knowledge that Burgoyne, the secretary, of whom I had always been suspicious, was no other than a man I had known previously under the name of D'Alton who made such a confession of Black Magic that I rejected him altogether as being impossible. Subsequently to that he comitted a felony, and underwent many months of imprisonment for it in Armley Gaol, Leeds. I did not know him under the name of Burgoyne and he took care that I should never see him. When I told Davidson that his secretary was a convicted felon, he made very light of it, so lightly, that I thought he must be as bad as Burgoyne. We got into communication with the detectives in Yorkshire, and it appears they were watching Burgoyne and the H. B. of L. all the time. They told us they knew all the time it was supposed to be a very big swindle, and they were ready to come down upon it at the right moment. I saved them the trouble by blowing it out of the water as I could, as soon as I knew that Burgoyne was a convicted felon and that Davidson upheld him. We knew the whole history of Burgoyne, and that he had been a curse to every one who employed him, a thorough deep-dyed scoundrel. We know all about him since he has been in America. He left a wife and family in England, but has married again there. The last I heard was that if he sees 2 or 3 men in the distance approaching his quarters he turns pale and trembles. It is supposed he has been guilty of something which puts him in mortal fear, and that he contemplates going off to Australia. It is too long a tale to tell you the whole of it.

If you know Thomas of Frodsham and mean him by your allusion, I can tell you about him. He has come entirely to grief and is sending begging letters to every one. He was a Medium in communication with the Colour Spirits with whom he appears to have had a pact, but on two occasions he nearly lost his life thro' them. The most apparently peacable Elementals, if a storm happens to come on, will become very violent and uncontrollable. The conflict of the elements seems to excite them to fury, and woe to the mortal, not being an Adept, who encounters them. Thomas has gone the way of all Mediums. I have investigated the circumstances as to a good many, and I find they all go wrong, sooner or later. It is the one thing to avoid. I should have very much have liked to have had a long talk with you personally, as one cannot put all these things down on paper. I am very much occupied in practical Occultism and that and my Profession leave me but little time to spare.

This very bad weather has prevented us going to Banbury and we have no cards to send. I am therefore obliged to content myself with wishing you a very Happy New Year, and success in whatever Occult pursuits you may be engaged in. Believe me,

Yours fraternally,

W. A. Ayton

Fryar Dissociates Himself (B.6.g)

Source: *Lucifer* I/2 (October 1887), 159.

Fryar wrote to Ayton in June 1886 that the Order's leaders had cheated him of money. Although he had acted as *poste restante* for "Theosi" or "Theon" [B.2.b], he now does not hesitate to adopt Ayton's theory of Hurrychund Chintamon as the adept behind the Order. This retraction was published in a slightly different form in *The Theosophist,* Supplement, March 1888, lxxix.

To the Editors of *Lucifer.*

For the purpose of correcting any prejudicial suspicion or erroneous misrepresentation of myself, arising from the insertion of the note at the end of the "Bath Occult Reprint Edition" of the "Divine Pymander" or as associated with the Society of the "H. B. of L.," known to me only through the names of Peter Davidson and T. H. Burgoyne, alias D'Alton, Dalton, &c., and whose secretary is announced to be "A convicted felon, and the supposed adept to be a Hindu of questionable antecedents," I wish it to be understood I have now no confidence, sympathy, or connection therewith, direct or indirect, since or even prior to the date hereof, viz., May, 1886.

Yours truly,

Robt. H. Fryar

8, Northumberland Place, Bath

A Warning and a Threat (B.6.h)

Source: *The Theosophist,* Supplement, June 1886, cxxxiv.

A CAUTION.

Information just received impels us to utter a word of caution to members of our Society with respect to an alleged occult Brotherhood which has been much discussed and lauded in Western countries. If the allegations sent us are true, it would appear that the Society in question is a catchpenny affair, promoted by disreputable persons for private gain; some worthy members of our Society and outsiders having been first duped and then utilized as honest decoys. The names and aliases of the reputed schemers of this movement have been given us, but will not be published at present.

After Ayton's revelations, the H. B. of L. is implicitly denounced, with the threat to publish the names and addresses of the persons responsible—presumably Davidson and Burgoyne.

Chintamon Again? (B.6.j)

Source: Theosophical Society Archives, Adyar.

This letter from Buck to Blavatsky continues their earlier correspondence [B.5.j, B.6.a]. Chintamon and Dayananda Saraswati had originally been named as the Hindu adepts who were to teach the Theosophical Society members practical occultism. On his expulsion from the Theosophical Society in 1879, Chintamon came to England and told the Society's members that Blavatsky and her masters were fraudulent. The same accusation was later made by Emma Coulomb, formerly a friend of Blavatsky in Cairo and later her employee in Adyar. The publication in December 1885 of Richard Hodgson's report to the Society for Psychical Research, referred to at the end of this letter, favored Coulomb's accusations.

Gorham Blake [B.4.d-e] was a member of the H. B. of L., and his letter was a report to the Committee of Seven that met in St. Louis (Page's hometown) in July 1886 to discuss the unsavory revelations. Buck was a neophyte of the Order, and had perhaps exploited his access to Blavatsky to find out more about it [B.5.j]. Now he seems to have decided to make amends.

Drs. Buck and Crawford
136 W. Eighth Street
Cincinnati, O. Aug. 10th 86

My Dear Sister.—

The enclosed may be of interest or use to you. *Gorham Blake* is the party from whom the "Colony grounds" Gold mines &c &c were to have been purchased. He is a member of the T. S. and apparently reliable in every way.—That the HBofL is *badly busted* there can be no doubt, but that these same parties will stop here is doubtful. Your old friend *Chintamon* apparently hurried to India to be in at the death *a la Coulomb,* but as nothing died *very dead,* at that time he may return here to help out this precious pair.

I send it to you for what it is worth. Of course you could get all this from other sources, but this is objective and vulgar enough to satisfy the *S. P. R.*

Yours truly,

J. D. Buck.

Blake Tries to
Summarize the Affair (B.6.k)

Source: Theosophical Society Archives, Adyar.

Peter Davidson gave instructions in the second half of 1885 for the prominent American H. B. of L. members to set up a "Committee of Seven" with a lodge system. It is a curious coincidence, at the very least, that Blavatsky told Olcott to sign his famous 1875 circular, "Important to Spiritualists" [B.1.a], with the same phrase.

William Oxley (born 1823) was one of the chief protagonists on the "Western" side of the debates that filled the spiritualist magazines in the 1880s, opposing the doctrines of reincarnation and karma and defending the possibility of communicating with the spirits of the dead. He ran a spiritualist circle which received "Angelic Revelations" (see W. Oxley, "His life and times, from a spiritual standpoint. Written by himself," in *The Medium and Daybreak*, 2 January 1885, 2-4). He was in touch with Emma Hardinge Britten (see Britten 1884, 203-205) and with the Theosophists, especially Sinnett, and was praised by Koot Hoomi (*ML* No. CXII) as the best of the English spiritualistic mystics. He contributed an excited account of the Cardiff Giant (a notorious fake) to *The Occult Magazine* II/13 (February 1886), 13-14.

Loudsville White Co Ga.   July 10th/86

To a Member of Committee of H. B. of L.—

Dear Sir,

I think that it is important that all information that can be obtained, all facts, connected with the subject coming before the Committee of Seven, should be made known and will therefore write the following.—I have been for over two months trying to get information from Burgoyne (or Dalton) and P. Davidson about the H. B. of L.—and have gathered sufficient to lead me to suppose that M. Theon, with Burgoyne as Sect'y—and Davidson as assistant, started the (branch of the) order, for the purpose of making money. The Mysterious M. Theon, Grand Master pro-tem of the Exterior Circle, the figure-head and director, Burgoyne or Dalton, the *Medium*, through as from occult influences give lectures and communications. And Davidson Prov'l Grand Master of the North, who prepares the matter for publication, also copies interesting Mysteries from old and rare books for the reading of Neophytes, attending to Correspondence and acting as Treasurer. They report some 270 members, and [sold?] some 1000 copies of the Occult Magazine, writing over different names nearly all the contents of the Magazine except that which is copied from books. They started the scheme for a Colony in Georgia, the Gold mine thereon probably being the attraction. They *reported* having £5000 subscribed, *but had none.* Arriving in Philadelphia they were confronted with charges from Bro Ayton, against *Burgoyne,* which both B and Davidson denied over their signatures. They came here and by words and actions soon shewed they were not what they represented themselves to be, that neither could be trusted or believed. They contradicted each other, and themselves. And Davidson getting sick of his Medium protege, acknowledged that the charges made by Mr. Ayton *were true.* That Burgoyne was an inspirational medium. And said that the grand mistake they had made was *in allowing the names of members of the order to be known to any but themselves.* If the members were unknown, they could not have been warned. There are satisfactory proofs to all, I think, that the charges made by Mr. Ayton *are true.*—Burgoyne says, he first met M. Theon in a park, where he (B) sat reading a book on occultism, on the same seat sat an old Gentleman of foreign appearance, who introduced himself by saying "you are young to read a book like that." They became acquainted and he invited B— to his house to dine, and he visited his house as a student every day for a long time. The man gave his name as M. Theon—one day he visited his house and learned that M. Theon and family had *mysteriously disappeared* and no trace of them could be found. Since that time Burgoyne has acted for M. Theon, and Corrinne (Theon's private Secty). Both B— and D— insist that Theon is in India. Burgoyne read me a letter from *William Oxley,* addressed to M. Theon, and his own reply in M. Theon's name. In *connection with this,* and Burgoyne, I will give copy of a letter rec'd by me from England today, as follows—

"you have hit it exactly that he (Burgoyne) is a Medium. He had acted as such sitting at circles before he was convicted. There is proof that before he was convicted he made the acquaintance and rec'd instruction from a Hindu then at Bradford named Hurrychund Chintaman. This man was an advanced Initiate, and swindled Madame H. P. B. and Col Olcott in 1879. Then embezzled 400 rupees from the T. Society and 4000 rupees from his employer, and was publicly expelled from the Theosophical Society, and bolted for England, where B— or Dalton took lessons of him in Magic before he was convicted. *Chintaman* swindled some people in Bradford, and left suddenly and could not be traced.—His leaving was *coincident* with (B's—or) Dalton's coming out of Prison. The probabilities are that the original Theon was *Chintaman*. I learned that the man he stole 4000 rupees from in India was dead, and that the T. S. was under a cloud with the Coulomb affair, and therefore he went back to India. Chintaman's son was also in London. My idea is that on Chintaman's departure from London, T. H. B. took the affairs into himself.—Supposing my conjecture to be right, Chintaman would probably put the Medium into communication with some of the evil kind of higher intelligences and hence all that has been done. He (B) came to see me for information, and had enough of Black Magic to boast that he had made an evocation. I did not believe him, but it showed his tendency."

By the above I think we can call the original M. Theon—Chintaman, and after he left T. H. B. took the alias, and with Davidson as a balance wheel, has run the machinery of the order, and rec'd its income. After satisfying myself fully about these individuals B and D.— and giving them every opportunity to explain, I requested them *to leave.* B— left for the Rail Road and D— with his family for a farm a few miles from here. The latter still receives money and registered letters, it is presumed from subscribers, as Davidson said he must make out of *the order,* the money he loaned to T. H. B. He stated that he had resigned active service in the H. B. of L.—and had no idea of continuing or having anything more to do with occultism, or Burgoyne, and wanted to get rid of him. He acknowledged that he had *fibbed a little* to help B— out of his difficulty. That Mr Ayton's charges *were true,* that

B. *was Dalton* and had been in prison, and did not deny it to
him. Also that B— was using the names of *Corinne* and
Stella, and other Alias were used by him often, and that B—
was an *inspirational medium and nothing else.* During my last
conversation with T. H. B— we fell into quite a merry
mood, and he, I think without knowing, personated at least
five individuals, his face and figure changing wonderfully,
and at one time looking exactly like the Photo of Dalton in
Prison. At the close [word illegible], while laughing at the
probable fury of some of his dupes when they heared of the
expose, T. H. B— made this remark, which should be
remembered. *"To make Gold, extract it from credulity."* Neither B or D are vegetarians, but rather coarse consumers of
fat pork, meats, tobacco etc, and have none of the fine feelings expected of members of the Ideal H. B. of L.—I believe
those parties would lead their followers into a most dangerous condition, that of negative obedience and debilitated,
Physical and Will Power, that they or their leaders or con-
trolls, by their superior Psychological power can bleed and
crush them. Give the members of the order *More Light*, for I
believe it is the intention of B. and D— to renew their efforts
at an early day, to issue their Magazine in a new dress, possibly in connection with some other publication, and continue their devil's work all the time. In the 1st Vol. of "Isis
Unveiled" we find on Page 53:

"We must confess that the situation appears to be
very grave. The control of mediums by such un-
principled and lying "spirits" is constantly becoming more and more general, and the pernicious
effects of *seeming* diabolism constantly multiply.
Some of the best mediums are abandoning the
Public rostrum and retiring from this influence,
and the movement is drifting Churchward. We
venture the prediction that unless Spiritualists set

about the study of ancient philosophy so as to learn to discriminate between spirits, and to guard themselves against the baser sort, twenty five years more will not elapse before they will have to fly to the Romish Communion to escape these *"guides"* and *"controls"* that have fondled so long.

With best wishes for the good of all honest investigators and students

I remain

Yours sincerely and fraternally

Gorham Blake.

Another Summary of the Affair (B.6.l)

Source: *The Theosophist* VIII (January 1887), 255-256.

The "Victim" was probably either the Yorkshire neophyte T. H. Holmes, or else T. H. Pattison, who was refused admission to the H. B. of L. but, like Holmes, was a personal "chela" (disciple) of Ayton's. The mention that Theosophists had complained about the lack of [practical] teaching touches the core of the H. B. of L.'s appeal. It was the Yorkshire neophyte's recognition of Burgoyne's handwriting, described here, that led to the unmasking of the former d'Alton by Ayton (the "active member").

The first paragraph tells an anecdote that was repeated by the novelist and Theosophist Gustav Meyrink in the Foreword to his German edition of Randolph's *Dhoula Bel* (Vienna: Rikola Verlag, 1922, 10-11). Meyrink here quotes an unnamed friend who supposedly knew both occultists well. Blavatsky was in Adyar, the friend says, when she suddenly cried out: "He's shooting at me, the Nigger!—Ah, now the Devil's got him." Randolph had loaded a pistol with the intention that the bullet would dematerialize in California and rematerialize in Blavatsky's heart, but at the last moment he lost his mind and shot himself.

Ayton says that Olcott himself, directly and personally, told Ayton exactly the same story, only changing the protagonist to Olcott instead of Blavatsky. (No matter that Randolph died in 1875, while the Founders reached Adyar in 1882.) Writers such as Maria Naglowska and Robert North have perpetuated this rumor of an "occult war" (Randolph [but largely by Naglowska] 1988, xxvii).

There is no evidence that Blake ejected Davidson and Burgoyne from his property at Loudsville; from Blake's own account [B.6.k] they seem to have parted "in quite a merry mood."

Correspondence.

_____

CAUTION.

Pseudo-Occultist Societies.

At the present time, when the very air seems to be full of whisperings of the Occult, may I be permitted to give a caution to all readers of *The Theosophist* as to joining so-called Orders or Societies professing to teach Occultism. The danger is exemplified in the history of a recent specimen of this class. I do not know how long exactly it had existed, but it first became active in 1884. It was evidently formed on the lines of the "Theosophical Society," but with special enmity to it. Knowing well that the members of that Society had complained of lack of teaching, it gave the largest promises of Occult knowledge to all comers, and tried to carry this out by copying in MSS., especially from the obscene works of the late P. B. Randolph, the Black Magician who made a stir in America some 20 years ago, and appropriately terminated his career by suicide, and, as it is said, getting up suddenly from an Incantation directed against the Theosophical Society and performing the "Happy Dispatch" with one of the instruments he had set before him as a symbol of his bitter hatred of the Theosophical Society.

By some means, its promoters had got hold of some real Oriental occult knowledge on one particular subject, which deceived a member who had made Occultism his study for years. There is good reason to suppose that they also practiced Black Magic against him, so as to throw a glamour over him. His position was such as to make his name important, to be used for their ultimate designs.

They professed to be in connection with a real adept, under whose instructions they acted. Occult knowledge was gleaned from rare books, or MSS., which were forwarded in succession to those who paid their guinea entrance fee, and 5s. for postage, &c. A high sounding name was given and a specious symbol of the order was fabricated, and also sent to neophytes, for a consideration. Reprints of important and rare books on the Occult Sciences were even made by the Society. A pretended formal, artfully contrived Initiation, was given to a few. They established also a monthly journal with articles in it, to which the names of Mejnour, Theon, and other celebrities were attached. They gained numerous adherents in England, America and even India.

Then, they added an astrologer to the Institution, whose name was duly advertised and his performance eulogised in their magazine. We shall see further on that this was fatal to them.

After a certain time, in conjunction with all this, there came out a scheme for buying a tract of land in some beautiful climate, and colonising it exclusively with their Initiates, who were to have the privilege of buying as many £10 shares in it, as they pleased. A temporary building was to serve, at first, as the place of Initiation, but in a few years a grand temple was to be built with all the accessories for the most elaborate rites and ceremonies of esoteric Magism. At what, we may suppose, they thought the propitious moment, there was issued forth the prospectus of this Colony Scheme. They had contrived, under cover of a partial and imperfect statement of facts, to get a provisional consent of certain of the members to become directors. Suddenly, a prospectus was issued forth of the Colony Scheme, with all these names put down as directors, without the Draft having first been submitted to them for their approval, which was virtually putting their names in without their consent. The prospectus was so bad on the surface that no city man would have looked twice at it. Several of those whose names were so fraudulently put in as directors, immediately wrote and demanded that their names should be withdrawn.

Almost simultaneously with the issuing of this swindling prospectus, one of the Yorkshire neophytes wrote to their astrologer to have his horoscope cast. In the handwriting of this astrologer, he recognized that of a man, who he had formerly the calamity to come across, who was well known about Leeds and Bradford, and who had ceased to afflict the eyes of the people of that part of the world by a seven months imprisonment in Armley Jail for a most tremendous swindle, since which he had disappeared altogether from view. The Yorkshireman having made quite sure by comparing the astrologer's handwriting with numerous letters in his own possession and that of others, and by this scrutiny finding that the handwriting identified him also as the Secretary to, and prime minister of the Order, he communicated the discovery to an active member who, for some time, had been very suspicious, and also happened to have letters and a photograph of the felon. This photograph was sent to another chief promoter of this knavish order, and was asked if he knew the original of that photograph. He aknowledged that he did, and was proud of the acquaintance, and was plainly quite indifferent whether he was a convicted felon or not, so long as he could help him to make money.

Upon this, without a moment's delay, every known member in England and America was written to and warned that its chief promoter was a convicted felon. This was done in time to prevent them making the haul of the £10 shares.

The convicted felon and his pal now fled to America, to the land in Georgia they were negotiating for, on which to plant the colony, evidently hoping at that distance to be able to still carry out the fraud. They were confronted on their landing by the Americans who had been warned, and they were well heckled as to the felony. A great controversy ensued, but it all ended in their being ignominiously ejected from the land they intended to purchase by the very intelligent and most honourable gentleman, the owner of it, who saw what knaves they were.

Notwithstanding all this, they, or one of them, continue to publish the magazine, and I have good reason to believe they still find dupes in America, in London, in England generally, and even in India, willing to send them guinea subscriptions, and perhaps even to buy £10 shares.

The Police say that, had it not been for the Yorkshireman above mentioned and those acting with him, it would have been one of the most gigantic swindles perpetrated for a long time:

The detectives had been watching them and knew that some fraud was contemplated.

I hope, therefore, I may be excused for giving this warning against Orders and Societies professing to teach Occultism, which is being brought into disrepute and ill odour by such abominable attempts, as above shortly, and only imperfectly narrated.

Yours faithfully,

A VICTIM

Blavatsky's Last Word
on the Affair (B.6.m)

Source: H. P. Blavatsky, *Collected Writings*, X, second ed. (Wheaton: TPH, 1974), 124-126. First published in *Lucifer* III/14 (October 1888), as "Lodges of Magic."

Blavatsky's insistence on mentioning once again the "Brotherhood of Luxor" of the 1870s and Olcott's certificate [see B.1.a] serves to complicate rather than clarify the situation. In that earlier period, Blavatsky had invited her doubters to "write to *Lahore* for information"—though without giving the address (*BCW*, I, 142; first published as "The Science of Magic," 1875). There is nothing here about Looksur [compare B.1.d]. Possibly Lahore was a blind (being almost an anagram) for Ellora, where the writer of *Ghost Land* [B.3.e] had become an adept. Olcott's early master Serapis told him that Blavatsky was "an *Ellorian*" (*LMW*, II, 42; Letter 12).

The remainder of Blavatsky's article is an answer to a letter from Ayton, included in her text, begging the Theosophical Society to found "Lodges in which something practical should be done." The same month (October 1888), against the advice of Olcott and Sinnett, Blavatsky started an Esoteric Section within the Theosophical Society, which Ayton immediately joined. (On these events, see also Gilbert 1987b.) In a footnote, Blavatsky dissociates the "Brotherhood of Luxor," mentioned by Mackenzie as having many members, from the secret body of the same name whose sole member, we now learn, was Olcott.

The suppression of Peter Davidson's name from this damning document "for past considerations" recalls his previous contributions to *The Theosophist* [B.3.e] and to the Society.

One of the most esteemed of our friends in occult research, propounds the question of the formation of "working Lodges" of the Theosophical Society, for the development of adeptship. If the practical impossibility of forcing this process has been shown once in the course of the theosophical movement, it has scores of times. It is hard to check one's natural impatience to tear aside the veil of the Temple. To gain the divine knowledge, like the prize in a classical tripos,by a system of coaching and cramming, is the ideal of the average beginner in occult study. The refusal of the originators of the Theosophical Society to encourage such false hopes, has led to the formation of bogus Brotherhoods of *Luxor* (and Armley Jail?) as speculations on human credulity. How enticing the bait for gudgeons in the following specimen prospectus, which a few years ago caught some of our most earnest friends and Theosophists.

"Students of the Occult Science, searchers after truth, and Theosophists who may have been disappointed in their expectations of Sublime Wisdom being freely dispensed by HINDU MAHATMAS, are cordially invited to send in their names to. . ., when, if found suitable, they can be admitted, after a short probationary term, as Members of an Occult Brotherhood, who do not boast of their knowledge or attainments, but teach freely [at £1 to £5 *per* letter?] and without reserve [the nastiest portions of P.B.Randolph's *Eulis*], all they find worthy to receive" (read: teachings on a commercial basis; the cash going to the teachers, and the extracts from Randolph and other "love-philter" sellers to the pupils!).[1]

If rumour be true, some of the English rural districts, especially Yorkshire, are overrun with fraudulent astrologers

---

[1] Documents on view at *Lucifer* Office, viz., Secret MSS. written in the handwriting of——(name suppressed for past considerations), "Provincial Grand Master of the Northern Section." One of these documents bears the heading, "A brief Key to the Eulian Mysteries," *i.e., Tantric* black magic on a phallic basis. No; the members of *this* Occult Brotherhood "do not boast of their knowledge." Very sensible on their part: least said, soonest mended.

and fortune-tellers, who pretend to be Theosophists, the better to swindle a higher class of credulous patrons than their legitimate prey, the servant-maid and callow youth. If the "lodges of magic," suggested in the following letter to the Editors of this Magazine, were founded, without having taken the greatest precautions to admit only the best candidates to membership, we should see these vile exploitations of sacred names and things increase an hundredfold. And in this connection, and before giving place to our friend's letter, the senior Editor of *Lucifer* begs to inform her friends that she has never had the remotest connection with the so-called "H (ermetic) B (rotherhood) of L (uxor)," and that all representations to the contrary are false and dishonest. There is a secret body—whose diploma, or Certificate of Membership, is held by Colonel Olcott alone among modern men of white blood—to which that name was given by the author of *Isis Unveiled* for convenience of designation,[2] but which is known among Initiates by quite another one, just as the personage known to the public under the pseudonym of "Koot Hoomi," is called by a totally different name among his acquaintances. What the real name of that society is, it would puzzle the "Eulian" phallicists of the "H. B. of L." to tell. The real names of Master Adepts and Occult Schools are never, *under any circumstances*, revealed to the profane; and the names of the personages who have been talked about in connection with modern Theosophy, are in the possession only of the two chief founders of the Theosophical Society.

---

[2] In *Isis Unveiled*, Vol. II, p. 308. It may be added that the "Brotherhood of Luxor" mentioned by Kenneth MacKenzie (*vide* his *Royal Masonic Cyclopedia*) as having its seat in America, had after all, nothing to do with the Brotherhood mentioned by, and known to us, as was ascertained after the publication of "Isis" from a letter written by this late Masonic author to a friend in New York. The Brotherhood MacKenzie knew of was simply a Masonic Society on a rather more secret basis, and, as he stated in the letter, he had *heard of, but knew nothing of our* Brotherhood, which, having had a branch at Luxor (Egypt), was thus purposely referred to by us under this name alone. This led some schemers to infer that there was a regular Lodge of Adepts of that name, and to assure some credulous friends and Theosophists that the "H. B. of L." was either identical or a branch of the same, supposed to be near Lahore!!—which was the most flagrant untruth.

Olcott's Version of the Affair (B.6.n)

Source: Henry S. Olcott, "M. 'Papus' on Occult Science," in *The Theosophist* XIII (August 1892), 696n.

Papus (Dr. Gérard Encausse, 1865-1916) was a prominent French occultist who had joined the H. B. of L. through his friend Barlet [see B.9.a], and who acknowledged Peter Davidson as his "master in practice." He left the Theosophical Society in 1890, having become convinced that Blavatsky was ignorant of Sanskrit and of Buddhism (see Godwin 1989, 23-24). Olcott's review of Papus's *Traité méthodique de science occulte* (1891) appeared at the same time as his account of the Brotherhood of Luxor's certificate [B.1.b]. The circular which he has before his eyes is Gorham Blake's letter [B.6.k].

M. Papus, however, again under the influence of personal prejudice, closes, or at least winks, his eyes whenever it suits his convenience, as may be seen from his recognition of that famous fraud, the H. B. of L., as a distinct school of occultism.

[Footnote to the foregoing] This "School of Occultism," now defunct, was a conspiracy for extracting money out of dupes, headed by a grocer of Leeds, a Spiritualist medium, named Thomas H. Dalton, who was convicted at the Leeds Borough Sessions of crime (*vide The Leeds Mercury* of Jan. 10, 1883) and sent to jail. Upon his release he passed under various *aliases* and, in co-partnership with another man—formerly an F. T. S.—concocted this fraudulent Society and called it the H. B. of L. (Hermetic Brotherhood of Luxor.) They offered gudgeons a most tempting bait, and issued advertisements offering to teach adeptship to all who had "become dissatisfied with the slow methods of the Theosophical Mahatmas," promising speedy psychical development under the training of Western initiates (viz., the convict grocer) who had devoted "twenty years" to occult research. Quite a number of our impatient and too credulous members were caught in the trap and some hundreds of pounds must have been taken in by the swindlers. The project of founding a colony in White County, Georgia, of members of the H. B. of L. with a view to surrounding themselves with the most favorable occult conditions (!) was launched, and the pretended initiates went there; but their dishonesty becoming soon exposed, the vendor of the land turned them out, and issued a circular letter showing them up, of which a copy is before me at this moment. In this circular, he says that the bait held out to the victim-colonists was the alleged existence of a gold mine on the estate, but that Dalton had one day said, laughing, "To make gold, extract it from credulity." All the occult teaching, save one chapter, they ever gave was filched from "Isis Unveiled" and other known works on the occult sciences. The other chapter was called "The Mysteries of Eulis," and was a compilation of sexual hints and pornographic information from a work entitled "Eulis," by that famous spiritual medium and sorcerer, the late Paschal Beverly Randolph, and from certain private instructions of his. The very name of Dalton's occult society was stolen from a document written by myself in the year 1875, of which I shall speak in the proper place.

THE H. B. OF L. IN AMERICA AND FRANCE (B.7)

Davidson Offers
Books and Crystals (B.7.a)

Source: Theosophical Society archives, Adyar.

The greater part of "Barrett's Magus" (Barrett 1801) is an unattributed transcription of Henry Cornelius Agrippa's *Three Books on Occult Philosophy* and the spurious *Fourth Book*. They were likely inspirations for the H. B. of L.'s rituals and use of the magic mirror [A.1.e-f, A.3.a]. For an advertisement for Davidson's mirrors, see the extract from the first number of *The Occult Magazine* [B.3.e]. For an idea of what these prices represented in money of the time (at £1=$5), see Davidson's notes on the cost of living [B.4.f]. He refers here to *The Theosophist* IV/6 (March 1883), which carried an article on magic mirrors with a preface by Blavatsky (*BCW*, IV, 356).

Loudsville Co. Georgia. U.S.A.   19/9/86

D. Sir,

Your letter of 17th Ulto has just reached me. Price of *Barrett's Magus*—The copy I have here complete £1.5.6d and postage 2/6d. I herewith send your Application Form for the venerated H. B. of L. and also a copy of the Rates. Please keep the latter away from the public as they are *private* and only for Members. As to Mirrors and *List of Books* you will find prices of such in the *Occult Magazine* a copy for *September* which I post you along with this letter. I can get you Agrippa's 4 Books if you wish. I have not them in stock just now; they are rather difficult to be had now as they are getting very scarce. American dollar is about 4.1d but value varies every day. As to prices of Rock Crystals I append a few. *Circle* and polished very fine:—1 inch diameter 25s.; 1-1/2 inches £2.2; 1-3/4—£3.3. 2 inches £4.4, 2-5/8 inches £10 &c &c. They are GUARANTEED *new, unsoiled* and *perfect*. They shew more wonderful phenomena than that described in *Theosophist*.

Now as to the *two* addresses I wrote you regarding. Understand this that my postal address is at *Loudsville* as above on the head of this letter, but note well that Loudsville is not a Money Order office but that all Monies must be made to me upon *Gainesville, Georgia,* as *Gainesville* is the nearest Money Order office to this place.

In enclosed Application Form you will also see that an *Astrological Chart* or *Nativity* is required. If you do not have this I can get you such calculated here by an Astrologer for a small fee of 6s. to cover his time and trouble. In such a case it will be necessary for you to send me the *Time* of your Birth, as near as possible, the *hour* if you can, and at least the day of the month and year, and likewise the PLACE.

Faith'y Yours,

Peter Davidson

Burgoyne Answers an Enquirer (B.7.b)

Source: Theosophical Society Archives, Adyar.

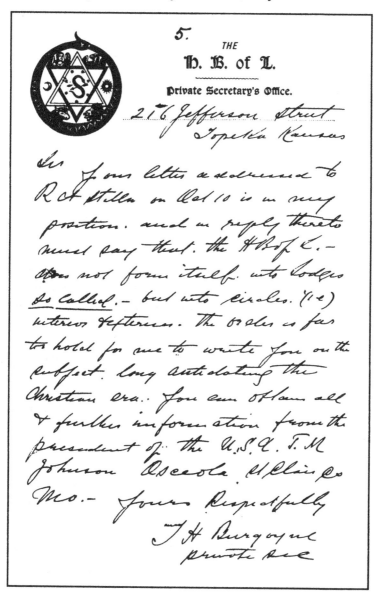

The facsimile shows the H. B. of L.'s seal. Otherwise the most noteworthy thing about this letter is the Private Secretary's weakness in spelling, punctuation, and grammar, which only served to increase the Theosophists' contempt for this unfortunate man.

The H. B. of L.
Private Secretary's Office
216 Jefferson Street
Topeka Kansas

Sir

Your letter addressed to R A Stella on Oct 10 is in my position, and in reply thereto must say that. the H. B. of L.— does not form itself into Lodges *so called.*—but into circles. (i e) interior & exterior. The order is far too hold for me to write you on the subject, long antidating the Christian era. You can obtain all & further information from the president of the U.S.A. T. M. Johnson Osceola St Clair Co Mo.—

Yours Respectfully

T H Burgoyne
Private Sec

Johnson Answers an Enquirer (B.7.c)

Source: Theosophical Society Archives, Adyar.

Thomas Moore Johnson (1851-1919) was a lawyer, a book-collector, a student of Neo-Hegelianism, and a lover of Neoplatonism and the works of Thomas Taylor. He was President of the H. B. of L. in America from the origin of the "Committee of Seven" in the fall of 1885, and also a member of the American Board of Control of the Theosophical Society, which he had joined in 1884 (Anderson 1963, 175). From 1881 to 1889 he edited *The Platonist*, in which he urged American readers to subscribe to *The Occult Magazine* and announced the plans for the colony (*The Platonist* II/10 [October 1885], 156, 157). *The Platonist* published several pieces over Burgoyne's name: an article on "The Kabbalah" (III/2 [January 1887], 106-112), and an unfinished work on "The Taro" (III/7 [July 1887], 354-357; III/8 [August 1887], 407-410; III/9 [September 1887], 478-482; III/11 [November 1887], 571-576; III/12 [December 1887], 655-660; IV/1 [January 1888], 41-47). They are of a noticeably lower literary and scholarly standard than most of the journal's contents, being mainly adaptations from P. Christian and Eliphas Levi. An earlier article on "The Chinese Taro" (*The Platonist* II/8 [August 1885], 127) was written by Ayton on the basis of a vision seen by an unnamed friend, but Burgoyne makes no reference to it.

Osceola, Mo.
Dec 25th 1886.

Dr. Sir:

Your favor of the 21st inst. is received.
1. The H. B. of L. is an occult organization of great antiquity.
It is of Egyptian Origin. This is all that I can say on this point.
2. I enclose a printed document, which will answer question
as to the objects, aims etc of the Order.
3. The entire control of the Order in this country is committed to a Central Council of Seven, and all applications for
membership must be addressed to the President thereof.
4. Any one desiring to become a member of the Order may
send his application to the President of the Council, stating
his age, sex, occupation etc. He should also send data for
horoscope, viz. time and place of birth should be given if
known. If *unknown*, send photograph (which will be
returned) and *personal description*—the fee for horoscope is
$1.00, to be remitted with application. The initiation fee is
$5.00, and annual due $1.25. Manuscript instructions are
sent to Neophytes.
5. The chief qualifications required in an applicant for admission are moral character, and an earnest, *genuine* desire to
know the *truth*. An inspection of his horoscope determines
whether an applicant has any *tendency* towards the occult.
6. The Order is not connected with Masonry.
7. The Order has in this country a comparatively large membership, and the number of applicants is rapidly increasing.
8. There are several members in Denver, Col.

Faithfully Yours,

Thos. M. Johnson
Pres. Amer. Cen. Coun.
H. B. of L.

To H. Lewis Esq.

Barlet Answers an Enquirer (B.7.d)

Source: Bibliothèque Municipale de Lyon, Fonds Papus 5.489. Translated from French.

Albert Faucheux (1838-1921) was an official in the French Registry Office, whose anagrammatic pseudonym was F.-Ch. Barlet. He never managed to obtain a posting in or near Paris, which made his researches and contacts with other occultists difficult but not impossible, as one can see from Guénon's article [B.9.c]. He was one of the first in France to join the Theosophical Society (in June 1880).

Arthur Arnould (1833-1895) was a member of the Paris Commune, for which he was condemned to death *in absentio* in 1872. After the amnesty of 1880 enabled him to return to France, he became a successful novelist under the name of "A.Matthey" (*Nouvelle Biographie Française*). After the death of Louis Dramard, President of the Isis (Paris) Lodge of the Theosophical Society (and a transcriber of H. B. of L. manuscripts), and a schism for which Papus was largely responsible, Arnould was given a charter by Henry Olcott in September 1888 for a new Lodge, the "Hermès." (See Godwin 1989, 14-16.)

Barlet encountered the H. B. of L. in the autumn of 1885 [see B.7.g], when the magazine *Le Magicien* asked him to make translations from *The Occult Magazine*. If Barlet was "Glyndon," this would account for his tardy appearance in the latter's pages. Here he lends his authority to the myth of the H. B. of L.'s Interior Circle as the "Mother Society" of the Theosophical Society, i.e. to its priority in time, an idea that led some French writers to think that it was hierarchically above the Theosophical leaders. See the opinion of J. Ferrand, in *Revue de Philosophie*, August 1913, 14-52, quoted in Guénon 1982, 25n.

Dear Sir and honored brother,

I hope that you will be good enough to excuse me, in general, if I am tardy in replying to you, and if I do so much more cursorily than I would wish; I am always so short of time.

The idea of the H. B. of L. is that its members, as you will have seen from the Declaration, work by themselves as far as possible (being only *guided*, not committed to any faith), and in the broadest possible liberty of thought. In addition, when I myself put a similar question to Mr. P. Davidson before I entered the H. B. of L., he replied to me that he was a member of the Council of the Theosophical Society. So you see that there is no objection on the part of the H. B. of L. to your belonging to any Society that seems to you able to reveal any corner of the difficult arcana; for my part, purely out of principle, I have always looked around everywhere from the moment I hear the announcement of anything occult. It seems particularly happy that the president of the French branch of the Theosophical Society should also receive from the Mother Society all that it offers to make known, from the moment that you pass the requisite conditions.—Finally, a different teaching will furnish you with points for comparison and very instructive themes for discussion, and I am convinced that it will be a pleasure to the H. B. of L. to reply to all the difficulties you may raise, as freely as you might wish.

Mr. P. Davidson will send you your horoscope (but only the figure and a few words on generalities, because a complete horoscope is an enormous task); if he has not done so, it is because of doubts that you definitely want to present yourself.—As you have replied to him directly (which was preferable by far), there is nothing more that I can do at present to be useful to you; I will just assure you once more of my sympathetic devotion, which is at your disposal and may be useful to you however and whenever you wish. I will only add one word, in response to your desires which are so natural and shared by us all, which is that, unless gifted with a special physiological disposition, you must expect to make *lengthy* efforts before getting practical results that are at all complete and satisfying.

For my part, it will give me great pleasure if you agree to answer from time to time some *theoretical* and *impersonal* questions, such as we students like to put to ourselves, so as to give us mutual aid through our discussions.

With all my good wishes for courage and optimism, I beg you, dear Sir and esteemed brother, to accept the assurance of my affectionate devotion.

Faucheux.

Bar sur Seine
5 September 1888.

Davidson Counsels a Neophyte (B.7.e)

Source: Bibliothèque Municipale de Lyon, Fonds Papus. Original in English.

This is one of the most valuable survivals among the H. B. of L. documents, touching as it does on very personal and serious matters, and showing Peter Davidson's efforts to be of real spiritual assistance to the neophytes.

After the death of his wife, Arnould tried to contact her through the exercise with the card given in "The Mysteries of Eros" [A.3.c] which Barlet correctly calls "Eulis." His meeting (according to Barlet's interpretation) with "elementals" and "elementaries" (present in great icy waves) and his efforts to communicate with his departed wife caused Peter Davidson to advise Barlet, in a postcard of 8 March 1889 (in same collection), to tell Arnould to stop the exercise.

The idea of contacting his dead wife was no mere whim of Arnould's, but was of the essence of the H. B. of L. Two ideas intermingle: one (which would have shocked Guénon) was that living men could contact the spirits of the dead, and that this was encouraged. The second is the central idea of the divine, bi-sexual monad. In the H. B. of L. it was only when the adept (or more usually, the dead person) reached the juncture of the sixth and seventh heavens (which coincided with the sixth and seventh degrees of the Order) that he finally and permanently reunited the sundered halves of the original monad, and it was this that thereafter sallied forth on its perpetual journey through the universe. Mead's quotations from *The Light of Egypt* [B.8.c] present a version of this doctrine. The same idea is essential to Randolph's system, where the interfusing of souls is one aspect of what he calls "blending." The question that remains is whether Arnould's contact with his wife was sexual. There are hints in other letters that it was, and if so, this would be absolutely concordant with the teachings of the H. B. of L. and of Randolph. Naturally, "sex" had a somewhat more refined meaning in the celestial spheres. See Part 1, Section 15, for more on this subject.

The idea that Love is at the basis of the occult corresponds to Theon's later teachings in the Cosmic Movement. According to Pascal Thémanlys, Theon said to Pascal's parents concerning "Eros": "*C'est un texte de nous qui n'a pas eu de chance*" (It's one of our texts which had no luck). Whatever he meant by "our," the remark is worth recording.

Explanation, which you will kindly send to him in the *Strictest confidence,* and sign your official designation please, in the Order viz. *Provincial Grand Master for France,* of the H. B. of L. Make this important matter *as confidential* and *private* as you can, please, as YOU WILL see the *necessity* of this.

Tell Mr. Arnould then that after a certain stage of occult advancement is reached there is no longer "mine" or "thine" as commonly understood, there is a new degree in fact of preferential Love. An Arch-Vril is formed and condensed in which the living forms of the affections are enabled to become embodied as was impossible formerly. If a man loved his wife before, he now loves her with a love of singularity enhanced more than a hundred fold, and she is enabled to demonstrate to him according to the measure of this abundance. Oriental Buddhist Initiates assert that in the states arising beyond, and superior to Devachan personal affection is *less and less*—but this is a gross and mighty— misnomer—a cold, heartless, *untrue* philosophy, for, in reality and in truth, affection and love become *intensely more concentrated.* They also assert that in order to renew the physical frame, man must die out of the affections that unite him to his kind. This I again repeat is an outrageous delusion, for in the Adeptship of the Divine Science progress is first made by cleansing loves from the *taint of self-desire,* then, by loving till we hold a creation of loves, living loves, fashioned in the heaven of our body, as the spirits of the glittering stars in the blue immensity of heaven.

The strange circumstances in all their phases attendant upon Mr. A. and his deceased wife are perfectly known to the *Masters* of Occult Science, and also the many ideas imperfectly given therein in his Extracts through the intervention of the Lady he alludes to. It is indeed a *Solemn Mystery* which has been performed between the two loving souls in the realms of the Spirit World. The plain truth of the matter is this: the husband has been in *dark Despair,* caused by the sorrow which happened unto him by the death of his loving wife. But, my Brother, there are *Mysteries within Mysteries* in the realm of soul-life, and one of them has been truly and solemnly enacted, by which indeed, he, the husband, has been saved from the awful fate which awaits the *Suicide*. The terrible states of mind in which the gentleman was—and in fact sometimes is still, for dark clouds of despair and sorrow still cross that sunny path which is partially being illumined *for him,* through the intensified and holy love of her who is so dear to him. *God is Love.* Her whose affections are now intensified a hundred fold in the soul-state in which she is, for ah, friend, never imagine with the cold, apathetic and unfeeling Orientals, that affection in its holy and sacred intensity, is ever blotted out in the realms of the blessed, upon the contrary, love and affection are very much stimulated there, and where genuine Love—*true* Love—has existed in all its ardour and devotion between two souls upon earth, rest assured beyond the vague shadow of a doubt that their Love *still exists,* and that the mere fact of *Death* happening, instead of being a barrier, or an obstacle in the way of such heartfelt devotion—that upon the contrary, all the delights of soul-sympathy are far more stimulated and intensified in their solemn ardour with the departed soul, than what formerly could have taken place upon earth.

As to the strangeness occurring in the phrasing of portions of the *Messages, Urania,* &c., this has been adapted for *a purpose* in view towards attracting the attention of those who are in a position to realize the truths of what has been simply related. The gentleman in course of time will be thoroughly able to appreciate the motives which the "Member" or "Child of the Divine Science" or "Sacred Circle" had in view for thus bringing such prominent phrases into notice. As I have already stated, and again I *emphasize* it; a solemn and sacred mystery has been most assuredly consummated in the soul-realms between the soul of himself, and that of his wife, as is clearly pointed out in the last passages of his "Extracts" alluding to the "interblending" or "interfusion of souls." But Mr. Arnould will not understand this mystery in its hyper degree until he has passed a *complete Initiation,* when the truths of such will be imparted to him, in a manner which will be unmistakable to him.

Papus Publicizes the H. B. of L. (B.7.f)

Source: *L'Initiation* II/7 (1889), 11-12. Translated from French.

Papus published a similar version of this five years later, in "Notices historiques sur l'occultisme contemporain," in *L'Almanach du Magisme*, 1894, 237-238. His informant was probably Barlet, his colleague in numerous occult societies [B.9.c]. The reference to a person who offered a secret manuscript for sale is either Burgoyne or Robert Fryar [B.3.b], though Fryar was the source, not the recipient, of the sexual magic manuscripts.

H. B. of L.

This mysterious abbreviation conceals the name of one of the most closed occult Societies in existence. We have had the greatest difficulty in obtaining information about it. On the one hand, we have heard extremely violent attacks against it; on the other, hints full of enthusiasm. As no one attacks anything that is not worth their while, we have pursued our investigations with the greatest possible impartiality. Here is an exact transcript of the information that one of the most authoritative members of the Society has given us:

Presenting itself as the newly-opened *Exterior Circle* of a very ancient center of initiation, the *H. B. of L.* sets out to develop *occult theory* from the point of view of the intellect and the Western world's own traditions, and to teach *a practice* that, contrarily to what is said by those ignorant of it, is free from every base element, leading only to the development of the *spiritual faculties*. To attain this goal, it provides its members with manuscript instructions and helps them in their studies and exercises, each one on a personal basis. It is absolutely false to say that these instructions, numerous and lengthy as they are, are always paid for. There are no charges other than an admission fee of about thirty francs, and an annual fee of five francs, as in every Society.

The origin of this legend of paying for the manuscripts came from a member of the most exterior circle who, breaking his oath, offered the first manuscript he received for sale to the first comer. This manuscript, it turns out, is incomprehensible without another one, and can only baffle the curiosity of the uninitiated. This is the source of those tales of manuscripts sold at high prices for initiation, which have been repeated in *Lucifer*.

According to information which we have reason to think accurate, this Society has many members spread over Egypt, India, Scotland, France, and America. Admission is very difficult, depending without appeal on the occult tendencies of the postulant, which are determined by the esoteric examination of his aptitude.

To sum up, it is difficult for us to judge this Society, in view of the obscurity in which it wraps itself. If we ever obtain corroborating explanations that may be useful to the public, we will publish them.

Barlet's Summary of the
H. B. of L.'s History (B.7.g)

Source: Jean-Claude Frère, *Vie et mystères des Rose+Croix* (Paris: Mame, 1973), 202-207. Translated from French.

This letter, whose writer and receiver are only indicated by initials, appears to be from Barlet to Augustin Chaboseau, who is reported rightly or wrongly to have exchanged his Martinist initiation with Papus. The content gives one every reason to accept it as genuine, even though the original source is not disclosed. Barlet's master is here revealed as Ayton, who was however not a Fellow but simply a graduate of Trinity Hall, Cambridge (Howe 1985, 10). On "Louis," the reputed author of *Art Magic* and *Ghost Land*, see B.3.e.

On the H. B.

The H. B. of L., whose complete name may be revealed only to its members, presents itself as the Exterior Circle, recently opened with the assent and under the auspices of an Order, which goes back without interruption to the utmost antiquity.

Its goal is to prepare those who have shown themselves worthy and capable for the development of man's transcendental psychic faculties. Its philosophical teachings are more secondary, being subordinated to practical spiritual development (not for the sake of phenomena or ritual magic, but aiming at the unfoldment of the higher faculties in every person).

Its method consists of personal advice and direction, given to each member in two ways: first, by sending him a graded series of manuscripts; second, by assigning him a special master (though a better word would be "coach"), whose job it is to issue these manuscripts to him as and when he thinks it appropriate, and who must also provide the instructions and explanations that the student requires, while leaving him, as far as possible, to work on his own. It is in fact a mutual education: the master assigned is simply an elder brother who reports to his own superior, with whom the student is put directly in touch when he desires it.

As in Martinism, each person knows only this superior and his own master, and is not permitted to make known the names of members without *their written authorization*.

Now here is the shadow-side:

When I was admitted into the Society, the representatives for Europe and America were Messrs. Davidson and Burgoyne, both in England, as President and Secretary of the Western Section. Above them was M.Théon, Chief of the Interior Circle, with whom one generally did not communicate directly, and whose residence, even, was not indicated. Above them, in turn, was an initiate of the Interior Circle whose very name was not given.

The Society, although recent, was then (1885) prospering; it seemed to have a number of lodges; it published some Hermetic brochures and a small journal that had been going for about two years. One of its members (of the Interior Circle) was credited with two works that have become very scarce, published anonymously as *Ghost Land* and *Art Magic.*

The Society was quite vigorously opposed to the Buddhist doctrines of the Theosophical Society, without however being either aggressive or personal. This brought down upon it repeated accusations, albeit timid and very vague, from the intolerant "society of universal brotherhood."

While this was going on, there arose—on which member's initiative I don't know, but anyway as a project outside of the Society—a proposal to sell shares in a colony, whose object was the elimination of poverty. Land, seeds, lodgings, and the first tools were to be offered gratis to unemployed people, who would then take on small annuities that would make them landowners. The circular, addressed exclusively to members of the H. B. of L., announced that a rich American engineer was offering vast tracts in Georgia (U.S.A.) at half their value (which later proved to be nonsense). A little later, Messrs. Burgoyne and Davidson were appointed by the board of the fledgling company (whose names were given) to go and see *in situ* whether these projects were practicable. No payments were demanded.

I have no idea of what success these proposals had among the members of the Society, but they had a predictable result. The man whom I had as my master (who was Fellow of a great English university, a title analogous to our *agrégation*), certainly very well versed in everything touching the occult, at least in theory, and master at the same time, I believe, of quite a number of other scattered members—who up to then had always spoken with respect, even admiration, of the Order, the Exterior Circle, and his own masters—suddenly started firing off circulars to everyone he knew, announcing that the colony project was a tremendous fraud, and, a few days later, that the H. B. of L. itself was nothing but a frightful fake set up by Burgoyne alone, perhaps with Davidson's consent, and that the existence of any Order or of any of the persons mentioned was a pure chimera.

This is what had happened:

When the colony project was aired, the master in question was informed that Burgoyne had been sentenced to about three months in prison—under the name of Dalton (I believe), which was his real one—for setting up, with an accomplice, a fraudulent employment agency. Confirmation of this fact came from comparing a photograph of Burgoyne (Secretary of the H. B. of L.) with that of Dalton as taken and furnished by the police; and Burgoyne, not without some difficulty, ended by admitting it. However, this sentence had been served several years before there was any occult publicity in England, and long before the foundation of the H. B. of L. as an Exterior Circle.

In addition, all the rest of the accusations which were being made in consequence were purely hypothetical. The police, for all their enquiries and solicitations, could find no fraud in the colony project, nor in the H. B. of L. But the Society was no less critically wounded, for that circular was of course the signal for the dissolution of most of the lodges.

What is one to think of these accusations against the Society? Mr. P. Davidson, who on his own account produced for me a series of certificates or letters going back to his childhood, has always sworn to me that the accuser's claims were absolute calumnies; that he himself had proofs that Théon and the Interior Circle of initiates existed. What I, for my part, saw of the case brought by my master against the Society, and even what he said afterwards—himself so competent—about the quality of the teachings, compared with the sworn statements of Mr. Davidson, all of whose correspondence shows him to be an excellent, devout, and thoroughly honorable man (this is the general opinion of him), have made me think, along with several friends, that the accusations involved considerable exaggerations and a precipitate rush to judgment.

The Society seems in no way involved in the crime committed earlier by Burgoyne (whom, by the way, I do not know at all). I myself have found great value in the H. B. of L.'s teachings, and have stayed loyal to it just as Mr. Davidson has, who has since impressed me with his rare courage. Persevering in the colony project, resumed on a much more modest scale, he and his family have gone to Georgia to be pioneers: to break new ground at his own expense and found there a model farm, in the hope of attracting other colonists and of forming the kernel of a model theosophic community for the future. But I don't believe that his hard labor has been rewarded: it seems that he has been through frightful tribulations, which he probably will not long withstand.

Up to now I have only got seven or eight manuscripts—there is a considerably larger number, and I would have received them last year, had it not been for the hard times through which Mr. Davidson has been. Those which I do have, at least, seem to contain a teaching as high as it is original. Our friend Papus will tell you himself what he thinks of it.

The first of the manuscripts is especially suggestive, its few pages filled with fundamental principles that are quite concealed, to escape the notice of the incompetent or inattentive disciple.

What is curious is that this manuscript, full of highly moral precepts and ideas both broad and deep (although unnecessarily outspoken) was written by this very Burgoyne, who has been accused of ignorance, swindling, and baseness.

It evidences, at least, a great power of assimilation. He has since published anonymously another, more complete work, which I haven't yet been able to obtain.

Burgoyne also went to America, I don't know exactly where; Mr. Davidson, with whom he emigrated, seems to have lost track of him.

The basis of the H. B. of L.'s teaching and practice is *love*, of course in its divine sense. Thus one develops one's psychism, intuition, and all the corresponding faculties, in preference to intelligence and exact science. It is remarkable, by the way, that certain passages in the letters attributed to Kant-Homi [sic] indicate analogous initiatic practices.

The conditions for admission are as follows:

Provide: (1) one's photograph; (2) one's horoscope (drawn up by the astronomical method), or, if one cannot do that, give the exact date (with the time if possible) and place of birth (with latitude and longitude)—enclosing five shillings for the work that has to be done.

Admission fee (to be paid after the examination of the photograph and the horoscope): £1.1.0 (one guinea).

Annual fee, which the professor may ask for (or may not), for the cost of his mailing and copies: five shillings = six francs.

(When I write to Mr. Davidson I will tell him that he may consider your entrance fee as paid, so that the delay of mailing will not hold up your definitive admission.)

Here is the address of Mr. Davidson, who will determine the admission (all the names must be written *exactly* like this, as the postal service is fairly poor)—but with the reservation that one must not send *postal orders* to this address, as they cannot be paid there:

Mr. Peter Davidson
Loudsville
White County, Georgia
U.S.A.

After admission is approved, you will be given the statutes, as it were, followed by a short profession of faith in the Society and a promise of secrecy to sign. And that is all.

After that you will be put in possession of the name of the Order and of its degrees, and you will receive the manuscripts from the person designated as your brother.

Chintamon Yet Again (B.7.h)

Source: Pierre Duvar, "Lumière d'Egypte," in *Le Lotus Bleu* VII/2 (April 1896), 80-83. Translated from French.

The interest in this review of *The Light of Egypt* from the official journal of the French Theosophical Society lies in its version of Ayton's Theon-Chintamon theory. The second and third paragraphs present a scenario that may not be entirely fantastic, viz. that Chintamon, expelled from the Society in India, did meet Davidson and Burgoyne. This could have been totally independent of their relationship with Max Theon.

The article mentioned in the second paragraph is: Jean Léclaireur, "Le secret du comte de Saint-Germain," in *Le Lotus Bleu* VI (September 1895), 319, who repeats the description of the Brotherhood of Luxor from Blavatsky's *Isis Unveiled* [B.1.d].

The founder of the H. B. of L. was one of the warmest welcomers of HPB when she and Colonel Olcott arrived in India from America around 1879. He left the ranks of the Aryo-Samajists in order to enter Theosophy, and was soon obliged to leave India for reasons of which any member of the T. S. who knows its history will be aware, thereafter living in England.

He knew through HPB that there still existed the débris of an old Egyptian occult fraternity which had once had its seat in Luxor (see Léclaireur on the Count of Saint-Germain), and of which one branch, the Brothers of Light (*Fratres Lucis*) had equipped Mesmer and taught Lévi. He made his plan: he would present himself as a high-grade initiate and, as such, remain prudently in the background.

In Scotland he met an occult researcher, D...: a sincere man who fell into this impostor's trap. Then a secretary, B..., joined, whose pseudonym hid a personality who also had no wish to make himself known, and who besides was only a business associate, not a real secretary, the latter being in fact C...'s own son.

They founded a journal, the *Occult Magazine*, and through it a business, the American occultist colony.[1] According to a tempting prospectus, immense tracts of land were to be bought in Georgia, in a county of incomparable richness, a sort of earthly paradise, so fertile as to give every promise of complete financial success.

Unfortunately for the proposed colony, the Grand Master, C..., who signed as "Théon" and whom the *Occult Magazine* made into "an exalted Adept of the venerable Order of the H. B. of L.," they were in too much of a hurry. As the shareholders were hesitating, references were given, putting forward individuals who had not even been consulted. Then protests broke out, suspicions were voiced, and the financial partnership collapsed, dragging with it the infant pseudo-fraternity of Luxor.

---

[1] The Hermetic Colony Association, Ltd., capital 500,000 francs, dividend in shares 4000 × 125.]

During the crisis, one of the Society's members was able to obtain photographs of Théon, which enabled Théon to be identified with C..., and his past reconstituted. Then they heeded the warnings of an eminent Theosophist. But from this moment on, C... swore enmity towards HPB, the Mahatmas, and everything Theosophical, which time has done nothing to lessen.

This, in short, is the abridged history of the H. B. of L., given here for the education of those unaware of it. Anyone who suspects that we may be exaggerating should look at the journal that they founded, the *Occult Magazine*[2] and read the advertisements printed on the cover.

As for its teachings, readers need only compare *Isis, Man*, and the *Theosophist* on the one hand with the works of Randolph on the other. They will then see for themselves that the compilers took the best of their journal from HPB, and the worst from the dangerous magic of Randolph.

---

[2] R. B. Murdoch, 451 Eglinton St., 1.25 francs per annum.

REACTIONS TO *THE LIGHT OF EGYPT* (B.8)

William Q. Judge (B.8.a)

Source: *The Path*, July 1889, 119-120.

This review is probably by the editor, William Q. Judge, who had a very ambiguous relationship with the H. B. of L. [see B.5.b]. However, he assumed that *The Light of Egypt* was by Emma Hardinge Britten [see B.8.d]. This misattribution was corrected in *The Path* for August, 150-152, where Burgoyne was denounced as responsible.

Some of Judge's rancor must have come from the innumerable American Theosophists who wrote to him enquiring about the Order and demanding practical training. It was largely his insistence that prompted the foundation of the Esoteric Section, which he then headed in America.

THE LIGHT OF EGYPT OR THE SCIENCE OF THE SOUL AND THE STARS. *Anon. (1889 Rel. Phil. Pub. House, Chicago $3.50.)* This is a paper-covered book of 292 pages to which the author is afraid to put a name. It is not by the editor of the R. P. J. because he is known to be a ridiculer of theosophical works, and this book is a plagiarism similar to Street's *Hidden Way*, only that here the author has assimilated doctrines put forth in such works as *Isis Unveiled, Esoteric Buddhism, The Secret Doctrine,* and *The Theosophist,* and then dressed them up in slightly different words. The method adopted to make it appear original is to omit citation of authorities and to denounce the doctrines of Karma and Reincarnation as applicable to this earth, while admitted otherwise. A whole chapter is devoted to Karma, but we find it illogical and very muddy. The theory of life-waves along the planetary chain, first put forward in *The Theosophist* and modified in *Esoteric Buddhism,* is adopted by the author as *hers,* after "twenty years of intercourse with the Adepts of Light." It is strange that it was not brought forward before in the author's other works. On page 85 we find a reproduction of what H. P. Blavatsky long ago said, "the fifth race is coming to a close, and already forerunners of the sixth race are among the people," and has repeated in her *Secret Doctrine* at p. 444, vol.2. After ridiculing Karma on the ground that if the first races had no Karma there could not be the present fall, the author proceeds to answer the question, "What is the real cause of so much misery in the world?", by gravely stating "it is the result of innumerable laws, which in their action and reaction produce discord in the scale of human development"—only another way of saying, "it is the result of Karma"—, and then devotes a page or two to proving it is Karma by showing the gradual degradation of man through the various ages. The preface astonished us, for the book is a rehash, pretty well done, of theosophical doctrines from first to last. A great blemish is the ignorant mistake of calling Karma, Devachan, and Reincarnation, "Buddhist doctrine," when mere tyros know they are Brahmanical Vedic doctrines taught to Buddhists. "What is new in the book is not true, and what is true is not new" but quite theosophical. Its numerous *ex cathedra* unsupported statements about nature are as refreshing as those in theosophical writings, lacking, however, the logical and reasonable force of the latter. The second part is devoted to astrology, and is merely another rehash of all that can be found in Lilly, Ptolemy, Sibley, and others. The book is by Mrs. Emma Hardinge Britten, and will no doubt be as good a business venture as her other two works.

H. P. Blavatsky (B.8.b)

Source: *Lucifer* IV/24 (August 1889), 522-523.

This review was written by the editor, Blavatsky (see *BCW*, XI, 385-386). The pamphlet to which she refers was the flyer advertising the lessons that became *The Light of Egypt*. Most of the points with which she takes issue are contained in the extracts from Burgoyne's polemical Preface [given in B.8.d]. The analysis promised at the end was entrusted to her secretary G. R. S. Mead [B.8.c].

Perhaps it was carelessness that caused Blavatsky, by reprinting verbatim Judge's review [B.8.a], to confirm his statement that *The Light of Egypt* was by Emma Hardinge Britten. She was perfectly well aware that Burgoyne was the author.

Hiram Erastus Butler edited *The Esoteric* at Boston and had his own sexual teachings. Blavatsky consistently equated his group with the H. B. of L., and wrote letters to the *Boston Globe* in 1888 that are full of hatred for both groups (see introduction to A.3.b). She made similar remarks at the 1887 American Convention. The only ascertainable connection, according to Mr. Gomes, is that Butler had joined the Theosophical Society in Rochester, NY, through Mrs. Cables, who was a prominent member of the H. B. of L. (see introduction to A.1.a).

Several months before the publication of this work, simply by glancing at a small pamphlet which gave a summary of the headings of its chapters, we had said: "This comes from the same hierarchy of unscrupulous enemies and plagiarists, of the Butler-Nemo and the 'H. B. of L.' clique." When we received it for review, and had read its first pages, we felt more than ever convinced that the quill which traced the author's introductory remarks and his reasons for its publication—was drawn from the same goose as the pen of Nemo, of the Hiram-Butler gang, who wrote *Theosophia* a few months ago.

We did not care to learn the name of its anonymous author or authors rather; we knew them by their landmarks and literary emanations. It was sufficient for us to read sneers about "the sacerdotalisms of the decaying Orient," vituperations against Karma and Reincarnation and the writers' (for there are several) impudently expressed declaration, that "the writer[s] only desires to impress upon the reader's candid mind the fact that his earnest effort is to expose that particular section of Buddhistic theosophy (esoteric so called) that would fasten the cramping shackles of theological dogma upon the rising genius of the Western race"—to recognize the author, rather by his donkey's ears than by his "cloven foot." However great the help given to that "author" by persons more intelligent than himself, his "ears" are plainly visible. We recognize them in the accusations of selfishness launched against the Eastern Masters and the qualification of *dogma* given to teachings more broadly Catholic and unsectarian than those of any other school the world over.

And now comes a corroboration of our idea in the shape of a complete *exposé* of the "author" whose wish was to *expose* "Buddhistic Theosophy." We might go farther than the "Path" and append to the review of the "Light of Egypt" the "author's" photograph. We have it from a double plate, one showing *** *before,* and the other *after,* the unpleasant and *arbitrary* ceremony of being photographed *gratis* by those in authority. The author and "adept" of "twenty years' occult study" is an old acquaintance, known in London and Yorkshire to many outside the large circle of his dupes and victims. But we pause to await further developments.

[A transcription of the *Path's* review (B.8.a) follows here]

We hope next month to give in *Lucifer* a detailed examination of this pretentions volume and to exhibit, by quotations and parallel passages, the outrageous character of its wholesale plagiarisms and the emptiness of its claims to authority.

Anonymous Theosophist (B.8.c)

Source: *The Theosophist,* August 1889, 699-700.

While some Theosophists may have been angry with the H. B. of L., they were hugely amused by *The Light of Egypt* and its surly polemics against the teachers of reincarnation and karma. The "dilapidated swastika" with which "Zanoni" signed his works is indeed angled, perhaps to resemble the letter Z. (The phrase in brackets is in the original.)

THE LIGHT OF EGYPT or *The Science of the Soul and the Stars.* By [here follows a sign that looks like a dilapidated Swastika]. Religio-Philosophical Publishing House. Chicago, 1889. 8vo., pp. 292.

This book professes to be an occult treatise, and occult it certainly is, for its meaning is exceedingly hidden. From the preface we learn that "for nearly twenty years the writer has been deeply engaged investigating the hidden realms of occult force," which investigations seem to have been excursions into "Kama Loka" of much the same order as those of Andrew Jackson Davis. "The chief reason urging to this step (the publication of the book) was the strenuous efforts now being systematically put forth to poison the budding spirituality of the Western mind, and to fasten upon its mediumistic mentality, the subtle, delusive dogmas of Karma and Reincarnation, as taught by the sacerdotalisms of the decaying Orient,"—so says the author. Here is a specimen of how the subject is handled. "A mediumistic nature will respond to error, because of the more potent thoughts of the writer, or, if we are over, sensitive, we may be superficial enough to respond to an erroneous idea through pure sentiment. These means have been seized upon by the Inversive Brethren, to enable them to fasten this re-awakening of the karma and re-incarnation delusion upon the sensitive minds and mediumistic natures of the

---

Western race. The most finely spun ideals of the 'the higher life,' of 'Devachan,' 'the Masters,' and 'blissful Nirvana,' have been and are continuing to be presented by a host of sentimental, spiritually sick, mystical writers to explain 'the glorious mysteries' of nature and 'the secret doctrine' of all religious philosophies, of which they themselves in real truth know very little, apart from the mediumistic ideas which are projected towards them by the Inversive Magic. The whole craze is merely a metaphysical delusion cast over their mentalities by means of a magnetic glamour." It would take a very large ocean of this kind of stuff to wash away the doctrines of Reincarnation and Karma! The work makes a very good counterfoil to Theosophic publications: It is decidedly amusing in parts, whereas in others it reads like the confused recollection of last night's dreams. Why it is called "The Light of Egypt" is a mystery which the author does not reveal. "The Light of Chicago" would seem to be a more appropriate title. Southern Illinois is nicknamed "Egypt"; or perhaps, there is a place called "Egypt" near Chicago, which is not marked on the map. Every American knows that Cairo at least is in the United States.

G. R. S. Mead (B.8.d)

Source: *Lucifer* IV/25 (September 1889), 54-64.

George Robert Stow Mead (1863-1933) had graduated from Cambridge, where he may have been drawn to Theosophy through his contemporary at St. John's College, Bertram Keightley (B.6.a; see Goodrick-Clarke 1992, 134). He met Blavatsky on her return from Europe to England in 1887, gave up his teaching job, and became her private secretary. After her death in 1891, he became the editor of *Lucifer*. This review is one of Mead's earliest writings. On the question of priority for the theory of "rounds," there was indeed a selection of "Mahatma Letters" published as "Fragments of Occult Truth" in *The Theosophist* during 1881, which sketched the theory although they did not contain all the information later given out in Sinnett's *Esoteric Buddhism* (1883). Subsequent editions of *The Light of Egypt* pre-empted this as a source by saying that "La clef hermétique" [A.2.b] was written as early as 1880.

Theon's later teaching, at least, contains the septenary idea. In the Cosmic Philosophy it is explained that after the six "periods of classification of matter" (like so many "big bangs"), the Seventh period, in which we are, will be one of progress both before and after the acquisition of the "glorious body."

This review contains essential extracts from *The Light of Egypt* on the doctrine of the bi-sexual monad. Mead's emotions are most strongly engaged by the H. B. of L.'s attitude to sex: that it is fundamental and primordial, and that at every stage of progress, even beyond the grave [B.7.e], sex continues and is an essential element of the path. This would have jarred painfully with the continence to which, as Blavatsky's pupil, the young man had committed himself.

54   *LUCIFER.*

The Astral Plague and Looking=Glass.

HOW SOME PEOPLE THINK THE SHADOWS OF THEMSELVES ARE OTHER FOLKS.

A SYSTEM of thought, new to the Western hemisphere, but old as the world itself, embracing in one synthesis religion, science and philosophy, is brought before our notice and claimed by its introducer to have been received from certain sources. It succeeds in arousing wide interest, in creating a new train of ideas, in attracting the attention of men and women of the most diverse nationalities, beliefs, tastes, gifts and attainments in every part of the civilized globe. And this simply in its broad outlines, by its ideas and innate force.

The introducer of the system says: "This is not my invention. I was taught it by others; neither do I know it in its entirety nor its last word. But even if you think me a deceiver, there's the system. Judge it on its own merits. What you have is but a sketch ; work out the details for yourselves."

The study is fascinating even for the superficial, and the curiosity of numbers is fiercely aroused. They would give worlds to know all, to work out the ideas in externals. "The key is within you," says the system. That was the great difficulty. Few could understand it. "If we had only a scientific primer with easy experiments ! " they cried.

So there was a great demand for primers, and trade became brisk ; and some worked it out this way, and some that, and there was a great disputing. And some clever but unscrupulous persons who did not love their brother students, arose and worked it out to their own satisfaction ; plausibly enough to all seeming, but cunningly devised to pander to the ambitions and desires of the curious ignorant ; and howled that they were greater, wiser, purer, better far than the original teachers, nay were the only true guides.

So these precocious and uninvited pupils set up a school of their own, and in the delirium of the plague which had now obtained firm hold upon them, began to spread abroad the insane charge that their late brother students in the original school were but poor dolts and weak past mentioning, and the teachers iniquitous depraved Satanities.

Perhaps it had not been so totally unpardonable if the system of these pretenders had been new and borne the stamp of essential difference from the school in which these ignoramuses had been such sorry outside surface pupils. That, however was beyond their attainments : they could not construct, they could but throw into confusion, destroy. Therefore with subtle ingenuity they stole and plagiarised, heaping together gold and silver, brass and iron and abominations, and threw over it a cloak of specious fascination and decent exterior. And by flattering the race-prejudices, pride, persons and presumptions of their victims, drew an eager crowd of flies around the garbage-bin which they had smeared with the sweet adulterated honey of falsehood and self-deception.

One thing alone they could not hide : abominations, as is their wont, must putrify, and the odour which thus arose, was most unsavoury.

THE ASTRAL PLAGUE AND LOOKING-GLASS.   55

The following is an extract from the New York *Path* of August :

"THE LIGHT OF EGYPT,"
OR THE SCIENCE OF THE SOUL AND THE STARS.

Some few years ago was started (about 1884) an order called " H. B. of L."
—or Hindu, Hermetic, or Hibernian Brotherhood of Luxor, as one may choose
—which, under pledge of secrecy, pretended to give occult information and
teaching to its members.   The "private secretary" of this was Mr. T. H.
Burgoyne, of whom a short biography has hitherto been written.   The instructions were to be free.   In August 1887, a circular was received by the members
of the order reading thus :

" To THE AMERICAN MEMBERS OF THE H. B. OF L.

Dear and Esteemed—"
[The first paragraph, for which we have no room, stated that because the
order was not sufficiently united the Private Secretary had determined upon a
plan of instruction, and then proceeds.   ED.]
" Those members who have read and *thought* upon the work just issued to
them, *The Mysteries of Eros*, will see that I have therein but briefly outlined
a few of the first principles, as it were—the ALPHABET only—of Occultism.   I
am, therefore, preparing an elaborate course of lessons giving the theoretical and
revealing the practical secrets of the science, which I am about to teach in connection with a series of lessons on the *Ancient Chaldean Astrology*.   This
system of Chaldean Astrology constitutes the basic principles from which ALL
doctrines, theories, systems and *practices* radiate, and *cannot* be found in *published works*.   I have thoroughly elucidated this science in the lessons, after
eighteen years of incessant labour, study and *practice*. *   Apart also, from this
series of lessons, I have in preparation a Special Course upon Egyptian and
Chaldean Magic, which will follow as a natural sequence.
" The actual teaching alone, connected with these lessons, will absorb the whole
of my time for *at least* twelve months, hence it is impossible for me to attempt
this work without remuneration.   I have, therefore, decided to form a Special
Class within our Order, for those who desire this sublime knowledge.   My
terms to each will be $60 for the complete course, payable quarterly in advance
(viz. $15).   Therefore, all wishing to subscribe will do me a special favour by
sending their names at once, so as to enable me to make the necessary preparations.
" In conclusion, I desire to impress upon each individual member who desires
to attain unto actual imitation [so printed and altered to *initiation* in ink.   ED.]
the great necessity of subscribing for this Elaborate Course in Occult Instruction,
as these teachings are not simply *metaphysical speculations*, but ACTUAL FACTS,
each and all of which have been verified by *actual experiences* in the great astral
soul-world of nature ; further, each fact and theory advanced is issued with the

---

* This *guru* must have begun then his "incessant labour, study and *practice* " when ten years of
age [?]   For, in the " Extract from a report of the proceedings at the Leeds Borough Sessions in the
Leeds Mercury of January 10, 1883," before us, we find that one Thomas Henry Dalton, later *alias*
d'Alton, *alias* Burgoyne, *alias* Corrini, Stella," etc., etc., grocer, was in that year 27 years old.   We
have undeniable proofs corroborated by a photograph that the " Burgoyne " of the " H. B. of L.,"
Dalton the enterprising (grocer) of Leeds, and the author of *The Light of Egypt*—helped of course by
several others whom we know—are *identical.*—[ED.]

56   *LUCIFER.*

knowledge, full consent and approval of our revered Masters, *the Hermetic Adepts* and guardians of ' *The Wisdom of the Ages.*'

Fraternally yours,

T. H. BURGOYNE,

Private Secretary.

Address, P. O. Box (   ) Monterey, California.

SYNOPSIS OF THE COMPLETE COURSE OF INSTRUCTION EMBRACED IN THE FOREGOING LETTER.

PART I.

OCCULTISM AND HERMETIC PHILOSOPHY.

" A full and complete course of twelve lessons, embracing the most arcane doctrines of the Hermetic Wisdom. This course is subdivided into *three* principal divisions containing *four* lessons each.

FIRST DIVISION.   Containing " *The Genesis.*"   " *The Alpha.*"—viz :
    I.   " The Involution of Spirit."
    II.   " The Evolution of Matter."
    III.   " The Laws of Crystallization—*the production of Forms.*"
    IV.   " The Origin of Life."

SECOND DIVISION.   Containing " The World of Phenomena."   " The Transition."
    V.   " Reincarnation "—Its truths, its *apparent* truths, *and its delusions.*
    VI.   " The Hermetic Constitution of Man." *Apparent contradictions reconciled.*
    VII.   " Karma "—Its real truths revealed and its oriental delusions exposed.
    VIII.   " Mediumship "—Its nature, laws and mysteries.

THIRD DIVISION.   Containing " The World of Realities."   " The Omega."
    IX.   " The Soul and its Attributes," *and the method of their unfoldment.*
    X.   " Mortality and Immortality," *and the processes of its attainment.*
    XI.   " The Dark Satellite," and the laws of the soul's annihilation.
    XII.   " The Triumph of the Soul." Adeptship—what it *is*, and *how* attainable.

N.B.—In the above lessons all argument or superfluous matter will be strictly omitted, and the laws, teachings and principles briefly and concisely stated. They will therefore contain the real gist and substance of what would otherwise be a very large book. The contents of Part I. contains about 100 pages. Part II, 260 pages. They will be *clear lithographs of the original*, produced by " *the Autocopyist.*"

PART II.

THE ASTRO-MASONIC SCIENCE OF THE STARS.

" Embracing a most thorough and complete course of 26 lessons, containing an elaborate exposition of the arcane mysteries of ASTROLOGY, giving also, in

THE ASTRAL PLAGUE AND LOOKING-GLASS. 57

detail, *The Ancient Chaldean System* of reading the stars. Scores of Horoscopes (chiefly those of public and historical characters) will be given as examples to demonstrate the absolute truth of planetary influence, according to the laws and rules contained in these lessons. The student will then *see for himself how* we read the past, *realize* the present, and *anticipate* the future.

PROGRAMME.

" The lessons will be issued with strict regularity, as follows, on the first Monday of each month, commencing with October. One lesson of the Occult series will be issued, and all questions thereon answered during the interim.

" Commencing upon the same date, the first lesson of the Astrological series will be issued and continued *fortnightly*. Consequently each student will receive one lesson upon Occult Philosophy and two lessons upon Astrology each month. The whole course occupying exactly one year."

The private secretary signed all his letters to the order with the symbol found on the title page of " The Light of Egypt." An inspection shows that the book is mostly a reprint of the instructions which were " lithographs of the original produced by the Autocopyist."

———

It will therefore be instructive to quote from the preface and give the table of contents of the " *Light of Egypt*."

" For nearly *twenty years* * the writer has been deeply engaged investigating the hidden realms of occult force, and, as the results of these mystical labours were considered to be of great value and real worth by a few personal acquaintances who were also seeking light, he was finally induced to condense, as far as practicable, the general results of these researches into *a series of lessons for private occult study*. This idea was ultimately carried out and put into external form ; the whole, when completed, presenting the dual aspects of occult lore as seen and realised in the soul and the stars, corresponding to the microcosm and the macrocosm of ancient *Egypt and Chaldea* and thus giving a brief epitome of *Hermetic philosophy*.

At the conclusion of the first part, we read—" We have written during the past *twelve months* probably as much as the ordinary human mind will be able to realise."

PART I.

SECTION I.

THE GENESIS OF LIFE.

I. The Realm of Spirit,
    The Involution of the Divine Idea.
II. The Realm of Matter,
    Evolution and the Crystallisation of Force.
III. The Origin of Physical Life,
    Progressive Expressions of Polarity.
IV. The Mysteries of Sex.
    Differentiations of the Biune Spirit.

SECTION II.

THE TRANSITION OF LIFE..

Incarnation and Re-incarnation,
    Its truths, Its Apparent truths, Its Delusions.
The Hermetic Constitution of Man,
    Principles versus Results.
    Contradictions Reconciled.
III. Karma,
    Its real nature and influence.
IV. Mediumship,
    Its Universal Nature, Laws and Mysteries.

* The italics are mine.— G.R.S.M.] By comparing them with the synopsis of the H.B. of L., just quoted the reader wi be edified.

58   *LUCIFER.*

SECTION III.
THE REALITIES OF LIFE.
I. The Soul,
    Its Nature and its Attributes.
II. Mortality and Immortality,
    Nature's Processes.
    The Appearance and the Reality.
III. The Dark .Satellite,
    The Sphere of Failure and Undeveloped Good.
IV. The Triumph of the Human Soul,
    Adeptship, Its Nature and *how* attainable.

PART II.
THE SCIENCE OF THE STARS.

To quote from the H. B. of L. instructions would be simply to reprint the "Light of Egypt."

It is interesting to notice that H. B. C., the private secretary of M. Theon the "Adept," signs himself with the identical "dilapidated swastica" of the "Author" of the "Light of Egypt." The object of the present paper is first of all to prove the source of the volume beyond refutation, and then to deal solely with the book itself and prove the perniciousness of its teachings. Burgoyne, d'Alton, H. B. Corini, M. Theon, Stella the Astrologer &c. &c. (all these being permutations and combinations of aliases of persons unfortunately too well known by many of us), with their schemes, occasional forced retirements from public life, rapid change of residence, mediumship and avowed practice of the foulest black magic, may be left to Karma.

And what is this "Light" which presumption, with reiterated claims of knowledge, professes to throw on the problem of being?

"Where now, O Egypt, where are thy diviners and ordainers of the hour? . . . . Thou shalt not, therefore, know what the Lord Sabaoth shall do. For this Egypt is the inefficacious Hyle."

Throughout the whole book the claim of having verified their assertions by actual experiment is again and again brought forward.

We recognize here the disease which has overtaken so many who have contacted the Astral Light. Do they not know that there are states far more material still than this external world of ours?

The skeleton of their body of doctrine is plagiarized wholesale from what they understand of Eastern cosmogenesis.* We read of (Re) incarnation, Karma, septenary rounds, principles, races, &c., the eighth sphere, cyclic progression, involution, evolution, the One Life and its two aspects, &c., &c. But what a tangled skein they have made of it! The threads are all thrown into inextricable confusion, and the spirit of the original gives place to excuses for the exercise of passion and indulgence. On this framework are patched together scraps from Swedenborg, the *Perfect Way*, the works of Lake Harris, and preeminently of the P. B. Randolph school, making, as a unity, I know not what sorry *olla podrida* of absurdities and obscenities. The word "obscenity" may perhaps

---

* In the H. B. of L. instructions (1884) we find a statement that the Races and Rounds are not taken from Mr. Sinnett's Esoteric Buddhism, but were written by a young student in 1882. Granting this to be true, which is by no means sure, the *Fragments of Occult Truths* published in the *Theosophist* since 1881, containing the substance of *Esoteric Buddhism*, may account for the fact.

THE ASTRAL PLAGUE AND LOOKING-GLASS. 59

startle the general reader of the volume under examination. The public exposition of their " Love " doctrine has been made in such generally guarded language that it may well deceive those who read in good faith and without a knowledge of the authors and their " secrets." We hope, however, to enlighten the public on some of these " mysteries."

Two subjects will be sufficient examples of their method. (i) Reincarnation and (ii) Karma.

(i)" In no case does the soul monad commence as a mineral and attain unto the animal or human upon the same planet, but it becomes latent on each alternate orb. For instance, the mineral atoms upon this earth will undergo a purely impersonal cycle upon *Venus (!) ** which is their next sphere, and then become incarnated within the vegetable circuit upon the next planet, and so on ; while the mineral atoms of the planet *Mars (!)* when they reach this planet, are purely impersonal beings and do not incarnate here as objective forms, but pass their cycle in the astral spaces, then enter material conditions again upon Venus."

" The talented author of ' Art Magic ' and ' Ghost Land,' who *for years* had investigated the various unseen realms of life for himself, gives the world the brief results of his *life-long* research in the latter work. Speaking upon re-incarnation the writer says : ' To my *dim apprehension*, and in view of my long years of wandering through spirit spheres, where teaching spirits and blessed angels guided my soul's ardent explorations, this brief summary of pre-existent states explains all that the re-incarnationists have laboured so sedulously to theorize upon. . . . *the universal and reiterated assertion of myriads of spirits in every stage of a progressive beyond*, convinced me there was no return to mortal birth, no retrogression in the scale of cosmic being, *as a return to material incarnations undoubtedly would be,†* and all the demands of progress, justice and advancement, are supplied by the opportunities offered the soul in the sphere of spiritual existence."

Oh the Summerland, the harps and streets of gold ! But why should the author who elsewhere insists on the *Cyclic* law of progression, quote the opinion of his " adept" friend to support his pet theory.

Is this the materializing of the spiritual or not? To this there can be but one answer. If such chaos-makers could have their own way, they would poison the pure spiritual state with the mephitic exhalations of their passionate lower natures, and make a " Hell " of " Heaven." If they could have comprehended the idea of the word *plane* or sensed the mystic meaning of the term *planet*, they would never have been guilty of such " inversive " delusion, or have so bedaubed the pure garments of spirit with the mire of matter.

As long as an attraction to the material exists so long will the monad return under the Law. These, on the contrary, would project the gross matter of their lower natures, unpurified, into the realm of Spirit. It is true that the Fixed must be transformed into the Volatile. But many processes and many days are necessary for the transformation, and every atom must be transmuted, the operator continually watching and aiding the Great Work. And this he must do alone. And, therefore, must he sleep and wake again and again returning to the .task.

All such material schemes have an attraction for surface-skimmers, as presenting a mind-picture which the vulgar can easily follow. This is not the method of true Occultism. The mystery of *Man* can never be told in words. One facet only at a time of the Stone of the Philosophers can be glimpsed at. Its unity must be sensed by the spirit.

(ii). Karma for Theosophists is a *law* affecting both spirit and matter. The School of Misrepresentation informs us that we believe that

* The Italics in all quotations are mine.—[G.R.S.M.]
† The " Adept " apparently places planes one above another and traces progress in a straight line [?].

60   *LUCIFER.*

"Karma at death remains somewhere or other down upon the astral planes of the planet, like an avenging demon, waiting anxiously for the period of Devachanic happiness to come to an end, in order to re-project the poor unfortunate soul once more into the magnetic vortices of material incarnation, where, with its load of bad Karma hanging like a mill-stone round its neck, it will, in all human probability, generate a still greater load of this theological dogma, and, consequently, at each re-birth it will sink deeper, unless the spiritual Ego can bring it to some consciousness of its fearfully sinful state."

This will be news for most of us. Surely we live and learn (mostly lies)! Now hear what comfortable words the·" Hermetic " doctrine teaches.

"Karma is not an active principle, but, on the contrary, it is a *crystallized force*."
    ·   ·   ·   ·   ·   ·
"*Karma is the offspring of everything.* . . . Races of men, species of animals, and classes of plants also evolve special racial Karmas *which constitute their astral world*. . . . . .
"*Karma is absolutely confined to the realms of the astral light,* and consequently is always subjective. . . . *When the soul leaves the planet the Karma disintegrates.* (!!)
" When the soul enters the spiritual states of the soul world (which Buddhists term Devachan), the power of its earthly Karma can never re-attract it to earth ; *its influence over the soul is for ever lost*."

Astral, very astral! The result of indigestion. And to think of credulity paying sixty dollars for so pernicious a disease! And if they will give sixty dollars for an acute attack of astral dyspepsia, what would they not pay for an indulgence in astral aphrodisiacs? Here we have a brew of such abominations from the astral materia medica. Those who have in their possession the MS. notes to *Eulis*, circulated by the H. B. of L., will recognize the hand of the same crew.*

---

* Extracts from the *Mysteries of Eulis*, by Dr. Pascal Beverley Randolph, 1882.
These *mysteries* were the most secret instructions of the *H. B. of L.*
"*Conclusion.* These are the fundamentals and all that is absolutely essential to anyone, for their application is as broad and varied as life itself ; a list of over one hundred powers attainable is given in the A—— M——,† which see. But there are certain sexive applications not therein given, amongst which is that of life-prolonging through a peculiar *rite* which usually weakens health and destroys life, but which, under proper conditions, absolutely strengthens and prolongs both ; this mystery is that of MAHICALIGNA—or the sexive principle of Eulis, and comes into active use in many ways, but principally in these seven :
    I. For purposes of increasing the brain and body power of an unborn child.
    II. Influencing one's wife or husband and magnetically controlling them.
    III. Regaining *youthful beauty, energy, vivacity, affectional and magnetic power*.
    IV. Prolonging the life of either the subject or actor, or either at will.
    V. Attainment of supreme White Magic of Will, *Affection or Love*.
    VI. For the furtherance of financial interests, schemes, lotteries, &c.
    VII. The attainment of the loftiest insight possible to the earthly soul.
These seven constitute a *crowning glory* of the System of Eulis."
Here follow long and detailed instructions, unfit for publication in any country. A hint or two may be given to show their general tendency. The seven problems are characterized as a "radical soul-sexive series of energies" ; further on we are told that "the great intent" is to be executed through the magic use of gender. "The mystery of Life and Power, seership and forecast, endurance and longevity, silent energy and mental force lies in the SHE side of God, the love principle of human kind and in the sexual nature of the homos. Outside of it all is cold and death, in it resides all Fire, Energy, procreant power (spiritual and all others) and the key unlocking every barred door in the realms that are.
"Fix this first principle firmly in your memory. Its basic form is ' Love lieth at the formation,' and love is convertibly Passion, Enthusiasm, Heat, Affection, Fire, God, ' master that.' . . . . Now I will teach you the grandest truth you ever dreamed of. It is this. Remember that the essence of all power, of whatsoever nature, character or kind ever resides in evolves out of and derives its impulsive energy from the *She* side of God . . . ." "You cannot master what is herein written in a day or month, for it requires long and severe study and *practice* to thoroughly comprehend it."
    † *Ansairetic Mystery*, a work by the same author.

THE ASTRAL PLAGUE AND LOOKING-GLASS.   61

"The twin souls are related to each other primarily as brother and sister, *and finally as man and wife. In this latter state their true meeting place is the plane of embodied humanity.* . . . . But whenever the two halves of the same divine Ego do meet, love is the natural consequence ; not the physical sensations produced by the animal magnetism of their sexual natures, but the deep, silent emotions of the soul . . . . this Spiritual love is the outcome of their Divine relationship, and *should never be set aside nor crushed by any worldly considerations. But, on the contrary, wherever possible, these pure intuitions of the soul should be obeyed* . . . If a female should marry under these circumstances and become the mother of children, *it will frequently transpire that the actual germs of spiritual life will be transmitted by this absent one, the external husband only provides the purely physical conditions for the manifestation of the spiritual offspring of the true lord. The rejected soul-mate, the spiritual bride-groom, is the real father, and very often the child born will resemble the image of its true parent.*"

" *To suddenly and completely suppress the natural functions of the sexual organism will do a great deal of physical and spiritual harm,* because the re-action will create violent discord with the ethereal constitution. *In fact, the complete suppression is almost as bad as the excessive use or sensual indulgence.*"

" No foreign or outside influence can absorb or annihilate the sexual qualities of the soul. It is therefore true that the masculine and feminine attributes of the soul cannot be destroyed as a whole. But the masculine portion may attract its feminine portion or soul mate, and the intense selfhood of its own dominant forces virtually destroy her manifested existence. This absorption, however, is a very rare occurrence and only transpires in the case of those magical adepts of the astral plane who have attained their psychological powers by a complete *polarization of all the truly human elements of their internal natures. Such magical adepts become the concentrated centres of spiritual selfishness,* but teach the external masses that self is the very demon they have conquered. . . . . It is from this magical school of thought that mankind have received the doctrines which teach that sex is only the appearance of matter, and not a *spiritual reality,* whereas, *nothing in this mighty universe is so manifest and so eternal as the male and female expressions of the Divine soul.* These adepts profess to have blended the two ; but they have simply polarized the one, and created a conscious selfhood of he other."

" Celibacy is a method that should be discouraged in all cases wherein the spiritual constitution of the organism is in a negative condition, and under the most favourable circumstances it is a very questionable practice unless the spiritual nature is sufficiently active to absorb and use *the etherealised atoms of the seminal fluid which has become dematerialised by the magnetic activities of Occult training.** Celibacy, then, must only take place when the animal nature has been so far evolved upward toward the higher principles *that the sexual propensities are susceptible of extending their vibrations to a higher plane of action.* In this case celibacy becomes an absolute necessity of further Occult progress."

" The human soul must be wholly evolved up out of the animal soul, *i.e.,* the sphere of undeveloped good in man's constitution must be developed, the animal forces and· appetites, instead of being conquered and chained like a wild beast as sought by oriental mystics, must be gradually developed and transformed or evolved into the human."

Very subtle indeed.† Love is a union of souls : a most excellent and righteous precept. But souls are male and female and each individual soul ever remains so and continues to aid in procreation, for "it frequently transpires that the actual germs of spiritual life will be transmitted by the absent one. . . And very often the child born will resemble the image of the true parent." So

---

* Truly one may say "I smell all horse pond, at which my nose is most indignant."

† The reader must bear in mind that the views brought forward in the present paper to combat the pernicious doctrines of these pseudo-teachers and pretended " Adepts " are meant only for those who believe in *Occultism* as a living fact and who seek to model their lives on its teachings. That the majority of us are capable of speedy success is extremely doubtful—still we can try ; we may advance a few steps on the journey and not sit still with folded hands in passive lethargy ; and so alone shall we gain courage to move boldly on, for face the task we must some day. But indeed in these latter times, that the doctrines of the great teachers of the past on this momentous question should receive even a just hearing is highly improbable. The two views contrasted are diametrically opposed to one another. It is for those alone who have made up their minds, to choose the Right or Left Path. The Middle is for those who doubt. Those therefore who do not yet believe in *Occultism* and that every act of their lives leaves its mark indelibly upon their moral atmosphere, cannot of course be expected to fully agree in the strong view brought forward, and for them it is not intended.

that these souls may prostitute their bodies wholesale, for "during the present cycle very few of these spiritual unions take place," and this, no·doubt, is quite to the satisfaction of such Don Juans. And thus we have a doctrine to encourage elective affinities ; sympneumata triumphant, astral prostitution preached as the divine law. And still these inconsequent babblers proclaim that when "the animal is evolved," celibacy becomes compulsory. But when shall the evolution of this monster cease ? we cry. This is the momentous question. Shall it be now and·within, or shall it be further indulged ? Shall the "Kingdom of Heaven" be put off to a dim and distant future, and "Hell" continue to reign triumphant, or shall the cry go forth "Choose ye, *this day*, what gods ye shall serve " ?

No doubt it is less damnable to their fellows that man and woman should weaken the passion of their thought sphere by an expression in act, and as legitimate a gratification as the self-preservative laws of society may provide. But to say such thoughts and acts are a *necessity* for man is a pernicious and frantic lie. The act is merely a curbing of the animal strength of the weak.

The pure in heart shall see, the pure in mind shall know, the pure in act shall be clad in the breast-plate of righteousness.

Marriage, it is true, is sanctified by the Churches ; and in this they show a practical common sense and a desire to keep the animal within certain bounds, but not even they preach its *necessity*.

True love of Humanity, the one religion, shows a nobler ideal, so that the *higher* ethics of Theosophy, as also the lives and teachings of the Nazarene and the Buddha, incalculate absolute purity, the virgin state, both of thought and act.

The crew of the piratical craft, sailing under the stolen flag of Egypt's hoary wisdom, with brazen impudence proclaim aloud that the exercise of the sex function is a *necessary* step in the conscious development of "Adeptship"! Indulge the animal, they howl, develop it, do not suppress it; do not slay the dragon, fatten it up, give it to eat! Such is their creed. St. George shall no more slay the Dragon, nor Bellerophon the Chimæra, nor Hercules the Hydra ; the Mysteries are overthrown and Chaos returns to its primæval slime. Progress is throttled and hurled into the yawning gulf of lust, and red Anarchy raises high its standards among the tents of men.

My brethren, can such things be ?

And so at this time, when the "budding spirituality of the West" begins to feel a surfeit of this same animal, and to "get its eye at length upon the knot that strangles it," begins to see this "Love" in its true colours and its poisonous influence on young and old ; this band of knaves would drag the pure white maid of LOVE down into darkness and chaotic mire, and oozing out an *ignis fatuus* of lust would send it forth to hover round the noisome fens of passion. Pure Love is love for all Humanity, "Divine Compassion." This love alone can teach man Justice.

It is indeed "Jehovah-God" whose constant exhortation was "Increase and multiply," that spreads such dire delusions. Thus the world is taught to look on such an act as Divine and God-appointed.

It is true that this function is a *fact* in nature, but by no means a divine fact any more than any other of the natural functions. Simply an animal fact, owing

THE ASTRAL PLAGUE AND LOOKING-GLASS. 63

to the evolution of matter, nothing more; but from the standpoint of that which is above the animal,—infernal. By this means, say these subtle tempters, the god within shall be strengthened. Aye, the false shadow "Jehovah"* but not "The God."

Man must be a perfect animal. Quite so: all his animal organs must be perfect. He has then the power of choice at every moment whether his body shall be the playground of the animal or the temple of the God.

It is sometimes argued that from physiological considerations, the exercise of every function is necessary and to refrain from the use of any function harmful. In extraordinary cases, when the individual is suffering from a veritable disease, it may be so, and then only if it is entirely beyond the control of the patient and becomes a sort of madness. But in the great majority of ordinary cases, a large percentage of the medical faculty, in one country at least, has declared the exercise of such functions unnecessary to health.† This is, of course, a purely material judgment, but why need we any further witness?

But indeed the perniciousness of preaching such an indulgence as *necessary* and its deadly attraction, especially for those who hanker after the occult, is by no means the prejudiced imagining of sentimental prudery, but an actual fact of experience. The poison is subtle. Astral alcohol is of finer aroma and taste than the destructive fire water of modern commerce.

The sanctified spilling of Abel's blood ‡ is the corollary of the doctrine of Twin Souls and biune sentimentalism. That sex is the outward expression of a law is true. But that there is anything of the nature of sex relationships in higher states within this material veil of appearances, of this absurd union which breeds multiplicity and is therefore a descent into matter, is absolutely false and unthinkable. Is this then the path of progress which leads to *Unity*; this a means to At-one-ment? §

But let no one imagine that we call the sex function unnatural. It is natural beyond a doubt: but natural to the animal; natural to man, while the animal predominates—but no longer than that.

" Love, pure and divine, is the grand keynote according to which all the harmonies of the Infinite Universe are tuned. Love is life and immortality, while the teachings and practice which insidiously or openly produce a contempt for *sex and love*, all tend toward the dark satellite and death, in its

* *Jod-hevah.*

† See reports of the White Cross Society in America, and also *Clinical Lectures and Essays* by Sir J. Paget, p. 291; *British and Foreign Medico-Chirurgical Review*, 1865, vol. i. p. 389, an article by G. M. Humphrey, M.D.; *Medical Times and Gazette*, 1872, vol. i. p. 239, article by Dr. Neale; *Vanguard*, Aug. 1889, article by T. S. Clouston, M.D.; *Ethics and Natural Law*, by Joseph Rickaby, 8vo, Lond. 1888.

‡ Use the physiological key of esoteric symbology. *Vide Secret Doctrine*, vol. ii. p. 125.

§ The reader will now be able to appreciate the brazen-faced impudence and falsehood of Hiram E. Butler of G. N. K. R. and "Esoteric" notoriety, a further development of the H. B. of L. imposture. In the *Press* of Boston for Feb. 3, 1889, the promoter of the "Call to the awakened" and "Esoteric College" is reported to have made the following answers to his interviewer's question: "Are the Theosophists throughout the country favourable to this movement?" "No, they hate us," responded Butler. "They hate us for our many virtues. Do you know, I am convinced that all the Theosophists, not excepting Mdme. Blavatsky herself, cling to the pernicious doctrine that the way to conquer the passions is to exhaust them through gratification. For an organization that embraces so frightful a heresy there is no hope, absolutely none." After this it is somewhat astonishing to find a favourable review of the "Light of Egypt" in *L'Initiation* of Paris, presumably a publication for the furtherance of Theosophy and Occultism.

64   *LUCIFER.*

awful and occult sense ; for just in proportion as *love* is displaced, *self* rushes in to fill the vacuum. . . . the whole teaching of Re-incarnation and Karma as taught by Buddhism, esoteric (?) or otherwise, is purely dogma ; it is *materialism* run to seed, combined with oriental speculations. It is a huge system of *selfishness, to work out good here for the sake of greater good hereafter.*"

And Theosophy inculcates selfishness ! That which teaches the divine Brotherhood of Man, the one religion, the sole bond of union between humanity, Divine compassion, is selfish ! Cannot these disloyal traitors to the truth, unloving sons of one fond mother, realise however vaguely the meaning of Sacrifice of·Duty ; are they still'too blind to see the narrow way that leads across the mountain peaks of self unto the smiling plains of sweet Compassion. As long as sorrowing human kind remain on earth, so long must we continue to think and do and speak for it, for therein we live and move and have our being.

So that at length, when possible and endurable, we may refuse the heavenly bliss of Devachan, to crucify ourselves afresh, most willing victims for our brothers' woes, and bearing the ever-growing burden of responsibility reach at length the Christ State of Nirmanakayas, to sorrow on until the feet of the last pilgrim soul have passed the narrow way.

These are they, who having suffered all and won through countless years Nirvanic bliss and an eternal rest ; yet when the prize is now within their grasp, refuse Nirvana for their great large love, not to another soul of sex, but to Humanity, a sexless unity, and on this most delusive plane their sad and weary brothers in the flesh ; and so in sympathy beneath this crushing weight of pain continue, till the Great Day " Be with us," when all shall be in Paranishpanna, where " We are one and the same and thou art one and the same ; this is the First Mystery, the Mystery of the Ineffable, before he came forth."

And all this sorrowful and weary waiting to help a few at most from time to time ; for even they are under the Great Law, the Absolute, and deaf mankind will neither hear nor yet perceive it. What work of Love can be compared to this, what higher ideal can be set before man as he is ? What story of earthly suffering, or of the cruel crying woes of those great souls all born before their time, lost children* of our mother, or even of the more familiar scene on Calvary, can ever shadow forth this love of *man* which passeth all understanding ? †

G. R. S. MEAD, F. T. S.

* *Infanti Perduti.*
† Those who desire to know how high an ideal of unselfishness theosophy can teach should read the " Voice of the Silence," translated by Mdme. Blavatsky and now in the press. It is impossible to imagine that so high an ideal can meet with one dissentient voice.

NOTICE.

American Theosophists who may have read in the August LUCIFER in "A Puzzle from Adyar" a reference to a report copied in the *Theosophist* from the *N. Y. Times,* and called by us "bungled and sensational" are notified that the qualification has no direct reference to that particular article, which is *not* " bungled up " and was written by *a friend.* Our remark was due to an oversight, the article was not read in the hurry, and was mistaken for some speech by Dr. Keightley at the Chicago Convention ; the editor having in mind shorthand reports in general, and having no idea of the identity of the two.—[ED.]

Emma Hardinge Britten (B.8.e)

Source: *The Two Worlds,* 8 May 1891, 301.

This review is presumably by Emma Hardinge Britten, the editor of the magazine. The deep hatred she had developed towards Blavatsky and the Theosophical Society since its move to India is shown not only by her fulsome praise of Burgoyne's work, but by her choosing to reprint the most inflammatory passages of his Preface.

The Light of Egypt; or, The Science of the Soul and the Stars.

This great work, which first appeared about two years ago, is now acknowledged—by some of the most scientific men of the day, and in especial—by many of the most profound students of occultism, to be one of the masterpieces, both of writing and instruction, of the age we live in. To the present writer, who has most carefully studied this sublime and truly-inspired treatise (or rather, it should be said, series of treatises), there is nothing comparable to it in the English language. The history, powers, and possibilities of the human soul, the world we inhabit, its place in the infinity of worlds in space, the laws, government, and inter-relations of these various worlds in the immensity of being, already known to man as the universe—these, and all the theories which deal with these gigantic problems, are discussed in plain, bold, nervous, yet truly scientific terms; and so adapted to the comprehension of the general reader, that none can mistake, and few (if any) dispute the surpassing powers of delineation displayed by the writer. The work, as a whole, is too unitary to admit of quotation in detail; but the 287 large pages of this noble volume will so well repay a steady perusal, that we feel no hesitance in referring a true student of Nature's deepest mysteries to the work itself.

The only pages that we can quote from, without marring that which precedes and follows them, are the succeeding few extracts from the author's preface, the perusal of which will at once place the reader *en rapport* with the objects of the publication.

PREFACE

The reasons which have induced the author to undertake the responsibility of presenting a purely occult treatise to the world are as follows:—

For nearly twenty years the writer has been deeply engaged investigating the hidden realms of occult force, and as the results of these labours were considered to be of great worth and value by a few personal acquaintances who were also seeking light, he was finally induced to condense, as far as practicable, the results of these researches in a series of lessons for private occult study. . . . Having served their original purpose—namely, of giving a brief epitome of Hermetic philosophy—circumstances have compelled their preparation for a much wider circle of minds. The chief reason urging to this step was the strenuous efforts now being systematically put forth to poison the budding spirituality of the western mind, and to fasten upon its mediumistic mentality the subtle and delusive dogmas of "Karma and Reincarnation," as taught by the Sacerdotalisms of the decaying Orient...

During the author's twenty years of personal intercourse with the exalted minds of those who constitute the brethren of light, the fact was revealed that long ages ago the Orient had lost the use of the true spiritual compass of the soul, as well as the real secrets of its own theosophy. As a race they have been, and still are, travelling the descending arc of this racial cycle, whereas the western race have been slowly working their way upward through matter upon the ascending arc. Already it has reached the equator of its mental and spiritual development. Therefore, the writer does not fear the ultimate results of the occult knowledge put forth in the present work during this, the great mental crisis of the race. . . . It is also necessary to state most emphatically that the writer does not wish to convey the impression to the reader's mind that their Orient is destitute of spiritual truth. On the contrary, every genuine student of occult lore is justly proud of the snow-white locks of old Hindustan, and thoroughly appreciates the wondrous store of mystical knowledge concealed within the astral vortices of the Hindoo branch of the Aryan race. In India, more than in any other country, are the latent forces and mysteries of nature the subject of thought and study. But alas! it is not a progressive study. The descending arc of the spiritual force keeps them bound to the dogmas, traditions, and external-isms of the decaying past, whose real secrets they cannot now penetrate. The ever living truths concealed beneath the symbols in the astral light, are hidden from their view by the setting sun of the spiritual cycle. Therefore, the writer only desires to impress on the reader's mind the fact that his earnest effort is to expose that particular section of Buddhis-tic theosophy (*esoteric* so called) that would fasten the shackles of theosophical dogma upon the rising genius of the western races. It is the delusive Oriental systems against which his efforts are directed, and not the race, nor the mediumistic individuals who uphold and support them, for *omnia vincit veritas* is the life motto of—THE AUTHOR.

POST-MORTEM DEBATES (B.9)

H. B. of L. and Brotherhood
of Luxor Equated (B.9.a)

Source: S. C. Gould, "Résumé of Arcane Fraternities in the United States," in *Miscellaneous Notes & Queries* XIV/11 (November 1896), 271.

Sylvester Clark Gould, of Manchester, New Hampshire, was an enthusiastic joiner of secret societies, and joined the H. B. of L. on 1 December 1885. He was the publisher of *American Notes & Queries* (also titled *Bizarre N. & Q.* and *Miscellaneous N. & Q.*), which carried many questions and articles on occult matters. Alexander Wilder was one of the most prolific contributors; John Yarker also wrote for the journal, and Robert Fryar and Peter Davidson advertized their publications in it. Shortly before his death in 1909, Gould was one of the founders of the Soc. Ros. in America, a body corresponding to the S.R.I.A. or "Societas Rosicruciana in Anglia," which had been founded in 1866.

Gould was in close contact both with Edouard Blitz, the introducer of Papusian Martinism to the United States, and with Peter Davidson, himself a Martinist. Since his information comes from that side, he equates Blavatsky's Brotherhood of Luxor [see B.1.b-d] with the H. B. of L. His placement of the H. B. of L.'s head in Illinois must refer to the "Hermetic Brotherhood of *Light*," a different order which began to appear in Chicago in 1895.

HERMETIC BROTHERS OF LUXOR.

The Hermetic Brothers of Luxor. An Ancient and Noble Order. Teaches that the divine scintillations of Eternal Spirit will each complete its own "Cycle of Necessity." This the only immortal portion of the Human Soul. The Brotherhood was divided into three grades, and these again sub-divided into three degrees, in America. The Order in America was somewhat modified from the Eastern form. It is referred to in a foot-note in "Isis Unveiled." This Brotherhood has had a somewhat checkered record, at one time it was dormant. It has, it is understood, in quite recent years, been revived, re-formed, and is at present in active life, the Head of the Exterior Circle being in Illinois.

Waite's Summary of the Affair (B.9.b)

Source: A. E. Waite, *A New Encyclopaedia of Freemasonry* (London: Rider, 1921), I, 349-350.

Arthur Edward Waite (1857-1942) was a keen proponent of the esoteric traditions of the West, as opposed to those of the East. He joined Anna Kingsford's Hermetic Society in 1884, became friendly with A.P. Sinnett and others in the London Lodge of the Theosophical Society, joined the Hermetic Order of the Golden Dawn in 1891 and the S.R.I.A. in 1902 (see Gilbert 1987a, passim). He knew Ayton, both in these groups and outside them, and evidently trusted his explanation of Theon being Hurrychund Chintamon [see B.6.k]—now transmogrified into "Christamon." Given Waite's reputation as a scholarly authority on every aspect of Western esotericism, this article became the accepted account of the H. B. of L., which, incidentally, was never connected with Freemasonry. For the photograph of Burgoyne in prison garb, see B.6.e.

HERMETIC BROTHERHOOD OF LUXOR

I have been informed by at least one American Mason of excellent standing that this association still exists in the United States and is unobjectionable in its present character. I have no particulars concerning it, and it would seem to be an obscure body. Its Masonic connections now, and at the beginning, may be limited to the fact that its male members are masons, but there are both sexes. It would not be necessary to mention it on such slender grounds, but it has been noticed in various publications belonging to the Brotherhood in an unofficial sense, while ridiculous periodicals like THE MASONIC AND ROSICRUCIAN RECORD have put forward spurious claims regarding it. It is distinctly an order with a past and that past is as follows. In or about the year 1880 an adventurer passing under the name of D'Alton was located at Baildon, near Bradford, and was making inquiries among occult students of the period. He was brought into communication with one who was well informed on matters appertaining to Alchemy, Magic and later Kabalism, one also who was a clergyman of the English Church and a Past Master of the Masonic Craft. The appearance and expression of D'Alton caused some hesitation about admitting him into anyone's house. He was dismissed by the cleric as soon as possible, but there was a feeling that he might return as a burglar. A few months passed away, and then D'Alton was convicted elsewhere of a very bad case of swindling.

Peter Davidson.—About the time that he came out of prison the clergyman mentioned received a letter from one Peter Davidson, inviting him to join an Occult Order under the title of the HERMETIC BROTHERHOOD OF LUXOR and stating that its secretary was Mr. Burgoyne, resident at Burnley in Lancashire. Inquiries were made and the respectability of Davidson was vouched for by an old friend of the Clergyman, who became a member thereupon. Many applied for admission and paid their entrance fees. The clergyman himself appears to have been unwisely active in securing subscribers among people of his own class and remitted their monies to Burgoyne, from whom he received in consequence a number of illiterate letters, giving hints about a great adept who was behind them. Certain suspicions were aroused and inquiries were made on the spot. It was ascertained that Burgoyne was in collusion with an ex-Brahmin—Hurychund Christaman—who had cheated various people at Leeds, Halifax and elsewhere. Other investigations proved that the handwriting of Burgoyne was identical with that of D'Alton. By means of a photograph Christaman was found to be in communication also with Davidson, to whom the clergyman wrote to ask if he was aware that the secretary of the HERMETIC BROTHERHOOD, under the alias of D'Alton, was a convicted felon. Davidson answered that he knew him as a great Occultist. Davidson was regarded therefore as implicated in the rascality of this confederate, and the known members of the order were communicated with, stating the facts of the case. Davidson and Burgoyne threatened legal action, but the police had been shadowing the latter since he left Armley Jail, and presently he fled with Davidson to America, presumably taking the considerable subscriptions which had been obtained under a pretense of purchasing land in America and erecting suitable buildings for an occult society.

Migration to America.—The police are said to have recognised that it might have proved an imposture of magnitude, had it not been stopped in time. The HERMETIC BROTHERHOOD was established duly in the States, but a photograph of D'Alton was obtained in his prison-dress and, together with one taken before his conviction, was sent by the clergyman to an American correspondent whom the Order had endeavoured to dupe. Copies of both were printed in juxtaposition, accompanied by an open letter addressed to all transatlantic members. Meanwhile Burgoyne had proved unendurable even to Davidson, who is said to have "turned him out" with a small sum of money, Burgoyne saying—a little tritely—as he went: "The way to make gold is to practice on the credulity of mankind." This time he fled to California, consequently upon the portrait disclosure. He had deserted his wife at Burnley and ultimately married another woman—I believe in the Far West. But he is said to have led a miserable life, in constant dread of reprisals on the part of those whom he had defrauded. At the sight of any stranger it is reported that he would go into hiding. He died under circumstances which I have not been able to ascertain. Davidson continued to turn Occultism into account and apparently the HERMETIC BROTHERHOOD remained in his hands. It must have lived down the rough unveiling of its original secretary. The interests of the Society seem to have been represented for a period by a monthly magazine under Davidson's editorship. It was called THE MORNING STAR.

Barlet and Initiatic Societies (B.9.c)

Source: René Guénon, "F.-Ch. Barlet et les sociétés initiatiques," in *Le Voile d'Isis* 30/64 (April 1925), 217-221. Translated from French.

René Guénon (1886-1951), who was one of the greatest esotericists of the twentieth century, frequented occult organizations for several years from 1905, including those connected with Papus, and received numerous initiations. His many allusions to the H. B. of L. supplied the clues that lead two of the present editors into these researches. Guénon's good relations with Barlet, who it seems entrusted Guénon with the insignia and documents of the Ordre Kabbalistique de la Rose-Croix (information kindly furnished from documents examined by Mr. Jean-Pierre Laurant) made him particularly well suited to speak of all the questions treated in the two *Voile d'Isis* articles. Barlet's materials included an incomplete set of the secret manuscripts in French, and correspondence including Davidson's letter of July 1887 [A.1.c]. Guénon doubtless used other sources, of which some can be found fairly easily but are somewhat unreliable if not actually misleading.

One of these is the series of articles by Narad Mani in *La France antimaçonnique*, an extremely bigoted Catholic magazine to which Guénon contributed at this period. The issue of 23 July 1914, 358, says that the "Hermetic Brotherhood of *Light*" was founded in 1895 in the U.S.A. This, and the mention of dissidence and rivalry, probably refers to the "Hermetic Brotherhood of *Light*," a different but obviously related order which began to appear in 1895 in Chicago. This suggests that the coincidence with the society mentioned by S. C. Gould [B.9.a] may not be purely fortuitous.

Guénon's statements that George H. Felt and Emma Hardinge Britten were *members* of the H. B. of L. raise the question of an H. B. of L., or its predecessor, existing in the 1870s. Felt is named as a member of the "Brotherhood of Luxor" by Mani (*La France antimaçonnique*, 11 January 1912, 21). Emma Hardinge Britten did belong as a child or teenage medium to more than one secret society that included important figures of occultism, including her friend Louis, the author of *Ghost Land* and *Art Magic* [B.1.a, B.3.e]. Besides maintaining complete secrecy about this author, and partial secrecy about the occult circles in which she had taken part, she also remained *incommunicado* on the subject of the H. B. of L. But her review of *The Light of Egypt* [B.8.d] shows that she was not ignorant of it, and anything but unsympathetic. Guénon's suggestion is that the author of *Art Magic* belonged to a society from whom the H. B. of L. received a certain inheritance, rather than to the H. B. of L. as a structured organization. This points to what we have mentioned in Part 1, Section 13, namely the striking continuity of thought among Randolph, the H. B. of L., Emma Hardinge Britten, and the early Blavatsky, which they all attributed to a mysterious source that was both Oriental and Western.

Felt's role in the early Theosophical Society has been undervalued. What he supplied was practical training to the inner circle, which may well have included the use of the magic mirror. Judge was his pupil in practice: see the anonymous "Reminiscence," in *The Path* VIII (February 1893), 343ss.

Guénon is wrong about Burgoyne's being denied access to American soil, even though he is correct [B.9.e] about the Theosophists furnishing documents to the American authorities about Burgoyne's past: probably the "double plate" photograph mentioned by Blavatsky in her *Lucifer* review [B.8.b]. A sworn statement by Burgoyne and Davidson [see B.6.g] seems to have got them past the Philadelphia immigration authorities.

Barlet's disagreable experience, mentioned by Guénon, refers to his membership in autumn 1907 of the "Centre Esotérique Oriental" of the conjuror and swindler Albert de Sarâk, also known to have founded in 1902 an "Oriental Esoteric Center of the United States of America, under obedience to the Supreme Esoteric Council of the Initiates of Tibet" in Washington D.C. Barlet became the Center's president for France, putting his authority and skills at Sarâk's disposal for several months, despite the many attacks which the latter deservedly received.

Stanislas de Guaita (1861-1897), a childhood friend of Maurice Barrès, abandoned a poetic vocation to devote himself to esotericism after meeting Joséphin Péladan (1859-1918). Guaita,

Papus, and Barlet acted together in all the decisive events of the infant occultist movement in France, notably in distancing themselves from the orientalism of the Theosophical Society, and in condemning Péladan as an apostate from the Ordre Kabbalistique de la Rose-Croix. Guaita seems to have had a good opinion of Peter Davidson. The Ordre Kabbalistique, like the H. B. of L., comprised nine grades.

Finally, Guénon himself had a definite kinship with the "continuity" mentioned above and in the Introduction. His early contacts were in the Parisian occultist milieu that was suffused with the Order's teaching, and his philosophic initiation was through contact with mysterious Hindus. A recent authority on Guénon suggests that this contact was not on the physical plane, but through what Randolph called "blending," and he calls *tulkus* (Robin 1992, 580-582). Under these influences, Guénon wrote polemics against the two targets of the H. B. of L.: Theosophy and simple-minded spiritualism. He loathed the doctrine of reincarnation, while his explanation of the "multiple states of the being" provided the metaphysical basis for the Order's more loosely-expressed doctrine of universal evolution. He expressed vigorous contempt for every modern occult group except the H. B. of L., and showed a definite respect for Theon. This was expressed first by not attacking him, as Guénon attacked almost every one of his contemporaries in the occult world; second, by according him the (unearned!) title of Dr.; and third, by avoiding mentioning him at all until forced to do so. Later Guénon appears to have revised his judgment, often speaking ironically of the "famous Tradition Cosmique." It should be added that, unlike Guénon, the H. B. of L. and its offspring and antecedents had no conception of the "greater mysteries." Any idea of absolute realization or of the supreme identity, so central to Guénon's thought, was foreign to them.

F.-Ch. Barlet and Initiatic Societies

By René Guénon

Before taking part in the beginnings of the movement that can accurately be called "occultist," F.-Ch. Barlet had been one of the founders of the first French Branch of the Theosophical Society. A little after this, he became involved with the organization known by the initials *H. B. of L.*, meaning *Hermetic Brotherhood of Luxor,*[1] which stated as its main goal "the establishment of exterior centers in the West for reviving the rites of the ancient initiations." This organization claimed origins going back to 4,320 years before 1881 CE: obviously a symbolic date, alluding to certain cyclical periods.[2] It pretended to be attached to an indigenously Western tradition, since, according to its teachings, "Hermetic Initiates have borrowed nothing from India; the apparent similarity between many names, doctrines, and rites of the Hindus and the Egyptians, far from showing that Egypt derived its doctrine from India, only shows clearly that the principal themes of their respective doctrines were derived from the same source; and this original source was neither India or Egypt, but the *Lost Island of the West.*" As for the form that the association had now assumed, this is what it says about itself:

> In 1870, an adept of the still-existing ancient Order of the original H. B. of L., with the permission of his brother-initiates, resolved to find a neophyte in

---

[1] There was also a *Hermetic Brotherhood of Light,* which seems to have been a dissident and rival branch. One might add that the name of *Luxor* also means "Light," even in a double sense if one breaks it down into the two words, *Lux* and *Or,* which have the same meaning in Latin and Hebrew respectively.

[2] These periods are the subject of the *Treatise on Secondary Causes* by Trithemius, whose explanation is part of the H. B. of L.'s teachings.

Great Britain who could correspond to his intentions. After having accomplished an important private mission on the Continent of Europe, he arrived in Great Britain in 1873 and succeeded in finding a neophyte whom he instructed gradually, after having satisfactorily tested him and had his letters of recommendation verified. The neophyte then obtained permission to establish an Exterior Circle of the H. B. of L., to make available to all who showed themselves worthy the form of initiation for which they were qualified.

On the brink of joining the H. B. of L., Barlet hesitated: was this compatible with his membership of the Theosophical Society? He put this question to his initiator, an English clergyman, who was quick to reassure him by saying that "he and his Master (Peter Davidson) were members of the Council of the Theosophical Society." Nevertheless, a scarcely disguised hostility was real enough between the two organizations, and had been so since 1878. At that time, Madame Blavatsky and Colonel Olcott had been expelled from the H. B. of L., having joined it in 1875 through the mediation of the Egyptologist George H. Felt. Perhaps it was in order to conceal this rather unflattering adventure of the two founders that *The Theosophist* claimed that the creation of the H. B. of L.'s Exterior Circle went back only to 1884. But oddly enough, the same *Theosophist* had reproduced in 1885 an advertisement from the *Occult Magazine* of Glasgow, the organ of the H. B. of L., in which there was an appeal to persons who desired "to be admitted as Members of an Occult Brotherhood, who do not boast of their knowledge, but teach freely and without reserve, all they find worthy to receive"—an indirect allusion, but clear enough, to the quite contrary behavior for which the Theosophical Society was reproached.

The latter's hostility would show itself plainly a little later, in connection with the founding of a sort of agricultural colony in America by the members of the H. B. of L. Madame Blavatsky found in this a golden opportunity to avenge herself for her own expulsion, and maneuvered in such as way as to get the Secretary-General of the Order, T. H. Burgoyne, banned from entry to United States territory. Only Peter Davidson, who held the title of "Provincial Grand Master of the North," went to settle with his family in Loudsville, Georgia, where he died a few years ago.[3]

In July 1887, Peter Davidson wrote a letter to Barlet in which, after having referred to "Esoteric Buddhism" as "an effort made to pervert the Western mind," he said:

> The true and authentic Adepts do not teach these doctrines of *karma* and *reincarnation* put forward by the authors of *Esoteric Buddhism* and other Theosophical works. . . . I know that the correct view and the esoteric meaning of these important questions are to be found neither in those works, nor in the pages of *The Theosophist*. One of the principal objects of the H. B. of L. is to reveal to those brethren who have shown themselves worthy the complete mystery of these solemn subjects. . . . One must add that the Theosophical Society is not, and has not been since the arrival in India of Madame Blavatsky and Colonel Olcott, under the direction or inspiration of the *authentic and real* Fraternity of the Himalayas, but under that of a very inferior Order belonging to the Buddhist religion.[4] I am speaking here of things I *know* and have learned from an unimpeachable authority: but if you have any doubts about what I say, Mr.

---

[3] After the H. B. of L. had been "put to sleep," Peter Davidson founded a new organization called *The Order of the Cross and the Serpent*. Another of the H. B. of L.'s exterior chiefs put himself at the head of a movement of a very different character, in which Barlet was also involved, but with which we need not occupy ourselves here.

[4] He refers to the organization whose leader was the Reverend H. Sumanagala, principal of the *Vidyodaya Parivena* of Colombo.

Alexander of Corfu has several letters of Madame Blavatsky, in one of which she *confesses* clearly what I tell you.

A year later, Peter Davidson wrote in another letter this rather enigmatic phrase: "The true Adepts and the veritable Mahatmas are assuredly members of our Order; but they appear as Mahatmas only for very important motives." At this point, towards the middle of 1888, Barlet resigned from the Theosophical Society, after the dissension that had arisen within the Isis Branch of Paris, and of which one can find echoes in the *Lotus* of that period.

It was also at about this date that Papus began to organize Martinism, and Barlet was one of the first people he called on to form his Supreme Council. It was understood, at first, that Martinism's sole purpose was to prepare its members for entry into an Order that could confer an authentic initiation on those who showed themselves able to receive it; and the Order which they had in view for this was none other than the H. B. of L., of which Barlet had become the official representative for France. This is why Papus wrote, in 1891: "Authentically occult societies still exist, possessing the integral tradition; I call for witness one of the wisest of Western adepts, my Practical Master, Peter Davidson."[5] However, this project did not succeed, and they had to content themselves, for Martinism's superior center, with the Kabbalistic Order of the Rose-Cross, founded by Stanislas de Guaita. Barlet was also a member of the Supreme Council of this Order, and, when Guaita died in 1896, he was designated to succeed the latter as Grand Master. But although he had the title, he never exercised its functions effectively. The Order, in fact, had no further regular meetings after the death of its founder, and later, when Papus was thinking for a moment of reviving it, Barlet, who by now was not frequenting any occultist

---

[5] *Traité méthodique de Science occulte*, p. 1039.

groups, declared that he was completely uninterested in it; he thought, and no doubt rightly, that such efforts, resting on no solid basis, could only lead to further failures.

We will not discuss the other more or less ephemeral organizations which Barlet joined, perhaps a little too readily; his great sincerity, his essentially honest and trusting character, hindered him in these circumstances from seeing that certain people were only trying to use his name as a guarantee of "respectability." In the end, these disagreable experiences put him on his guard and led him to doubt the usefulness of all associations whose initiatic pretensions hid almost no real knowledge, and which were merely a pretext for people to adorn themselves with more or less pompous titles; he had seen through the vanity of all these exterior forms, from which the truly initiatic organizations were entirely detached. A few months before his death, while speaking to us about a new, so-called Rosicrucian society imported from America which he had been invited to join, he told us that he would have nothing to do with it, because he was absolutely convinced (as we ourselves were) that the true Rosicrucians never founded any societies. We will end with this conclusion, reached by him at the end of so much searching, and which may well cause a good number of our contemporaries to reflect—if they are willing, as the H. B. of L.'s teachings say, "to learn to know the enormous difference between intact truth and apparent truth," or between genuine initiation and its countless imitators.

Some Corrections (B.9.d)

Source: "Periodical Literature," in *The Occult Review*, May 1925, 326-327.

Outside Theosophy, *The Occult Review* was the only serious esoteric periodical in Britain during this period, and it kept its readers in touch with the periodical literature of Europe and America. This was probably written by A. E. Waite [see B.9.b].

The second and later issue of *Le Voile d'Isis* returns to F. C. Barlet and his connection with occult societies. He was an original founder of the Theosophical Society in France, but left it in 1888; of the Martinist Order about that period; and was on the Supreme Council of *L'Ordre Kabbalistique de la Rose-Croix*, which was established by Stanislas de Guaita but was destined to languish and finally pass out of existence after the death of the latter in 1896. But that which is most curious is the full account of Barlet's connection with the Hermetic Brotherhood of Luxor and the representations made concerning it at this late day of the subject, considering that its real position has been known publicly in England since 1921 and privately for many years past. It began to be heard of in this country chiefly through the activities of Peter Davidson, behind whom was a convicted felon named Burgoyne, while behind Burgoyne was a fraudulent ex-Brahman, passing as Hurychund Christaman. This was about 1880. As the result of investigations made by the late Rev. W. Alexander Ayton, a well-known theosophist, occult student and writer, Burgoyne and Davidson fled to America, where the former posed as Provincial Grand Master of the North. Burgoyne died in California and Davidson in Georgia, but at a much later period. It was evidently from America that the latter opened communication with Barlet and also with Papus, who was completely taken in and described Davidson as *mon maître en pratique*. The Hermetic Brotherhood of Luxor referred its foundation to B.C. 4320, but the root-matter of its teaching was to be sought in "the Lost Isle of the West," presumably meaning Atlantis. Our French contemporary says that its official organ was *The Occult Magazine* of Glasgow—which we remember far in the past; but we think that this is a mistake: in any case the Brotherhood was represented for a period in America by *The Morning Star*, under the auspices of Peter Davidson. Barlet's experience of occult societies seems to have been extensive as well as peculiar, but in the end it is said that he found vanity alone in all external forms. As regards the vast majority at least, we express our concurrence and offer our salutation to the memory of F. C. Barlet.

Guénon Tells All (B.9.e)

Source: René Guénon, "Quelques précisions à propos de la H. B. of L.," in *Le Voile d'Isis* 30/70 (October 1925), 592-595. Translated from French.

This is an amplification of the article on Barlet [B.9.c], occasioned by the comments in *The Occult Review* [B.9.d]. On Barlet's adherence to the H. B. of L., see B.7.d, where he says he joined in 1885.

The undue emphasis given by Guénon to the Order of the Cross and the Serpent probably derives from a statement in *La France antimaçonnique* of 23 July 1914, 358, that this order was still under Davidson's direction and devoted to the Philosophie Cosmique. Davidson does mention the Order of the Cross and the Serpent in *The Morning Star* during the first years of the new century, but mainly to publicize the ideas of Holden E. Sampson, author of *The Message of the Sun and the Cult of the Cross and Serpent* (London: Philip Wellby, 1904). *The Morning Star* began to introduce the Philosophie Cosmique in 1903, and by 1905 was devoted almost entirely to the diffusion of Theon's new teachings.

Narad Mani is the probable source for Guénon's allegation that Blavatsky had been expelled from the "Brotherhood of Luxor" shortly before leaving New York for India (*La France anti-maçonnique*, 26 October 1911, 465). It remained for Guénon to extend the expulsion to Olcott (Guénon 1982, 25), and to identify this brotherhood with the H. B. of L. of Davidson and Burgoyne. Guénon clears up Ayton's misidentification of Theon with Chintamon, but he confuses the issue by seeming ready to believe Barlet's idea that Theon was the son of Paulos Metamon. The degree of Guénon's ignorance of Theon is a measure of the latter's reticence.

The Arya Samaj was founded not in 1870 but in 1875, the same year as the Theosophical Society—a circumstance that struck Olcott as significant and encouraged him in (temporarily) uniting the two societies.

Some Particulars Concerning the H. B. of L.

By René Guénon

The *Occult Review* of May 1925, in reviewing the article we contributed to the *Voile d'Isis* on the relationship of F.-Ch. Barlet with various initiatic societies and especially with the H. B. of L. (Hermetic Brotherhood of Luxor), has added some information about the latter which is unfortunately incorrect, for the most part, and we think it best to rectify it by amplifying our previous article.

To begin with, when Barlet was affiliated with the H. B. of L., its headquarters had not yet moved to America. Barlet's affiliation must even have been a little earlier than the publication of the *Occult Magazine*, which appeared in Glasgow during the two years 1885 and 1886, and of which we have before us a complete run. This magazine was certainly the official organ of the H. B. of L., whose motto it carried on its masthead: *Omnia vincit Veritas*. We made no mistake in this, contrarily to what our English colleague seems to believe. At this period, Peter Davidson was living at Banchory, Kincardineshire, in New Brunswick [sic], and it was only towards the end of the year 1886 that he left to settle in Loudsville, Georgia, where he was to pass the rest of his life. It was much later that he edited a new magazine called *The Morning Star*, which was the organ of the *Order of the Cross and the Serpent*, founded by him after the H. B. of L. had been "put to sleep."

Then again, it was in the *Occult Magazine* of October 1885 that the note was inserted, explaining for the first time the project of organizing an agricultural colony of the H. B. of L. in California. This note was signed with the initials of T. H. Burgoyne, Secretary of the Order (and not "Provincial Grand Master of the North," a title which belonged to Davidson). There was much about this project in the following numbers, but the idea of founding a colony in California was quickly abandoned, and their sights were turned to Georgia. It was even announced that Burgoyne would be in Loudsville from 15 April 1886 onwards, but he was not, thanks to the intervention of Madame Blavatsky to which we alluded. In the past, Burgoyne had been sentenced for swindling; Madame Blavatsky, who knew this fact, took steps to obtain documents containing the proof of it and sent them to America, in order to have Burgoyne denied residency in the United States. Thus she avenged the expulsion from the H. B. of L. of herself and Colonel Olcott eight years before, in 1878. As for Davidson, whose honesty never gave rise to the slightest suspicion, he did not have to "flee to America," as the *Occult Review* has it; neither was there any way of stopping him from settling in Georgia with his family, to become the first seed of the future colony, which however never developed as hoped.

The editor of the *Occult Review* says that behind Davidson there was Burgoyne, which is inaccurate because their respective posts implied no kind of subordination of the former to the latter. Even more surprisingly, he claims that behind Burgoyne was an "ex-Brahman" named "Hurychund Christaman." There is a peculiar misunderstanding here that requires some explanation. Madame Blavatsky and Colonel Olcott had joined the American Branch of the H. B. of L. towards the month of April 1875, through the agency of George H. Felt, who called himself a Professor of Mathematics and Egyptology, and with whom they had been put in contact by a journalist named Stevens. One consequence of this affiliation was that, in the spiritualistic séances that Madame Blavatsky was then giving, the manifestations of the famous "John King" were soon replaced by those of a so-called "Serapis." This happened precisely on 7 September 1875, and it was on 17 November of the same year that the Theosophical Society was founded. About two years later, Serapis was in turn replaced by a certain "Kashmiri Brother." What had happened was that Olcott and

Madame Blavatsky had in the meantime made the acquaintance of Hurrychund Chintamon (not Christaman), who was certainly not the chief, secret or otherwise, of the H. B. of L., but the representative in America of the Arya Samâj, an association founded in India in 1870 by Swami Dayânanda Saraswatî. In September or October 1877, in the words of Madame Blavatsky, "an offensive and defensive alliance" was formed between the Arya Samâj and the Theosophical Society. This alliance was broken in 1882 by Dayânanda Saraswatî himself, who expressed himself pretty forcibly at that time on the subject of Madame Blavatsky. She, for motives that we have not been able to explain, later displayed an absolute terror of Hurrychund Chintamon; but what is important in all this is that her relations with the latter coincided exactly with the moment when she began to detach herself from the H. B. of L.; and this point is enough to refute the statement in the *Occult Review.*

It remains now to seek an explanation for this mistake. May it not have been a simple confusion, due to the partial similarity of the two names Chintamon and Metamon? The latter name is that of Madame Blavatsky's first master, the magician Paulos Metamon, of Coptic or Chaldean origin (it has never been possible to determine which), whom she had met in Asia Minor as early as 1848, then rediscovered in Cairo in 1870. But, one will ask, what connection could that person have with the H. B. of L? To answer that question we are obliged to inform our colleague on the *Occult Review,* who seems not to know it, of the identity of the real head, or to be more exact the Grand Master of the "Exterior Circle" of the H. B. of L. This Grand Master was Dr. Max Théon, who would later create and direct what was known as the "Cosmic Movement." It is this, moreover, that explains the part that Barlet, formerly representative of the H. B. of L. in France, took in the Cosmic Movement from its beginnings—that is, if we are not mistaken, from 1899 or 1900. As to the origin of Dr. Max Théon, which has always remained very mysterious, we have only one witness, but one which deserves to be considered seriously: Barlet himself, who should have known what he was talking about, assured us that Théon was actually the son of Paulos Metamon. If that is true, then the whole matter is self-explanatory.

We did not want to bring into our preceding article persons who are still alive, and that is why we abstained from naming Monsieur Théon, to whom we had only alluded in a note. But after the contribution of the *Occult Review*, it is necessary to set the record straight in the interests of historical truth. It is even to be hoped that these explanations will bring forth others, for we do not claim to have cleared away all the obscurities at a stroke. There must still be some people who witnessed the facts in question, and, since certain questions are now raised, could they not reveal what they know about them? The many years that have now elapsed since the H. B. of L. ceased its activity surely gives them every liberty in this respect.

BIBLIOGRAPHY

(Contains the works cited in the editors' contributions: Part 1, introductions and notes to the documents. A more complete list of sources is to be found in the more specialized works by the editors. These publications are cited in this bibliography.)

Agenda de Mère [= Mirra Alfassa, "The Mother"]. Paris: Institut de recherches évolutives, 1978-1981. English edition: *Mother's Agenda.* 8 vols. New York: Institute for Evolutionary Research, 1979.

Amadou, Robert. "Les Archives de Papus à la Bibliothèque municipale de Lyon." *L'Initiation,* April-June 1967, 75-91.

Anderson, Paul R. *Platonism in the Midwest.* Philadelphia: Temple University, 1963.

Art Magic, or Mundane, Sub-Mundane, and Super-Mundane Spiritualism. New York: Britten, 1876.

BCW. H. P. Blavatsky. *Collected Writings.* Compiled by Boris de Zirkoff. 15 vols. Wheaton: Theosophical Publishing House, 1950-1991.

Barrett, Francis. *The Magus, or Celestial Intelligencer.* London: Lackington Allen, 1801. Reprinted Weiser, n.d.

Blavatsky, H. P. *Isis Unveiled.* 2 vols. New York: Bouton, 1877.

———. *The Secret Doctrine.* 2 vols. London: Theosophical Publishing House, 1888.

———. *The Letters of H. P. Blavatsky to A. P. Sinnett.* New York: Stokes, 1925.

Bricaud, J. *L'Abbé Boullan, sa vie, sa doctrine et ses pratiques magiques.* Paris: Chacornac Frères, 1927.

Brieu, Jacques. "Esotérisme et spiritisme." *Mercure de France,* May 1907, 139.

Britten, Emma Hardinge. *Autobiography of Emma Hardinge Britten.* Manchester: John Heywood, 1900.

———. *Nineteenth Century Miracles.* New York: William Britten, 1884.

Burgoyne, Thomas H. *The Language of the Stars.* Denver: Astro-Philosophical Publishing Co., 1892.

———. *Celestial Dynamics; a Course of Astro-Metaphysical Study.* Denver: Astro-Philosophical Publishing Co., 1896.

Burgoyne. See *LOE.*

Cahagnet, Alphonse L. *Magnetic Magic, A Digest of the Practical Parts of the Masterpieces of L . A. Cahagnet, H. F. T. S., Arcanes de la future dévoilés, and Magie Magnétique. Now translated for the first time from the French by the Editor, with the portrait of the Author.* Privately Printed for Subscribers, 1898.

Campbell, Robert Allen. *Mysteries of the Hand Revealed and Explained: The art of determining, from an inspection of the hands, the person's temperament, appetites, passions, impulses, aspirations, mental endowments—character and tendencies.* St. Louis: J. W. Campbell & Co., 1879.

———. *Phallic Worship: An Outline of the Worship of the Generative Organs, As Being, or as Representing, the Divine Creator, with Suggestions as to the Influence of the Phallic Idea on Religious Creeds, Ceremonies, Customs and Symbolism—Past and Present.* St. Louis: R. A. Campbell & Co., 1887.

Caracostea, Daniel. "Lettres de H. P. B. à Arthur Arnould." *Le Lotus Bleu* 93/3 (March 1988), 60-66.

Chacornac, Paul. *Grandeur et Adversité de Jean Trithème, Benédictin, Abbé de Spanheim et de Wurtzbourg (1462-1516), La Vie, La Légende, l'Oeuvre.* Paris: Editions Traditionnelles, 1973.

Chanel, Christian. Review of *H. B. of L. Textes et documents secrets...*, *Politica Hermetica* 3 (1989), 146-152.

———. "De la 'Fraternité de Louxor' au 'Mouvement cosmique': l'oeuvre de Max Théon (contribution à l'étude des courants ésotériques en Europe à la fin du XIXème siècle et au début du XXème siècle." Doctorat d'Etat, E.P.H.E., Section Ve, 1994.

———. "Max Théon and the Theosophical Society." Paper read at the American Academy of Religion, Chicago, 1994. [1994a]

"The Church of Light. Its History and Principles." Undated pamphlet, issued in or after 1985.

Clymer, R. Swinburne. *The Book of Rosicruciae.* 3 vols. Quakertown: Philosophical Publishing Co., 1947.

Conger, Margaret. *Combined Chronology for Use with the Mahatma Letters... and the Letters of H. P. Blavatsky.* Pasadena: Theosophical University Press, 1973.

Curry, Patrick. *A Confusion of Prophets. Victorian and Edwardian Astrology.* London: Collins & Brown, 1992.

Davidson, Peter. *The Mistletoe and Its Philosophy.* Loudsville: Davidson, 1892.

———. *The Violin.* Glasgow: Porteous Bros., 1871 and reeditions.

Deveney, John Patrick. *Paschal Beverly Randolph. A Nineteenth Century Black American Spiritualist and Sex Magician.* Albany: SUNY Press, forthcoming.

"The Founders of the Church of Light." *The Church of Light Quarterly* 45/1 (1987), not paginated.

Fryar, Robert H. *Sub-Mundanes; or, The Elementaries of the Cabala: Being The History of Spirits, Reprinted from the Text of the Abbé de Villars, Physio-Astro-Magic. Wherein is asserted that there are in existance on earth rational creatures besides man.* Bath: Fryar, 1886. A reissue of the translation by P. A[yers], 1680.

Fryar, Robert H., ed. *Sexagyma, A Digest of the Works of John Davenport—"Curiositates Eroticae Physiologiae" and "Aphrodisiacs and Anti-Aphrodisiacs," with a Bio-Bibliographical Memoir of the Author.* Bath: Privately Printed for Subscribers, 1888.

Ghost Land, or Researches into the Mysteries of Occultism. Boston: E. H. Britten, 1876.

Gilbert, R. A. *A. E. Waite, Magician of Many Parts.* Wellingborough: Crucible, 1987[a].

———. *The Golden Dawn and the Esoteric Section.* London: Theosophical History Centre, 1987[b].

Godwin, Joscelyn. "Saint-Yves d'Alveydre and the Agarthian Connection, Part I." *Hermetic Journal* 32 (1986), 24-34.

———. *The Beginnings of Theosophy in France.* London: Theosophical History Centre, 1989.

————. "The Hidden Hand." Four parts. *Theosophical History* N. S. III/2-5 (1990-1991).

————. *Arktos: the Polar Myth in Science, Symbolism, and Nazi Survival.* Grand Rapids: Phanes Press, 1993.

————. *The Theosophical Enlightenment.* Albany: SUNY Press, 1994.

Gomes, Michael. *The Dawning of the Theosophical Movement.* Wheaton: Theosophical Publishing House, 1987.

Goodrick-Clarke, Clare. "Mead's Gnosis: a Theosophical exegesis of an ancient heresy." *Theosophical History* IV/4-5 (Oct. 1992-Jan. 1993), 134-148.

Greenfield, Allen. "Notes on P. B. Randolph and the Hermetic Brotherhood of Light." *LAShTAL: a journal of Thelemic magick in theory and practice* IV/1 (1992), [5-9].

Guénon, René. *L'Erreur spirite.* Paris: Editions Traditionnelles, 1952 (First ed., 1923).

————. *Formes traditionnelles et cycles cosmiques.* Paris: Gallimard, 1970.

————. *Mélanges.* Paris: Gallimard, 1976.

————. *Le Théosophisme, histoire d'une pseudo-religion.* Augmented ed. Paris: Editions Traditionnelles, 1982 (First ed., 1921).

H. B. of L. Textes et documents secrets de la Hermetic Brotherhood of Luxor. Milan: Editions Archè, 1988.

Hamill, John, ed. *The Rosicrucian Seer: Magical Writings of Frederick Hockley.* Wellingborough: Aquarian Press, 1986.

Harrison, C. G. *The Transcendental Universe.* Ed. Christopher Bamford. Hudson, NY: Lindisfarne Press, 1993.

Hermes Trismegistus. *The Divine Pymander of Hermes Mercurius Trismegistus.* Bath: Robert H. Fryar, 1884.

Higgins, Godfrey. *Anacalypsis: An Attempt to Draw Aside the Veil of Saitic Isis; or an Inquiry into the Origin of Languages, Nations, and Religions.* 2 vols. London, 1836.

Howe, Ellic, ed. *The Alchemist of the Golden Dawn: the Letters of the Rev. W. A. Ayton to F. L. Gardner and Others, 1886-1905.* Wellingborough: Aquarian, 1985.

————. "Fringe Masonry in England, 1870-85." *Ars Quatuor Coronatorum* 85 (1972), 242-295.

Jennings, Hargrave. *The Rosicrucians, Their Rites and Mysteries.* London: J. C. Hotten, 1870. 4th revised ed., 1888.

————. *The Letters of Hargrave Jennings.* Ed. Invictus. Bath: Robert H. Fryar, 1895.

Johnson, Paul. *In Search of the Masters: Behind the Occult Myth.* South Boston, VA: Author, 1990.

————. *The Masters Revealed. Behind the Myth of the Great White Lodge.* Albany: SUNY Press, 1994.

Judge, William Q. *Practical Occultism.* Pasadena: Theosophical University Press, 1980.

Laurant, Jean-Pierre. *Le sens caché selon René Guénon.* Lausanne: L'Age d'Homme, 1975.

————. "Albert Jounet: un 'Kabbaliste chrétien' à la Belle Epoque." *Bélisane* 1977, 123-128; 1978, 21-34.

Levi, Eliphas. *Transcendental Magic*. Trans. A. E. Waite. London: Rider, 1896. Reprint: Samuel Weiser.

————. *The Mysteries of Magic, A Digest of the Writings of Eliphas Levi, with Biographical and Critical Essay by A.E. Waite*. London: Redway, 1886.

Letters from the Masters of Wisdom. Ed. C. Jinarajadasa. 2 vols. Adyar: Theosophical Publishing House, 1917, 1925.

Levin, Martin. "The Gnostic Cosmology of Max Theon." *Eco-Gnosis* 2 (February 1988), 8-23.

LOE. The Light of Egypt, or, The Science of the Soul and the Stars. 2 vols. Vol. I: Portland, OR: Green Dolphin Bookshop, 1969; Vol. II: Denver: H. O. Wagner, 1963. (First eds., 1889, 1900).

Mackenzie, Kenneth R. H. *The Royal Masonic Cyclopaedia*. London, 1877. Reprinted Wellingborough: Aquarian, 1987.

Mackey, Samson Arnold. *Mythological Astronomy*. Norwich: Author, 1823. Reprinted Minneapolis: Wizards Bookshelf, 1973.

ML. The Mahatma Letters to A. P. Sinnett from the Mahatmas M. and K. H. Transcribed and compiled by A. Trevor Barker. 3rd revised ed. Adyar: Theosophical Publishing House, 1979 (First ed., 1924).

Mani, Narad. "Baptême de Lumière, Notes pour servir à l'Histoire de la Société dite Théosophique." *La France Antimaçonnique*, various issues from 1911-1912.

Mariel, Pierre. *Dictionnaire de sociétés secrètes en occident*. Paris: Culture, Arts, Loisirs, 1971.

Möller, Helmut, and Ellic Howe. *Merlin Peregrinus. Vom Untergrund des Abendlandes*. Würzburg: Königshausen & Neumann, 1986.

Nahar, Sujata. *Mother's Chronicles*. 3 vols. Paris: Institut des Recherches Evolutives, 1985-1989.

Nock, A. D., and A.-J. Festugière. *Corpus Hermeticum*. 4 vols. Paris: Société d'Editions "Les Belles Lettres," 1972-1978.

ODL. Olcott, Henry Steel. Old Diary Leaves. 5 vols. Adyar: Theosophical Publishing House, 1895-1935. We cite the 2nd ed. of vol. I (1941).

Owen, Alex. *The Darkened Room*. Philadelphia: University of Pennsylvania Press, 1990.

Philipon, René. *Stanislas de Guaita et sa bibliothèque occulte*. Paris: Dorbon, 1899.

Randolph, P. B. *Clairvoyance; How to Produce It, and Perfect It, With an Essay on "Hashish, Its Benefits and Its Dangers." Also, "How to Make the Magic Glass, or Mirror of the Dead, by means of which the Oriental Magi are said to have held intelligent commerce with spirits."* Boston: Albert Renne & Co., 1860.

————. *The Guide to Clairvoyance and Clairvoyant's Guide...Also, a Special Paper Concerning Hashish....* Boston: Rockwell & Rollins, 1867.

————. *Seership! The Magnetic Mirror. A Practical Guide to those who Aspire to Clairvoyance-Absolute. Original and Selected from Various and Asiatic Adepts*. Boston: Randolph & Co., 1870.

————. *The New Mola! The Secret of Mediumship! A Hand Book of White Magic, Magnetism, and Clairvoyance. The New Doctrine of Mixed Identities. Rules for obtaining the phenomena, and the celebrated Rules of Asgill, a Physician's Legacy, and the Ansairetic Mystery.* Toledo: Randolph, 1873.

————. *Eulis! The History of Love . . . Being the Third Revelation of Soul and Sex.* Toledo: Randolph, 1874.

————. [and Maria Naglowska]. *Sexual Magic,* ed. and trans. Robert North. New York: Magickal Childe, 1988.

Ransom, Josephine. *A Short History of the Theosophical Society.* Adyar: Theosophical Publishing House, 1938.

Regardie, Israel. *The Golden Dawn.* St. Paul: Llewellyn, 1984.

Robin, Jean. *Le Royaume du Graal: Introduction au mystère de la France.* Paris: Trédaniel, 1992.

Saint-Yves d'Alveydre. *Mission de l'Inde en Europe; Mission d'Europe en Asie.* Nice: Bélisane, 1981 (First ed., 1886).

Scott, Alan. *Origen and the Life of the Stars.* Oxford: Clarendon Press, 1991.

Sédir, Paul. *Les miroirs magiques.* Paris: Chamuel, 1895.

Spierenburg, H. J. "Dr. Rudolf Steiner on Helena Petrovna Blavatsky." *Theosophical History* I/7 (1986), 159-174.

Thémanlys, Claire. *Un Séjour chez les Grands Initiés.* Paris: Publications Cosmiques, 1931.

Thémanlys, Pascal. *A Way of Meditation in the Light of the Kabbalah.* Jerusalem: Argaman, 1973.

Théon, Max. "Comment il faut considérer le magnétisme." *Journal du Magnétisme et de la Psychologie,* 5 February 1899, 62. [1899a]

————. "Le devoir des hommes libres." *Journal du Magnétisme et de la Psychologie,* 5-20 July 1899, 297. [1899b]

[Theon, Max?] "La quatrième Evocation." *Revue Cosmique* III/4 (April 1904).

[Theon, Max, and Mme. Theon] *La Tradition Cosmique.* 6 vols. Paris: Bibliothèque Chacornac/Publications Cosmiques, 1903-1920.

Vallee, Jacques. *Messengers of Deception: UFO Controls and Cults.* New York: Random House, 1980.

Villars, Abbé N. de Montfaucon de. *Comte de Gabalis.* London: The Brothers, 1913.

Waite, A. E. *The Mysteries of Magic, A Digest of the Writings of Eliphas Lévi, with Biographical and Critical Essay.* London: Redway, 1886.

Webb, James. *The Flight From Reason.* London: Macdonald, 1971.

Welton, Thomas. *Mental Magic. A Rationale of Thought Reading, and its attendant Phenomena....* London: Redway, 1884.

INDEX OF NAMES

Made in the USA
Middletown, DE
24 August 2024